DISMANTLING EVERYDAY DISCRIMINATION

Perspectives on Sexual Orientation and Gender Diversity

Marie Lucia Miville, Series Editor

DISMANTLING EVERYDAY DISCRIMINATION

Microaggressions Toward
LGBTQ People Second Edition

Kevin Leo Yabut Nadal

 AMERICAN PSYCHOLOGICAL ASSOCIATION

Published by
American Psychological Association
750 First Street, NE
Washington, DC 20002
https://www.apa.org

Order Department
https://www.apa.org/pubs/books
order@apa.org

In the U.K., Europe, Africa, and the Middle East, copies may be ordered from Eurospan
https://www.eurospanbookstore.com/apa
info@eurospangroup.com

Typeset in Charter and Interstate by Circle Graphics, Inc., Reisterstown, MD

Printer: Gasch Printing, Odenton, MD
Cover Designer: Gwen J. Grafft, Minneapolis, MN

Library of Congress Cataloging-in-Publication Data

Names: Nadal, Kevin L., author. | American Psychological Association.
Title: Dismantling everyday discrimination : microaggressions toward LGBTQ
    people / By Kevin Leo Yabut Nadal.
Description: Second edition. | Washington, DC : American Psychological
    Association, 2023. | Series: Perspectives on sexual orientation and
    gender diversity series | Includes bibliographical references and index.
Identifiers: LCCN 2022043383 (print) | LCCN 2022043384 (ebook) |
    ISBN 9781433840159 (paperback) | ISBN 9781433840166 (ebook)
Subjects: LCSH: Discrimination. | Sexual minorities--Mental health. |
    Sexual minorities--Psychology. | Microaggressions.
Classification: LCC HM821 .N33 2023 (print) | LCC HM821 (ebook) |
    DDC 305--dc23/eng/20220921
LC record available at https://lccn.loc.gov/2022043383
LC ebook record available at https://lccn.loc.gov/2022043384

https://doi.org/10.1037/0000335-000

Printed in the United States of America

10 9 8 7 6 5 4 3 2 1

This book is dedicated to every young person who has ever been bullied for being who they are. I hope they realize that they are not alone.

This book is for my children. I hope they learn that regardless of how they identify in the future and regardless of with whom they fall in love, they are perfect.

Contents

Preface

When I published the first edition of this text, titled *That's So Gay! Micro-aggressions and the Lesbian, Gay, Bisexual, and Transgender Community* (Nadal, 2013), the world was a much different place. While I was writing the book in 2012, the United States was starting to become more accepting of lesbian, gay, bisexual, transgender, and queer (LGBTQ) people. Federal law had recently prohibited hate crimes based on sexual orientation and gender identity, and LGBTQ people were finally able to serve openly in the U.S. military. LGBTQ people were more visible in the media—via celebrities (e.g., Laverne Cox, Ellen DeGeneres, Anderson Cooper, Elton John) and television shows (*RuPaul's Drag Race, Glee, Modern Family*). And before his reelection in 2012, President Barack Obama had become the first sitting president of the United States to publicly come out in support of same-sex marriage.

However, there were many ways in which LGBTQ people were still being overtly discriminated against. At the start of 2013, same-sex marriage was legal in only nine states (Massachusetts, Connecticut, Iowa, New Hampshire, Vermont, New York, Maine, Maryland, and Washington). Further, many state laws prohibited LGBTQ people from adopting children, and federal law did not view sexual orientation and gender identity as protected classes when it came to workplace discrimination. Overt homophobia and transphobia were still prevalent across all sectors of society—from school systems to media to families—with phrases like "That's so gay!" being commonly heard in many settings and contexts.

In these ways, 2013 was not so different from the decades prior. As a Filipino American child of immigrants growing up in the 1980s, some of the earliest messages I remember were about gender conformity (e.g., "Stop acting like a girl," "Boys don't cry," and "You're such a *bakla*"—the derogatory Tagalog term for gay or transgender). As a closeted queer teen in the 1990s, I heard the word "faggot" at least once a day, but typically more. Sometimes, groups of bullies made weird high-pitched noises as I walked down the hall, which I discovered later was their way of mocking my femme voice. Daily, these boys asked my female friends if I was gay, why I was gay, and why I just didn't tell everyone. My female friends would tell me, and I just laughed it off. If I couldn't even admit to myself that I was gay, how was I ever to admit it to anyone else? And if I couldn't admit to being gay, how would I ever be able to tell the teachers that I was being harassed? I'd have to tell them that the boys called me a "faggot," which, in my head meant that I would be admitting to being something I wasn't ready for.

By the time I was in college, I was surrounded by more liberal peers— people who did not aggressively antagonize LGBTQ people but who were also not aware of their homophobic or transphobic language (e.g., commonly saying things like "That's so gay" or "No homo" in their everyday conversations). More subtle forms of bias persisted throughout my early adulthood— with family members and strangers commonly asking me if I had a girlfriend or a wife, or heterosexual women telling me that they wanted me to be their new "gay best friend." Meanwhile, homophobic slurs were also commonly yelled at me while I walked down city streets—each time triggering a fear that this would be the day I was targeted by a hate crime.

In sharing these personal stories, I hope you might understand why I wrote this book. These nine chapters illustrate how LGBTQ people still navigate hate and ignorance—with examples of how bias manifests both overtly and subtly. These experiences have a profound effect on the lives of the people who encounter them—something to which I can attest from both empirical research and personal experience. A continual life lesson I learn is that even if the world changes for the better—with the legalization of same-sex marriage, federal protections for LGBTQ people in the workplace, and more widespread acceptance of LGBTQ people—everyday homophobia and transphobia persist. So long as trans and queer people are still targeted by violence and systemic oppression, or LGBTQ youth are still being bullied or kicked out of their homes, or LGBTQ people are still encountering microaggressions in their everyday lives, the fight for equity and justice will continue. And I sincerely hope you will join me.

Acknowledgments

Thank you to the American Psychological Association, particularly Division 44, Society for the Psychology of Sexual Orientation and Gender Diversity, for supporting the first and second publications of this text. I am eternally grateful to my mentor, Dr. Derald Wing Sue, for introducing me to the concept of microaggressions and for taking me under his wing. I thank all my mentors for believing in me throughout the years, particularly Dr. Jeannett Castellanos, Dr. Alfiee Breland-Noble, and Dr. Elizabeth Fraga. *Maraming salamat* to my family of origin, especially my parents, Charity and Leo Nadal, for sacrificing so much so that I could have the most opportunities. Thank you to my chosen family for demonstrating unconditional love—especially at times when I needed it most. Finally, thank you to the family I've created—my husband and my children—for giving me the inspiration to wake up every morning to do the things that I do. I promise I will always fight to make the world a better place for you, every single day of my life.

DISMANTLING EVERYDAY DISCRIMINATION

AN INTRODUCTION TO MICROAGGRESSIONS

Understanding Definitions and Impact

Jonathan is a 42-year-old biracial man of Filipino and Haitian descent who interchangeably identifies as **queer** or **gay**. Recently, Jonathan started working a government job in a suburb in Michigan. Though he generally enjoys his new position, he finds himself frequently encountering situations at work that he describes as "cringeworthy." For example, many of his coworkers use homophobic language in the workplace (e.g., saying, "That's so gay" when describing something that they don't like). Other times, people have teased him about not having a girlfriend, while other coworkers have expressed interest in setting him up with women they know. Although Jonathan is comfortable with his queer identity with his family and friends, he feels uneasy about sharing his identity with coworkers, due to their insensitive behaviors. So, he opts to simply ignore these comments, while passively looking for other job opportunities.

Stephanie is a 28-year-old South Asian American woman who is currently in a romantic relationship with a 27-year-old Black American woman named Debbie. Stephanie identifies as **bisexual** and has openly done so since she was 18 years old, and Debbie identifies as a **lesbian**. Over the past 10 years,

https://doi.org/10.1037/0000335-001
Dismantling Everyday Discrimination: Microaggressions Toward LGBTQ People, Second Edition, by K. L. Y. Nadal

Stephanie has had relationships with people of different **genders**; however, for the past 4 years, she has dated only cisgender women. She had two other romantic relationships with women before Debbie, with whom she has been in a monogamous relationship for the past year.

Stephanie decides to bring Debbie to her 10-year high school reunion back home in California. Although some of Stephanie's current friends know she is bisexual, many of her classmates had not heard. At the reunion, Stephanie sees a former classmate, Tom, whom she greets; she then introduces Debbie to him as her girlfriend. Astonishingly, Tom replies with "What? Are you a lesbian?" Stephanie replies, "Well, no; I'm actually bisexual, but I don't think that really matters, does it?" Tom laughs and says, "Well, I guess not . . . So—I'm single, and you two are very beautiful women. What are you both doing later?" Stephanie and Debbie look at each other and roll their eyes; they leave politely, feeling belittled and upset.

Agnes is a 20-year-old Latina **transgender** woman who is visiting a metropolitan university in Atlanta for the first time. After attending a community college for the past 2 years, she is interested in transferring to one of the local 4-year universities to pursue a career in fashion design. Thus, she visited several campuses within a 50-mile radius that offer her major. Agnes makes an appointment to see the local admissions counselor, so that she can discuss requirements, financial aid, and other logistical information.

FIGURE 1. A Queer Black Couple Sharing a Tender Moment

Note. Photo courtesy of Rodnae Productions.

When Agnes first arrives on campus, she approaches the security guard at the front desk; he looks at her, snickers, and asks to see her identification. Without hesitation, she pulls out her driver's license and hands it to him. Because Agnes's photo on the ID is one of her before her **gender affirmation surgeries**, the man says to her, "This isn't you. This is a man!" Agnes replies with "That is me. I'm transgender." The security guard hesitates, looks her up and down, and says, "Wait, so do you have a penis?" Agnes, embarrassed, tries to politely answer his question by replying, "I really don't think that's any of your business." However, she refrains from yelling at him or getting visibly upset, since she knows he has the power to let her into the building. He grants her permission to enter—smiling condescendingly and creepily as she walks through the turnstile. Meanwhile, Agnes walks away feeling dehumanized, furious, and hurt.

WHAT ARE MICROAGGRESSIONS?

While all of the scenarios in the book are fictional, including the opening vignettes, they are inspired by the types of experiences reported by lesbian, gay, bisexual, transgender, and queer (**LGBTQ**) people whom I have encountered over the past 20 years through my work as a professor, therapist, and community organizer. Each scenario represents the experience of **microaggressions**. Microaggressions are types of everyday discrimination that are typically subtle or even well-intentioned in some cases and are most often experienced by people of color, LGBTQ people, women, religious minorities, people with disabilities, and people of other marginalized groups. In contrast to outright assaults and hate crimes (or conscious prejudicial treatment motivated by fear or dislike of "the other" and intended to hurt people), microaggressions are typically more covert or innocuous in nature—sometimes intentional, sometimes unintentional—communicating hostile, insulting, or negative messages about people of oppressed groups. Research has found that microaggressions can occur in various settings (e.g., schools, workplaces, families) and have a detrimental impact on people who experience them, including mental health issues, difficulties in coming-out processes, or the development of trauma symptoms (Torino et al., 2019).

Although there are myriad ways that **racism**, **sexism**, **heterosexism**, **cissexism**, and **genderism** manifest differently, many authors in the fields of psychology and education began to describe a new trend in discrimination towards the end of the 20th century. Because of changes in public opinion and policy in the United States, it has become unacceptable and offensive for Americans to express blatantly discriminatory thoughts, statements, or behaviors toward minority groups in public settings. People of dominant backgrounds (e.g., white Americans, men, heterosexuals) may believe that they are good people who believe in equality and may choose not to associate with those who are blatantly racist, sexist, or heterosexist. For example, because most white Americans associate the term "racism" with white supremacist groups, they may fail to recognize the biases and stereotypes that they hold about people of color (Dovidio et al., 2016). Similarly, many heterosexual cisgender people may consider themselves to be good and open-minded because they do not engage in hate crimes or blatant discrimination toward queer or **trans** people; however, they still "may be oblivious to the ways that they harass or insult LGBTQ individuals (or allow others to)" (Nadal, Rivera, & Corpus, 2010, p. 219). So, although political correctness may lead to fewer instances of blatant discrimination (e.g., hate crimes; racial, sexist, and homophobic slurs), it may also result in the lack of awareness of one's unconscious biases and unintentional behaviors.

According to Sue et al. (2007), there are three types of microaggressions. The first type, **microassaults**, are defined as the use of explicit derogations either verbally or nonverbally, as demonstrated through name-calling, avoidant behavior, or discriminatory actions toward the intended victim (e.g., making a derogatory joke about Asian Americans or telling a Latinx person to "go back where you came from"). While such language can be interpreted as hostile and derogatory by the many people who hear it, people who engage in such behavior may rationalize their actions as being jokes or justified political opinions that are not reflective of any racial biases.

The second type of microaggression, **microinsults**, are often unconscious and are described as verbal or nonverbal communications that convey rudeness and insensitivity and demean a person's heritage or identity. For instance, when a person with a disability is spoken to patronizingly, or when a woman is told she is not capable of something, a subtle message is sent that these individuals are inferior to the dominant group (i.e., able-bodied people or men). Although the perpetrator did not explicitly say derogatory words, the target may experience such comments as degrading, and although the perpetrator may not have intended any offense, they target may react negatively.

The last type of microaggressions, called **microinvalidations**, are also often unconscious and include communications that exclude, negate, or nullify the realities of individuals of oppressed groups. Examples include a white American professor telling a student of color that they complain about racism too much or a white male colleague telling a woman of color colleague that she is angry or hostile. Such messages, although seemingly innocuous, indirectly invalidate the racial or gendered realities that a person faces on a regular basis.

These same three microaggression categories have been applied to the lived experiences of LGBTQ people (Nadal, 2018; Nadal, Rivera, & Corpus, 2010). Perhaps the most common forms of microassaults are the homophobic and transphobic slurs and violent language that LGBTQ people hear on a regular basis. Overhearing words like "faggot," "dyke," or "tranny"—which are commonplace phrases heard by LGBTQ youth in their school systems (Kosciw et al., 2020)—can be damaging to LGBTQ people, regardless of whether the terms are used jokingly or are intentionally directed at LGBTQ people. Further, when comedians, actors, or other public figures use transphobic or heterosexist language in their jokes, scripts, or social media posts, they complicitly encourage violence towards trans and queer people. For instance, in 2021, comedian Dave Chappelle released a Netflix special in which he expressed an array of transphobic prejudices. In doing so—and refusing to apologize or acknowledge any harm—Chappelle demonstrated a lack of empathy for trans people (especially Black trans women and trans women of color) who are violently targeted or killed by hate crime homicides every year.

Microinsults, which are often unconscious and unintentional, can affect LGBTQ people in many ways. For example, a subtle glare of disgust or shock when an LGBTQ couple displays affection to each other conveys someone's feelings of discomfort or disapproval toward LGBTQ people. Similarly, if a coworker or family member consistently **misgenders** someone (i.e., referring to a trans or **nonbinary** person with the wrong pronoun)—particularly when they had already been informed about a person's gender identity or have been corrected multiple times—the perpetrator communicates a lack of understanding or acceptance of their trans colleague or family member.

Finally, an example of a microinvalidation (or a statement that excludes or nullifies people's realities and lived experiences) would include a heterosexual person's vehemently denying that they are homophobic after an LGBTQ person confronts them about an enacted bias. Similarly, comments like "It's all in your head" or "You're too sensitive" negate the ways that LGBTQ people (and other **minoritized** people) may perceive or interpret situations. Such microinvalidations have also been referred to as **gaslighting**, in that the person from the historically dominant group attempts to convince the person from the historically marginalized group that they psychologically inept and have a distorted sense of reality (Johnson et al., 2021).

Over the past 2 decades, hundreds of empirical studies have investigated the impacts of microaggressions on people of historically marginalized groups, namely, people of color, women, religious minorities, and people with disabilities (Nadal, 2018; Torino et al., 2019). Specific to microaggressions and

LGBTQ people, Nadal, Rivera, and Corpus (2010) proposed a theoretical taxonomy—hypothesizing about the various types of microaggressions LGBTQ people face. Empirical literature began to increase significantly shortly thereafter, with a few key qualitative and quantitative studies that highlighted the pervasiveness of microaggressions in the lives of LGBTQ people (e.g., Balsam et al., 2011; Nadal, Issa, et al., 2010, 2011; Nadal, Skolnik, & Wong, 2012; Nadal, Wong, et al., 2011; Platt & Lenzen, 2013; Shelton & Delgado-Romero, 2011; Wright & Wegner, 2012). Consistent to all these studies was the notion that LGBTQ people could easily identify microaggressions they had experienced and that such encounters had tremendous impacts in their everyday lives.

With this nascent literature, I published my text *That's So Gay! Micro-aggressions and the Lesbian, Gay, Bisexual, and Transgender Community* (2013)—the original text of this current revision—hopeful that it would inspire an entire area of research. By 2015, there were dozens of empirical studies on heterosexist and transphobic microaggressions (Nadal et al., 2016), and a special issue on anti-LGBTQ microaggressions was published in the *Journal of Homosexuality* (Nadal, 2019a). Newer studies on LGBTQ microaggressions focus on more nuanced experiences and intersectional identities, including LGBTQ people of various religious backgrounds (Lomash et al., 2019), LGBTQ college students (Winberg et al., 2019), and LGBTQ youth (Munro et al., 2019). Further, multiple scales have been created to attempt to quantitatively measure microaggressive incidents and assess their relationships with multiple psychosocial outcomes (Fisher et al., 2019; Nadal, 2019b; Resnick & Galupo, 2019). A decade after the original taxonomy presented in 2010, research supports that anti-LGBTQ microaggressions are pervasive and can result in many negative outcomes and disparities for LGBTQ people—ranging from depression to substance use issues to body image issues.

WHAT THIS BOOK COVERS, WHAT YOU WILL GET FROM IT, AND WHOM IT IS FOR

The purpose of this book is to highlight the microaggressions that LGBTQ people face on an everyday basis and to examine the impacts that such experiences have on mental health. Building off the first edition of *That's So Gay* (originally published in 2013), it felt necessary to address all that has happened within and toward LGBTQ communities in the past 10 years. When the book was first published, the concept of microaggressions was still fairly new—especially in the context of anti-LGBTQ discrimination. Overt heterosexism and transphobia were still quite common and pervasive—

particularly in the media, in school systems, and other institutions. Back then, demonstrating pro-LGBTQ stances often came with a cost; for example, if politicians or celebrities vocalized LGBTQ-affirming views, they were often deemed queer or trans themselves, were questioned on their own morality, and even lost popularity (and sometimes elections). Nowadays, the majority of the country is more in support of LGBTQ rights than against it—which generally might mean less heterosexism or transphobia but may also mean more nuanced microaggressions directed toward LGBTQ people. Thus, writing and revising this book also meant an opportunity to guide people in navigating and addressing microaggressions, which hopefully could be helpful in their everyday lives.

In this book, the topics covered in each chapter are similar to those in the first edition. However, each chapter has been revised significantly, with new research, more relevant examples, and even updated language to replace dated terminology from a decade prior. In Chapter 1, I review the historical currents of acceptance and rejection of LGBTQ people in society and trace the research literature on the psychological effects of discrimination on LGBTQ people and other historically marginalized groups. In Chapter 2, I comb through a finer level of race, gender, and LGBTQ research to reveal the taxonomy of microaggressions that I use as a lens to focus the research review and examples in subsequent chapters. In Chapters 3, 4, and 5, I provide an overview of the current theoretical and empirical literature involving micro-aggressions toward various LGBTQ people and subgroups. Chapter 3 is focused on microaggressions targeting queer, lesbian, gay, bisexual, pansexual, and other nonheterosexual people, and Chapter 4 focuses on microaggressions targeting transgender, **gender nonconforming**, and nonbinary people. Chapters 5 through 7 explore how intersectional identities influence microaggressions faced by LGBTQ people of color, LGBTQ people with disabilities, LGBTQ older adults, LGBTQ people of diverse sizes, LGBTQ people of religious and nonreligious communities, and LGBTQ youth. Finally, in Chapters 8 and 9, I offer practical guidance on how to identify and deal with microaggressions as they occur, discussing implications for policy, clinical practice, and more.

Vignettes are presented throughout the text; they describe microaggressions that may be conscious (i.e., the perpetrator may be conscious of their actions but might not recognize any negative consequences), unconscious (i.e., the perpetrator may be completely oblivious to their statements or behaviors), intentional (i.e., the perpetrator may have been purposeful in hurting or offending another but may rationalize their actions or deny the behavior as problematic), and unintentional (i.e., the perpetrator did not mean to hurt or offend another person). Most examples of microaggressions involve hetero-sexist or transphobic biases but may also illustrate how other identities and situational contexts may affect how such microaggressions are perceived or handled.

For people who have been targeted by microaggressions firsthand, I hope this book can be validating—demonstrating situations encountered in their own lives, while normalizing their reactions. For individuals who have committed microaggressions (consciously, intentionally, or not), it may be difficult to recognize that their behaviors may have had a negative effect on others. I hope this book can highlight how these actions may hurt others, so readers can become more aware of their own biases, challenge themselves to change behaviors that negatively affect others, and educate and confront others about microaggressions to prevent future traumas for LGBTQ people and other groups.

Readers of all backgrounds can benefit from this book. First, it can serve as a resource for researchers who are interested in further understanding how microaggressions may influence LGBTQ people's everyday lives. Through the literature review, researchers can gain a sense of what empirical work has already been done, so that they can brainstorm future research questions to initiate or build upon. Furthermore, practitioners in the helping professions—such as psychotherapists, psychiatrists, social workers—can use the book to attain an understanding of how microaggressions negatively affect their clients' or patients' lives—potentially assisting them in building stronger therapeutic relationships and conceptualizing treatment plans that may be effective for them. Educators, trainers, and professors may use this book to educate their students, trainees, and colleagues about heterosexism, genderism, and microaggressions; meanwhile, managers, consultants, and company presidents may find this book to be a helpful source for understanding the types of dynamics that may affect their work environments.

The book can also be extremely useful to laypeople of all professional and educational backgrounds. I bold key terms and include a glossary in every chapter as a way of educating readers about the varied terminology currently used about, among, or by LGBTQ people. Perhaps people who have a friend or family member who has just "come out of the closet" can find this text beneficial in gaining some basic knowledge about LGBTQ experiences while learning about the various elements that either strengthen or hurt a relationship. Moreover, in addition to the vignettes, I include anecdotal examples from the media, qualitative research, and nonfiction narratives. In doing so, I hope that people will see how microaggressions may manifest in every element of life and affect the spectrum of LGBTQ-identified people.

I include discussion questions throughout each chapter as a way for readers to gain some insight into their own beliefs, opinions, or biases. Because personal attitudes, values, and worldviews may have an impact on the ways that people interact with others, it is important to critically reflect about our impact on others. It may be helpful for readers to examine these discussion questions on their own first, before discussing them with peers. For example, perhaps readers can journal about some of their responses to these questions independently before engaging in discussions with classmates or colleagues. Educators and instructors may use these discussion questions as a way of eliciting thought-provoking insights from their students and allow honest dialogues to occur. As with any discussion, facilitators must assess participants' sense of personal safety and willingness to share in a public setting. For instance, emotionally provocative questions can be reserved for groups with established trust and rapport. Finally, because being an effective clinician means developing and maintaining self-awareness of how one's biases and worldviews may affect work with clients, psychologists and other mental health practitioners may use these questions to assist in exploring countertransferential issues and other emotional processes that may impede their efforts to be culturally effective.

FIGURE 2. An Interracial Gay Couple Laughing and Lounging at Home

Note. Photo courtesy of Ketut Subiyanto.

Reflecting on the Opening Vignettes

Think back to the vignettes about Jonathan, Stephanie and Debbie, and Agnes. Why did they feel hurt? In the first vignette, Jonathan is distressed about his coworkers' subtle heterosexism, especially their heterosexist language. When people say: "That's so gay," they may not necessarily be thinking about gay people, but may have just become accustomed to equating "gay" with "bad" or "weird." And when his coworkers assume that Jonathan is heterosexual, they may not be conscious or intentional in conveying their views of heterosexuality as the norm. However, their actions indirectly communicate their biases. While Jonathan appears to have a strong support network outside of work, he may not want to bother them about work problems, which may result in internalized feelings. If Jonathan does choose to confront his coworkers, he may worry about putting his job at risk or creating a tense and hostile work environment that would worsen the current situation. His situation is exemplary of the many difficult decisions LGBTQ people make when they face workplace microaggressions.

The vignette of Stephanie and Debbie demonstrates the kinds of microaggressions that can occur in an instant. When Stephanie introduces Debbie to her former classmate, Tom, two microaggressions occur sequentially. First, he assumes that she is a lesbian and does so in a way that makes Stephanie feel like she must justify her bisexual identity. Second, Tom objectifies both women and demonstrates his misogynistic views by presuming that they would want to engage in a "three-way" with him. In these types of quick microaggressions, both Stephanie and Debbie must decide immediately how to react. They can choose to angrily vocalize their disgust to Tom, or they can choose to smile or ignore the interaction. In this case, the couple chose to be polite and nonconfrontational (albeit rolling their eyes in disapproval). Perhaps they believed that this passive–aggressive behavior would be enough for him to take the hint that they were not pleased with his comment, or perhaps they just wanted the interaction to be over so that they could continue to have a pleasant evening.

In the third vignette, Agnes's driver's license does not match her current gender presentation, resulting in the security guard giving her trouble and asking an invasive question. He is rude throughout the interaction, laughing and smiling at her in a condescending and disparaging way. As do Stephanie and Debbie, Agnes chooses to remain as calm as possible, primarily because she knows that she needs to cooperate with him to arrive at her appointment on time. However, perhaps she begins to wonder whether this is the type of institution that she would want to attend; perhaps other people on campus would be disrespectful toward her and would discriminate toward transgender people in general.

In all three vignettes, the perpetrators of the microaggressions may have no idea that they committed a microaggression. Jonathan's coworkers who make heterosexist and **heteronormative** comments may not recognize that their actions and statements convey their belief that heterosexuality is the norm, whereas LGBTQ people and experiences are abnormal. If they were to be confronted regarding their behavior, they might simply say that they ask everyone about their relationships and that phrases such as "That's so gay" are harmless because they aren't meant to disparage gay people. Stephanie's old classmate, Tom, may not recognize his comment was offensive and declare, "I was just joking." Perhaps Tom genuinely thought he was being funny and did not really expect that the two women would take him up on his offer. Tom might also assert that his comment was complimentary because his intention was to flatter two women who he thought were attractive. It is also conceivable that Tom could react with hostility and tell the two women that they were overreacting or needed to stop being "angry lesbians"—both which are common retaliations for lesbian, bisexual, or queer women who confront their perpetrators.

Similarly, the security guard in Agnes's case may simply be unaware of the way he treated her. He might also say that he was "just joking," or that he was simply following standard university procedures because her driver's license photo did not correspond to her physical appearance. On the other hand, perhaps he is aware of his transphobic attitudes and biases and mistreated Agnes intentionally. If this were the case, then perhaps the microaggression was blatant, conscious, and deliberate. However, because Agnes does not know the security guard's exact intention, she simply walks away with a spectrum of feelings—not knowing whether she handled the situation correctly or whether she should take further action. Perhaps if the guard had simply refused to let her into the building and explicitly told her it was because of her gender presentation, she would be better able to label his comments as overt discrimination. If that were the case, she might then report it to someone from the university or seek other appropriate measures. Instead, she leaves feeling confused and agitated, among other emotions.

Furthermore, the vignette of Agnes reflects a common experience for transgender people, particularly for those who have more difficulty in **passing** (i.e., the ability to be regarded as a member of the sex or gender with which one identifies). Many trans or nonbinary people who do not undergo hormonal treatments or gender-affirmation medical procedures may maintain physical appearances that match their sex assigned at birth (hence not matching the gender they feel internally and psychologically). Even when some trans or nonbinary people do undergo hormone or medical treatments, they might still not fully "pass" (sometimes referred to as living in **stealth**), and experience discrimination accordingly. On the contrary, some trans people who transition and now "pass" may still encounter microaggressions because people may not know of their trans identity. For instance, if someone who identifies as a transgender man (i.e., assigned female at birth), underwent surgery and is taking hormones, he may be treated as any cisgender (i.e., nontransgender) man would; as a result, perhaps people may make transphobic or heterosexist remarks to him or around him. So, although not directed at him, these could still be considered microaggressions.

Across all three scenarios, the perpetrators of the microaggressions (Jonathan's coworkers, Tom, and the security guard) are not inherently bad people. Rather, they are people who have been socialized to develop heterosexist and cissexist biases. In fact, I believe they can potentially learn to become more LGBTQ-affirming people, if they were given opportunities to learn and reflect. So, whether readers of this text find themselves as targets or well-intentioned people who hurt others without knowing, it is my hope that the research-based data in this book will help everyone feel validated and understood. I also sincerely hope that all readers might learn new LGBTQ affirming tools that can help identify practical steps to furthering equities for all people.

GLOSSARY OF KEY TERMS

bisexual A sexual orientation that is based on having sexual attractions toward more than one gender and the identity that is developed based on these attractions.

cisgender A term used to describe someone who identifies with their sex assigned at birth; someone who is not transgender. The term **cis** is commonly used as a shortened form of cisgender.

cissexism The negative attitudes, biases, and beliefs perpetuated across systems and held about transgender or nonbinary people, as well as the discrimination that occurs as a result.

gaslighting The process of manipulating others to question their own realities and perceptions—often relating to dynamics involving power, privilege, and historically marginalized identities.

gay A sexual orientation that is based on having sexual attractions toward one's own gender and the identity that is developed based on these attractions. The term is often reserved for gay men; however, many women also identify as gay.

gender A socially constructed category that is used to classify people, based on their sex assigned at birth, adherence to masculinity or femininity, or other personality traits, behaviors, expressions, or identities.

genderism The ideology that reinforces the negative evaluation of gender nonconformity or the incongruence between sex and gender.

gender nonconforming The trait or identity of not adhering to gender role expectations.

heteronormative Assuming heterosexuality as the norm; assuming that individuals would engage in traditional heterosexual lifestyles, behaviors, and relationships.

heterosexism The negative attitudes, biases, and beliefs perpetuated across systems held about queer, gay, lesbian, and bisexual people, as well as the discrimination that occurs as a result.

lesbian A woman whose sexual orientation is based on sexual attractions toward her own gender and the identity that develops because of these attractions.

LGBTQ An acronym used as an umbrella term to describe people who do identify with diverse sexual orientation and gender identities—typically referring to lesbian, gay, bisexual, transgender, and queer or questioning people, but also inclusive of other identities such as asexual, nonbinary, genderqueer, pansexual, demisexual, and others. Sometimes a plus sign is used (LGBTQ+) to be more inclusive of other identities.

microaggressions Verbal, behavioral, or environmental indignities that communicate hostile, derogatory, or negative slights and insults toward members of oppressed groups.

microassaults The use of explicit derogations, either verbally or nonverbally, such as name-calling, avoidant behavior, or discriminatory actions toward the intended victim.

microinsults Verbal or nonverbal communications that convey rudeness and insensitivity and demean a person's heritage or identity.

microinvalidations Communications that are often unconscious and exclude, negate, or nullify the realities of individuals of oppressed groups.

minoritized A term used to describe people of historically oppressed groups. While "minority" was once a commonly used term, it does not accurately describe groups that are not numerical minorities; further, many oppose the term because it can convey a lower status. Thus, "minoritized" is used to signify that certain people are treated as subordinate groups, due to oppression.

misgender To refer to someone—especially someone who is of trans or nonbinary experience—with pronouns that they do not use to identify themselves.

nonbinary (or non-binary) A term used to describe someone who does not subscribe to gender binaries (i.e., they do not identify exclusively as women or men). Nonbinary can also be used as an umbrella term for other gender identities that do not conform to gender binaries (e.g., genderqueer, agender, bigender, gender fluid, *māhū*, two-spirited, or gender nonconforming).

passing The ability to be perceived as a member of a historically privileged group; for trans people, it is the ability to be seen as the gender that someone identifies with or as a gender identity in which they may avoid violence or discrimination.

queer An umbrella term used to identify individuals who are not heterosexual. While initially an antigay epithet, the word has been reclaimed as an empowering identity.

racism The negative attitudes, biases, and beliefs perpetuated across systems and held by people about nonwhite people (e.g., Black, Indigenous, Asian, or Pacific Islander people), as well as the discrimination that occurs as a result.

sexism The negative attitudes, biases, and beliefs perpetuated across systems and held about women or femme-identified people, as well as the discrimination that occurs as a result.

stealth The experience of transgender people not being perceived as transgender; the experience of a transgender person being perceived and treated as a cisgender person of their gender identity.

trans A shortened version of the world "transgender," often used as an umbrella term for people of transgender experience (e.g., nonbinary people, genderqueer people).

transgender An umbrella term that can be used to refer to anyone for whom the sex they were assigned at birth is an incomplete or incorrect description of themselves.

1 A BRIEF HISTORY OF LGBTQ PEOPLE AND CIVIL RIGHTS

FIGURE 1.1. The LGBTQ Center Marching at the NYC Pride Parade

Note. Photo courtesy of Following NYC.

https://doi.org/10.1037/0000335-002
Dismantling Everyday Discrimination: Microaggressions Toward LGBTQ People, Second Edition, by K. L. Y. Nadal

In the past decade, there has been a significant cultural shift toward the acceptance of LGBTQ people in the United States. In 2009, President Obama signed The Matthew Shepard and James Byrd, Jr. Hate Crime Prevention Act, which made it a federal crime to assault an individual because of their **sexual orientation** or **gender identity**; previously, hate crimes were only considered to be based on race, color, religion, sex, or national origin. In 2010, President Obama signed the law that repealed "Don't Ask, Don't Tell," which formerly prohibited gays and lesbians from serving openly in the military. In 2015, via *Obergefell v. Hodges*, the Supreme Court of the United States (SCOTUS) ruled that state bans on same-sex marriage were unconstitutional, thereby legalizing same-sex marriage across the United States. In 2022, GLAAD (formerly known as the Gay and Lesbian Alliance Against Defamation) reported a significant increase in the number of LGBTQ characters in broadcast television as well as the highest percentage of LGBTQ-identified characters in television history (11.9% across prime time scripted broadcast television shows; Townsend et al., 2022). Finally, in 2020, SCOTUS ruled that LGBTQ people were protected under Title VII of the Civil Rights Act of 1964, making workplace discrimination toward LGBTQ people illegal on the federal level. Such systemic changes reflect the overall shift in American culture's greater awareness and acceptance of LGBTQ people—the Pew Research Center indicates that only 51% of Americans were in favor of **homosexuality** being accepted in 2002, and that the number had risen to 72% in 2019 (Poushter & Kent, 2020). It is hypothesized that some of these positive gains may be why the number of LGBTQ-identified young people has increased significantly, with nearly 10% of young people identifying as LGBTQ (Conron, 2020).

While these examples of LGBTQ equality are viewed as huge gains for LGBTQ people, there are many ways that **institutional discrimination** manifests toward LGBTQ people. First, many laws (especially on state and local levels) overtly target or discriminate against LGBTQ people. In fact, the Human Rights Campaign (HRC; 2021) cited that while there were 370 pro-LGBTQ bills proposed across the United States in 2020, and that 47 of those LGBTQ-affirming bills passed into law, there were 175 anti-LGBTQ bills proposed in 2020 and four were signed into law. For example, on state and local levels, there have been many attempts to silence LGBTQ people and communities—particularly as they relate to public school education and young people's health care. For instance, in 2022, the state of Florida passed Senate Bill 1834, more popularly referred to as the "Don't Say Gay Bill"; its intention is to prohibit the discussion of sexual orientation or gender identity among elementary schoolchildren, because it is believed such discussions are not age- or developmentally appropriate for young people (Lambda Legal, 2022). In 2022, the governor of Texas issued an order that restricted transgender minors' access to gender-affirming medical care—citing that adults or treatment providers who participated in such care would be engaged in "child abuse" (Conron et al., 2022). So, despite efforts for institutions like educational and health care systems to become more inclusive and accepting of LGBTQ people, anti-LGBTQ laws and policies make it difficult to sustain pro-LGBTQ stances, programs, organizations, or environments.

HRC (2021) also noted that only 23 states prohibit housing discrimination based on both sexual orientation and gender identity, and only 22 states prohibit public accommodation discrimination due to sexual orientation and gender identity. One state (Wisconsin) prohibits both sorts of discrimination based on sexual orientation only. Only 18 states prohibit discrimination in education based on sexual orientation and gender identity; two states (New Mexico and Wisconsin) protect against sexual-orientation-related discrimination but not gender identity. So, even if some state legislatures are not actively introducing or passing anti-LGBTQ laws, many states do not have laws to protect LGBTQ people when they encounter discrimination.

On the federal level, one law that overtly targets LGBTQ people includes the Food and Drug Administration (FDA) policy that has banned blood donations, since 1983, from men who have ever had sex with men (Varriage, 2019). In 2015, the FDA lifted the ban and began to permit blood donations from gay, bisexual, and queer men who have refrained from any sexual contact with other men in the past year. In other words, if a queer man is sexually active, practices safe sex, and gets tested regularly, he would not be permitted to donate blood unless he was celibate for a year. Similarly, if two men were married and in a monogamous sexual relationship, they would not be eligible unless they abstained from sexual contact for a year. Meanwhile, a heterosexual who was sexually active with multiple sex partners, did not practice safe sex, or did not get tested regularly would be eligible to donate and would not have to abstain from any sexual activity for a year. Critics have cited how the policy was both illogical and unconstitutional (Varriage, 2019)—especially given that all donated blood is tested for any diseases or infections before it is redistributed.

For many LGBTQ people, **interpersonal discrimination** remains a blatant part of life. LGBTQ people—particularly those who reside in areas where overt heterosexism and **transphobia** are culturally accepted—may encounter blatant discrimination, harassment, and **bullying** in their daily lives. Casey et al. (2019) found that over half of their LGBTQ sample of 489 participants had experienced overt discrimination, including slurs (57%), violence (51%), and sexual harassment (51%). One third of participants (34%) reported harassment regarding public bathroom use, and over half of the sample (53%) reported experiencing microaggressions. Such findings suggest some societal progress, in that a study from almost 2 decades prior (Herek et al., 2002) found 94% of participants reported being a victim of a hate crime in their lifetime. Yet, compared with a study from just 10 years prior (Herek, 2009), in which half of participants described verbal harassment due to their sexual orientation, the pervasiveness of discriminatory experiences appeared to remain similar.

Similarly, the 2019 National School Climate Survey found that 59.1% of LGBTQ-identified students felt unsafe at school because of their sexual orientation, 42.5% because of their gender expression, and 37.4% because of their gender identity (Kosciw et al., 2020). The same report noted that nearly a third of LGBTQ students skipped at least 1 day of school in the past month and that those who were harassed regularly had lower grade point averages than those who were less harassed. Anti-LGBTQ stigmas remain pervasive in many families, and few programs or interventions are targeted to help families be more LGBTQ-affirmative (Parker et al., 2018). So, although there many believe that anti-LGBTQ discrimination may decrease in younger generations, research indicates that LGBTQ youth today may still feel unsafe in their schools and home environments.

Furthermore, many studies have shown that LGBTQ individuals experience high levels of psychological distress (or **minority stress**) because of the systemic and interpersonal oppression they encounter due to their sexual orientation or gender identity, which may then result in various mental health disparities (I. H. Meyer, 2015). Many studies suggest that LGBTQ persons are at higher risk of suffering from mental health problems (e.g., depression, substance abuse) and physical health issues such as high blood pressure (Casey et al., 2019; Flentje et al., 2020). An earlier study revealed lesbian and gay people were 2.5 times more likely to have a mental health problem in their lifetime compared with their heterosexual counterparts (I. H. Meyer, 2003), whereas another study reported that LGBTQ youth were more likely to be depressed than their heterosexual counterparts (Almeida et al., 2009). Thus, microaggressions and minority stress are public health issues because they can significantly harm LGBTQ people and affect their abilities to live happy and healthy lives.

LGBTQ PEOPLE THROUGHOUT WORLD HISTORY

To best address microaggressions, it would be helpful to examine some of the known experiences of LGBTQ people throughout history. Although most elementary books documenting the history of the world neglect to state so, LGBTQ people have existed since the dawn of time. Egyptian hieroglyphics depict the tomb of royal servants Khnumhotep and Niankhkhnum (who lived in the 25th century BCE); they are credited as being the first same-sex couple identified by name (Parkinson, 2013). In ancient Greece, same-sex relationships were found between Greek men as early as the 7th century BCE (Dover, 2016). During this time, a woman poet named Sappho of Lesbos wrote about her relationships with women, which is where the term "lesbian" is believed to have originated (Stern, 2009). Famous leaders such as Alexander the Great, Julius Caesar, and Marc Antony are documented as being bisexual or having same-sex sexual and romantic relationships, and same-sex marriages in both Rome and Greece were viewed as legal and acceptable during their reigns (Stern, 2009). In North America, Indigenous tribes had accepted **two-spirited**, transgender, or **gender nonconforming** people long before settler colonialism (Crawford-Lackey & Springate, 2019). In Southeast Asia, trans and queer people have been well documented: the *babaylan* of the pre-colonized Philippines were viewed as gender fluid spiritual healers (Hanna, 2017) and the *kathoey* or ladyboys of Thailand are considered to be a third gender (Käng, 2014). These examples demonstrate that **homosexuality**, **bisexuality**, and **gender nonconformity** are not new concepts and have existed across the world.

While many religious groups may view homosexuality as an "abomination," it is important to note that even the Bible describes same-sex romantic relationships. In the first book of Samuel, a romantic relationship is described between David (often known as the underdog who slayed Goliath) and a man named Jonathan (Harding, 2016). In the Book of Ruth, a letter is written from Ruth to a woman named Naomi, stating,

> Where you go, I will go; where you lodge, I will lodge; your people shall be my people, and your God my God. Where you die, I will die—there I will be buried. May the Lord do thus and so to me, and more as well, if even death parts me from you. (Ruth 1:16–17)

While scholars have debated whether Ruth and Naomi had an actual romantic relationship (because Naomi was the mother of Ruth's late husband), the passage does describe the love between two women. It is also read at heterosexual Christian wedding ceremonies often, and many people are unaware that the passage is written from one woman to another. So, although Bible passages are commonly used to argue against homosexuality, people fail to acknowledge scripture in which same-sex relationships are evident.

Despite these instances of LGBTQ people in the history of the world, it became common beginning in the Middle Ages for countries to criminalize homosexuality and convict many LGBTQ people, particularly gay men, of **sodomy** (Bronski, 2011). The act of punishing sodomy was common in many European countries (particularly those with strong Christian influences).

For example, the Buggery Act of 1533, which was enacted by King Henry VIII of England, was an antisodomy law that lasted for 3 centuries and made "buggery" (or sex between two men or sex between a man and a beast) punishable by hanging (Nadal, 2020).

In the 19th and 20th centuries, countries like Brazil, France, Indonesia, and the Netherlands began to decriminalize homosexuality or lessen the punishments for engaging in homosexual acts. However, in most countries (including the United States), LGBTQ people were still being punished during this time (Bronski, 2011). One notable example occurred in 1895, when famous writer Oscar Wilde was convicted in England for "gross indecency" and sentenced to 2 years of hard labor in prison (Stern, 2009). Meanwhile in the United States, the first documented targeted arrest of a group for sodomy was in 1903, when the New York Police Department raided a bathhouse and arrested 12 men on sodomy charges (Chauncey, 1994). Such instances were commonplace for the next 60 or 70 years. In fact, it was not until 1961 that a U.S. state (Illinois) removed a sodomy law from its criminal code (Nadal, 2020). And while 20 states in total had repealed their sodomy laws by 1979, many of these repeals came after long legal battles (Bronski, 2011).

In addition to being punished for sodomy, LGBTQ people were also criminalized throughout the history of the United States, even if they were not involved in any same-sex sexual behavior. For instance, in 1953, President Dwight Eisenhower issued an executive order dismissing all **homosexuals** from federal employment—targeting both civilian and military positions (D'Emilio, 2012). This presidential order only reinforced the notion that LGBTQ people were not to be trusted, were allowed to be treated as second-class citizens, or both.

Furthermore, it was not long before this that homosexuality was first believed to be a mental illness, which eventually shaped the stigmas and perceptions of LGBTQ people today (Nadal, 2020). Sigmund Freud is usually credited with first defining sexual orientation as one's attraction toward men or women and defining people as heterosexuals and homosexuals. He also believed that homosexuality represented a less than optimal outcome for psychosexual behavior but should not be considered an illness (Drescher, 2015). However, in the early 1900s, physicians, sexologists, and psychologists began to view homosexuality as a pathology in contrast to heterosexuality, which was viewed as normal behavior (Drescher, 2015). In the 1950s, the *Diagnostic and Statistical Manual of Mental Disorders* (*DSM*) listed homosexuality as a "sociopathic personality disturbance" (van den Berg, 2017, p. 849), which eventually led to decades of psychiatrists and psychologists attempting to "cure" homosexual people of their "disorder" through electroshock therapy, lobotomy, hormone and drug treatments, and even castration

(Nadal, 2020). None of these treatments were viewed as effective, which eventually led to both the American Psychiatric Association and American Psychological Association discontinuing their view of homosexuality as a mental disorder in 1973 and 1975, respectively (Glassgold, 2017).

While antigay sentiment continued throughout the United States, uprisings occurred in places like Los Angeles and San Francisco in the 1950s and 1960s. However, the 1969 Stonewall Uprisings (formerly known as the Stonewall Riots) in New York City are typically viewed as the "birth" of the LGBTQ rights movement in the United States. When NYPD police officers raided the Stonewall Inn—a bar in the Greenwich Village neighborhood in Manhattan— bar patrons (many who were transgender women and queer, homeless youth) fought back, and an uprising ensued (Bronski, 2011; Chauncey, 1994). The following year, communities in New York, Los Angeles, and San Francisco held marches in their local cities, leading to more visibility of LGBTQ people in major metropolitan areas and eventually Pride parades. In the next few years, several strides toward LGBTQ rights occurred, including the first "out" lesbian and gay Americans elected to public office: Kathy Kozachenko in Ann Arbor, Michigan, in 1974; Elaine Noble in Massachusetts in 1975; Allan Spears in Minnesota in 1976; and Harvey Milk in San Francisco in 1977 (Ring, 2015).

CONTEMPORARY LGBTQ ISSUES IN THE UNITED STATES

Over the past 5 decades, there have been myriad other national events and issues that have exemplified the struggle for LGBTQ rights in the United States. While there were many gains for LGBTQ rights—including the removal of homosexuality as a psychological disorder from the *DSM* in 1973, the end to "Don't Ask, Don't Tell" in 2011, and federal legislation protecting LGBTQ people from hate crimes in 2009—numerous issues demonstrate that the fight for LGBTQ rights is still ongoing. Examples include (a) the anti-LGBTQ sentiment that emerged from the HIV/AIDS crisis in the 1980s and continues to the present day; (b) the increase in media attention regarding anti-LGBTQ hate crimes (particularly after the murder of Matthew Shepard in 1998 and the increase of Black transgender women being murdered in the late 2010s); (c) the fight for same-sex marriage in the United States that became more visible at the brink of the century; (d) the focus on anti-LGBTQ teen bullying that occurred in 2010; and (e) the recognition of disparities affecting LGBTQ people (ranging from LGBTQ involvement in the criminal justice system to homelessness and poverty).

HIV/AIDS

In the early 1980s, the HIV/AIDS virus was first discovered in New York City and San Francisco. Because it was found mostly in gay men, it was initially labeled as the "Gay Disease," resulting in a national antigay sentiment, particularly from religious groups (Bronski, 2011). During this time, gay and bisexual men who were diagnosed with HIV/AIDS began to experience a dual discrimination because of their sexual orientation and HIV status; many were fired from their jobs, evicted from their homes, and shunned by their family members and friends (Nadal, 2020; Vitiello & Nadal, 2019). In the late 1980s, there were thousands of reported cases of antigay harassment and victimization, with close to one fifth of these involving biases relating to HIV/AIDS (Nadal, 2018). This anti-LGBTQ sentiment is still pervasive today, as demonstrated by the members of fundamentalist Christian groups who have continually and publicly denounced LGBTQ people, even protesting LGBTQ events and LGBTQ funerals, with signs like "God Hates Fags" or "AIDS Kills Fags."

Hate Crimes

A **hate crime** can be defined as a criminal act in which the victim (individual or group) is targeted because of their actual or perceived race, color, religion, national origin, ethnicity, disability, or sexual orientation (Herek, 2017). Hate crimes manifest in multiple ways, including violent physical assaults, violent threats (e.g., hate mail, biased and hostile phone calls), and property damage (e.g., vandalism, fires, bombings). While hate crimes have been pervasive throughout the history of LGBTQ people across the world, they may not have been recognized or studied as such until more recent years. It was not until 1990, that the term "hate crime" was officially named on a federal level by the U.S. judicial system (Willis, 2008).

In 1999, hate crimes against LGBTQ people came to the forefront of mainstream media when Matthew Shepard, a young gay white man, was killed in Laramie, Wyoming, because of his sexual orientation (Dunn, 2010; Nadal, 2020). With heinous details shared through a much-publicized court trial (and the public outcry that followed), Shepard's murder eventually led to changes in hate crime legislation on local, state, and even federal levels. In fact, the Hate Crimes Bill, which was passed by Congress and signed by President Obama in 2009, is also known as The Matthew Shepard and James Byrd, Jr. Hate Crimes Prevention Act.

One murder that occurred 2 decades prior to Matthew Shepard was the 1978 murder of Harvey Milk—a 48-year-old gay white man and one of the first openly gay people to be elected to local government (Eyerman, 2012). While not deemed a hate crime murder—due to the lack of hate crime laws at the time and the other motives involved in the killings of Milk and San Francisco Mayor George Moscone—the murders of both Shepard and Milk are traditionally deemed as watershed moments in LGBTQ history. However, what is often overlooked are the hundreds of other LGBTQ hate crime victims (especially trans people or queer people of color) who did not receive the kind of media attention paid to Shepard or Milk, who were both gay white men (Nadal, 2020).

First, although antitransgender hate crime murders have been prevalent throughout history, the number of trans victims has never been properly documented or counted. In fact, because gender identity was not deemed a protected class in hate crime law until 2009, hate crime reports involving transgender people would have been labeled as being due to sexual orientation or would have been erased or ignored altogether. The first International Transgender Day of Remembrance was held in November 2009 to remember the 200 or more transgender people across the globe who had been killed within that past year and the hundreds of murders of transgender people throughout US history (Chang & Skolnik, 2017).

Second, hate crimes against LGBTQ people of color have also been pervasive over time but may not have received as much media attention as those against Shepard or Milk. For example, in 2003 (just a few years after Shepard's murder), a 15-year-old lesbian Black American woman named Sakia Gunn was murdered in a hate crime in New Jersey (Townsend, 2012). Although several thousand locals (mostly LGBTQ people of color) attended her funeral services, the event remains relatively unknown in public discourse, suggesting that hate crimes committed against people who are both racial and sexual minorities may not be nationally publicized, as compared with white LGBTQ people. In fact, even when the Orlando Pulse massacre occurred in 2016—in which 49 people were gunned down at the Pulse nightclub in Orlando, Florida—many news outlets failed to mention that the majority were people of color and that most were Latinx and Puerto Rican (Ramirez et al., 2018). Thus, the racialized experiences of LGBTQ people of color are erased, even in tragedy or death.

Two decades later, hate crimes are still a pervasive problem, particularly affecting trans people and queer people of color, and most especially Black trans women and trans women of color. Some notable victims include Jorge Steven López Mercado, a queer Puerto Rican who was burned, dismembered, and decapitated in 2009; Mark Carson, a Black gay man who was shot point-blank in the face in New York in 2013; and Muhlaysia Booker, Chynal Lindsey, and Brittany White, three Black transgender women who were murdered in

Dallas, Texas, in 2019 (Nadal, 2020). For the past several years, LGBTQ media outlets have documented the number of trans people who were killed that year; in 2020, there were 44 trans people murdered in the United States—the highest number ever recorded, with transwomen of color being most targeted (Sonoma, 2021).

Marriage Equality

In 2004, Massachusetts became the first state to legalize same-sex marriage. Five other states and Washington, DC, followed suit by 2011. However, despite these victories, there were also setbacks. For example, after same-sex marriage became legal in California in June 2008, a vote in favor of Proposition 8 in the November 2008 election banned it. That same year, same-sex marriage was also banned in two other states, and adoption by LGBTQ people was also banned in the state of Arkansas. However, in 2013, SCOTUS ruled that the California's Proposition 8 was unconstitutional, and in 2015, SCOTUS ruled that all same-sex marriage bans were unconstitutional, thus legalizing same-sex marriage across the United States. Since then, the Pew Research Center (2019) reported that in general, the US population's views of same-sex marriage have changed significantly (from 60% opposed in 2004 to 61% in favor in 2019); however, the number of people opposed to same-sex marriage (39%) represents how many still hold overt anti-LGBTQ biases.

Anti-LGBTQ Bullying

In the fall of 2010, six LGBTQ youth committed suicide in the span of weeks. While teen suicide is not a new phenomenon, these six individuals gained national attention because they were all reported to have committed suicide due to their peers bullying them because they identified or were perceived as LGBTQ. One of these young people was Seth Walsh, a 13-year-old from California who was bullied every day by his peers at school for being gay. After being taunted on a regular basis, he finally could not handle the agony and hanged himself from a tree in his backyard. On the other end of the country was Tyler Clementi, an 18-year-old college freshman at Rutgers University in New Jersey, whose roommate posted a streaming video of him on the internet having sex with another man, without Clementi's knowledge. Clementi, who was allegedly a closeted gay man, was reportedly humiliated, posted a suicide note on Facebook, and jumped off the George Washington Bridge after the cyberbullying had occurred.

Following these events, nationally syndicated sex columnist Dan Savage initiated the national "It Gets Better" campaign, which aimed to increase awareness about LGBTQ bullying and discourage LGBTQ youth from viewing suicide as a viable option. Celebrities and everyday people made videos sharing personal messages and stories of triumph, including LGBTQ celebrities (e.g., Adam Lambert, Lady Gaga, Tim Gunn, Neil Patrick Harris) and LGBTQ **allies** (e.g., Kathy Griffin, Barack Obama, Hillary Clinton). Media correspondents, psychologists, and others publicly hypothesized reasons why bullying existed, and why bullying toward LGBTQ youth led to a trend in suicide. Some explained how school systems were not protecting LGBTQ young people or creating a safe space for them, while others hypothesized that parents and educators were not teaching their children that bullying was wrong and could have severe consequences. Regardless, the surge of teen suicides has led to an increased awareness of anti-LGBTQ bullying, as well as the struggles that LGBTQ youth still face in current times.

Criminal Justice System

In recent years, there has been an increase of attention regarding LGBTQ disparities in the criminal justice system, the foster care system, and poverty (see Nadal, 2020, for a review). Through the documentary *Free CeCe*, actress LaVerne Cox assisted in publicizing the story of CeCe McDonald—a Black trans woman who was serving time in prison for fighting back during a hate crime. Media stories have also emerged about trans women who are harassed and brutalized by police officers; incarcerated LGBTQ offenders who are violently victimized in prisons; and incarcerated trans people who are housed in prison facilities that do not match their gender identities (Nadal, 2020). Further, researchers reported how LGBTQ people (especially trans people of color) are disproportionately affected by homelessness and poverty; studies found that LGBTQ people are 2 to 13 times more likely than cis heterosexual people to be homeless (Coolhart & Brown, 2017) and that trans people are 2 or 3 times more likely than cis people to live in poverty (James et al., 2016). Studies also found that LGBTQ youth are overrepresented in the child welfare system (McCormick et al., 2017) and that a significant number of incarcerated LGBTQ offenders spent time in foster care (Irvine & Canfield, 2016).

Given these numerous systemic inequities, it is crucial to examine how societal biases toward LGBTQ people may play a role. For example, many LGBTQ youth become homeless after running away from abusive homes or being kicked out or disowned by their parents. Meanwhile, some LGBTQ people (especially trans people of color) may have difficulty obtaining employment due to employers' transphobic or homophobic biases. Accordingly, many LGBTQ people may live in poverty, and some LGBTQ people may turn to

FIGURE 1.2. Young Queer and Trans Friends Celebrating Pride

Note. Photo courtesy of Rodnae Productions.

criminal or illegal activities as a means of survival. Thus, discrimination may not only affect people on an individual level, it may also result in systemic obstacles for entire subgroups and communities.

THE MANIFESTATION AND IMPACT OF LGBTQ DISCRIMINATION

A growth in empirical literature has described the many ways discrimination has negatively impacted people's mental health. This section explores the previous psychological research regarding various forms of discrimination, including (a) anti-LGBTQ hate crimes; (b) heterosexism and monosexism; and (c) transphobia, cissexism, and genderism. I define each of these terms and describe how each type of discrimination has influenced the lives of LGBTQ people as well as how each may lead to mild to severe psychological consequences.

Hate Violence

One way in which violent discrimination manifests toward LGBTQ people is through acts of hate violence, also known as hate crimes. Previous authors have described an array of reasons why perpetrators may commit hate crimes against LGBTQ individuals, such as perpetrators' discomfort with LGBTQ people, perpetrators' own discomfort with themselves, and/or their desire to possess power over another individual (Herek, 2017; Nadal, 2020). Previous research suggests that unlike race-based and religious-based hate crimes, anti-LGBTQ hate crimes are not motivated by historic antecedents; for instance, highly publicized racially charged court cases and terrorist acts often result in increased racial and religious hate crimes, whereas historic LGBTQ cases do not increase anti-LGBTQ hate crimes (King & Sutton, 2013). One study that examined FBI files of hate crimes between 1987 and 2003 found that perpetrators of anti-LGBTQ hate crimes were more likely to have committed their crimes alone, with LGBTQ victims dying by blunt force trauma (instead of gunshot) and victims being found naked or partially exposed (Davis, 2018).

Some studies reveal how people in general perceive hate crimes and are often less empathetic toward LGBTQ people. For instance, one study showed that people who maintain strong antigay biases often place blame antigay hate crime on victims (Lyons, 2006), while another study found that people had more empathy for victims of hate crimes based on religion, ethnicity/national origin, and disability than they did for victims of hate crimes based on sexual orientation or race (Griffin, 2010). Thus, it is evident that biases toward LGBTQ people still exist and may even negatively affect the ways that individuals view LGBTQ people who are victimized.

Previous studies found that hate crimes toward LGBTQ people involve more brutal violence and result in more serious injuries to their victims, with patterns of harm such as overkill, brutality, excessive mutilation, and aggravated assault, as well as the use of weapons such as guns, baseball bats, knives, clubs, blunt objects, chains, vehicles, ropes, and restraints (Briones-Robinson et al., 2016). One study found gay and bisexual men were more likely to experience hate crime-related sexual assaults than gay and bisexual women (Rothman et al., 2011). Another study revealed that homophobic sexual assaults occurred for both men and women, resulted in significantly more posttraumatic stress disorder (PTSD) symptoms than other types of assaults, and had a long-term effect of more than 2 years (Rose & Mechanic, 2002).

Hate crimes are very prevalent for transgender people in general and even more specifically for transgender women of color (James et al., 2016; Walters et al., 2020). One study found that hate crimes toward transgender and gender nonconforming people are especially violent and that transgender victims are targeted for violence for more complex reasons than their **gender variance** (Stotzer, 2008). Another study, with 629 trans women in San Francisco, found that about half reported a transphobic hate crime but only half of those were reported to police (Gyamerah et al., 2021). One study found that trans people were more likely than cisgender lesbian, gay, bisexual, or queer people to report heightened levels of threat, vulnerability, and anxiety when learning about hate crimes (Walters et al., 2020). Finally, researchers who analyzed data from the National Crime Victimization Survey found that trans participants experienced 86.2 victimizations per 1,000 participants, in comparison with 21.7 victimizations per 1,000 cis participants; trans women participants were also significantly more likely than cisgender men to identify their victimizations as hate crimes (Flores et al., 2021).

It is necessary to recognize that when examining hate crimes, particularly hate crimes based on sexual orientation and gender identity, actual statistics are likely incorrect for a few major reasons. First, hate crimes toward LGBTQ people tend to go underreported by survivors, particularly because of fear of retaliation by their attackers and because of the fear of discrimination or **retraumatization** by police officers and the criminal justice system (Nadal, 2020; Nadal, Quintanilla, et al., 2015). Further, LGBTQ people who are still "in the closet" may not want to report hate crimes in order to avoid revealing their sexual or gender identity, while others may blame themselves for being victimized. Sometimes, LGBTQ people who are victimized by hate crimes may connect to emotions like shame, guilt, embarrassment, and fear, which then prevents them from reporting hate crimes when they occur (Herek, 2000). Furthermore, because of the heterosexism and transphobia that are often common and pervasive within the criminal justice system, hate crimes toward LGBTQ people may not be labeled as such by police officers and prosecutors, resulting in a severe underreporting of anti-LGBTQ hate crimes (Palmer & Kutateladze, 2021; Ruback et al., 2018). As a result, it is common for anti-LGBTQ perpetrators to be convicted of less punishable charges and serve shorter sentences because their crimes were not determined to be hate crimes.

Hate crimes toward LGBTQ people are also misreported and misinterpreted due to the lack of uniform data collection across different jurisdictions, as well as whether reports are based on the number of victims or biased incidents. For example, according to the Federal Bureau of Investigation (FBI; 2021), in 2020 there were a total of 8,052 single bias incidents (with 11,472 victims) across the entire country—suggesting that most hate crimes involve multiple victims per incident. When examining the data on victims alone, 20% of the hate crime victims were determined to have been targeted by sexual orientation bias (or 2,229 victims), and 2.7% of the incidents involved gender identity bias (or 302 victims). Meanwhile, when looking at the incidents alone, it appears that there were 1,110 hate crime incidents based on sexual orientation bias and that 266 hate crime incidents were based on gender identity bias. The breakdown of these hate crimes based on sexual orientation include (a) antigay (male): 673 incidents; (b) anti-lesbian, gay, bisexual, transgender (mixed group): 306 incidents; (c) antilesbian (female): 103 incidents; (d) antibisexual: 17 incidents; and (e) antiheterosexual: 11 incidents. Specific to gender-identity-related hate crimes, 244 antitransgender incidents and 58 anti–gender nonconforming incidents (FBI, 2021).

Some researchers have examined how LGBTQ people experience and cope with hate crimes. While victims of any crime may experience significant psychological distress, previous research has found that hate crimes toward LGBTQ people may also have more severe psychological consequences than nonbias crimes, with survivors reporting symptoms like depression, anxiety, and posttraumatic stress disorder (Boroughs et al., 2015). For gay men specifically, some research has suggested that gay survivors of hate crimes experience both immediate and long-term physical consequences and severe psychological distress (e.g., insecurity, lack of safety, low self-worth; Scheer et al., 2021). Hate crime victims may blame themselves and develop an internalized heterosexism, and they may learn to believe that being LGBTQ is bad, deficient, or a punishment (Paterson et al., 2019). Furthermore, previous research has suggested that victims of hate crimes may still experience psychological distress for long periods of time after their incidents; one earlier study found that there were no significant differences in the amount of anxiety between recent hate crime victims and victims of crime more than 5 years earlier (Herek et al., 1999). A newer study found that while LGBTQ survivors of hate crimes may initially feel empathy and vulnerability when learning about other LGBTQ people experiencing hate crimes, they are more likely to show less empathy and may even victim-blame over time (Paterson et al., 2019). Taken together, these two studies demonstrate some long-term psychological consequences for LGBTQ survivors of hate crimes, perhaps involving self-blame and other internalized feelings.

Intersectional identities may also factor into one's experience of hate crimes. One study reported that 70% of anti-LGBTQ murder victims are people of color but that only 55% of the total number of reported hate crimes involve LGBTQ people of color (Dixon et al., 2011). Another study revealed that while LGBTQ people of color from poor and working-class backgrounds experience more physically violent hate crimes than middle-class LGBTQ white people, middle-class LGBTQ white people were more likely to perceive their violent experiences as severe (D. Meyer, 2010). Trans women of color of lower socioeconomic statuses are particularly vulnerable to hate crimes because of their multiple oppressed identities (James et al., 2016; Stotzer, 2008). Thus, when examining hate crimes, it is crucial to consider how other social identities influence the type of hate crime, the severity of the hate crime, the intention of the perpetrator, and the coping mechanisms and psychological outcomes of the victims.

Finally, research has shown that when a hate crime occurs, LGBTQ people may experience a **vicarious traumatization**. This means that even though LGBTQ individuals were in no way involved in the hate crime (i.e., they were not present, they do not know the victim personally, or they do not live anywhere near the scene of the crime), their fundamental assumptions of benevolence and meaningfulness of the world (and of other people) were challenged (Bell & Perry, 2015; Noelle, 2002). Other terms to describe this phenomenon include **historical trauma** or **collective trauma**, with the former describing the type of trauma that is passed across generations of people of historically marginalized groups and the latter describing the types of traumas that people experience in reaction to a traumatic event affecting someone in their community or with a shared identity (Nadal, 2018). Often, experiencing vicarious traumatization could even negatively impact one's own mental health and self-worth, regardless of any personal connection to the victim (Bell & Perry, 2015; Noelle, 2002).

To illustrate this, when the Orlando Pulse Massacre occurred in 2016, many LGBTQ people (especially LGBTQ Latinx people and LGBTQ people of color) were vicariously traumatized (Nadal, 2020). Although they may not have ever met any of the victims, the event may have had negative consequences on LGBTQ people's **worldviews** or mental health. Because many LGBTQ people frequent queer bars and nightclubs—even viewing them as "queer sanctuaries" that temporarily protect them from heterosexism and trans-phobia (Nadal, 2020, p. 40), many LGBTQ people became more concerned or vigilant about their safety, while others reported an increase in psycho-logical distress and trauma symptoms (Ben-Ezra et al., 2017; Jackson, 2017; Stults et al., 2017). LGBTQ Latinx people and other LGBTQ people of color reported feeling especially distressed due to their feelings of connection to the Pulse victims (with shared similar intersectional identities) and their frustrations that issues of race and ethnicity were erased or ignored when dis-cussing the tragedy (Ramirez et al., 2018). Thus, it is crucial to recognize that hate crimes do not only negatively affect the victims (or families of victims); they can also have a detrimental impact on entire communities, including LGBTQ people.

Heterosexism and Monosexism

Although it may be less acceptable for hate crimes to occur and more acceptable for people to be more accepting of LGBTQ people in general American society, anti-LGBTQ sentiment is still enacted and experienced in multiple ways—overtly and violently (e.g., hate crimes), systemically (e.g., heterosexist laws), and interpersonally (e.g., discrimination, microaggressions). Prior to the now commonly accepted use of the term "microaggressions," scholars had conceptualized everyday forms of antigay, antilesbian, antibisexual, and antiqueer biases in various ways. First, sexual prejudice was initially described as "all negative attitudes based on sexual orientation" (Herek, 2000, p. 19)—with biases involving negative views about LGBTQ behaviors, LGBTQ individuals, and LGBTQ communities. Herek (2000) noted that sexual prejudice was a preferable term to **homophobia** because homophobia implies that one has a fear of homosexuals, whereas sexual prejudice describes the bias, aversion, or negative perception of LGBTQ people. Second, Burn et al. (2005) defined *antigay harassment* as "verbal or physical behavior that injures, interferes with, or intimidates lesbian women, gay men, and bisexual individuals" (p. 24). For example, when adolescents (particularly heterosexual young men) use words like "faggot" or "homo" as a way of insulting or hurting others, they may not necessarily be accusing someone of being gay but are instead insinuating that they are weak or less masculine. Similarly, when adolescents (and adults) use the word "gay" as a synonym for bad, undesirable, or weird, individuals may not necessarily be using the term to insult gay people (Burn et al., 2005). Yet, even if they do not do so consciously, someone who uses such biased terms might subconsciously believe that LGBTQ people are inferior or bad, and these terms can cause distress and hurt for LGBTQ people who hear them. One study found queer college students who heard the term "That's so gay" were more likely to report feelings of isolation, more headaches, and poor appetite (Woodford et al., 2012), while another study found that hearing both "That's so gay" and "No homo" predicted increased binge drinking and substance use (Winberg et al., 2019).

Silverschanz et al. (2008) defined *heterosexist harassment* as "insensitive verbal and symbolic (but nonassaultive) behaviors that convey animosity toward nonheterosexuality" (p. 179), with two main manifestations: (a) personal or direct experiences and (b) ambient or indirect experiences. Personal experiences are situations when a person is directly targeted due to their sexual orientation (i.e., being called a "dyke" or "queer"), while ambient experiences include situations when LGBTQ people are indirectly targeted (e.g., someone making homophobic jokes in front of an LGBTQ person).

Modern heterosexism or modern homonegativity were two other terms that described less overt forms of discrimination toward LGBTQ people, or societal ways in which heterosexual people are celebrated or normalized while nonheterosexuals are pathologized (Cowan et al., 2005; Walls, 2008).

Sexual stigma refers to "negative regard, inferior status, and relative powerlessness that society collectively accords to any non-heterosexual behavior, identity, relationship, or community" (Herek, 2007, p. 906), with three main types (a) enacted stigma, (b) felt stigma, and (c) internalized stigma. *Enacted* stigma describes the overt behavioral expression of sexual stigma (i.e., the traditionally overt, old-fashioned heterosexism). *Felt* stigma involves instances where LGBTQ individuals may modify their behavior to avoid difficult and dangerous situations or enacted stigma. For instance, an LGBTQ person may not share their **sexual identity** to someone in their family, even if the said family member had not said anything overtly heterosexist or biased against LGBTQ people, because they worry about that person's reactions. Finally, *internalized* stigma involves the integration of one's sexual stigma into one's value system. For example, if a person has internalized negative feelings toward and perceptions of LGBTQ people, it may be difficult for them to acknowledge their own sexual orientation; relatedly, if a heterosexual person has learned sexual stigma about LGBTQ people, they may behave in discriminatory ways consciously (e.g., using homophobic slurs, bullying LGBTQ individuals) or unconsciously (e.g., not having LGBTQ friends, avoiding movies with LGBTQ characters).

Finally, scholars have also described the types of discrimination that bisexual people experience specifically. The term **biphobia** was used to describe how people hold prejudicial attitudes or enact discrimination onto bisexual people (Mulick & Wright, 2002). However, the terms *biphobia* and *homophobia* have both decreased in usage—likely because a phobia clinically involves irrational or terrifying fears of certain things (and most people with heterosexist bias aren't typically viscerally terrified by gay, bisexual, or queer people). The term **monosexism** emerged shortly afterward—being defined as "the privileging of sexual attraction to one sex or gender, from heterosexual, gay, and lesbian communities" (Roberts et al., 2015, p. 554). Monosexism is derived in the notion that people are either exclusively heterosexual or nonheterosexual—failing to understand the fluidity of both gender identity and sexual attraction, or that enforcing binaries—especially within LGBTQ communities—is simply a reiteration of societal heterosexism.

Transphobia, Cissexism, and Genderism

In the field of psychology, there are three major terms that are used to describe the discrimination and prejudice that transgender people may experience. *Transphobia* can be defined as "an emotional disgust toward individuals who do not conform to society's gender expectations" (Hill & Willoughby, 2005, p 533), while *genderism* is "an ideology that reinforces the negative evaluation of gender non-conformity or an incongruence between sex and gender" (Hill & Willoughby, 2005, p. 534). Cissexism has been used more recently to depict the systems of oppressions affecting trans and nonbinary people (Velez et al., 2021). Transphobia may be a parallel term to homophobia, in which individuals are fearful of gay, bisexual, and lesbian people, while genderism may be a parallel term to heterosexism, which describes the subtle ways that individuals may be prejudiced toward gay, bisexual, and transgender persons. Cissexism may also be akin to heterosexism—focusing on both the systemic and interpersonal manifestations of antitrans bias.

While it is likely that our changing society may encourage individuals to be less racist, less sexist, and even less heterosexist, it is possible that cisgender people (both heterosexual and queer) may maintain transphobic or genderist views. This may be due to the rigidity of **gender roles** in U.S. society, particularly with **gender role expectations** in which men and women are expected to dress, look, act, and speak in **gender conforming** ways. Furthermore, because gender conforming people tend to fixate on **gender presentation**, many may show overt fear or disgust toward any transgender person.

Although there have been great strides toward transgender rights in the past decade, there remains a dearth in academic literature that highlights their experiences with discrimination or cisgender people's attitudes toward them (Worthen, 2016). The few empirical studies and reports regarding transphobic discrimination inform many of the obstacles that transgender people experience. One study from 2 decades ago found that 60% of participants had been victimized (e.g., experiencing harassment by strangers on the street, verbal abuse, assault with a weapon, sexual assault) because of their gender identity, while 37% of their sample reported economic discrimination, such as being fired, demoted, or unfairly disciplined (Lombardi et al., 2002). Another study revealed how trans people encounter a range of discriminatory experiences in their families—describing everything from physical violence, open hostility, to indifferent or neglectful responses from parents; participants also reported that they were forced out of their homes during adolescence (or chose to leave because of the hostile environment in which they were living) due to rejection and violence (Koken et al., 2009). Scholars have applied minority stress theory (a model used to describe how systemic and interpersonal discrimination negatively impacts the physical and psychological health of LGBTQ people and other minoritized groups) to reveal how trans people may regularly navigate hate speech, physical and/or sexual assault, and social ostracization (Hendricks & Testa, 2012). One study reported similar realities for trans people (e.g., harassment, violence) but also revealed the notion of "silent harassment," in which people stare or whisper about trans people, which in turn results in feelings of intimidation, marginalization, or othering (Ellis et al., 2016).

The first large-scale comprehensive report regarding the everyday lives of transgender people was the National Transgender Discrimination Survey (Grant et al., 2011). In this study, which included 6,450 transgender people across the United States and Puerto Rico, the following findings were reported:

- Survey respondents experienced unemployment at twice the rate of the population, with trans people of color reporting 4 times the unemployment rate.

- Ninety-seven percent (97%) of those surveyed reported experiencing harassment or mistreatment on the job.

- Forty-seven percent (47%) had experienced an adverse job outcome, such as being fired, not being hired, or being denied a promotion.

- Fifteen percent (15%) of transgender people in the sample lived on $10,000 per year or less—4 times more likely than general population.

- Nineteen percent (19%) of the sample had been or were homeless, 11% had faced eviction, and 26% were forced to seek temporary space.

- Nearly half of the sample (41%) had reported a suicide attempt in their lifetime, as compared with the national average of 1.6%.

Several years later, results from the U.S. Transgender Survey (a study that included 27,715 participants from the United States and its territories) were released (James et al., 2016). While findings regarding workplace discrimination and poverty were similar, results illuminated experiences within health care, educational systems, the criminal justice system, and more. Examples include the following:

- Nearly one fourth (23%) of participants reported not seeking health care out of fear of being discriminated against by doctors.

- Thirty-nine percent of the sample reported severe psychological distress, and 7% reported a suicide attempt in the prior year (12 times higher than the general population).

- Over half (54%) who were out or perceived as trans in their K–12 schools were verbally harassed, and nearly one quarter (24%) were physically assaulted.

- More than half (58%) reported being harassed by police, and 22% of those who were arrested in the prior year believed it was because of their gender identity.

- Only 11% of the sample reported having a government identification card with their preferred name.

Thus, it is evident that trans people face extreme discrimination on interpersonal levels (e.g., from their families, coworkers, or peers) and systemic levels (e.g., having higher rates of unemployment, poverty, and homelessness). Now, let's examine how these cumulative experiences with discrimination affect queer and trans people's mental health.

PSYCHOLOGICAL CONSEQUENCES OF DISCRIMINATION

There has been an abundance of previous literature that has described the psychological distress and mental health problems that LGBTQ individuals develop because of overt sexual discrimination; these include everything from suicidal ideation, depression, anxiety, and trauma (Nadal, 2018; Sutter & Perrin, 2016; Velez et al., 2021). Integrating minority stress theory, other authors have examined the **minority stress** that is experienced by LGBTQ people (i.e., the chronic, consistent stress that is related to stigmatization and marginalization because of one's sexual orientation or gender identity; Hendricks & Testa, 2012; I. H. Meyer, 2015). Such stress can often create hostile and distressing home, work, and social environments, which may potentially result in mental health problems like depression, anxiety, posttraumatic stress, and internalized homophobia (Herek & Garnets, 2007; I. H. Meyer, 2015). Discrimination and stigmatization are also predictors of physical health issues (e.g., cardiovascular disease, diabetes) as well as health-risk behaviors (e.g., substance use, risky sexual behaviors, overeating; Mereish & Taylor, 2021). Multiple forms of victimization and trauma exposure are significantly related to increased sick days, anxiety, depression, substance use, and suicidality (Kassing et al., 2021). Further, studies support that when LGBTQ people face microaggressions, they are susceptible to a variety of mental health problems, including depression, anxiety, and posttraumatic stress (see Nadal, 2018, for a review). Thus, when LGBTQ people are victimized in any way, they are at risk for both mental and physical health problems—making the study of microaggressions (which is covered more extensively in the next chapter) a public health issue.

DISCUSSION QUESTIONS

For General Readers

1. Have you experienced overt discrimination, anti-LGBTQ violence, or hate crimes in your life? How have you reacted to these occurrences? How have they made you feel?

2. Have you experienced microaggressions in your life? How have you reacted to these occurrences? How have they made you feel?

3. Did your educational systems or media teach you about the history of LGBTQ people in the United States or in the world? If so, what do you remember? How do you feel about this?

For Psychologists, Educators, and Other Experts

1. How do institutional and systemic discrimination negatively affect the people you serve?

2. What can you do in your field or organization to combat microaggressions that your clients, students, or constituents face in their everyday lives?

GLOSSARY OF KEY TERMS

allies People from historically privileged groups who understand the influence of oppression and show solidarity to people from historically marginalized groups.

biphobia An emotional disgust toward individuals whose sexual orientation is bisexual; a fear of people who are sexually attracted to more than one gender.

bisexuality The identity or description of being romantically or sexually attracted to more than one sex or gender.

collective trauma A group's shared sense of psychological distress upon witnessing or observing a horrific event or public tragedy.

gender conforming The trait or identity of adhering to gender role expectations.

gender identity An individual's personal sense of identification as male, female, more than one gender, no gender, or something else.

gender nonconformity The act of not adhering to societal gender roles, particularly regarding identity, presentation, or behaviors.

gender presentation Perceptions of a person as male, female, or another gender identity—based on how they are dressed, look, and/or act.

gender roles Expectations defined within specific societies and cultures about culturally appropriate behaviors, norms, and values for men and women, based on gender.

gender variance A behavior, style of dress, or identity that does not conform to standard ideas of what it means to be a woman or man.

hate crime A criminal act in which the victim is targeted because of their actual or perceived race, color, religion, national origin, ethnicity, disability, sexual orientation, or other identity. Also known as "hate violence."

historical trauma The collective psychological distress that is felt over time and across generations of a group of people who share an identity, affiliation, or circumstance.

homophobia An emotional disgust toward people who are sexually attracted to people of their same sex; a fear of nonheterosexual people.

homosexuality The identity or quality of being romantically or sexually attracted to members of one's own sex.

homosexuals An outdated term describing people who are only romantically or sexually attracted to members of their own sex.

institutional discrimination The unfair and biased indirect treatment of a person based on operating procedures, policies, laws, or objectives of systems or organizations.

interpersonal discrimination The unfair and biased treatment of another person based on one person's prejudice or stereotypes about one of the other person's identities.

intersectional identities The unique combination of individuals' multiple social groups (e.g., race, ethnicity, gender, sexual identity, gender identity, age, religion, size) and the identification, experiences, and worldviews that result from these combinations.

minority stress The excess psychological distress caused by prejudice and discrimination.

monosexism The belief, biases, or actions that promote monosexuality (either exclusive heterosexuality and/or homosexuality) as the only legitimate or right sexual orientation.

retraumatization The act of being traumatized again by a reminder of a past violent or life-threatening event.

sexual identity The process of developing a personal sense of self as a sexual being; encompasses one's sexual orientation and gender identity.

sexual orientation A personal and social identity based on one's sexual attractions, behaviors expressing those sexual attractions, and membership in a community of others.

sodomy A dated term used to describe the sexual act involving anal or oral copulation, or sexual acts between a human and an animal.

transphobia An emotional disgust toward individuals who do not conform to society's gender expectations; a fear of transgender or gender nonconforming people.

two-spirited A term in North American Indigenous cultures used to describe people who are neither male nor female; often referred to as a "third gender."

vicarious traumatization The notion that people of a certain social group will experience moderate to severe psychological distress when a member of the same social group is victimized.

worldview The collection of beliefs and perspectives from which one sees and interprets the world, based on one's cultural identities and life experiences.

2 A REVIEW OF MICROAGGRESSION LITERATURE

FIGURE 2.1. Two Young Queer Women of Color Smiling

Note. Photo courtesy of Bran Sodre.

https://doi.org/10.1037/0000335-003
Dismantling Everyday Discrimination: Microaggressions Toward LGBTQ People, Second Edition, by K. L. Y. Nadal

As reviewed in Chapter 1, there has been a growth in literature that supports how discrimination in general has become much subtler, more innocuous, or more coded, rather than blatant, obvious, and direct. So, while it is known that assaults based on race, gender, sexual orientation, ethnicity, religion, and other identities still occur and have detrimental impacts on oppressed groups, it has become less acceptable or less "politically correct" for such interactions to transpire in everyday life. For instance, while race-based hate crimes may still be pervasive in American society, research has found that racism in everyday interpersonal interactions have become more indirect—being labeled as modern racism, symbolic racism, and aversive racism (Sue et al., 2007). Scholars have used similar concepts to describe more insidious forms of discrimination toward LGBTQ people; these include sexual prejudice, antigay harassment, modern heterosexism, and others (Nadal, Rivera, & Corpus, 2010). This chapter briefly reviews the trajectory of microaggression literature—citing how the term was first conceptualized, how it became popularized, and the types of research that have emerged today. While further chapters cover in more detail the research microaggressions toward various LGBTQ people (e.g., lesbian, gay, bisexual, and queer people; trans and non-binary people; LGBTQ with multiple marginalized identities), this chapter also demonstrates the difficulty in labeling microaggressions, empirically measuring microaggressions, and combatting the naysayers who are committed to negating or challenging microaggressions as a legitimate area of study.

IDENTIFYING AND MEASURING MICROAGGRESSIONS

Scholars have described how one challenge with more subtle or less violent manifestations of discrimination is that the intent of the culprit is harder to prove—often resulting in a different type of distress from when one is overtly targeted (Sue et al., 2007; Torino et al., 2019). For example, if someone is targeted violently by a hate crime—especially if the perpetrator verbally and clearly uses homophobic, transphobic, or racist language when assaulting the person—the victim or survivor may have no doubt that they are being targeted because of their sexual orientation, gender identity, or race. While undergoing such an attack would be extremely traumatizing and debilitating, the targeted person does not have to spend a lot of extra cognitive energy debating whether the act was biased. They may engage in other self-blaming and other self-deprecating thought processes, but at the very least they know intellectually that they were targeted because of their identity group.

Conversely, when a covert racially charged interaction occurs between two parties, one person (typically a person of color) may perceive something to be racially motivated, while the other person (typically a white person) may provide many other explanations other than race. Imagine a scenario in which a white woman is riding in an elevator by herself. After she travels up a few floors, the elevator stops, and a Black man enters the elevator. Right at that moment, the woman moves a few feet slightly to the right, while grabbing onto her purse tightly.

People with different worldviews may have different reactions to and justifications for the woman's behaviors. First, some may believe that race was not involved in the interaction, presuming good intentions (e.g., maybe the woman moved to the side of the elevator to allow the man to "have more room"). The woman may also claim she coincidentally held her purse at the exact moment the man entered through the door or that she would have done so when anyone, of any race or gender, entered. Yet, others may perceive race as the primary motivating factor in her behavior: Because of her anti-Black stereotypes, she grabbed her purse as an irrational fear.

Regardless of the woman's intention, the man who notices her behavior may have an array of reactions. First, he may not think anything of it and may believe that the woman coincidentally clutched her purse without any racial motivations. Second, there is a chance that he did notice the behavior and did attribute it to race. There is also the potential that he is accustomed to such experiences (because they occur so frequently); therefore, he might claim to not be bothered by the interaction. On the other hand, there is the possibility he does perceive the woman's behavior as racially charged; accordingly, he may react with an array of emotions, like anger, frustration, hurt, and sadness *because* these types of situations occur regularly.

Further, deciding how to respond to subtle or more coded forms of discrimination can be challenging. For example, the Black man on the elevator may believe that the incident was racially motivated; however, it may be challenging for him to "prove" his hypothesis to the woman. If he did confront her, she could deny his accusations and provide an alternative rationalization (which in turn could cause him more distress or conflict). She could also turn it around on him and accuse him of being hostile or violent toward her. Yet, if he chooses to simply ignore the incident, she will not learn the impact of her behavior, and he may regret not addressing the situation.

Scholars have described the process of deciding how to react to microaggressions, particularly where there could be both positive and negative potential outcomes or repercussions, as a "Catch 22" (Sue et al., 2007, p. 279). Some people always confront microaggressions, potentially leading to consistent arguments and subsequent psychological stress. Other people may rarely or never challenge microaggressions that occur, potentially resulting in internalized emotions like guilt, resentment, or anger. Some people in these situations may learn to "pick their battles" and only confront micro-aggressions they believe are worth fighting for, or in which they believe the perpetrator may be capable of listening or willing to learn from their behaviors.

Relatedly, scholars have also highlighted the notion of **microinterventions**, or strategies that people (e.g., targets, allies, bystanders) can use to cope with or address microaggressions (Sue et al., 2019). For instance, some targets of microaggressions may learn to directly stop or deflect a microaggression immediately (e.g., "I don't agree with what you said") or challenging stereo-types (e.g., "I may be Black, but I'm not dangerous"; Sue et al., 2019, p. 130). Some targets of microaggressions may feel unable to address microaggressions individually, so they may turn to external support or reinforcement. While more of these microinterventions will be described throughout the text, situa-tions like the scenario above illustrate the complexities of microaggressions and the psychological toll on their targets—a theme that will be presented throughout this text.

Parallel to this process in reacting to microaggressions, researchers who *study* microaggressions have had similar struggles with how to address people who challenge their work. Given that intention and internalized processes might feel very difficult to prove, it becomes easier for naysayers to say that microaggressions are invalid, not real, or misinterpretations by the target. In fact, Sue, Capodilupo, Nadal, and Torino (2008) described how early contrarians to microaggression research depicted people of color as "overly sensitive, out of contact with reality, and even paranoid" or that the bur-geoning field of microaggressions was "pure nonsense" (p. 277). In these ways, the academic reactions to the study of microaggressions themselves may parallel the diverse reactions of people in the elevator incident. While the targets may perceive incidents as being influenced by dynamics such as race, gender, sexual orientation, and so forth, the perpetrators may claim to have good intentions, may rationalize or intellectualize their behaviors, or attempt to gaslight the targets into believing that they are paranoid or psychologically inept (Johnson et al., 2021). Sue, Capodilupo, Nadal, and Tornio (2008) argued that when perpetrators are successful in convinc-ing others that microaggressions are nonexistent or nonsensical, they dem-onstrate that individuals from privileged backgrounds or who come from positions of power really do have the "power to define reality" (p. 277). But first, let's review the previous literature on microaggressions to understand more context.

LITERATURE REVIEW OF RACIAL AND GENDER MICROAGGRESSIONS

Dr. Chester Pierce, who was a psychiatrist and professor at Harvard Medical School, first introduced the term racial microaggressions in the 1970s when identifying the subtle discrimination toward Black Americans in the media (Pierce et al., 1977). For the following 30 years or so, the term had been described sparsely in various areas of psychology and education. Notably, Dr. Daniel Solórzano et al. (2000) highlighted the different microaggressions that students of color encountered on various college and university campuses. Despite these few efforts, most research involving racial discrimination during this time focused mainly on overt, blatant forms of racism, and the concept of microaggressions was generally invisible in academia.

In 2007 I was a doctoral student at Teachers College–Columbia University in New York where I was mentored by one of the most revered counseling psychologists—Dr. Derald Wing Sue—and I was a member of the team that reintroduced racial microaggressions in an article in *American Psychologist* (Sue et al., 2007). We described the ways that the United States had become more politically correct and how racism was much more masked and covert. We presented a theoretical taxonomy, highlighting the different types of racial microaggressions that people of color may face in their everyday lives. These included the following:

- *Alien in one's own land:* experiences in which people of color may be treated like perpetual foreigners. (e.g., telling a Latinx, Asian American, or Indigenous person "You speak good English" or persistently asking them "Where are you from?" even though they persistently respond that they are "American")

- *Criminality/assumption of criminality:* incidents in which people of color are stereotyped to be deviant or criminals. (e.g., a police officer who pulls over a Black male driver for no reason or a store owner who follows a Black woman around in a store while she is shopping)

- *Second-class citizen:* experiences in which people of color receive substandard service (e.g., a taxicab driver who passes a person of color for a white customer; a group of people of color are seated at the back of the restaurant or near the kitchen when there are plenty of seats in front)

- *Ascription of intelligence:* incidents in which people of color (typically Black, Latinx, or Indigenous) are assumed to be less intellectual or uneducated, or when East Asian or South Asian Americans are assumed to be the "model minority" (e.g., when someone tells a Black American that they are "so articulate" or when a Chinese American is automatically presumed to be good at math or sciences)

- *Assumption of inferiority:* experiences in which people of color are assumed to be poor or in substandard careers (e.g., when someone assumes people of color reside in poorer neighborhoods or when someone presumes a person of color is "the help")

- *Color blindness:* incidents in which people of color are told by white people that they "don't see race" (e.g., after a person of color confronts a white person on their biases, and the white person replies, "That's absurd. I don't see color; I just see you!")

- *Denial of racial reality:* statements in which someone invalidates the experiences with racism that people of color encounter regularly (e.g., a white person's telling a woman of color that she is paranoid or "oversensitive" to racial issues)

- *Pathologizing cultural values/communication styles:* experiences in which people are viewed as abnormal or deviant for their cultural behaviors, traditions, or ways of communicating (e.g., someone tells a Middle Eastern student to "be more aggressive; you're in America now" or insults her for the food from her culture that she eats for lunch)

- *Denial of individual racism:* statements in which someone defensively denies that they are racist or engaged in racist behaviors (e.g., after being confronted about a microaggression, someone says, "I'm not racist. One of my best friends is Black!")

- *Environmental racial microaggressions:* subtle racially discriminatory messages that are communicated through institutions, media, government, and other systems (e.g., when media portrays people of color in stereotypical or negative ways, when corporations do not have any people of color in any leadership positions)

Since this taxonomy was originally presented, many qualitative studies focusing on racial microaggressions emerged—covering perspectives of Black Americans, Asian Americans, Latinx Americans, Indigenous People, and Multiracial People (see Sue, 2010, for a review). A racial microaggression measure titled the Racial and Ethnic Microaggression Scale also emerged, identifying quantitatively six subscales of racial microaggressions that people of color may encounter in their everyday lives (Nadal, 2011).

While these publications and subsequent studies on racial microaggressions began to emerge, dialogues regarding microaggressions affecting other marginalized groups did too. In 2010, I presented a comprehensive taxonomy on gender microaggressions toward women, based on previous literature studying related variables like subtle sexism, **objectification**, and **benevolent sexism** (see Nadal, 2010a). Themes included:

- *Sexual objectification:* experiences in which women are viewed as sexual objects (e.g., when women are catcalled as they walk down the street or when men touch women's backs as they walk past them in a crowded bar or restaurant)

- *Assumptions of inferiority:* incidents in which women are viewed as intellectually or physically inferior (e.g., presuming a woman would not be capable of carrying a heavy box or telling someone that women are not good leaders)

- *Assumptions of traditional gender roles:* experiences in which women are presumed to maintain stereotypical gender role norms (e.g., when women are expected to cook or clean at home, or asked to plan the office holiday party)

- *Use of sexist language:* statements that subtly or overtly demean women (e.g., when people freely use the word "bitch" or "skank" to describe women)

- *Denial of individual sexism*: statements in which a man defensively denies that he is sexist or engaged in sexist behaviors (e.g., a man who says, "How dare you accuse me of being sexist. I have two daughters!")

- *Invisibility:* incidents in which women receive substandard treatment from men (e.g., when a woman is overlooked for service by a male bartender at a crowded bar)

- *Denial of reality of sexism:* statements in which someone invalidates the experiences with sexism that women encounter regularly (e.g., a man's telling a woman that she is "angry" or "hypersensitive" to issues regarding sexism)

- *Environmental gender microaggressions:* subtle discriminatory messages that are communicated through institutions, media, government, and other systems (e.g., when media portrays women as sexual objects, when corporations do not have any women in any leadership positions)

Eventually, studies on gender microaggressions toward women materialized, citing the various kinds of microaggressions that target women

FIGURE 2.2. A Queer Asian American Family Flying a Kite in Seattle

Note. Photo courtesy of PNW Productions.

(Capodilupo et al., 2010) as well as the various ways in which women react to gender microaggressions (Nadal et al., 2013).

Besides race and gender, microaggression taxonomies regarding other populations began to develop. Some theoretical models focused on perspectives of multiracial people (Johnston & Nadal, 2010), religious minorities (Nadal, Issa, et al., 2010), and people with disabilities (Keller & Galgay, 2010). I was involved in a lot of this microaggression literature and research, as both an advanced doctoral student at Teachers College–Columbia University and later as an early career professor at John Jay College of Criminal Justice–City University of New York. I wanted to ensure that anti-LGBTQ microaggressions were also discussed in the literature; thus, I aimed to conceptualize a sexual orientation and gender identity microaggression taxonomy and began researching how subtle discrimination negatively impacted LGBTQ people's lives.

TAXONOMY OF LGBTQ MICROAGGRESSIONS

The first step in creating a taxonomy focusing on microaggressions experienced by LGBTQ people was to consult with others who would be as passionate about studying the topic as I was, so, I called upon two doctoral student colleagues—David Rivera and Melissa Corpus. David (a self-identified gay Latino man) had previously conducted research on racial microaggressions encountered by Latinx people; Melissa (a self-identified gay Filipina American woman) had conducted extensive research on lesbian and bisexual women, particularly lesbian and bisexual women of color. Our task was simple: to review previous literature on LGBTQ discrimination while using our own professional and anecdotal knowledge to create a list of the various categories of microaggressions that LGBTQ people encounter in their daily lives. We were consciously aware that we did not have any transgender people on this task force and that all three of us identified as cisgender. We also recognized that we did not represent a completely diverse group of racial and ethnic backgrounds, as we were all either Latino or Filipina/o. Thus, we consulted with our personal and professional networks, which included transgender women and men, other LGBTQ people of color, LGBTQ white people, bisexuals, and others, to create a comprehensive list of microaggressions that targeted LGBTQ people.

Our proposed theoretical taxonomy on sexual orientation and gender identity microaggressions cited eight distinct categories of microaggressions that may target LGBTQ people (Nadal, Rivera, & Corpus, 2010). Themes included:

- *Use of heterosexist or transphobic terminology:* statements in which someone uses derogatory heterosexist or transphobic language toward LGBTQ people (e.g., saying words like "faggot" or "dyke" or "she-male"; using phrases like "That's so gay!")

- *Endorsement of heteronormative or gender normative culture and behaviors:* incidents in which an LGBTQ person is expected to act like or be heterosexual (e.g., a heterosexual person telling a queer friend not to act "gay" or "flamboyant" or to "tone it down" in public, or a cisgender parent forcing their child to dress according to their sex assigned at birth)

- *Assumption of universal LGBTQ experience:* experiences in which heterosexual people assume all LGBTQ persons are the same (e.g., stereotyping all gay men as interested in fashion or interior design or assuming all lesbian women act or look "butch")

- *Exoticization:* incidents in which LGBTQ people are dehumanized or treated as objects (e.g., heterosexual people stereotyping all LGBTQ people as being the "comedic relief" or a cisgender man who enjoys having sex with transgender women but is not open to a committed, romantic relationship with them). For LGBTQ people of color or LGBTQ disabled people, exoticization may also involve being sexualized due to their racial or ethnic backgrounds or their disability statuses.

- *Discomfort/disapproval of LGBTQ experience:* experiences in which LGBTQ people are treated with disrespect and criticism (e.g., when a stranger glares at an affectionate lesbian couple or a heterosexual person tells an LGBTQ person they are "going to hell")

- *Denial of the reality of heterosexism or transphobia:* incidents in which people deny that heterosexism and transphobia exist (e.g., a coworker telling a queer friend that she's being paranoid thinking someone is discriminating against him, or someone telling a nonbinary person that they should stop complaining)

- *Assumption of sexual pathology/abnormality:* experiences that stigmatize LGBTQ people as hypersexual, sinful, or sexual deviants (e.g., someone comments that all gay men have AIDS or are child molesters, or that all trans women are sex workers)

- *Denial of individual heterosexism:* statements in which people deny their heterosexist and transgender biases (e.g., saying, "I am not homophobic, I have a gay friend!")

Numerous studies empirically supported this taxonomy, and quantitative measures emerged (Nadal, 2019a), demonstrating how this proposed model was valid and representative.

CHALLENGES IN ADDRESSING MICROAGGRESSIONS

Before going further into the literature, it is important to revisit the aforementioned notion that it is difficult to name or prove microaggressions—as a target or even as a researcher—particularly when the behaviors are not overtly biased (e.g., there is no use of overt or violent heterosexist or transphobic language when enacted). In such cases, a person may question whether the incident even occurred at all or whether the instance was motivated by sexual orientation or gender identity (real or perceived). Akin to the earlier scenario of the Black man in the elevator, an LGBTQ person who experiences a microaggression may (a) choose to confront their perpetrator, (b) choose to ignore it altogether, or (c) choose to "pick their battles" and only address the microaggression if they believe it may be worth it. They may also choose to utilize a microintervention described by Sue et al. (2019), such as educating the perpetrator or "making the 'invisible' visible" (p. 136). In making their decisions (which sometimes may need to be made within seconds), they will consider contexts, intentions, and potential consequences; and often they will never know if they made the best or most effective choice. Thus, in some ways, the decision-making process of deciding how (or if) to address the microaggression might be as stressful as the micro-aggression itself.

Sometimes it is not readily clear whether something should be considered a microaggression or simply labeled as overt or violent discrimination. To address this, it is necessary to revisit the concept of a microassault, a type of microaggression that is considered more old-fashioned discrimination, in that often manifests through name calling, avoidant behavior, or discriminatory actions toward the intended target. One of the main differences between microassaults and traditional, overt forms of discrimination is the intention and the consciousness of the perpetrator. If an individual blatantly, intention-ally, and violently calls someone a "faggot," "dyke," or "tranny" (i.e., they are actively aware that they made the statement, and they intended to ridicule or hurt someone for their sexual orientation), then observers might con-sider this to be a traditional, overt form of discrimination. However, perhaps someone may use a homophobic slur in an unconscious or unintentional way, which might cue an observer to label it more as a microaggression. For example, when two male teens are joking with each other and they call each other "faggots," they sometimes are not even conscious that they have used the word. If confronted by a passerby or authority figure, they may realize in retrospect that they should not have used such language, but in the moment, they may not have even been aware of what they were saying. Similarly, if these same two male teens were calling each other "faggot" and an LGBTQ person overheard the conversation, this could be considered a microaggression because the intention of the two boys was not to offend anyone around them; instead, the boys may report that they were using language that they viewed as playful and that they were not even thinking about anyone's sexual orientation when using the word. Thus, they may not view anything wrong with their behavior and may continue with such behavior because they really do not think that any parties are hurt. Because of their lack of consciousness, intention, or both, their behavior may be viewed as microaggressive.

On the contrary, because microinsults and microinvalidations are typically more subtle and may be enacted by perpetrators who are well-intentioned or unaware of their actions, some targets or observers may question their need to intervene. For example, imagine that a grandparent asks their LGBTQ grandson if he has a girlfriend, or tells their granddaughter that she looks so pretty when she wears dresses, that grandparent may not recognize that they might be engaging in what would be a microinsult (a comment or action that may demonstrate one's bias that people should be in hetero-sexual relationships or that people should conform to gender role norms).

As a result, their grandchild (or anyone who hears the comments) may choose to not confront their grandparent for a variety of reasons (e.g., not wanting to offend them, not wanting to argue with them, or presuming their grandparent would be invalidating or cause further harm). Relatedly, if an LGBTQ person hears a person at a family party impart a microinvalidation like "Homophobia doesn't exist anymore," they may not have the emotional capacity to engage in educating them, they may not feel that it is not worth the effort, or both.

Another complication with identifying and measuring microaggression is that the origins of the term "microaggression" itself have been a source of controversy. First, some people argue that the term is a misnomer because "micro" conveys that the encounters are small, when in fact they have huge impacts. Dr. Chester Pierce, who coined the term, asserted that the "micro" refers to the manifestation of the bias and not the impact (Torino et al., 2019). In other words, engaging in such behavior—particularly when not maliciously intended—would not be as powerful as a violent or hostile, physical, or verbal aggression. Yet, the behaviors may still be considered as types of aggressions because of the impact and consequences they have for the people who endure them.

Relatedly, many people incorrectly use the word **macroaggression** to refer to instances of overt discrimination; however, macroaggressions refer to the ways that bias is enacted through systems, policies, and institutions (Torino et al., 2019). "Macro" refers to the manifestation of the bias (i.e., the power of systems). While some scholars initially referred to these as systemic microaggressions (e.g., Nadal, Wong, et al., 2011), the term *macroaggression* is used in this text to describe covert discrimination that manifests through systems.

Throughout this book, myriad microaggression examples are presented, with some vignettes that may straddle the fine line between microaggressions and overt forms of discrimination. In such cases, discussion points are offered to provide insights on how to approach each situation. Either way, it is evident that microaggressions can be tricky and nuanced—one reason why it is crucial for people to learn more about them. In the next chapter, we examine the ways that microaggressions manifest for specific LGBTQ subgroups, beginning with lesbian, gay, bisexual, and queer people.

DISCUSSION QUESTIONS

For General Readers

1. How have you reacted when you experienced or witnessed microaggressions in your life?

2. Reviewing the various taxonomies presented on microaggressions based on race, gender, sexual orientation or gender identity, what types of microaggressions have you experienced or witnessed in your life?

3. In reviewing the examples presented, have you committed any microaggressions before?

For Psychologists, Educators, and Other Experts

1. What types of microaggressions do you notice most in your work with your clients, students, or constituents? How do you handle them?

2. How do you handle microaggressions when they occur with your coworkers or supervisors?

GLOSSARY OF KEY TERMS

benevolent sexism The act of promoting and maintaining traditional gender role norms, in which women are deemed inferior to men, often manifested through paternalistic or chivalrous thoughts or behaviors toward women.

exoticization The act of portraying or regarding a person or thing as uniquely different or out of the ordinary; while often well-intentioned, such behaviors may be representative of biases related to dehumanization, objectification, oversexualization, or other stereotypes.

macroaggression Systemic and institutionalized forms of bias and oppression toward historically marginalized groups.

microinterventions Communications or behaviors that are employed in response to microaggressions, as a way of validating perceptions of historically marginalized groups while offering support, encouragement, and reassurance.

objectification The act of degrading or dehumanizing someone, akin to treating them like objects; in academic literature, used typically to describe the sexualization of women.

3 SEXUAL ORIENTATION MICROAGGRESSIONS

Experiences of Queer, Lesbian, Gay, Bisexual, and Pansexual People

FIGURE 3.1. Two Young Black Queer Men Displaying Affection

Note. Photo courtesy of Uriel Mont.

https://doi.org/10.1037/0000335-004
Dismantling Everyday Discrimination: Microaggressions Toward LGBTQ People, Second Edition, by K. L. Y. Nadal

In Chapter 1, a brief history of discrimination toward lesbian, gay, bisexual, and transgender people was presented. This review included everything from the sodomy cases that punished men who had sex with men to the Matthew Shepard and James Byrd, Jr. Hate Crimes Prevention Act, which was the federal legislation that protects people who are victims of a crime due to their sexual orientation or gender identity. The academic literature involving heterosexism, monosexism, and transphobia was also reviewed—highlighting the previous research over the past 4 decades that has examined the impacts of discrimination on the lives of LGBTQ people. The term *microaggression* was defined, citing a more common manifestation of discrimination that LGBTQ people (and people of other marginalized identities) may encounter in their everyday lives. Microaggressions were further discussed in Chapter 2, and a taxonomy involving the types of microaggression experienced by LGBTQ people was presented.

The next several chapters focus specifically on microaggression incidents, highlighting actual perspectives of LGBTQ people. Using the taxonomy of sexual orientation and gender identity microaggressions presented in Chapter 2, I discuss examples of each of the categories from my own research, as well as some excerpts from LGBTQ people in contemporary media and literature. Voices from various LGBTQ subgroups are shared in subsequent chapters, emphasizing the diverse microaggressions based on sexual orientation and gender identity, as well as the intersections of race, ethnicity, gender, immigration status, religion, and age. This chapter discusses microaggressions based on sexual orientation, underscoring experiences of lesbians, gay men, and bisexual, queer, **pansexual**, and **asexual** people.

For the sake of brevity, I use *queer* to describe the umbrella group of people who are minoritized due to their sexual orientation; I will use specific terms like *lesbian, gay, bisexual,* and *pansexual* when referring exclusively to those groups. While I recognize that older generations (particularly older gay men) may have aversions to the term "queer" (typically due to personal or collective histories of trauma or violence), I also recognize that many LGBTQ people have reclaimed the word "queer" as a form of resistance (Rand, 2014). I also acknowledge that taking back the word "queer" has resulted in LGBTQ scholars and community leaders disrupting oppressive systems via queer theory and **queer studies** (see Eng & Puar, 2020; Ghaziani & Brim, 2019; Nadal & Scharrón-del Río, 2021). Finally, because I also understand that LGBTQ youth are becoming use more diverse terminology to identify themselves (particularly with a growing number of young people using terms like "pansexual" or "nonbinary"; Watson et al., 2020), I acknowledge that using "queer" as an umbrella term might feel appropriate at the time of this writing but that it might become outdated shortly after.

A REVIEW OF SEXUAL ORIENTATION MICROAGGRESSIONS

When the literature on sexual orientation microaggressions began to grow at the start of the 21st century, a few key studies introduced the ways that microaggressions may manifest for queer people. First, Shelton and Delgado-Romero (2011) conducted a study with 16 self-identified lesbian, gay, bisexual, or queer people to describe microaggressions that they experienced as clients in psychotherapy sessions. Using focus groups, participants' responses were analyzed and classified into several major themes, including (a) the assumption that sexual orientation is the cause of all presenting issues, (b) avoidance and minimizing of sexual orientation, (c) making stereotypical assumptions about LGBQ clients, and (d) the assumption that LGBQ individuals need psychotherapeutic treatment. Second, Nadal, Wong, et al. (2011) examined how sexually minoritized people react to and cope with microaggressions, citing emotional, behavioral, and cognitive processes. Participants also reported the various types of mental health problems that resulted due to microaggressions, including depression, anxiety, and trauma. Finally, participants divulged a spectrum of macroaggressions, including biases from the media, the government, their cultural groups, their school systems, and their religions.

In a qualitative study utilizing focus groups, Nadal, Issa, et al. (2011) aimed to validate the taxonomy presented by Nadal, Rivera, and Corpus (2010). After asking participants to think about the subtle types of discrimination they had encountered in their lives, researchers used a directed content analysis to examine if queer participants' responses matched those presented in the taxonomy. Nearly all original categories were supported; these included (a) use of heterosexist terminology; (b) endorsement of heteronormative culture and behaviors; (c) assumption of universal LGBTQ experience; (d) exoticization; (e) discomfort with or disapproval of LGBTQ experience; (f) denial of the reality of heterosexism; and (g) assumption of sexual pathology, deviance, or abnormality. (See Chapter 2 for a description of these categories.) One new category emerged: physical threat or harassment.

Other qualitative studies have investigated themes of heterosexist microaggressions too. First, in a qualitative study by Platt and Lenzen (2013), similar themes emerged, with a few new themes including: "undersexualization" (i.e., incidents in which loved ones showed ambivalence when learning of their sexual orientations but showed discomfort when the queer person brought home a romantic partner) and "sinfulness" (i.e., incidents in which people convey beliefs that nonheterosexual identities or relationships are morally wrong, typically based on religious values). Second, in a qualitative study with 10 bisexual white women, Bostwick and Hequembourg (2014) identified themes based on bisexuality: (a) hostility denial/dismissal, (b) unintelligibility (or incidents in which people convey confusion or lack of understanding about bisexuality), (c) pressure to change, (d) not being treated as legitimate members of the LGBTQ community, (e) dating exclusion by people of other sexual orientations, and (f) hypersexuality. Third, Deutsch (2018) interviewed 11 asexual people and reported several themes of microaggressions, including (a) invalidation, (b) sexual normativity/romantic normativity, (c) pathologization, (d) ignorance, (e) general LGBTQIAP+ prejudice, (f) dehumanization, (g) rejection, (h) disappointment, (i) infantilization, (j) tokenization, and (k) sexual threats and pressure.

For the first study (which consisted of a general queer sample), it appears that the new themes (undersexualization and sinfulness) might fit best under the "discomfort/disapproval" category, based on their descriptions. For the two latter studies, many themes may align with taxonomy categories, but emphasize how those experiences may be felt differently by bisexuals or asexuals. For instance, "unintelligibility" might be a specific type of "discomfort or disapproval" encountered by bisexual people, whereas "hypersexuality" (or incidents in which people bias bisexuals as being highly sexually active) may be a specific type of "assumption of sexual pathology" that targets bisexual people. Similarly, "sexual and romantic normativity" might be a specific type of "endorsement of heteronormative culture or behaviors," while "tokenization" might be a kind of "exoticization"—all faced by asexuals in nuanced ways.

Quantitative literature has also attempted to assess sexual orientation microaggressions and their influences on psychological health, particularly for LGBTQ college students. First, to measure microaggressions based on **homonegativity**, Wright and Wegner (2012) created the Homonegative Microaggressions Scale, a 45-item measure that revealed that homonegative microaggressions were linked to poor self-esteem and internalized oppression for lesbian, gay, and bisexual people who are targeted. Wegner and Wright (2016) validated the scale further and revealed four subscales: (a) assumed deviance, (b) second-class citizen, (c) assumptions of gay culture, and (d) stereotypical knowledge and behavior. Using this scale, other researchers found that homonegative microaggressions predicted posttraumatic stress (J. L. Robinson & Rubin, 2016) and alcohol use. Second, Woodford et al. (2015) created the LGBQ Microaggressions on Campus Scale to specifically investigate the types of subtle discrimination queer college students face. With 35 items and four subscales: (a) microinvalidations, (b) heterosexist

FIGURE 3.2. Two Queer Latina Women Making Each Other Laugh

Note. Photo courtesy of Felipe Balduino.

and heteronormative expectations about LGBQ people (microinsult), (c) LGBQ people as immoral and dangerous (microinsult), and (d) environmental microaggressions (i.e., microaggressions manifested through systems and institutions). Using the scale, studies found that LGBQ microaggressions predicted outcomes like alcohol use (Kalb et al., 2018), depression, and attempted suicide (Woodford et al., 2018). Finally, Nadal (2019b) developed the Sexual Orientation Microaggressions Scale (SOMS) with five unique subscales: (a) environmental microaggressions, (b) microinvalidations, (c) assumption of pathology, (d) enforcement of binary gender roles, and (e) heterosexist language. In a study that utilized the SOMS and examined differences between queer subgroups, Bolwell (2021) found that more frequent experiences of sexual orientation microaggressions significantly predicted depression.

VOICES OF QUEER, LESBIAN, GAY, AND BISEXUAL PEOPLE

This section revisits the LGBTQ microaggression taxonomy while including the additional categories presented in Nadal et al. (2011). Within each category are quotes from various sources, including previous qualitative literature and examples from contemporary media and literature.

Use of Heterosexist Terminology

This theme is characterized by incidents in which queer people are called derogatory names, teased with cruel words, or subjected to hearing biased language around them. Sometimes such language is used intentionally to berate or offend a queer person; other times, people may not even realize they are using homophobic language because it is part of their everyday speech. For example, saying, "That's so gay" when referring to something that is odd, unpleasant, or unappealing has been a common behavior for many people—especially youth—dating back to the 1980s. One media depiction of this process is through the television show *Pen15*, a comedy set in the year 2000 that focuses on the lives of 13-year-olds. In an era in which phrases like "That's so gay!" were part of everyday vernacular for American youth, one character, Gabe, struggles with his sexual identity because of the homophobic culture that such language creates; he even ends up participating in heterosexist bullying toward an effeminate peer classmate (Ian) as a way of deflecting his own confusion about his sexuality (Fallon, 2020). Such defense mechanisms are quite common, as research finds that many queer people use homophobic language toward others as a way of compensating for their own internalized heterosexism (Chonody et al., 2012). Research also finds that when queer youth hear such language (especially when they are questioning their own identities), such experiences can have a detrimental impact on their identities, behaviors, and mental health (Mathies et al., 2019; Winberg et al., 2019; Woodford et al., 2012).

Using homophobic language may often be used as a weaponizing way to insult someone; for some, to be labeled as a "faggot" or "dyke" would be considered the ultimate insult. When using such terms toward another person, the speaker might not actually believe that the targeted person is gay or lesbian; rather, the expressions may reflect the person's need to assert their **power** (or, for cisgender men specifically, their masculinity), while also reflecting their own unconscious biases that queer people are bad, weak, weird, or inferior (Pascoe, 2011). Overt uses of these homophobic slurs as insults have been quite common in many feature films, with examples including *Can't Hardly Wait* (1999), *Stuck on You* (2003), and *Horrible Bosses* (2011). Similarly, the use of "fag" or "faggot" had been historically prominent in hip hop lyrics, with common perpetrators being Eminem, Tyler the Creator, and J. Cole. In the movie *Moonlight* (Jenkins, 2016; the first movie about an LGBTQ main character to win an Academy Award for Best Picture), one of the earlier scenes involves a 9-year old Chiron (nicknamed "Little") asking his new mentoring figures what a "faggot" is—indicating that he is already being bullied for his perceived sexuality.

Heterosexist language and sexist language are often interchangeable, both contributing to a culture of **toxic masculinity**—originally defined as "the constellation of socially regressive male traits that serve to foster domination, the devaluation of women, homophobia, and wanton violence" (Kupers, 2005, p. 714). However, given the link between toxic masculinity and transphobia (Capous-Desyllas & Loy, 2020), **white supremacy**, **settler colonialism**, and **cisheteropatriarchy** (Buenavista et al., 2021), more intersectional definitions acknowledge how toxic masculinity is harmful for people of all historically minoritized groups.

Microaggressions involving heterosexist language have also been documented in qualitative research. In one of my studies, a gay male divulged,

> I recently opened up to my friend about [being gay] and he's a guy . . . and just the other day I was at his house, and we were talking about other people, and he would describe them as like 'faggot,' and it would get to me. (Nadal, Issa, et al., 2011, pp. 243–244)

Another gay male participant related the following:

> For me when somebody says in the street, 'Hey faggot' I look around but [then I realize] they're not talking to me. I was so worried, it's just so challenging. It's embarrassing. Even if it's not toward me, it's still embarrassing. (Nadal, Wong, et al., 2011, p. 31)

Both cases illustrate how "faggot" is used so casually, particularly by adolescent boys who want to tease or convey weakness or femininity in other boys. And even if not directed at them, queer people in earshot are emotionally affected.

There have been many instances that reveal how lesbian and bisexual women and girls have been bullied with heterosexist language too. In one personal narrative, a bisexual woman recalls an incident during her childhood, in which she was holding hands with her best friend:

> They turned, saw us holding hands, and the taunting began. One said: "Chocolate and Chip, holding hands!" and the other responded "Oh gross, what lez-bos!" Today, I know that they were derogatively referring to us as lesbians. Back then, we had to demand to know, "What are you talking about?" Finally, they gave us a hint, saying that we were two of the same thing, like a chocolate chip cookie, and that it was disgusting. We should not hold hands because we were both girls and doing so made us "lez-bos." (Phillips, 2005, p. 116)

When children or adolescents use heterosexist language, they often might simply repeat phrases they hear from adults or from television and not fully understand the meaning behind their words. Yet, LGBTQ people who hear these words may feel scared, unsafe, sad, and alone.

Relatedly, many heterosexist terms are so ingrained into everyday vernacular that people do not recognize their impact. In a news article that described the bullying phenomena with LGBTQ youth, Preston Witt, a gay man from Alabama, recalled an experience from his childhood in which a term was used so freely by students and even a teacher:

> In my elementary school during PE, there was a favorite dodgeball game of all the students called "Smear the queer." I still, at that time, did not realize, "Oh, I'm gay," but the whole premise of the game bothered me. I remember saying to the coach, "Can we play a different game—I don't like that game. [My teacher then made me] "the queer" [for the day]. . . . The whole premise of the game is that all the students run around and throw balls at the student designated as the queer . . . very similar to the old idea of stoning. (Cox, 2009, para. 2–3)

This type of heterosexist language aligns with previous literature that found that many students regularly overhear homophobic or heterosexist remarks by their own teachers and other staff members; in fact, a recent study found that over half (52.4%) of the LGBTQ youth sample ($N = 16,713$) heard teachers or other staff members make homophobic comments, while two-thirds of the sample (66.7%) heard teachers and other staff make disparaging remarks about gender identity or expression (Kosciw et al., 2020). Often, this language may be purposefully hurtful and offensive; other times, individuals may not even be aware of the impact of the words that they use. Regardless of intention, an underlying heterosexist bias is communicated, which may especially be harmful to queer children who are developing their sexual identities.

Endorsement of Heteronormative Culture and Behaviors

This type of microaggression occurs when heterosexuality is conveyed as being the "normal" sexual orientation, while all other sexual orientations are viewed as abnormal, immoral, or wrong. While these biases can emerge in overt ways (e.g., someone saying that heterosexuality is "natural" and that homosexuality or bisexuality is "against God's will"), they can also come out in subtle ways (e.g., presuming a teen girl would have or want a boyfriend).

When it comes to these manifestations of heteronormative messages, it appears that women are often taught or criticized about their ways of dress, while men are often taught or criticized about their ways of speaking or behaving. The 1999 movie *But I'm a Cheerleader* depicts a camp where adolescent girls and boys are sent when their families suspect that they may be lesbian or gay; there, the teenagers are taught the "proper" ways to act, talk, and dress as heterosexuals, as well as "appropriate" ways to interact with the opposite sex and their own sex. Relatedly, the 1996 film *The Birdcage* involves an adult man who was raised by two gay men. Upon returning home for a visit, he asks his parents to hide their sexual orientations and to mask their feminine or flamboyant traits, to impress his fiancée's parents. While both movies are meant to be comedic (and even satirical), they depict the types of pathologizing messages that are often taught in families and by society in general about queerness.

A lesbian discussed how her parents communicated these heteronormative messages:

> [My mother] knows that I'm a lesbian, but she is in denial. She doesn't want to see it, so I have to act a certain way. You know, act heterosexual, not mention anything about me having a girlfriend or anything like that to make her feel uncomfortable or make her say anything offensive toward me. So, I have to act completely differently at home. (Nadal et al., 2010a, p. 244)

In another study, a nonbinary Latinx participant said,

> Being that I did come from a Latino family, it's very taboo to be gay, and definitely spent most of my youth trying to conform to the ideals of my family that I should be feminine, I should have long hair, you know I should wear make-up, I should date boys. (Cerezo et al., 2020, p. 74)

Similarly, a queer Latina participant shared: "Family do force that I'm supposed to be a feminine woman and I'm actually a lot more masculine than they would like" (Cerezo et al., 2020, p. 74).

These types of messages are not just learned within families; they are also expressed by other aspects of society. Another lesbian participant describes an experience with a stranger:

> My girlfriend . . . she dresses a little boyish. [And this man] looks at her and . . . he kept telling her, "Why do you dress like that? You're a girl, what are you doing? You're supposed to wear, you know, girly clothes. . . . Why do you dress like a guy? Why do you look like a guy?" (Nadal et al., 2010a, p. 245)

While gender policing is problematic in general, this quote exemplifies how being evaluated or regulated by a stranger can feel particularly threatening and violent.

Similar messages about gender role expectations can also be communicated outside of the family. For instance, in a study on LGBTQ perceptions of the criminal justice system, one Latina lesbian described how police officers treated her gay male friend:

> [He] was very flamboyant. I guess he had some sort of guys harassing him. And the cops came. . . . They diffused the situation but there was also this, like,

> underlying thing where, like, he kind of deserved it for being so out. (Nadal, Quintanilla, et al., 2015, p. 466)

Because of treatment like this, some queer people may learn that they "need to act straight" (Nadal, Quintanilla, et al., 2015, p. 467) to survive or avoid violence.

Direct and indirect heteronormative messages can also be taught in school systems, often being conveyed by educators themselves. For instance, the mother of a gay adult son recalled an interaction in which an elementary school teacher had shared concerns about her son's behavior:

> I had one teacher tell me during a parent teacher conference, "Well, I have some concerns about him that during recess he prefers to be with the girls and not with the boys." And I said, "Was he struggling academically because of it? If not, well then that's his decision." (Cox, 2009, para. 11)

In this case, the teacher may not realize their biases regarding how boys or girls should behave or whom they should befriend. While the teacher may have good intentions in sharing this information with the student's mother, the indirect message that is conveyed is that acting differently from the heterosexual norm is blameworthy and even punishable.

Finally, when people presume that others are heterosexual when their sexual orientation has never been announced or discussed, they are assuming that heterosexuality is the norm. For instance, when a new male employee is hired at a workplace and his coworkers make blanket comments like "Do you have a wife and kids?" his coworkers are presuming that people are heterosexual, unless told otherwise. In an essay about the lack of LGBTQ+ people in the sciences, Dr. Jon Freeman (a gay male professor and neuroscientist) revealed: "During a single tenure-track job interview in 2011, thirteen people asked me: 'Do you have a wife?'" (Freeman, 2018, para. 1). One lesbian professor describes a similar experience:

> Questions regarding previous boyfriends, current boyfriends, and my desire to have children were on the rise from my colleagues. In addition, I was invited to express opinions regarding "controversial" topics such as gay rights, same-sex marriage, and same-sex parenting. Did I know any of those "dykes, queers, and candy-ass faggots?" (Wiebold, 2005, p. 131)

Again, while the narrators' coworkers (or potential coworkers) may be well intended in wanting to know about their personal lives and political stances, they also make them feel uncomfortable when they presume that they are heterosexual. Often, this can cause stress for queer people who feel the pressure to announce their sexual orientation or "come out" publicly in the workplace, even though it is never a requirement for their heterosexual counterparts to do so.

When queer people hear heteronormative statements in any environment (e.g., families, schools, churches), they often feel uneasy, unsafe, or invalidated—especially if they are struggling with their identities. Even if the perpetrator of the microaggressions appear well intentioned or benevolent, their behaviors communicate their lack of acceptance or potential rejection of LGBTQ people. Thus, some queer people make intentional choices to not disclose their identities to their families or friends, and because their loved ones may be oblivious to their heteronormative biases and behaviors, they may not understand why.

Assumption of Universal Queer Experience

Microaggressions under this theme occur when a heterosexual person assumes that all queer individuals are the same or have identical trajectories, interests, or lives. Sometimes some of the opinions are stereotypical (e.g., all lesbians are butch or like sports; all gay men are feminine and like fashion or theater; or all bisexual people are promiscuous or polyamorous). For example, a Black lesbian shared: "I have heard, 'I wouldn't be able to tell you were a lesbian,' you know because I don't have typical lesbian traits" (Weber et al., 2018, p. 548). In another study, one gay man described how a friend stereotyped him based on his sexual orientation:

> One day I had asked my friend, "because he was on the football team, and he was the most popular, and I said, you know, 'I want to try out for football.' He just stood there and kind of laughed at me. I felt, you know, 'What are you laughing at?' He was like, 'Come on, you're gay! You can't play football!'" (Nadal et al., 2010a, p. 245)

In both scenarios, there is a clear assumption that queer people are supposed to abide by certain gender role styles and behaviors. Even if comments were in jest, they were deemed hurtful.

Bisexuals also endure stereotypes—from heterosexuals as well as from gays and lesbians. In *Bi Lives: Bisexual Women Tell Their Stories,* Orndorff (1999, wrote:

> Bisexuality is the sexual orientation of a person who is attracted to people of both sexes. This does not mean that every bisexual person feels the need to be involved with both a man and a woman, or that they will have sex with anyone who is available to them. It does not mean, as some lesbians believe, that bisexual women are not serious about any relationship they have with a woman, because (they believe) bisexual women would place more importance on any relationship with a man. Yet, these are some of the misconceptions that gay and straight people have about bisexuals. While there are bisexuals who fit these stereotypes, I have not found many of them. (p. 1)

Sometimes others may assume that a typical queer experience can be applied to all. For example, while it is common for some people to believe that coming out of the closet is a normative and necessary experience, some cultures may view the process as being superfluous, excessive, and gratuitous (Nadal & Corpus, 2013). For instance, in qualitative research with gay immigrant men from the Philippines, one interviewee stated, "The Americans are different, darling. Coming out is their drama" (Manalansan, 2003, p. 27). Because sexuality is unspoken among Filipino families (for both heterosexuals and LGBTQ people), this individual does not view coming out as a necessary aspect to his identity. Thus, when someone makes a judgment about a queer person (especially a queer person of color, queer immigrant, or queer religious person) as not being out to everyone in their lives, the individual falsely assumes that this is a common and essential experience for all. Such presumptions may potentially result in a queer person feeling invalidated or abnormal, even if their situations are common or understood.

Sometimes individuals of a certain minoritized community (e.g., ethnic minority groups, LGBTQ people) are expected to be familiar with everyone else in the community, even though that would be impossible, since a community may contain millions of people. When this manifests, there are three main possible reasons for the perpetrator to do so: (a) they assume that *all* people of the group know each other or are friends, (b) they hope to create a bond with the person, or (c) they want to appear to be nondiscriminatory and open-minded. Although well intentioned, these behaviors result in offending, stereotyping, reducing, or tokenizing their target.

Other microaggressions related to this theme occur when queer people are asked to serve as "spokespersons" for their entire community. For example, a lesbian educator described the process of conducting workshops, and how people often assume that their experience was representative of all LGBQ people, "Despite our representations of a variety of identities, we do not represent all queers and their communities: It is important that we make this distinction clear" (Glasgow & Murphy, 1999, p. 220). Like previous literature that has found that tokenizing people of color and asking them to represent an entire group is distressing (Sue, 2010), asking queer people to do the same can be microaggressive as well.

Exoticization

Exoticization microaggressions are evident when queer people are viewed as a form of entertainment or objectified because of their sexual orientation or queer identity. For example, gay men may be viewed as a source of comedic entertainment, whereas bisexual women may be viewed as sexual objects. One gay man shared how people in his life assumed he was living a "fantastic and fabulous" lifestyle because he is gay:

> No, I'm not. I'm really not. It's not like I never do that, but it's not like I am out. I haven't done that in twenty years. . . . What bothers me are—where I get a little annoyed or where I feel weird about it is when I feel like they're using me as a fantasy projection for what they wish their life was. (Nadal et al., 2010a, p. 246)

Another gay male participant described an interaction in which he felt like he was expected to be an entertainer: "I feel like straight people kinda think it's funny how I behave . . . you know what I mean . . . like it's amusing to them" (Nadal et al., 2010a, p. 246).

Feeling exoticized or objectified is a very common experience for bisexual women; specifically, bisexual women may especially feel sexually objectified by heterosexual men. For example, one bisexual woman stated, "I'm more wary of being objectified by men than by women. When I first started sleeping with Josh, I felt it. I think he objectified me sexually in a way that I've never experienced with a woman" (Orndorff, 1999, p. 65). This type of sentiment was shared by a bisexual female participant in one of my studies who revealed the types of interactions she tended to have with heterosexual men: "A lot of guys would think, you know, because I'm into both guys and girls that I'll be like down with the threesome kinda thing, and it's like ugh, get over yourself" (Nadal et al., 2010a, p. 247). Because women in general are heavily sexually objectified in American society (and across the world), bisexual women may be stereotyped as especially oversexualized, which often leads to microaggressions. And due to rampant systemic sexism in American culture, the perpetrators of these microaggressions are typically unaware of the impact—continuing their behavior and negatively impacting others.

A final example of an exoticization microaggression toward queer people is when people proudly claim that they "have a gay friend." Such a statement may be considered a microaggression based on the context, the intention of the speaker, and how the people around them interpret it. In one study, a gay white man disclosed:

> I often hear, "I love that you are gay." Like it is cool, and you are welcome that I am gay. And another one I hear all the time is, "I always wanted a gay best friend." Yeah, it is cool, I am glad it is tokenized, I am glad I can do this for you. (Weber et al., 2018, p. 548)

Similarly, one lesbian educator described the types of people she encountered when she conducted LGBTQ-related workshops: "The participants I fear the most are heterosexuals who say 'Well, I have a gay friend. . . .' Often such a comment reflects a stagnation in what should be their evolving understanding of homophobia" (Glasgow & Murphy, 1999, p. 220). In these situations, people claim to be gay-friendly to denounce their homophobia or to appear to be good allies.

Discomfort With or Disapproval of Queer Experiences

A microaggression under this category consists of instances in which a heterosexual, whether aware or unaware, shows their displeasure of or apprehension toward nonheterosexual people. Historically, this may have been considered more overt, in that people were very vocal about their disdain and condemnation of queer people. For example, in the 1970s, Anita Bryant (an entertainer and Miss America runner-up) created a Christian group called "Save Our Children" in which she advocated against any gay rights laws. She publicly campaigned against any state legislation that protected the rights of gay and lesbian people, stating they were immoral and would corrupt or abuse children (Bronski, 2011).

When the disapproval of another person's sexual orientation is violent and overt, it may constitute more of an overt violent act of heterosexism, whereas when the disapproval is viewed as well intentioned, it may be perceived as more of a microaggression. One demonstration of these juxtapositions is from the television series *Pose*. When Damon, a Black gay teen is violently kicked out of his home because his father finds a gay pornographic magazine (Chappell, 2018), he finds himself homeless in New York City. It is later revealed that all the other trans and queer characters had similar storylines—representing how common it was LGBTQ youth to become homeless due to being kicked out of their homes or running away from violent environments. These types of disapprovals are clearly more overt and would not best depict microaggressions. However, in a later episode, Pray Tell, a Black gay man returns to his hometown to make peace with his family of origin, as he prepares for his death after his battle with AIDS. There, he is met by his aunt who says "Save the soul from eternal damnation . . . I never stopped loving you. Hate the sin. Love the sinner" (Upadhyaya, 2021). Such commentary, while very hurtful and overt, might best demonstrate a microassault—in that his aunt genuinely believes she is saying something positive and benevolent, unaware of the actual homophobic content, nor its harmful impact on her nephew.

It is common for microaggressions that convey disapproval to come from acquaintances or strangers in public places; however, other times, these may come from family members, coworkers, and friends. A lesbian participant in one of my studies (Nadal et al., 2010a) described the microaggressions she experienced in public, particularly when she was with her girlfriend:

> I was with my girlfriend on the train, and she was holding me and kissing me, and there were people sitting there, and they just made a face. They didn't— I didn't see them say anything to us. It's just the face—you can kind of tell, the manner, their facial expression is kind of like "Whoa." (p. 247)

In the same study, a gay male participant shared a similar story: "One time I was kissing my boyfriend on my front porch, and this guy walked by us and started chuckling" (p. 247).

In these two interactions, the offenders may not be forthright in their dissatisfaction, shock, or other negative reactions to the same sex couples showing affection toward each other. However, their peers, glares, laughter, and facial expressions (which may or not be fully conscious or intentional) may convey their discomfort with queer people, while also having a detrimental impact on the couple that is targeted.

Another way in which these types of disapproval microaggressions may manifest is when individuals disclose their sexual orientation to family members and friends. Sometimes this disapproval is overt, in that someone hurtfully disowns their family member or tells them that "they are going to hell" or that "they will be condemned." Other times, it is generally negative, but may get better over time. As an example, in the television series *Love, Victor*, the protagonist eventually comes out to his mother, who disapproves of his disclosure—admittedly due to her religious and cultural beliefs as a Catholic Puerto Rican (White, 2021). While she eventually comes to accept her son's sexuality, she engages in numerous microaggressions like asking Victor to not disclose his identity to his younger brother, whom she deemed too young to understand, or referring to her son's boyfriend only as his friend.

Coming out experiences can also be bittersweet, especially when a family member or friend appears to be accepting but still says indirectly hurtful things. In an interview, actress Portia de Rossi discussed how she came out to her grandmother:

> I wasn't planning on it, but I knew I wouldn't avoid it. So, she made the mistake of asking me about my love life, and I said, "It's great. I'm very, very happy, and we've been together for eight months, and everything is wonderful." And she said, "What's his name?" And I took a deep breath and said, "Ellen DeGeneres." . . . First thing she said was, "Well, this is a very bad day." It was the most honest reaction I've ever had. Then she said, "Darlin', you're not one

of those." It took her two minutes of being angry and upset and frustrated and disgusted—and then she just held her arms out to me and said, "I love you just the same." (Kort, 2005, p. 46, para. 9)

While it appears that the outcome was more positive at the end of their interaction, hearing a family member being "angry" and "disgusted" about one's sexuality or listening to a loved one deny one's sexual orientation retains some microaggressive qualities, and may cause hurt or frustration for the queer person who hears it. One gay man reflected:

> My upbringing told me that being gay was wrong [or] "morally depraved." As an only son, I was expected to get married and have a son to perpetuate the family name. . . . Deep down, I knew "the unspeakable truth," that I was a gay man. Yet I had a deep-seated fear of how the process of coming out would impact relationships with my family. After coming out, my worst fears initially came true. I lost the support of my parents and initially did not have contact with them. . . . Ultimately, the relationship settled into an uncomfortable silence about my life as a gay man. "Don't ask, don't tell" was the only way to maintain a connection with them. (O'Brien, 2005, pp. 97–98)

Through this narrative, we learn how the author reported receiving different types of direct and indirect messages that being gay was bad or immoral. After he did come out to his family, his parents appeared to not have reacted well and even halted communication with him, which could be one indication of their disapproval of his sexual identity. However, while it seems that they had eventually opened communication with their son, their relationship was tainted with an "uncomfortable silence" about his life as a gay man that would likely include anything related to his romantic relationships, friends, and LGBTQ community activities. This type of silence fits all the criteria of a microaggression. While they may no longer be divulging their discomfort or their disapproval of his sexual orientation, their silence indirectly communicates that they are not completely accepting or celebrating of this part of their sons' life.

For bisexual people, microaggressions that convey discomfort or disapproval often come in the form of others questioning their sexual identity. One bisexual female participant from one of my studies (Nadal, Issa, et al., 2011) described an experience where she felt insulted:

> I went to a taping of [a talk show] recently, and it was an episode about gay marriage and gay issues and [the host] had everyone in the audience wear T-shirts that they gave us that said either "straight" or "gay" or whatever on them. It was really cheesy, but they didn't have a shirt that said "bi." They had a straight shirt, a gay shirt, and then a shirt with a question mark on it. I was like, "What the fuck is this?" I'm like, my sexual orientation is *not* a question mark. I didn't like how it could be implied that I'm confused. (p. 248)

A common microaggression toward bisexual people is when people convey that they are "confused." One bisexual woman stated: "When I was first coming out as bisexual, I noticed that heterosexual and homosexual people were saying the same things to me. 'You have to make a choice. You're on a fence. You're confused'" (Orndorff, 1999, p. 111). When a **monosexual** individual (i.e., someone who practices exclusive heterosexuality or exclusive homosexuality) makes such statements, they demonstrate their biases against bisexual people.

Criticizing or devaluing someone's identity, realities, or experiences is a common type of microaggression for pansexual, **demisexual**, asexual, or **aromantic** people as well—groups who may often be told that their sexual orientations or identities are unfounded or illogical. In a study (Deutch, 2018) examining asexual people and microaggressions, one example of an invalidation included someone being told "'How do you know you're asexual if you've never had sex?'" (p. 17), while an example of being pathologized was someone being told "There's got to be something wrong with you. . . . Maybe it's a hormone thing" (p. 20).

Finally, it is crucial to note that bisexual, pansexual, and other queer people may experience microaggressions from lesbian and gay people, while also feeling microaggressions from heterosexuals. A bisexual woman describes the reaction she had from gay and lesbian friends whenever she entered a new relationship:

[That] is what being bisexual is; sometimes I'll fall in love with woman and sometimes a man. This gave me my first long-term experience of what it was like to negotiate my bisexual identity with a man, the fears it raised in both him and me. I wondered if I could ever be satisfied dating just one sex. Although gay and lesbian friends were primarily happy that I found someone they loved, they couldn't completely hide their disappointment that that person was a man. Conversely, straight friends seemed a little too happy that that person was a man. (Carrubba, 2005, pp. 44–43)

This narrative exemplifies the two types of microaggressions bisexual people may feel. From lesbian and gay people, they may feel invalidated when they *are not* supported when they enter heterosexual relationships; however, from heterosexual people, they may feel invalidated because they are "too" supported when they enter heterosexual relationships.

Assumption of Sexual Pathology, Deviance, or Abnormality

This theme includes microaggressions in which heterosexuals believe that queer individuals are sexually promiscuous, odd, or even violent. Sometimes this can take the form of comments and statements that are meant to be hurtful and demeaning. For example, when Christian fundamentalist protestors hold up signs at LGBTQ events with phrases like "AIDS kills fags," their intention is to offend the LGBTQ people who see them or hear them. These might be considered microassaults, in that they are conscious and intentional; however, depending on the context, such statements may also feel like overtly hostile threats of physical and/or psychological violence.

However, there are some microaggressions in which the perpetrator consciously decided to vocalize something, without realizing the impact it would have on others. As mentioned earlier, if the intention was to offend or hurt, it may be considered an overt act of heterosexism; however, if the intent was benevolent or oblivious, it might be better classified as a microaggression. In one of my studies (Nadal, Wong, et al., 2011), a gay male participant stated, "One of the kids that I knew in high school, he just came out of nowhere and just said that all gay people have AIDS" (p. 28). Perhaps the offender did not realize there were gay people in the room, or perhaps he thought he was making a factual statement. Yet, because he was conscious of his words but perhaps did not intentionally mean to offend, this might be classified as a microassault. A similar example occurred in 2021 when rapper Da Baby made some homophobic (and stigmatizing HIV-related) comments at a concert. He said, "If you didn't show up today with HIV, AIDS, [or] any of them deadly sexually transmitted diseases that'll make you die in two to three weeks, put your cell phone lighter up," which he followed with, "Fellas, if you ain't sucking dick in the parking lot, put your cellphone lighter up" (Stafford, 2021). While Da Baby later apologized for his comments, his language was problematic not only for its vitriolic and stigmatizing content but also because he was spreading misinformation about HIV/AIDS.

While the previous examples demonstrate microassaults (overt but not necessarily malicious acts or comments) regarding sexual stigmas toward queer people, many subtler microinsults also fall under this category. Such statements or behaviors may not intentionally or consciously be verbalized to upset or hurt the recipient. Rather, the perpetrator's biases and stereotypes about queer people are simply conveyed indirectly through their remarks or actions. For example, in a narrative written by a gay male college student (Meiner, 2000), the author described a phone call that he had with his mom:

> [I] get one message. It's from my mother. I'll call her and see what she wants. "Yes, Mom, I'm practicing safe sex. . . . And yes, I'm getting another AIDS test in April when I get my physical. . . . Yes, Mom, I'll see you at Easter . . . bye-bye." My mother says she will be supportive of my "lifestyle" but all she does is send me "cute" articles on gay issues that she cuts out of the newspaper. I think she's very concerned that I'm going to contract AIDS and "leave her." (p. 300)

While the mother in this scenario may believe she is supportive of her son's sexual orientation, she still maintains biases (either consciously or unconsciously) that all gay men have AIDS. While there are indeed a disproportionate number of gay men who contract HIV/AIDS, stereotyping this to be true of all gay men would be considered microaggressive. Such statements also convey that gay men are sexually irresponsible, while also stigmatizing queer sex in general; in addition, they fail to recognize the systemic or external reasons that might increase risky sexual behaviors, such as stigmatized sexualities, discrimination, and minority stress.

A common bias about queer people is that they would be sexually assaultive or coercive toward heterosexuals. One gay white man stated, "I think some people feel uncomfortable . . . like dealing with gay people in general. It's like, 'Oh, my God. . . . They're gonna make a pass at me' or something like that" (Wilson et al., 2020, p. 43). One specific bias that heterosexual men sometimes maintain is the irrational fear that gay or queer men would rape them. Such a trope was demonstrated in the 2005 film *Wedding Crashers* in which Vince Vaughn's character is molested by a queer male character, who is portrayed as stalkerish, awkward, and creepy (Baur, 2016). Similarly, the 2015 film *Get Hard* starring Kevin Hart and Will Ferrell demonstrated this fear (and conflation) of queer sex and sexual assault—with one scene describing what they believe Ferrell's character would need to do sexually to survive prison (Baur, 2016).

While both scenes are meant to elicit a few laughs, each promotes longstanding homophobic biases, which could be experienced as microaggressions to any audience member watching the film. Further, each example attempts to humorously depict the "gay panic" that heterosexual men may feel when they are in the presence of queer men—a fear that has been used as a defense in court cases to justify the killings of LGBTQ people (Tomei & Cramer, 2016). Perhaps most problematic about the second example is that sexual assault in prisons is a serious problem, particularly for incarcerated LGBTQ people who are brutalized regularly by other inmates and even by correctional officers (Beck, 2014).

Assumptions of sexual deviance may also apply to lesbian or bisexual women. One lesbian psychiatrist described an interaction with a heterosexual patient:

A neighbor who knew that I was a lesbian mentioned this to [my patient] Ruth. In the next session, she confronted me and without exploring the issue adequately, I told her it was true. She became angry and frightened, stating that she wanted to be referred to another therapist because she was afraid that I would attack her sexually. I almost burst out laughing at that old stereotype of lesbians, but calmly told her that was not going to happen. (Bjork, 2004, pp. 102–103)

This interaction is akin to what a bisexual woman in one of my studies (Nadal, Issa, et al., 2011) shared: "Well, in my case, I've actually had some friends stop being my friends, because they were like, 'Oh, since you're bisexual and you might try come on to me' so they stopped being my friend" (p. 249). This stereotype that a queer would automatically "hit on" or sexually assault someone implies a bias that queer people do not have any control of their sexual urges or desires. It can feel especially insulting because it suggests these queer people would have no standards and be attracted to anyone, regardless of physical attractiveness, personality, or other traits.

These stereotypes may also apply to the trope that queer people (particularly gay or bisexual men) would be child molesters. While there is a vast amount of research that finds that child molesters tend to be heterosexual men with pedophilic desires for young girls, many people still stereotype gay men as pedophiles with sexual desires for young boys (Nadal, 2020). One gay male former schoolteacher shared, "I remember being very careful about interacting with the kids. Because I was gay, I knew that people made assumptions and kept watch over me . . . like we were all sexual predators or something" (Nadal et al., 2010a, p. 250). While others did not explicitly accuse the gay man of being a child molester, their microaggressive behaviors led him to believe that they could not trust him around their children.

Denial of the Reality of Heterosexism

These microaggressions occur when people deny the occurrence of heterosexism or monosexism; sometimes this transpires when someone denies that they are homophobic, while other times people deny that heterosexism exists at all. For example, when queer people confront perpetrators on their microaggressive behavior, the perpetrator can sometimes react defensively and assert that their intention was not to be offensive. While some queer people may appreciate an explanation, others may believe that the individual is merely creating excuses instead of admitting fault. One example includes a scenario described by a gay man in one of my studies (Nadal, Issa, et al., 2011). At first, the interaction may be considered an "exoticization" microaggression; however, the second part of the interaction may be best classified under this microaggression category:

> This woman came up to me one night and she said . . . I think I made some joke or something and she said, "Do you know who you remind me of?" and I knew what was coming, I just knew what was coming. She's like, "You're just like that Jack on *Will and Grace*. You're so funny." And I looked at her, and I said,

"Ma'am, no offense, but that's actually not a compliment." And she was like, "What do you mean? What do you mean? No, no, I was saying you're funny, and you're cute, and you dress nice." (p. 246)

Perhaps the gay male in this scenario would have reacted more positively if she apologized for offending him or for stereotyping him. However, because she did not, he left feeling dissatisfied and upset. Moreover, because she is unable to recognize that her statement may be based on her biases toward gay men, she may continue to offend in the future.

Sometimes people may commit microaggressions in which their statements invalidate queer people's realities, particularly in overcoming the heterosexist discrimination they encounter on interpersonal or systemic levels. One lesbian recounted a story in which her professor invalidated the realities related to her same-sex relationship:

My professor, who is overseeing my dissertation in [chemistry], really wants me to become a professor of [chemistry]. And I tried to explain to him that it wasn't very easy for me, that there are very few jobs, and they are all like in Ohio or Oklahoma or in places I personally wouldn't want to live. And also, I have a partner. . . . And so, I didn't appreciate his guilt trip when I decided to leave the academy and his sort of lack of understanding around, Do I give up my personal life and who I am and maybe go to a place where I have to be closeted just because he think I should? And I would say his lack of understanding might be a subtle form of discrimination. (Nadal et al., 2010a, p. 249)

Finally, sometimes queer people (and people of other marginalized groups) do not report discrimination because of their fears of how others will react. For example, many children will not tell their teachers or principals about bullying because they may somehow be blamed for their actions. In a news article, a mother revealed how she tried to talk to school officials about her gay son being bullied, revealing: "I spoke with principals over the years and got the typical responses: 'Oh well, he needs to toughen up' or 'Oh, it's usually his fault'" (Cox, 2009, para. 32).

Physical Threat or Harassment

This category of microaggressions can be classified as microassaults. Offenders' overt homophobic biases create a dynamic that causes fears in others; yet, the aggressor does not cause any physical harm, making it feel less violent. To illustrate, a gay man described a situation:

I was at a hotel party . . . and the night before we had a good time. The next morning, there were some really rough dudes. . . . This guy asked me if I was gay, and I was like, "Yeah." And he backed up out of his chair and he said,

"Oh, we're all walking around in our boxers here. What were you thinking?" I didn't know what was going to happen, but I felt a little uncomfortable . . . a little bit unsafe. (Nadal et al., 2011, p. 30)

Similarly, a gay male college student wrote about how his fraternity brothers found out about his sexuality and wanted to kick him out, primarily because of his sexual orientation:

Members and alumni begin to fear that the Iowa Delta Chapter of Sigma Phi Epsilon will be labeled as the "gay house." They fear they will lose potential new membership to other houses. To them the only "logical" choice, instead of acceptance and support, is to make the faggot's life miserable, and they find a loophole in the bylaws to deactivate me. They hurl slurs and verbally harass me, my friends, and my parents. Threats of physical violence became frequent. Due to my circumstances, I am deactivated, but of course a repeal process is never explained to me. (Meiner, 2000, p. 301)

So, while the narrators do not reveal physical abuse or assaults, feeling unsafe and being threatened can have a profound impact on people's mental health and psychological well-being.

MACROAGGRESSIONS

Finally, macroaggressions involve elements in the systems or institutions that send denigrating messages to LGBTQ people. For example, when watching television shows that do not portray any LGBTQ characters (or only portray them negatively or stereotypically), LGBTQ people may feel invalidated or insulted. Such experiences are akin to research on sexual stigmas, which reveal how LGBTQ people just "feel" unable to disclose their sexual orientations or feel safe because of heteronormative environments (Herek, 2007). However, there are some macroaggressions that involve biases in actual systems and policies—including schools, government, and media. For instance, one queer woman described a school policy:

They would give detention at any moment like doing anything with the person of the same sex and then they would say, "You know, you should keep that to yourself because parents will complain, students will complain" and I'm like "Why would they complain it's not like I'm doing anything to them" and they're like, "No, it's wrong, you shouldn't do it because it makes other people uncomfortable." It actually bothered me because why can't I be myself, you know, it shouldn't be a problem. If other people can have boyfriends, you know . . . really promiscuous people making out in the hallway, you're trying to get to class and . . . they just keep doing whatever they're doing on the lockers and everything but if I was to hold hands with my girlfriend it would be like "What are you doing?" (Nadal et al., 2011, p. 36)

Another gay male participant described heterosexist macroaggressions in government:

> I was in the Army and they [had] the . . . "don't ask, don't tell" rule. Well, you're there and you feel freakin' terrified if anybody found out that you were that way. So that really pissed me the hell off. So, I just kind of kept to myself, you know. I mean, if at some point, I develop a close-knit relationship with one of my battle buddies, then I'm pretty much need to shut up and keep your mouth like this [gesture of zipping lip] and just don't let it get out there. (Nadal et al., 2011, p. 36)

Both examples demonstrate how heterosexist policies that denigrate their identities may result in psychological distress. Conversely, when policies are queer affirming, positive outcomes may emerge; many studies indicated that mental health outcomes improved for many LGBTQ people after same-sex marriage was legalized across the United States, demonstrating how battling systemic oppression can be good for LGBTQ health outcomes (Hatzenbuehler, 2016).

Within the LGBTQ umbrella, macroaggressions can negatively impact certain subgroups. For instance, asexuals (sometimes referred to as **aces**) have reported feeling excluded or ostracized from LGBTQ organizations. An asexual person shared the following:

> One of my teachers told me that I should consider going to the LGBT Center on 13th Street. And I looked at their schedule and they have like nothing for asexual people. And it's pretty much . . . Lesbian, Gay, Bi, and Trans and that's it. They have nothing for aces, nothing for intersex people, nothing for aromantics, nothing for nonbinary. (Deutsch, 2018, pp. 25–26)

Exclusion from what is perceived as a general or mainstream LGBTQ community is a common experience for other LGBTQ subgroups too—including LGBTQ people of color, LGBTQ people with disabilities, LGBTQ elders, and others. Such perspectives are described more in Chapters 5 through 7, which consider how intersectional identities play a part in dynamics within LGBTQ communities.

CASE STUDIES

To demonstrate the types of sexual-orientation-related microaggressions that queer, lesbian, gay, bisexual, and pansexual people may experience, three fictional case studies are provided. In reviewing the scenarios, readers are encouraged to reflect upon personal reactions as well as potential strategies for coping with such experiences.

The Microaggression of Silence Within Families: The Case of Nicole

Nicole is a 28-year-old white, Irish American, lesbian woman who grew up in a suburban neighborhood outside of Philadelphia with her parents, her older brother, and her younger sister. Nicole has always known that she was a lesbian and disclosed her identity to her parents when she was a junior in college. Initially, her parents were shocked and asked her a lot of follow-up questions, like "Are you sure?" and "How do you know you're gay if you've never had a boyfriend?" She replied with "Yes, I'm sure!" asking her father, "How do you know you're straight if you've never had sex with a man?" and her mother, "How do you know you're not gay if you've never had sex with a woman?" While the interaction was a bit awkward at first, Nicole's parents both told her they love her and will try to learn to accept her "decision."

Since coming out 8 years ago, Nicole has noticed that her parents had never made any direct mention of her sexuality, usually changing the topic when Nicole talks about LGBTQ-related political issues, or when she shares that she is attending events like the Pride Parade or queer poetry nights. Her parents have never said anything overtly homophobic to her, yet she feels sad and invalidated because they do not make the same efforts that they do with her heterosexual siblings. She observes her parents consistently asking her brother and sister when they plan on getting married, if they're dating anyone special, and when they plan on "giving them grandchildren." Meanwhile, neither parent has asked Nicole about her dating life, if she has plans to have a family, or if she will be able to "give them grandchildren."

Nicole recently began a serious romantic relationship with a woman named Andrea and is considering bringing her home to meet the family for Thanksgiving. Because she had never brought a girlfriend home before, Nicole is extremely distressed by the situation. While she can talk to Andrea and some friends about how she is feeling, she decides to seek a psychotherapist to guide her on whether she should bring her girlfriend home and whether to confront her parents about their perceived discomfort with her sexuality. In therapy sessions, Nicole connects to her feelings of anger, sadness, and disappointment with her parents. She explores the jealousy that she feels toward her siblings, particularly because of how they are favored because of their heterosexuality. She also begins to realize that having a lack of explicit support from her parents is almost as hurtful as not having support from them at all.

Microaggressive Environments and Bullying: The Case of Daniel

Daniel is a 14-year-old Mexican American high school freshman who lives at home with his mother, his father, and 12-year-old sister. The family lives in a typical middle-class, predominantly Mexican American neighborhood in a small Southwestern town. The high school that Daniel attends is also predominantly Latinx, with about three fourths being Mexican American. Because of the small community that they live in, Daniel has known most of his classmates since he was a child. However, Daniel presently has very few friends, particularly male friends, because classmates consistently tease him or bully him because they assume he is gay.

The bullying began several years ago, when Daniel started to become more involved in the arts (particularly in theater and dance) and when he started to develop close friendships with girls. During his physical education classes, Daniel was often the last to be picked for teams; the boys often called him a "sissy" or a "fairy" and told him that he "played sports like a girl." Sometimes his teachers heard these comments, but they usually just ignored them and told the kids to concentrate on the game. Daniel usually tried to brush off these hurtful statements in public; however, when he got home, he often cried alone in his room, without being able to tell anyone in his family about what happened that day.

In high school, the bullying continued, and Daniel tried to find excuses to skip class, particularly gym class, so that he wouldn't be teased. He also learned to avoid specific areas of the school because he knew that certain bullies gathered there, often laughing at him as he walked by. In his other classes, he often heard homophobic comments (from both teachers and classmates) that made him feel insulted and sad. For example, in his sex education class, his teacher was discussing the issue of families and marriage. When another student raised her hand and asked about gay sex, the teacher responded, "No, we'll only be learning about normal sex in this class." A month later in his social studies class, his teacher asked students to discuss unsung women heroes in U.S. history. When one of Daniel's classmates brought in an article about trans activists Sylvia Rivera and Marsha P. Johnson, the teacher berated the student with, "The assignment was to find real women historical figures, not whatever these two are." While the rest of the class laughed, Daniel subtly pretended to laugh too, so others wouldn't suspect he was queer.

Numerous other incidents like this happened at his school, and Daniel continued to feel disheartened and alone. He didn't want to tell his friends about being bullied because he feared he would have to admit to being queer—something he wasn't even 100% certain about anyway. He began to become so depressed that he found himself crying nightly and sleeping for 10 hours every night. His family noticed this behavior but didn't know what to do. When he told his mother that he wanted to kill himself, she panicked and took him to the emergency room.

Microaggressions Within LGBTQ Community Spaces: The Case of Sean

Sean is a 32-year-old Hmong American man who works as a licensed clinical social worker at the local LGBTQ community center in an urban city in the Midwest. When Sean first took the job, he was very excited to work there, particularly because he had a passion for working with LGBTQ people and advocating for their mental health needs. When Sean was hired, he "outed" himself immediately as a bisexual man to his supervisor, Jennifer. He asked her if there other openly bisexual people who worked at the center. Jennifer, a Black lesbian, informed him that there were bisexual women employees, but that she was not aware of any openly bisexual men. However, she assured him that the work environment was very "bisexual friendly" and very diverse in every other way.

When Sean started meeting his coworkers, everyone was very friendly with him. People oriented him to the office protocols and stopped by to say "hi" often. While he liked everyone in the office, Sean realized that most of his coworkers assumed he was gay because of the subtle comments he heard them make. For example, in one of his staff meetings, there was a discussion about how to make the center more accessible and welcoming to underrepresented groups within the LGBTQ umbrella, particularly to transgender people and LGBTQ people of color. When someone raised her hand and said, "What about the bisexuals?" a gay male coworker named Ben blurted: "Well, we have lots of bi women here, and we all know that bisexual men don't exist!" While most people laughed, Jennifer awkwardly looked at Sean, wondering if she should say something. After sharing brief eye contact with each other, they both remained silent.

Situations like these continued in the workplace for the next few months. Sean decided not to say anything because he figured that they were simply being ignorant and because he was accustomed to hearing monosexist language in every other aspect of his life. A few months later, Sean began dating a woman named Sophia. When he brought her to an office social gathering, he introduced her to his coworkers as his girlfriend. Some colleagues were polite, albeit with puzzled looks on their faces; some coworkers asked incessant questions to both Sean and Sophia about their relationship. One asked Sophia if she is bothered that Sean has been sexually involved with men; another asked Sean if he liked having sex with men or women more. Both Sean and Sophia were uncomfortable with the questions, but they each answered them politely. However, Ben, one of Sean's coworkers, was vocal about his disapproval, stating, "So when did you *become* bisexual?" Sean angrily replied, "I've *always* been bisexual, and you'll always be a jerk," before he walked away feeling even more furious than before.

CASE STUDY DISCUSSION

As the three cases demonstrate, microaggressions toward queer people can take many forms. In the first scenario, we were introduced to Nicole—a lesbian woman who does not feel that her parents support her sexual identity. While she does not have any tangible "evidence" to support this (i.e., they have never said anything overtly homophobic to her since she came out to them), she recognizes their behavior toward her is different from their behavior toward her heterosexual siblings. This type of situation is difficult to address for many reasons. First, because there is a lack of LGBTQ-supportive behaviors (as opposed to an omnipresence of overtly homophobic statements or behaviors in other families), Nicole may question whether she is being oversensitive or whether her perceptions are reality based. As a result, Nicole may have difficulty confronting her parents because she may be afraid that they may dismiss her accusations or tell her she is being paranoid.

Second, because this conflict occurs within a family environment, there are many other factors to take into consideration, such as dynamics with other family members, family history, communication styles, and an array of differing worldviews. Microaggressions toward LGBTQ people are quite common within families because there is often one sole LGBTQ family member (Nadal, Issa, et al., 2011). Accordingly, that person may feel unsupported or without any allies to stand in solidarity with them, resulting in a weight they carry themselves. Further, it may be challenging to confront micro-aggressions within families because individuals may want to avoid family conflict and tension. So, while Nicole is currently bothered by her situation, she may choose to hold back her feelings, as a way of maintaining some harmony within the family.

In the second case, we further our understanding of the relationship between bullying and microaggressions through the case of Daniel—a 14-year-old high school freshman who has been bullied for several years, primarily because of his involvement in the arts and his friendships with girls. Most of the bullying is extremely overt (e.g., his classmates call him names like "sissy" or "fairy"); however, some of the bullying may be more difficult to label if he did want to tell an authority figure (e.g., when his classmates laugh when Daniel walks by in the hallway, how can he prove that it is directed toward him or that it is malicious?). Moreover, the bullying appears to be condoned (e.g., teachers not punishing students for using homophobic terms, teachers making heterosexist comments, perpetuating harmful stereotypes about LGBTQ people). Perhaps one reason the situation has become so intense is because Daniel has not been able to discuss his experiences with anyone. While his family and some friends seem generally supportive, talking about these hurtful incidents with them would force him to acknowledge his identity. Thus, like many young people who struggle with their sexual identities, he represses his feelings, eventually taking a toll on his mental health.

The third scenario describes a microaggression that may often occur within LGBTQ community spaces: microaggressions against bisexual people. Bisexuals are often labeled (by heterosexual and lesbian or gay people) as being "confused," incapable of maintaining monogamous romantic relationships, or of being overly sexual. Bisexual men particularly are often viewed as "pretending" to be bisexual instead of fully accepting a gay identity. A scene from the popular television show *Sex and the City* has the four main characters talking about the bisexual man that Carrie Bradshaw is currently dating. Carrie, perplexed by bisexuality, states, "I'm not even sure bisexuality exists. I think it's just a layover on the way to Gaytown" (Garis, 2016). A similar sentiment occurred on the series *Insecure* in which Molly, one of the lead characters, is dating a man who admits to having sexually experimented with another man once before. When discussing this with friends, Molly's best friend, Issa, says, "Why can't Black men explore their sexuality without being labeled as gay, or bi, or whatever?" which prompts Molly's response of "Because I want my man to be a man" (Brathwaite, 2016). Biases like these invalidate the existence of bisexual men, while also enabling microaggressions against bisexuals (such as those encountered by Sean).

Sean is a bisexual man who is actively involved in serving LGBTQ community members; in fact, he has devoted his career to working with LGBTQ people and advocating for their mental health. However, at his workplace, there are several "jokes" and other types of comments made that promote people's views of monosexuality. Sean tries to ignore these types of biased views, but he becomes more upset as they persist on a semiregular basis. Because these sorts of microaggressions occur between members of two marginalized groups, they may be complicated to address. Studies find that bisexual women have reported feeling targeted by lesbians, and lesbians have reported feeling targeted by bisexual women (Nadal et al., 2011). However, because both groups are oppressed by heterosexual society, two outcomes may occur: (a) it may be difficult for individuals to recognize when they are the perpetrator of microaggressions because they are also the victims of such incidents, and (b) some may argue that these kinds of microaggressions might feel less threatening than those coming from the group with power and **privilege** (e.g., heterosexuals). Thus, it is possible that Ben (Sean's gay male coworker) may have difficulty in admitting his bias against bisexuals because of his minoritized identity. Perhaps Sean ignored or excused these comments because they were coming from gay or lesbian people, instead of from heterosexuals (which he may view as being more oppressive). Perhaps a microaggression committed by someone from a **target group** (e.g., LGBTQ people, people of color, women, persons with disabilities) may feel different than a microaggression committed by someone of a **dominant group** (e.g., heterosexuals and cisgender people, white people, cis men, or able-bodied people) because of the power and privilege involved. Either way, it is important to recognize that microaggressions can occur even within marginalized communities and can still be hurtful to their recipients.

In all three of these scenarios, a few themes emerge. First, in each scenario, there are some incidents that are much more blatant and obvious, while others might be well intentioned and not malicious in any way. For instance, when Nicole's parents asked her if she was "sure" she was a lesbian, their intention may not have been to insult her; rather, they may just be "concerned" about their daughter's well-being and want to ensure that she is happy. Similarly, when Sean's coworkers ask him and his girlfriend relentless questions about their relationship, they may claim to be well intentioned and simply curious.

In each of the scenarios, there are several people who serve as support systems for the individual—Nicole has her girlfriend and her psychotherapist; Daniel has his family and an intimate group of friends; and Sean has his girlfriend, Sophia, and his supervisor, Jennifer. Sometimes these individuals appeared to be helpful (e.g., Nicole's psychotherapist seems able to guide her in working through her issues). Sometimes they may seem stumped as to how to react (e.g., Sean's supervisor is unclear whether she should address the microaggression at the staff meeting). And sometimes they may not even know what is going on at all (e.g., Daniel's parents are not even aware he is being bullied). Having allies or accomplices who can assist people who are targeted by any type of discrimination is very important. **Allies**—those who are vocal in their knowledge of oppression and demonstrate a desire to show solidarity with people in historically marginalized groups—can help to validate a person's perceptions, feelings, and realities. Meanwhile, **accomplices** can use their privileged identities to advocate for the target of microaggressions, especially through challenging systems and institutions, so that the individual does not feel they must always fight for themselves. When people have more social support, they are likely to better cope with the microaggressions, leading to more optimal mental health.

Finally, in each of the scenarios, the reactions of all three individuals reflect the wide range of processes and responses that people have when dealing with microaggressions. Daniel, the queer teenager who is persistently bullied, has tried to avoid the perpetrators of microaggressions while repressing his true emotions when the microaggressions do occur. Nicole, the lesbian whose parents are not openly supportive of her sexual identity, has chosen to seek mental health treatment and is debating whether to confront her parents about her feelings. Sean, who experiences microaggressions in the workplace, has chosen to ignore the microaggressive comments; however, he is no longer able to contain his emotions and finally unleashes his anger toward his coworker. Regardless of how each scenario is ultimately handled, each person will have experienced a notable amount of distress. Similar types of processes are described in the next chapter, focusing on the impact of microaggressions toward transgender, nonbinary, and gender nonconforming people.

DISCUSSION QUESTIONS

For General Readers

1. What types of microaggressions do you believe occur often toward lesbian women? Toward gay men? Toward bisexual women? Toward bisexual men?

2. What types of sexual orientation microaggressions do you notice in various institutions (e.g., your workplace or school) or systems (e.g., government, media, religious)?

3. What would you do if you were in Nicole's situation? Daniel's situation? Sean's situation?

For Psychologists, Educators, and Other Experts

1. How might you improve your cultural competence in working with queer people?

2. What techniques or methods would you use in working with Nicole, Daniel, or Sean?

3. What countertransference issues would you have toward Nicole, Daniel, or Sean?

GLOSSARY OF KEY TERMS

ace A term used to refer to an asexual person.

accomplice A person from a historically privileged group who shows solidarity with members of historically marginalized groups by actively challenging systems of oppression.

ally A person who is vocal in their knowledge of oppression and demonstrates a desire to show solidarity with people in historically marginalized groups.

aromantic An individual who does not experience romantic attraction toward others or lacks interest in romance or romantic relationships altogether.

asexual An individual who does not experience sexual attraction toward others or lacks interest in sex or sexual activity altogether.

cisheteropatriarchy A system of oppression in which cisgender, heterosexual men maintain power over women, queer people, trans and nonbinary people, and other marginalized groups.

demisexual An individual whose sexual orientation typically involves experiencing sexual attraction toward someone after making a strong emotional connection with them.

dominant group A group of people in a society with greater power and privilege, due to their majority status or historical authority.

homonegativity Denigrating beliefs about nonheterosexual people.

monosexual One who identifies as exclusively heterosexual or homosexual.

pansexual An individual whose sexual orientation is not defined by gender, in that they have the potential to be sexually, romantically, or emotionally attracted to people of all gender identities and sexual orientations.

power The ability to define reality and to convince other people that it is their definition.

privilege A right, favor, advantage, or immunity, specially granted to one individual or group, and withheld from another.

queer studies The critical study of issues relating to sexual orientation and gender identity, centering the history and experiences of non-heterosexual and transgender people.

settler colonialism The act of people migrating to a new land or area and displacing or outnumbering the indigenous inhabitants who have historically lived in or cultivated the land or area.

target group A group of people in a society with less power and privilege, due to their minority status or historical marginalization.

toxic masculinity A set of traits, typically internalized in cisgender men, that promotes violent, competitive, misogynistic, heterosexist, transphobic, or generally oppressive attitudes or behaviors toward women, LGBTQ people, and other historically marginalized groups.

white supremacy The belief system that white people are a superior race to all other racial groups and that white people should dominate global society—typically to the exclusion, genocide, or dehumanization of other racial groups.

4 GENDER IDENTITY MICROAGGRESSIONS

Experiences of Transgender, Gender Nonconforming, and Nonbinary People

FIGURE 4.1. Nonbinary Friends Expressing Themselves via Fashion

Note. Photo courtesy of Rodnae Productions.

https://doi.org/10.1037/0000335-005
Dismantling Everyday Discrimination: Microaggressions Toward LGBTQ People, Second Edition, by K. L. Y. Nadal

So far, I have provided definitions and examples of microaggressions—often referred to as "the new face of discrimination." In the first two chapters of this book, I described what microaggressions are and how they manifest, while revealing how they detrimentally affect LGBTQ people and other marginalized groups. In Chapter 3, I provided examples of sexual orientation microaggressions, highlighting microaggressions that queer, lesbian, gay, bisexual, and pansexual people face. This chapter discusses microaggressions based on gender identity, highlighting the experiences of transgender, gender nonconforming, and nonbinary people.

A REVIEW OF GENDER IDENTITY MICROAGGRESSIONS

Let's begin by reviewing some of the previous literature on gender identity microaggressions. There is a dearth of research on transgender people and microaggressions, which reflects the lack of literature focusing on transgender people in general. Through the PsycInfo database (an abstracting and indexing database of psychology-related literature from the 1600s to the present), a search of the keywords "transgender" and "discrimination" in November 2021 yielded 1,612 entries. Comparatively, a search combining "discrimination" with "gay," "lesbian," and "bisexual" yielded 2,578, 2,269, and 1,638 hits, respectively. It is likely that many of the 1,612 articles may not actually be reflective of transgender experiences but are included because authors use umbrella terms like "lesbian, gay, bisexual, and transgender." For instance, many research studies that use "LGBTQ" in their titles are assumed to be applicable to transgender people but do not include any or many **trans** participants in their research—further perpetuating the silencing or erasing of trans communities (Fiani & Han, 2019). Moreover, by lumping these groups together, readers may presume that queer and trans people, identities, and lived experiences are interchangeable, resulting in a lack of specific care or understanding of trans people. Thus, it is important to review some basic terminology involving transgender people, as a way of fully acknowledging the various nuances of trans people as well as how microaggressions may affect them on systemic, institutional, and interpersonal levels.

In the Introduction and Chapter 1, I defined some basic terms, including *transgender* and *trans* (umbrella terms that can be used to refer to anyone for whom the sex they were assigned at birth is an incomplete or incorrect description of themselves); *gender identity* (an individual's personal sense of identification as male or female or another gender), and *gender nonconforming* (the trait or identity of not adhering to gender role expectations). All three of these definitions are important because they help us to understand who is included in the transgender umbrella. While *cisgender* people (i.e., individuals who identify with their sex assigned at birth) tend to think of transgender people as being **transsexuals** and others who physically transition, the transgender umbrella can also include *nonbinary* people (i.e., those who do not conform to any gender at all or who identify with a third gender). For example, **genderqueer** is an umbrella term that individuals may use when they identify as neither a man nor a woman or when they identify as both man and woman. In North American Indigenous cultures, a third gender is often referred to as *two-spirited*; in Hawaiian indigenous cultures, a third gender is referred to as *māhū*.

Furthermore, people who **gender bend** (also known as **gender benders**) may also be classified under the transgender umbrella. Gender benders may include people who perform **drag**, as well as **cross-dressers** who may dress in gender nonconforming ways often, occasionally, or sometimes. As an example, a **drag queen** or **drag king** may only gender bend during performances, and a cross-dresser may reserve gender bending for special occasions (e.g., nights "out on the town"). Sometimes people who gender bend do not identify as transgender or LGBTQ at all; in fact, many identify as heterosexuals with a more fluid gender identity, thus further supporting that gender identity and sexual orientation are independent concepts and self-identities.

Learning these definitions is also necessary because it helps one to grasp why microaggressions (and overt discrimination) remain common and pervasive towards trans people. Because most Western societies accept, promote, and teach others a **gender binary**, many cisgender people may have difficulties in recognizing that there are alternative ways to experience or express gender other than exclusively female or exclusively male. This gender binary promotes heteronormativity, in which all people are expected to act in accordance with their sex assigned at birth and subsequent gender roles. In Chapter 3, queer people described how others judged, mocked, or punished them when they behaved in gender nonconforming ways (e.g., boys who acted "effeminately" or girls who participated in "masculine" activities). However, for trans people, this gender binary may result in even more microaggressions, primarily because **cis** people are extremely uncomfortable that trans people's identities or physical appearances (or both) may not match what is traditionally "male" or "female."

The gender binary may impact various subgroups under the transgender umbrella differentially. First, gender presentation is a huge factor in understanding one's experiences with discrimination. As mentioned in Chapter 2, transgender people who do not medically transition or have gender-affirming surgeries may have difficulty in "passing" as their self-identified gender (i.e., their physical appearance does not match the gender that they identify with or feel most comfortable with). As a result, cis people may hold prejudicial attitudes toward these individuals, which may lead to microaggressions and more overt forms of discrimination. On the other hand, transgender people who do transition (i.e., those who have the access or resources to medically transition, complete gender affirmation surgeries, or take hormonal treatment) may have an easier time in "passing," which may reduce the discrimination that they encounter. However, this may result in experiencing different types of microaggressions because they are assumed to be cisgender (e.g., a coworker who does not know a transgender person's history may make a transphobic remark).

It is crucial to be aware that there are many reasons why trans people do not physically or medically transition. Because transgender people are often kicked out of their homes as youth and have difficulty gaining employment because of discrimination (Nadal, 2020), they may have difficulty in earning enough money to sustain their lives, let alone paying for hormone or medical treatments. Further, if they do not have access to full-time jobs, or their employers do not provide transgender-friendly health services or insurance benefits, they may not have the resources to get the treatment that they need. Third, some transgender people simply view a medical or hormonal transition as unnecessary to their gender identity development or personal journeys (Pardo & Devor, 2017). Some of these individuals are comfortable with their physical bodies not matching their transgender identities or internal self-concepts. For others, because they recognize that they do not have the resources to attain the medical treatment needed to transition, they learn to be comfortable with maintaining the appearance of their sex assigned at birth. Finally, some nonbinary, gender fluid, or gender nonconforming people may be comfortable with their physical bodies, but they do not want to be identified as either male or female; thus, medically transitioning from one binary gender to another would not be salient or required (Budge & Orovecz, 2017).

Moreover, because of the gender binary, transgender people who do transition may experience discrimination based on their perceived gender or gender presentation (Davis, 2017). For example, transgender women who "pass" may encounter similar forms of misogyny and sexist microaggressions as cisgender women (e.g., they may be sexually objectified, viewed as intellectually or physically inferior; Arayasirikul & Wilson, 2019; Nadal, Skolnik, & Wong, 2012). Meanwhile, trans men, when perceived as cisgender men, may be expected to adhere to the same rigid gender roles as cis men (e.g., they may be expected to be emotionally strong, masculine, or chivalrous; Rogers,

2019). So, while some gender identity microaggressions can be encountered by a spectrum of trans people, perceived gender itself can heavily influence one's discriminatory experiences.

The first known study to focus specifically on the impacts of gender identity microaggressions on transgender and gender nonconforming people was Nadal, Skolnik, and Wong (2012); the researchers used a qualitative, focus group method with transgender female and male participants ($N = 9$) to classify the spectrum of gender identity microaggressions. As in the previous microaggressions studies on queer people, there were several categories that validated the taxonomy presented by Nadal, Rivera, and Corpus (2010). These included: (a) use of transphobic and/or incorrectly gendered terminology, (b) assumption of universal transgender experience, (c) exoticization, (d) discomfort with/disapproval of transgender experience, (e) endorsement of gender normative and binary culture or behaviors, (f) denial of existence of transphobia, (g) assumption of sexual pathology/abnormality, (h) physical threat or harassment, and (i) denial of individual transphobia (see Chapter 2, this volume, for a brief description of these categories). However, in the current study, there was one category that emerged that was significantly different from the prior studies with queer people: "denial of bodily privacy" (or ways that transgender people's bodies are often objectified or exoticized, particularly through others' insidious and entitled questions). Galupo et al. (2014) also proposed another theme for trans people: "questioning of legitimacy of identities."

One critique of the limited literature on microaggressions is that there is little written about the diversity of the transgender umbrella group—particularly in the lack of research focused on genderqueer, nonbinary, gender nonconforming, **bigender**, or **agender** people (Chang & Chung, 2015; Nadal et al., 2016). In other words, while there has been some growth in literature on trans men and trans women, very little literature centers the experiences of nonbinary people. However, some emerging scholarship illustrates how microaggressions manifest in the lives of nonbinary people. Pulice-Farrow et al. (2020) examined the responses of 200 gender nonconforming and 190 agender participants regarding the sorts of microaggressions committed by romantic partners. Data was coded and categorized into three themes: The first was identity parsing, or microaggressions based upon presuming one's identities were in two opposing dimensions (e.g., real vs. presented self, public vs. private self, masculine vs. feminine). The second theme involved microaggressions regarding binary assumptions of gender/sex, and the third theme was labeled "transition-dependent" or microaggressions that involved trans' or nonbinary people's transitions.

Finally, some quantitative studies have examined how microaggressions affect the lives of transgender and nonbinary people. First, Parr and Howe

FIGURE 4.2. A Black Nonbinary Drag Performer Striking a Pose

Note. Photo courtesy of Greta Hoffman.

(2019) found that transgender participants' responses to "gender identity non-affirmation or denial microaggression events" (i.e., a list of situational prompts based on qualitative literature) were linked to myriad mental health issues, including sadness, hopelessness, and suicidal ideation.

Second, Nadal (2019b) created the Gender Identity Microaggressions Scale (GIMS), which consists of five subscales: (a) denial of gender identity, (b) misuse of pronouns, (c) invasion of bodily privacy, (d) behavioral discomfort, and (e) denial of societal transphobia. Utilizing the GIMS, Coco (2021) found that nonbinary people were more likely to encounter microaggressions than binary cisgender people. Finally, Woodford et al. (2017) found that trans college students who reported more environmental microaggressions (e.g., lack of gender-neutral restrooms on campus) were likely to report poorer academic outcomes.

VOICES OF TRANSGENDER AND GENDER NONCONFORMING PEOPLE

This section begins by revisiting the categories from the microaggression taxonomy presented by Nadal, Rivera, and Corpus (2010), plus the new additional themes mentioned previously. However, it focuses on the microaggressions from the perspectives from transgender people via examples from previous research and contemporary media and literature.

Use of Transphobic Terminology

This category of microaggressions includes instances in which others used denigrating language about or toward transgender people. Sometimes transphobic or genderist language was used intentionally to insult or berate a transgender person. In one of my research studies (Nadal, Skolnik, & Wong, 2012), a transgender man talked about an incident he had encountered before fully transitioning:

> I remember one time before I transitioned when I first moved to New York; I was on the train with my roommate, who was a non-transgender woman of color. A young African-American guy was like, "Yo, yo . . . is that a dude or is that a woman?" (p. 70)

In the same study, a trans woman mentioned similar transphobic language:

> I was walking one time to the post office, and I had just recently had my lips done and a little five-year-old kid said, "Daddy, daddy. Hey daddy, that's a shemale." So, he never referred to me as a man. He referred to me as . . . a shemale. (p. 65)

In both cases, the enactors of the microaggression were clearly conscious about their actions. While they may not have intended to directly insult the transgender target, their transphobic words were hurtful and insulting. What is even more disheartening is that the second example includes a transphobic remark that was made by a young child, which signifies how children can learn hurtful language at such an early age.

Sometimes people may use transphobic or genderist language that is unconscious and unintentional. For example, it is common for cisgender people (heterosexual and even queer people) to use the word "tranny" when describing transgender people. In the film *Lingua Franca* (Sandoval, 2019), the main character, Isabel, is a trans Filipina woman who is a caretaker of an older woman. In one of the scenes, she is cleaning up while her client's grandson and his friends are in the room. Not knowing her trans identity, the men begin using transphobic slurs when talking about their sexual exploits including: "Was she a fucking tranny or something?" and "Whatever it was." In a matter of a few seconds, Isabel is subjected to hearing transphobic language that is verbally violent ("tranny" is often deemed as having similar derogatory and demoralizing undertones as the N-word or "faggot"), as well as language that is dehumanizing in more coded ways (a trans person being described as an "it").

Misgendering (or the use of incorrect gender pronouns when describing someone) is also considered transphobic language. When someone intentionally uses wrong pronouns to describe a transgender person, it may be considered a microassault, in that the speaker is conscious of their decisions and often convicted in their stances about gender. With these situations, these individuals may still claim that they are not transphobic and they do not have any biases toward transgender people. A known example in the media is the controversy surrounding J. K. Rowling (author of the *Harry Potter* books); after a series of controversial tweets that were deemed transphobic, she released a statement that included further biased language. She wrote,

> I want trans women to be safe. At the same time, I do not want to make natal girls and women less safe. When you throw open the doors of bathrooms and changing rooms to any man who believes or feels he's a woman . . . then you open the door to any and all men who wish to come inside. (Rosenblatt, 2020, para. 11)

Based on this language, it appears that the author wants people to believe that she cares about trans people; however, she also propagates problematic notions that a transgender woman is merely a "man who believes or feels he's a woman."

Sometimes, misgendering may be less intentional and might be considered a "slip up." An example of this type of microaggression that later went viral online was an instance that occurred shortly after Demi Lovato disclosed their identity as nonbinary (and their use of "they" pronouns") in 2021. A paparazzi reporter asked musician Lizzo if she would ever collaborate with Lovato—using "she" and "her" pronouns in reference to Lovato. Lizzo corrected the reporter first by saying "they" and then explaining "Demi goes by 'they'" (Chung, 2021, paras. 4–5). The paparazzo can later be heard thanking Lizzo for the correction, demonstrating their acknowledgment of misusing Lovato's **gender pronouns**. In a different example, singer Sam Smith disclosed their nonbinary identity in 2019; a year later, singer Shaun Mendes publicly referred to Smith using male pronouns. However, shortly after, he offered a public apology, saying it completely "slipped his mind" (Koenig, 2020). Accordingly, perhaps, this example may be viewed as a microinsult because it was unintentional and not meant to be malicious, while also demonstrating how an enactor of a microaggression can hold themselves accountable for their mistake.

One form of misgendering is the act of **deadnaming**, or the act of referring to a trans person by their name assigned at birth instead of the name they now use. Like misgendering in general, such behaviors may be unintentional (e.g., a loved one who is accepting of their trans family member but occasionally errs in referring to them by their birth name and apologizes immediately). However, deadnaming can often be intentional and malicious—with some people doing so as a way of sharing their convictions or beliefs about the rigidity of gender.

Sometimes people make jokes about trans people under the guise of comedy. For example, for years, comedians like Ricky Gervais and Dave Chappelle have misgendered or deadnamed Caitlyn Jenner in their comedy sets. After public backlash ensued, they respond that they were simply joking—often citing the rise of politically correct culture or the end of free speech (Black, 2021). However, hearing such language can be damaging to transgender people (who may feel dehumanized and ridiculed) as well as to cisgender people (who may learn that it is acceptable to make jokes at transgender people's expense). Being aware of misgendering others is important, as research has supported that being misgendered is common for transgender people and can cause psychological distress (McLemore, 2018).

Endorsement of Gender Normative Culture and Behaviors

This theme describes instances in which transgender people are expected to subscribe to the gender binary, by subscribing to a gender normative culture and participating in gender normative behaviors. Often such comments made to transgender and nonbinary people are not meant to be malicious; people may believe that they are simply stating their opinions and that their thoughts are logical, or that they have a right to free speech. Further, such statements are usually based on one's convictions that there are only two rigid genders. To demonstrate this, in 2020, after basketball player Dwayne Wade and actress Gabrielle Union announced that their daughter identified as transgender, there was some backlash from some hip-hop artists, including Young Thug, who tweeted: "All I wanna say to dwade son is 'GOD DONT MAKE MISTAKES'" (Cachero, 2020). A year later, Bethenny Frankel faced some backlash when she made negative comments on her podcast that were deemed transphobic. She discussed her discontent about children being taught about gender pronouns in school, and later described how "a person with a penis who identifies as a girl" had recently attended her daughter's summer camp and shared a cabin with other girls (Shatto, 2021, para. 6). Such comments demonstrate the biased transphobic beliefs that equate gender and sex, and that the only "real" men or women are cisgender. In these specific cases, these messages negate the lived experiences of trans youth, which can be particularly damaging, given that trans and nonbinary youth suffer from more mental health disparities than cisgender youth (Hawke et al., 2021; Rimes et al., 2019).

In one of my studies (Nadal, Skolnik, & Wong, 2012), a transgender man (who was in the midst of transitioning at the time of our interview) described how his coworkers questioned his ability to do physical work. He shared: "[My coworker] said, 'This is a man's job type thing, you know'" (p. 67). Perhaps this was because his coworkers didn't assume he was masculine enough; perhaps they still stereotyped him as being a woman who would not be capable of completing a physically arduous task. Similarly, in the movie *Transamerica* (Tucker, 2005), there is a scene in which the main character Bree Osbourne (played by Felicity Huffman) is at dinner in a restaurant with her mother. Although Bree identifies and presents as a woman (and despite the presence of other people at the table), her mother expected Bree to be chivalrous and pull out her chair for her as she sat down. The underlying message that was communicated in this instance was that Bree was "still a man" and was expected to engage in the same chivalrous behaviors that are expected of cisgender men.

Finally, sometimes transgender people experience microaggressions in which others invalidate their gender identity when they are upset with them. For example, in one of my studies (Nadal, Skolnik, & Wong, 2012), a transgender woman participant described one romantic relationship she had with a man:

> I went out with a guy, also. At first when he thought I was a woman, he would open the car door for me. He would do this, he would do that, he would bring me flowers. And when I told him that I was transgender, he stayed with me, I'm not going to say he didn't. But when we would fight, he would say, "But you're a man, why should I treat you this way?" (p. 134)

Again, while the cisgender man in this scenario may have seemed to be somewhat accepting of the transgender participant, he still did not view her as a "real" woman. He chose to be chivalrous and generous with her when he was happy with her; however, he was mean and degrading when upset with her. These types of microaggressions have been reported as common occurrences for trans people in romantic relationships with cis people—particularly for trans women in romantic relationships with cisgender heterosexual men (Pulice-Farrow et al., 2017).

Assumption of Universal Transgender Experience

This theme of microaggressions occurs when individuals presume that all transgender people are the same. Many of these assumptions can be based on negative stereotypes that are learned through religion, the media, and other sources; others may be based on generalizations based on personal experiences. For instance, in the movie *Transamerica* (Tucker, 2005), when one of the characters, Toby, learns of the protagonist's transgender identity, he makes a comment alluding to the notion that transgender people could not be Christian. In response, Bree (the protagonist) replies, "My body may be a work-in-progress, but there is nothing wrong with my soul." Oftentimes it is assumed that LGBTQ people could not possibly be religious or spiritual, because they are "choosing" something that is "against God's will." However, alluded by the quote above, people of all gender identities can be spiritual, have connections to a higher power, and try their best to be morally good people.

Sometimes transgender people are stereotyped based on what is viewed in the media. Serrano (2007) wrote about how there is a disproportionate number of transgender women who are portrayed as sex workers on television and in movies:

> The popular assumption that trans women deliberately transform ourselves into sexual objects also explains why we are so frequently depicted in the media as sex workers. The fact that trans female sex workers have reached the status of "stock characters" is of particular interest, as such depictions are at complete odds with other cissexual presumptions about transsexuality. Media representations of trans people that do not involve sex work typically go out of their way to stress the fact that transsexuality is an extraordinarily rare phenomenon, and to promote the idea that transsexuals are sexually undesirable. So, it is unclear why, being as rare and undesirable as we supposedly are, we seem to make up such a significant percentage of sex workers on TV and in the movies. (p. 261)

This stereotype that transgender women are sex workers parallels a narrative from a transgender woman in one of my studies (Nadal, Skolnik, & Wong, 2012). She described going to the police station when she and another transgender friend were targets of a crime. She stated: "The detectives in the victim's unit asked if we were prostitutes. So, I said, 'I'm not a prostitute, why are you saying that?' He said, 'Because all you transsexuals are all prostitutes'" (p. 65).

Finally, a transgender participant in the same study described how people assume that after transitioning that all transgender people would have the same identities, lifestyles, and interests:

> In my experiences, [people] play certain male gender roles that are like super normative and I'm just like, "No, I don't play that. That's not me." There's so much of that that exists that it's hard to figure out how do you balance between being who you are and wanting [to] be respected and also not want [to] complicate it as well. (Nadal, Skolnik, & Wong, 2012, p. 65)

Thus, cisgender people have some stereotypes and assumptions about transgender people that they assume are true of all people within the transgender umbrella. Again, while the perpetrators of these microaggressions may be well intentioned, they may be communicating their true feelings of judgment or disapproval of transgender people.

Exoticization

There are many microaggressions that occur when transgender people are dehumanized or treated like objects. This may often occur when transgender people are viewed as "sexual objects" instead of human beings with any feelings. A Latina trans woman divulged:

> [Men often tell me], "You're not girlfriend material. All I want from you is that sexual asset and that whole thrill of being with a transsexual and go on with my life and act like you never exist." Now, not only am I being objectified and sensationalized, I'm being less than human. (Nadal, Skolnik, & Wong, 2012, p. 66)

Trans people can also be viewed as "tokens": token girlfriends, token boyfriends, or even token friends. One participant shared, "Even if they don't even like you, just because you're a tranny, they want you in their collection" (Nadal, Skolnik, & Wong, 2012, p. 66)

Finally, there are many ways in which transgender people can be viewed as "unique" or "bizarre" or "different" instead of being viewed as people. To illustrate this, in the movie *The Crying Game*, one transsexual character's transgender identity was revealed to the audience when her penis was shown during a love scene with a cisgender male character. The movie caused quite a stir at the time, as it was one of the first times that a transgender female character was portrayed in a mainstream movie as being "beautiful"—a word that was even used by the film's director. While the plot included several other dramatic and suspenseful story lines, reviewers used words like "comedic," "sexual extremism," and "perverse" to describe the film (Kotsopoulos & Mills, 1994). Because of this one transgender character and her "big secret," the movie was viewed as comedic, perhaps signifying that cisgender people view transgender people as "perverse" people for their entertainment. Other historical examples of transphobia in Hollywood are documented in the 2020 documentary *Disclosure: Trans Lives on Screen* (Feder & Scholder, 2020)—with examples including *Ace Ventura: Pet Detective*, *Bosom Buddies*, and *Tootsie*. Featuring interviews with trans artists and activists like Laverne Cox, Jen Richards, Chase Strangio, and Tiq Milan, the documentary argued that the blatant transphobia in the media increases transphobic biases in the audiences who consume them.

Discomfort With or Disapproval of Transgender Experience

These types of microaggressions occur when individuals express discomfort with or disapproval with transgender people or identities; they are often conscious, in that the individual is aware of their uneasiness. Other times, these behaviors may be unconscious, in that the individual does not even know they are reacting or acting in such a way. Sometimes these types of statements and behaviors may be unintentional, in that the individual may know that they are uncomfortable but do not know the negative impact such statements and behaviors have on the individual who experiences it.

An example of overt disapproval involves a trans Latina woman who shared the following:

> When I was 16, [my father] basically looked me in the eyes, and he said, 'I love you. You're always going to be my son. But you know you are going to die of AIDS, right?' And I . . . [pause] that's a horrible thing to say to your kid. (B. A. Robinson, 2018, p. 391)

Of note, this father misgenders the speaker by referring to her as "his son" while also presuming that all trans or queer people die of AIDS. This instance demonstrates how one brief incident can result from so many biases.

In another example, a transgender participant in one of my studies (Nadal, Skolnik, & Wong, 2012) shared a story in which both a classmate and a romantic interest shared disapproval of her transgender identity:

> I was in school and was getting to know this gentleman. I didn't feel comfortable in telling him that I was transgender because I wasn't too sure how I feel with him yet. There was this girl in my class who I had thought she knew I was transgender because we go to the gym together. She tried to question my gender and she [also] found out I was talking to that gentleman. One day, I happened to walk down the same block as he was, and he moved to the left and I kept moving forward. He waved "hi," but it was like he was ashamed, like I was a disease. I was definitely hurt. In the end, I found out she told him that I was a man. (p. 66)

This instance demonstrates how unspoken avoidant behaviors can demonstrate one's discomfort while causing so much pain for a person who is targeted.

Some microaggressions may influence one's worldview or overall perceptions about other people. One trans man described interacting with certain cisgender people:

> I pay real close attention to how I get treated in different spaces. I noticed that when I'm in an environment with mostly straight but sometimes also queer men, who know of my transgender history, the ways in which they treat me versus

the way in which they treat non-transgender men are like absolutely very clear. (Nadal, Skolnik, & Wong, 2012, p. 66)

This type of scenario demonstrates the more subtle types of microaggression that are harder to define or articulate. Because it may be more difficult to point out (i.e., it is often a "feeling"), it may be more challenging to confront an individual on any microaggressive behaviors.

This type of coded, unspoken microaggression may be common for transgender people when they try to find employment. For example, one trans woman illustrated the issue this way:

> I remember a lot of them looking at me . . . and taking the paper. I gave them my resume, and "If we have an opening, we'll call you." Even though in the window it says, "Now Hiring," they go, "If we have an opening, we'll call you." So, they would say that, but they didn't just come out and go "how dare you, hell no we ain't gonna hire you." But they did say it, it was just they watch what they say cause there were witnesses. (Nadal, Vargas, et al., 2012, p. 132)

Again, while the person perceived the employer was being transphobic, the lack of "evidence" may make the individual feeling confused or paranoid.

Assumption of Sexual Pathology, Deviance, or Abnormality

This category includes microaggressions in which transgender people are assumed to be sexually pathological, deviant, or abnormal. Like the examples shared in the previous chapter regarding queer people, transgender people may be assumed to be sexually promiscuous or be diagnosed with HIV/AIDS. A transgender woman shared an encounter in which an emergency medical technician (EMT) accidentally touched her blood: "She said, 'I have kids, I can't believe this. Oh my God. I touched that person! I touched that person's blood. I touched that person's blood!'" (Nadal, Griffin, et al., 2012, p. 68). Because it is likely that this EMT encounters blood on a regular basis; her harsh reaction to a trans person's blood exemplifies her bias towards trans people in general or a specific stereotype that trans people were HIV-positive.

While trans women balance microaggressions in which people convey disgust or disapproval, they also encounter situations in which cis men proposition them, simply wanting to use them sexually.

A transgender woman in one of my studies (Nadal, Skolnik, & Wong, 2012) revealed:

> A lot of men objectify or sensationalize me for being transgender and the first thing is "Will you suck my dick?" And I'm like you know, I don't even like oral sex so why don't you just say "Hello, my name is. . . ." (p. 68)

Denial of the Reality of Transphobia

This category of microaggressions involves instances (most often statements) in which cisgender people deny that transphobia and discrimination is a reality in the life of transgender people. Oftentimes, these types of invalidations may be well intentioned, in that the person simply wants to provide a rationalization for the transgender person. For example, in a post to the *Microaggressions Project*, a relative told a transgender person who was upset about being mistreated by a medical professional, "I don't know why you're so upset about this. You should really be more tolerant of people who don't get it." Comments like these can be very invalidating to transgender people who undergo bias and discrimination on a regular basis. Further, given that this cisgender person will never know what transphobia feels like, the comment could be labeled a form of "**splaining**," or "an act in which an outsider speaks for or provides rationale to marginalized groups, especially on issues of oppression" (Johnson et al., 2021, p. 1030).

In one of my studies (Nadal, Vargas, et al., 2012), a trans woman described the reaction she got from a friend after being verbally assaulted on the street. "I went home, I started crying and my friend said, 'Don't feel bad.' And I said, 'but didn't you just see what happened?'" (p. 134). Again, the friend in this scenario may simply be trying to be supportive and encouraging, perhaps even hoping that the individual would not "dwell" on a negative and obviously hurtful event. However, such a comment may invalidate the transgender person who simply wants a friend to comfort her and to authenticate that she has a right to feel the way that she does.

Physical Threat or Harassment

Like the threatening behaviors toward queer people described in the previous chapter, these sorts of microaggressions may occur toward transgender people. Again, if a behavior were clearly assaultive (i.e., it connotes clearly intentional, overt, physically abusive behavior or emotionally abusive behaviors), it would not be considered microaggressive. In the movie *Boys Don't Cry* (Peirce, 1999), which tells the story of Brandon Teena—the transgender male teen who was assaulted, raped, and killed for being transgender—the actions of the perpetrators are clearly hate crimes. However, physically threatening microaggressions towards trans people include instances where someone may not necessarily feel their life is in danger; rather, they feel extreme discomfort because the perpetrator creates a hostile or emotionally unsafe environment.

A scene in the movie *To Wong Foo, Thanks for Everything, Julie Newmar* (Kidron, 1995) involves Chi Chi Rodriguez, a drag queen played by John Leguizamo, being followed by several of the male citizens in a small rural town. While the young men did not overtly tell Chi Chi that they disapproved of her or that they were going to physically harm her, it was clear that Chi Chi felt very threatened by their hostile body language. While another young male townsperson came to "rescue" Chi Chi from the tense situation, there was a potential that something awful could have happened. However, because nothing occurred, it might not be classified as an assault without any overt physical or verbal harassment. Yet, perhaps it could be labeled a microaggression.

This type of microaggression has also been documented in the research. For example, in one of my studies (Nadal, Skolnik, & Wong, 2012), one transgender woman described an encounter in which she felt extreme discomfort because of the threatening behavior of others:

> I can remember when just walking in the street . . . I could have been with my friend, and someone could have said . . . "Those are men. . . ." And they would actually walk up to us. . . . You know . . . all make faces, laugh, and tell other people in front of us. Some people would come up to us . . . call us names . . . and that can happen from time to time. When I used to live in the projects, I also had a very hard time. . . . And every time I walked out, I swear even little kids, they would say "You got balls!" You know, everyday it was a horror story . . . kids . . . parents would tell their kids like 6 years old 7 years old . . . their [sic] so young. . . . You know . . . a lot of the guys used to . . . you know. . . . I used to walk by . . . and they would be like . . . "No that's a dude" . . . and then "No that can't be," those would come up to me and look at me. . . . It was always really hard for me. (p. 68)

In this scenario, the behaviors of the perpetrators are intentionally and consciously hurtful. However, these may be considered microaggressions because they cannot quite be classified as harassment as they consist of comments that are often said under people's breaths (even from little children). While physical and emotional assaults are viewed as criminal behavior, these types of acts may not be, and thus, may be classified as microaggressions.

Denial of Bodily Privacy

This microaggression category appears to be unique to transgender people and not pervasive in the research with queer people. Transgender people across the spectrum are often subjected to personal questions about their bodily parts. Because transgender people are often in various stages of transition, many cisgender people may feel privileged in finding out about transgender people's bodies. When cisgender persons "discover" a transgender person's sex assigned at birth, they often feel angry or betrayed that the transgender person did not tell them initially. However, Bree Osbourne, the main character of *Transamerica* (Tucker, 2005) said it best when she proclaimed, "Just because a person doesn't go around blabbing her entire biological history to everyone she meets doesn't make her a liar."

In my research with transgender people (Nadal, Skolnik, & Wong, 2012), it was common for them to be asked very private questions about their bodies. One transgender woman shared:

> I'm very open about being transgender inside the school and he went and told some students that that's a man and students looked at me and were like, "What, that's not a man. Look at her face and she has breasts. That's not a man." So, they were standing and looking at me like I was a circus freak, you know . . . as usual. (p. 69)

A transgender man shared a similar incident: "And then he came up to me and said, 'Yo, yo, you have a dick or pussy? A dick or pussy?'" And I was just like, "Why does it matter?" (Nadal, Skolnik, & Wong, 2012, p. 70). Finally, in another study with transgender participants (Singh & McKleroy, 2011), one male participant shared, "I would hear coworkers snicker behind my back at work and had friends at college who would ask what was in my pants. Not cool" (p. 38). Being on display and susceptible to public commentary can feel very invalidating, dehumanizing, and belittling for transgender people. Yet, the cis people who make such statements may not realize how much their words may affect the trans people who hear them.

Questioning of Legitimacy of Gender Identities

This theme, proposed by Galupo et al. (2014), involves societal and interpersonal invalidations of transgender identities and presumptions of gender inauthenticity. For example, one gay trans man described:

> When I first came out to one friend and explained that I was now gay as well as trans, she seemed confused and told me, "You don't have to become a man just to get with another guy. You can get plenty of guys and stay female!" I tried to explain there is a world of difference between being with a man as a straight woman versus as a gay man. . . . What really confused me was that she's bi and polyamorous. . . . If any of my friends "got" it, I'd expected it to be her! (p. 465)

Another trans man illustrated a similar example:

> A friend who's one of those heteroflexible girls who has a boyfriend was getting really handsy and flirty with me when she was drunk. "When I'm drunk, I get

really gay," she said. It hurt me that she was still seeing me as a woman, but I shrugged it off. (p. 465)

Both examples describe some of the subtle ways that trans people are misgendered beyond pronoun usage or pathologization; their friends can also covertly communicate that they do not view their gender identities as legitimate or authentic.

MACROAGGRESSIONS

Previous research has found that transgender people experience a significant number of systemic macroaggressions in their everyday lives. While other groups—namely, people of color, women, queer people, and people with disabilities—are exposed to a many macroaggressions through systems, institutions, and environments, there are many unique macroaggressions that seem to affect transgender people specifically (Nadal, Skolnik, & Wong, 2012; Woodford et at., 2017). Some of the major manifestations of systemic discrimination that have been reported include (a) public restrooms, (b) the criminal justice system, (c) health care, and (d) government-issued identification and public assistance.

In terms of public restrooms, it is a common, everyday struggle for transgender people who must decide which public restroom to use. If they use the restroom of the gender they identify with, they may be viewed as intruders and be met with people who will label them as sexual predators or deviants. If they use the restroom of the gender they do not identify with, they may also be harassed by those who believe they don't belong there. One trans man stated:

> When I use the bathroom, I tend to withdraw and use the handicap bathroom. People are always looking at me like . . . their perception of me is like "Just use the male bathroom. And I'm thinking . . . do I wanna engage with my male co-workers who might freak out? Or if I want to use the women's bathroom . . . what that brings up for women and seeing my presence in there." (Nadal, Skolnik, & Wong, 2012, p. 72)

Again, while using a public restroom may seem so innocuous to cisgender people, this very simple everyday behavior may cause distress for a transgender person.

Regarding the criminal justice system, transgender people are often placed in prisons and other facilities based on their sex assigned at birth (especially their genitalia) and not their gender. This may lead to inappropriate activities like strip searches by individuals of different genders or harassment by law enforcement officers. C, a transgender man, described an incident of being arrested and strip searched in front a group of other arrestees. One transgender woman participant recalled the treatment she received at a police station when she and her transgender friend were the victims of a crime:

> Can you hurry up and write your statements? Because it's late and we all have families. So do you wanna write a statement or do you want to leave?" And I just said [to my friend] "Write your statement because something happened to you" and so she was gonna write it . . . and the detectives were passing by, and they said . . . (singing) "transformers . . . men up in disguise" . . . just like that. . . . I said, "What the hell?" . . . I said these are the detectives. I said "Wait, wait, wait . . . don't write anything. They're gonna throw this in the garbage— they want us to leave." (Nadal, Skolnik, & Wong, 2012, p. 73)

While many groups may encounter discrimination within the criminal justice system, perhaps the type of discrimination encountered by transgender people is much more overt and vocalized than that directed toward other groups.

Within the health care system, transgender people are often met with interpersonal microaggressions (i.e., specific health care workers enacting microaggressions), but sometimes there are systemic microaggressions (also referred to as macroaggressions), in which the system displays its lack of competence in serving transgender people. One transgender female participant described one interaction she had:

> The ambulance lady came to pick me up. And she asked me when was the last time I got my period. And I looked at her and I said, "I don't get no periods, sweetie, I'm transgender." Once I told her that, as soon as they put me in the chair in the hospital, she told ALL the doctors what I was, ALL the nurses, and everybody came up to me looking at me. And the pain kept on getting stronger. I started getting agitated. I started going crazy. I got up, ripped the IV off with the blood gushing and I flipped on all of them. I said "You know what, I'm not here for y'all to look at me and to find out what the hell I am. I am here for you to help me." (Nadal, Skolnik, & Wong, 2012, p. 74)

The trans person in this scenario simply needed medical assistance; yet the second her transgender identity was discovered, she was treated like a science experiment. Although none of the doctors or nurses explicitly said anything discriminatory, she felt belittled and dehumanized.

Concurrently, health care systems tend to be transphobic in that they do not cater to the needs of transgender people. For example, most insurance companies do not cover trans-related medical costs (i.e., hormones, gender-affirming medical treatments, etc.). One trans person disclosed:

> There are transgender-specific issues such as access to medical care and hormone treatment. It is unaffordable to pay for hormones when it costs $25

> for [a] one-month supply. Health insurance does not always cover it, and if
> it is, it is very minimal. The problem is also with obtaining hormones, like one
> day you're in and one day you're out. (Bith-Melander et al., 2010, p. 215)

While social class may play a role in the transition process, even trans
people with families of higher socioeconomic statuses may become estranged
from their families, which may lead to difficulties in paying medical costs.
So, macroaggressions in the health care system may potentially affect transgender people of all social classes.

Finally, participants described how government-issued identification is a
major challenge because of the requirement to report gender. One participant
shared:

> I have to get my passport redone and I literally have to make an Excel spread-
> sheet. It's like, well, in order to get my passport gender marker changed, I have
> to first submit a letter to the selective service explaining why I'm not eligible
> for the draft. Then, I have to get a copy of my birth certificate, which I don't have
> because it says the wrong name and gender, so I can't use it. So, I have to first
> change that. And then I would have to go the social security . . . uhhhh . . . as
> I think about it, I was like ohhh my God . . . I have a migraine. (Nadal, Skolnik,
> & Wong, 2012, pp. 74–75)

Again, while many marginalized groups (e.g., people of color, women,
queer people, persons with disabilities) may experience a range of macroaggressions, they may take for granted many privileges, including having a
government identification that matches their identities, being grouped with
the gender they identify with, or feeling safe using a public restroom.

CASE STUDIES

Now that we are familiar with the types of microaggressions encountered by
transgender, nonbinary, and gender nonconforming people, three fictional
case studies are presented to demonstrate how people navigate gender
identity related discrimination. Upon reading these scenarios, pay attention
to any emotional reactions, as well as potential interventions that could be
useful for the person who is targeted.

Microaggressions at School: The Case of Destiny

Destiny is a 17-year-old Filipina American transgender woman who lives
in a major metropolitan city on the West Coast. She is the youngest of four
children (with one older brother and two older sisters who are 5–8 years

older than she). She was assigned a male gender at birth and given the name Dennis, and she lived in a close-knit Filipino family when she was growing up. Because her father was out of the picture, her single mother had always worked full-time, and her older siblings spent a lot of time taking care of their youngest sibling. When she was 4 or 5 years old, she loved playing "dress up" with her sisters. Because her mother did not buy her any dresses, she would ask her sisters if she could try on their clothes and makeup. They granted her requests and enjoyed putting on short performances for each other while participating in their own fashion photo shoots and fashion shows.

When Destiny was a young adolescent, she thought that maybe she was just a gay man—mainly because she knew she was attracted to other boys. However, as she grew older, she started to realize that playing "dress up" wasn't just a stage; it was how she felt most comfortable in every aspect of her life. She started to buy her own makeup and dresses and started to dress as a woman in private, when her family was not at home. By the time she was 16 years old, she eventually felt more comfortable wearing women's clothing in public. She eventually told her sisters and two close friends that she was transgender; all were supportive.

Destiny is about to start her senior year in high school and decides that she wants to live her life as a woman. At the urging of her sisters, she first "comes out" to her older brother and her mother at the same time. While they were definitely shocked (e.g., her mother cried hysterically at first) and confused (e.g., her brother said, "Are you sure you're not just gay?"), they both told her that they would support her decision but that it would take them a while to get used to it. When Destiny mentions that she wants to finish high school as a woman, her mom begs her not to, saying, "It will be too hard for you! I don't want you to get hurt." However, Destiny assures her that she is ready and that she doesn't want to "live a lie" anymore.

To prepare herself for her senior year of high school, Destiny sets up a meeting with Dr. Kaner, her high school principal. When Destiny shows up to the meeting dressed as a woman, Dr. Kaner looks at her irritably, but allows her into his office. Destiny then tells him that she is transgender and that she wants to live her life as a woman. She also states that she hopes the school would commit to creating a safe environment for her. Dr. Kaner responds by saying, "I can't promise you that it's going to be safe. Kids will be kids." He adds, "Plus, it's your decision to dress like that, so you can always choose to dress as a normal person if you don't want to get into any trouble." Destiny is shocked by his lack of support, but asks, "Well, I was wondering if I could use the faculty bathroom from now on, because I know they have private unisex bathrooms." He replies, "No, you still have to use the men's bathroom;

we can't make special requests for any student." Destiny nods in under-standing, leaves his office, and cries.

Unintentional Transphobic Microaggressive Language: The Case of Jan

Jan is a 21-year-old nonbinary Black person, who uses "they" pronouns but generally prefers to not be labeled with any pronouns at all. While Jan was assigned female at birth, Jan has always felt different from other family members, friends, and classmates. As a child, Jan refused to wear the dresses that Jan's mother often wanted Jan to wear, opting to dress in more **gender-neutral** clothing like sweatshirts and jeans. Most people just assumed that Jan was as lesbian, based mainly on Jan's gender presentation (which for most of Jan's childhood was as a "butch" teenage girl). However, Jan never identified as being gay or lesbian; instead, Jan always just felt "neither." And because Jan knew that others would be confused or not accepting towards Jan's identity, Jan decided to keep on "checking off" any "female" boxes on applications and forms, just because it was "easier."

Jan went to college in a southern state that was several hours away from Jan's family. Moving far away was important for Jan because it would give Jan the opportunity to explore romantic and sexual relationships, as well as **gender expression**, differently, since Jan would not have to worry about running into family members or friends. During the first week of school, Jan thought it would be best to meet other LGBTQ students, so Jan decided to go to the university's LGBTQ Resource Center and attend a LGBTQ Pride Club meeting. When Jan first started making friends, Jan disclosed identifying as "transgender" and "gender nonconforming." While most of the other students in the organization identified as lesbian and gay, Jan was the only one who identified as transgender. Despite being the only one, Jan tried not to let this be bothersome; in fact, Jan just assumed that there were very few transgender people altogether and was happy to just be around LGBTQ people. However, to ensure that transgender issues were being addressed in the organization, Jan decided to run for one of the elected officer positions and won.

One of the things that Jan had always been clear about with new friends or acquaintances was that Jan did not identify as either female or male and therefore would prefers either "they" pronouns or to simply be referred to as "Jan." When Jan mentioned this at the first board meeting, everyone was respectful about the request and promised Jan that they would try to abide by this. Jan was thankful for their sensitivity, even assuring to correct them each time they used a gendered pronoun.

Despite everyone else's promise to abide by Jan's request, people still referred to Jan as "she" or "her" whenever they made mention of Jan. For example, Ethan, the president of the organization, said: "So you all know we have a new board member, Jan. I was wondering if someone can help familiarize her with some of the basic procedures?" Before others could volunteer, Jan politely smiled and corrected the mistake, playfully saying, "Remember, it's just Jan!" Ethan was embarrassed, apologized, and continued to ask for a volunteer before continuing with the meeting. These subtle mistakes transpired a few more times at the meeting with others. Similarly, Jan would lightheartedly interrupt whoever was speaking, while correcting them in the same way as Ethan. Each time, the individual would apologize, and the meeting would continue. However, by the time it was the fourth or fifth time that Jan was correcting the individual, Jan wondered if people were annoyed by the disruptions or if others even really cared about Jan's feelings regarding their gender pronouns. Jan decided not to say anything for the rest of the meeting, even though others referred to Jan as "she" a few more times.

After the meeting, Jan decided to talk to Ethan, the president of the organization, who is a gay white cisgender male. Jan shared the feeling that the others were not taking the request seriously and how their actions made Jan feel marginalized, invisible, and upset. Ethan apologized, stating that he didn't want Jan to feel this way. He then added "I think people have trouble not referring to you as a 'she' because you look like a woman. Maybe if you had surgery or took hormones or something, people might be able to remember to not use pronouns." Jan was more baffled that Ethan didn't realize that what he was saying was hurtful and offensive. Instead of arguing with him, Jan meekly stated, "Okay, I see how it is" and walked away. Jan quit attending the LGBTQ Pride meetings altogether.

Microaggressions Encountered by Those Who Pass: The Case of Sid

Sid is a 45-year-old transgender man of Native American and Irish descent living in the northeast. Sid knew he was transgender since childhood. In fact, he "came out" to his parents when he was 17 and began hormone treatment on his 18th birthday. While initially shocked, his parents gradually grew supportive. Because they were a working-class family, they told him that he would have to pay for his own medical expenses. So, while going to college, Sid lived at home and worked two part-time jobs, to save money. By the time he graduated at 26 years old, he had saved enough money to finally start his gender-affirming reconstructive surgeries—first his top surgery and then his bottom surgery.

After graduating from college with a double degree in computer sciences and visual arts, Sid decided to pursue a career in graphic design. He worked for several smaller companies in more entry-level positions for years, before his most recent stint as an assistant editor for a major fashion magazine. While Sid enjoys his job very much (and has made several friends at work), he sometimes wonders if his colleagues know he is transgender. When he was hired, Sid consciously decided not to tell anyone about his history and to live in stealth. He always thought that if cis people do not announce that they are cis, then he does not need to announce his trans identity either.

Over the past year, Sid has started to become more acquainted with a couple of coworkers who are around his same age. Many of these coworkers, who are cisgender, heterosexual women, have expressed a desire to spend time with Sid outside of work. One week, one of his coworkers, Liz, invited Sid to come to a friend's birthday party that was taking place at a gay male bar. She told Sid, "Oh my gosh, you're going to love it; there are these trannies who host this drag show at midnight. It's hilarious!" Sid, who did not know how to react, was initially silent. Liz, who noticed Sid's discomfort, stated, "I hope you're not offended that I assumed you were gay. You are, right?" It was at this moment that he decided to "out" himself to Liz, explaining, "Hey Liz, I really like you and would like to get to know you better, but there is something you should probably know about me." He continued to tell her that he was transgender and taught her that the word "tranny" is offensive. Liz apologized for being insensitive, stating that she "really didn't know better." She thanked him for sharing his history, before proclaiming, "I wouldn't have even known. You look like a normal man!"

CASE STUDY DISCUSSION

As the three cases demonstrate, there are many ways that microaggressions toward transgender people can manifest. In the first scenario, Destiny began to discover her transgender identity when she was a young child. When she played dress up with her older sisters, she started to realize that this was not a phase; it was something that felt normal and right for her. While there were some family microaggressions that she experienced (e.g., her brother asked her, "Are you sure you're not just gay?"), most of the cissexist microaggressions in this scenario occurred when she met with her high school principal, Dr. Kaner. In general, Dr. Kaner is very dismissive of Destiny, declaring that he cannot do anything to protect her from any harassment or discrimination. He also presumes that Destiny's transgender identity is a "choice"—invalidating her reality and self-concept. Finally, while the system is not built to accommodate transgender students (e.g., there are no gender-neutral restrooms), Dr. Kaner makes no attempts to assist Destiny, conveying that trans people are unimportant or not worthy of being helped. Because of all these microaggressions, Destiny feels extremely distressed, likely not knowing how she will be able to make it through her senior year of high school.

In the second case, we learn of Jan, an individual who identifies as a gender nonconforming person. While Jan was assigned female at birth and does not take any hormones, Jan would prefer to not be referred to as any gender. At an LGBTQ student organization meeting, Jan shares how they would like to be identified and initially, Jan's peers agree. However, when others have difficulty obliging this request, Jan tries to discuss this with the president of the organization, who is eventually dismissive, suggesting that Jan should undergo surgery or take hormones so that people would not be confused. This type of conflict signifies that even well-intentioned queer people can engage in gender identity microaggressions. It also signifies that people may often blame the transgender person, instead of holding themselves accountable. Because many cisgender people may view transgender people's requests as being "inconvenient," it may be difficult for them to change their behaviors. In fact, many cisgender family members and friends of transgender people may slip up with transgender people's new names or pronouns. Perhaps an occasional slipup may be more tolerable to a transgender person if the perpetrator recognizes it immediately (and independently) and apologizes for it right away. However, if the perpetrator does not recognize or adjust the hurtful behavior, transgender people may feel as if their feelings or identities are not valid or accepted.

Finally, the third scenario describes how some transgender people may "pass," which may lead to specific types of microaggressions that people who cannot or do not pass may not encounter. So, while people's discomfort may be more identifiable with nonpassing transgender people, transgender people who do pass may be exposed to microaggressions because others do not even recognize that they are transgender. In this case, Sid has been working at a company for over a year, and no one knows that he is transgender. When his coworker, Liz, invites him to a birthday party at a gay bar, a few microaggressions occur. First, she uses the word "tranny" very casually when describing the drag queens that host a show at the bar. While she probably used the word in jest, it offended Sid when he heard it. Second, when Liz assumes that Sid is "probably" a gay man, she forces Sid to out himself, instead of allowing him to share his sexual identity (both his sexual orientation and his gender identity) of his own accord. Perhaps he would have divulged this information on his own independently and when he felt most comfortable; however, he now feels obligated to tell her all about his history, when he perhaps does not want to. A final microaggression is when Liz tells Sid that she thought was a "normal man"—signifying that being transgender is abnormal and that being cisgender is normal. While this may be meant to be a "compliment" (i.e., telling Sid that he "passes" very well), it can be construed as reflecting Liz's biases about trans, nonbinary, and gender nonconforming people.

In each of the scenarios, the intentions of the perpetrators may or may not be malicious. Dr. Kaner, the high school principal, may not directly want to upset Destiny by failing to accommodate her needs at school; rather, he may genuinely believe that he is making the fairest decisions by not "favoring" anyone. Ethan, the LGBTQ college student organization president, may sincerely believe that he is justified in telling Jan that Jan's requests for not using gender pronouns is unreasonable. His intention may not be to be hurtful; rather, he may feel he is standing up for himself and what he perceives as an irrational desire. Finally, Liz, the coworker, may honestly believe that she did not say anything offensive. She may believe she was trying to be kind in reaching out to her coworker whom she wanted to get to know better. When Sid outed himself to her, she may feel apologetic about using the word "tranny" because she did not know there was anything wrong with using the word. Thus, it appears that until Liz was confronted (or others pointed out her microaggressive behavior), she would not have recognized any fault. Many cis people will develop unconscious transphobic biases because they have been socialized with overt and covert transphobic messages, embedded in every aspect in society. Keeping these issues in mind, the next chapter explores how adding intersectional identities may affect experiences with microaggressions.

DISCUSSION QUESTIONS

For General Readers

1. What types of microaggressions do you believe occur often with transgender women? With transgender men? With gender nonconforming people?

2. What types of gender identity microaggressions do you notice in various institutions (e.g., your workplace or school) or systems (e.g., government, media, religion)?

3. What would you do if you were in Destiny's situation? Jan's situation? Sid's situation?

4. How could systems and institutions (e.g., government, school systems, media, or policies) assist each character in their experiences with microaggressions? How could these systems have been helpful in the past to prevent these microaggressions altogether?

For Psychologists, Educators, and Other Experts

1. In what ways might you improve your ability to work with transgender, nonbinary, or gender conforming people?

2. What types of countertransference issues would you have with Destiny, Jan, or Sid?

GLOSSARY OF KEY TERMS

agender A term used to classify people who do not identify themselves with a gender.

bigender A term used to classify people who identify themselves with at least two genders.

cis A shortened version of the word "cisgender," a term used to describe someone who identifies with their sex assigned at birth; someone who is not transgender

cross-dresser An individual who wears clothing that is typically worn by another gender.

deadnaming The act of referring to a trans or nonbinary person by their name assigned at birth, instead of their chosen name.

drag A term traditionally used to describe when an individual dresses in a gender that they do not typically identify with.

drag king A cisgender woman or nonbinary person who performs masculinity, usually for the purpose of entertaining.

drag queen A cisgender man or nonbinary person who performs femininity, usually for the purpose of entertaining.

genderqueer An umbrella term for gender identities other than cisgender female or cisgender male.

gender bending An informal term to describe the behavior of actively transgressing or defying traditional gender roles.

gender binary The belief that there are only two genders: male and female.

gender expression The way people perform their gender roles.

gender-neutral A description of something or someone as being unassociated with female or male.

gender pronoun The pronouns that people use to describe themselves and that should be used by others to describe them. Examples include "she/her/his" "he/him/his," "they/them/theirs," "ze/zir/zis," or to use no pronoun at all.

splaining An act in which a member of a historically dominant group (e.g., men, white people, cisgender people, heterosexual people) speaks for or provides rationale to people of historically marginalized groups (e.g., people of color, women, LGBTQIA+ people) about topics related to oppression or injustice. The term is derived from "mansplaining" or "whitesplaining."

transsexual An individual who utilizes various interventions to medically transition into the gender they most identify with.

5 INTERSECTIONAL MICROAGGRESSIONS

Experiences of LGBTQ People of Color

FIGURE 5.1. An Interracial Lesbian Couple Cuddling in Bed

Note. Photo courtesy of Tim Samuel.

One of the biggest difficulties in understanding microaggressions is whether such instances occurred because of one singular identity (e.g., one's sexual orientation) or because of multiple identities (e.g., one's sexual orientation and race). Throughout this text, there have been many examples of micro-aggressions that are primarily likely because of singular identities. Yet, perhaps some of the examples may have also been influenced by one's multiple identities. Let's revisit two of the microaggression incidents that I have described in the Introduction. First, there was the case of the same-sex couple, Stephanie and Debbie, who attended Stephanie's 10-year high school reunion. Stephanie, who is Asian American, and Debbie, who is a Black American, were both "jokingly" propositioned by one of Stephanie's former male classmates, after he learned they were a couple. Let's also recall Agnes, a 20-year-old trans Latina woman who was harassed by a security guard because her identification did not match her gender presentation.

While both cases clearly involve microaggressions regarding sexual orientation or transgender identity, perhaps there were other social identities that influenced the scenarios. In the first scenario, perhaps both race and gender influenced the microaggression. Would Stephanie and Debbie have been pro-positioned (and subsequently objectified) if they were both men? Is there a possibility that the male classmate exoticized both women because of their racial backgrounds, which led to his sexual proposition? In the second scenario, could it be possible that race and age (and maybe even social class) influenced the microaggression? If Agnes was white or older, would she have had an easier time getting through security? While her social class may not be as obvious, could it be possible that she would have been treated better if the security guard perceived her as being wealthy or upper class? It is entirely possible that these other identities did indeed have an influence on the ways that these individuals were treated. However, because these identities were not clearly addressed or articulated, it may be much more difficult to identify, leaving the victim to feel more confused and emotionally distressed.

The complexities of dynamics and situations being influenced by multiple identities has been described thoroughly through **intersectionality theory**. First proposed by Kimberlé Crenshaw (1989) to understand the ways that Black women encounter and navigate racism and sexism, the theory has been more recently used to understand the ways that systemic oppression nega-tively impacts various groups with multiple marginalized identities. Although people may interpret the theory differently, intersectionality understands how people with multiple marginalized identities (e.g., LGBTQ people of color, LGBTQ people with disabilities) may encounter more frequent or complex forms of discrimination than their singular identity counterparts (e.g., LGBTQ white people, able-bodied LGBTQ people), which may result in increased psychological distress and everyday challenges. Further, when studying intersectionality, scholars have advocated for the need to explore interlocking types of oppression (e.g., racism, sexism, heterosexism) instead of trying to measure the concepts individually (Ferguson, 2021; Lewis et al., 2017).

This chapter discusses **intersectional microaggressions**, or microaggressions that are encountered because of one's intersectional or multiple marginalized identities (Nadal, Davidoff, et al., 2015). First, I discuss power and privilege, to understand the complexities of intersectional identities, particularly within the LGBTQ umbrella. Next, I provide a brief review of previous literature on intersectional microaggressions. Finally, in this chapter, I highlight the lived experiences and perspectives of LGBTQ people of color (LGBTQ POC).

UNDERSTANDING POWER AND PRIVILEGE IN LGBTQ COMMUNITY SPACES

In Chapter 3, I first introduced the concepts of power and privilege. *Power* in its most general form can be defined as the ability to define reality and to convince other people that it is their definition also. On the other hand, *privilege* refers to a right, favor, advantage, or immunity, specially granted to one individual or group, and withheld from another. Throughout the text, I have written about how LGBTQ people may have less power and privilege due to the heterosexism and genderism that occur on systemic, institutional, and interpersonal levels. However, it is important to recognize that power and privilege does exist within LGBTQ community spaces—creating a culture of what is considered normative, while resulting in an array of dynamics between various LGBTQ subgroups.

First, it becomes necessary to acknowledge that while LGBTQ research has been somewhat minimal for the past century in the United States and abroad, and that majority of the existing LGBTQ literature and media has focused almost exclusively on able-bodied, cisgender, white American lesbians, and gay men (Fiani & Han, 2019). Thus, members of these subgroups have unconsciously set the cultural norms, behaviors, and standards of beauty for everyone else, regardless of race, gender, gender identity, ability, and other identities. For example, LGBTQ people who are able-bodied, cisgender, gay, male, and white are often viewed as having the most power and privilege in the community. When someone identifies with more than one of these descriptions, the more power and privilege they will have. When someone identifies with few or none of these descriptions, the less power and privilege they will have.

So, let's discuss how this might manifest within a general LGBTQ community. First, consider the standard of beauty that has been predominantly promoted in gay male culture: the young, able-bodied, thin or athletic, masculine-presenting white man. In this case, there are many people with financial or institutional power who can perpetuate this standard of beauty: the film and television producers who only cast actors who fit this type in mainstream and LGBTQ media, the owners of gay bars and restaurants who only hire bartenders and staff members who fit this type, the editors of gay male magazines who only use these types of models, the owners of gay establishments who do not install wheelchair accessible ramps, and the managers or bouncers of LGBTQ clubs who refuse to admit others who do not fit this description.

At the same time, individuals who do fit this picture (particularly those who match all these characteristics) hold power and privilege without even recognizing it. They have the power of assuming that their experiences are the norm and that their physical looks are most desirable. They also are likely to receive certain privileges (e.g., rights, favors, advantages) without recognizing them as such. In fact, they may not even consciously realize that they have an easier time getting admitted into certain establishments; that they get better treatment by bartenders, servers, or others; or that certain magazines and establishments cater to them. Meanwhile, any other gay man who does not fit that description (e.g., gay men of color, gay men with disabilities, gay men who are fat or deemed overweight, gay men who are older) may feel deficient, inferior, or second-class, while also potentially being treated as such.

Furthermore, it is necessary to emphasize that with any social identity, individuals with privilege may not recognize they have privilege (see McIntosh, 2003). For instance, able-bodied people in general may not even think twice about wheelchair access to buildings. Because they have the privilege of belonging to the dominant group of other able-bodied persons, they may unconsciously uphold the expectation that most buildings will have entrances and walkways that they can utilize. Unless someone points out the privilege to them, they may live their life not realizing the ways that their life is easier because of the group that they belong to. Moreover, when someone is oppressed in one identity but privileged in another, it may be even more difficult for them to recognize the power and privilege they may have. For instance, when a gay white man feels marginalized and oppressed because of the many ways that heterosexism has negatively impacted his life, it may be difficult for him to recognize the ways that he has privilege because of his race or his gender. When a lesbian woman of color feels marginalized or oppressed because of the many way that both racism and heterosexism have negatively impacted her life, she may not be able to easily recognize the power or privilege she has that a transgender person or a person with a disability would not. Because of this, it is important for people of any marginalized or targeted group to recognize that there are likely to be other social identity groups in which they do have power and privilege. Otherwise, people may remain defensive and be unable to hear or validate the realities of others.

Discussing types of power and privilege among LGBTQ people is helpful in understanding the dynamics and tensions that may occur between groups. Sometimes LGBTQ people with other marginalized identities (e.g., LGBTQ POC, LGBTQ people with disabilities, LGBTQ older adults) may feel excluded or disconnected by other LGBTQ people with privileged identities (LGBTQ white people, able-bodied LGBTQ people, LGBTQ young adults), leading to even further isolation among some LGBTQ people and groups. Other times, people with privileged identities may be genuinely oblivious to the ways they are privileged, leading to microaggressions that are often unconscious or unintentional. Thus, it is important for all individuals to recognize the areas where they have power and privilege as well as the domains where they have less power and privilege. In doing so, dialogues can continue within LGBTQ communities, hopefully resulting in more unity and less marginalization.

LGBTQ PEOPLE OF COLOR AND DISCRIMINATION

Over the past 3 decades, there has been a steady growth in literature that has focused on the psychological, physical, and behavioral outcomes that result from the discriminatory experiences faced by LGBTQ POC, namely, Black, Latinx, Asian, Pacific Islanders, and Native American people in the United States (Balsam et al., 2011; Cyrus, 2017; Nadal, 2018; Sutter & Perrin, 2016; Toomey et al., 2017; Velez et al., 2021). However, some authors have noted that most of these articles pertaining to LGBTQ POC have focused on the "deficit model," in which they concentrate mainly on the negative aspects of their lives, including substance abuse, HIV/AIDS, and health disparities (Velez et al., 2021). For example, there have been many studies that have described how Latino gay men and other Latino **MSM** (or men who have sex with men) report a higher prevalence of health disparities than white gay men and white MSM (see Ibañez et al., 2009, for a review).

In the past 2 decades, there have been some notable studies that examined the types of discrimination that LGBTQ POC face (a) within American society in general, (b) within a general LGBTQ community, and (c) within their own racial and ethnic communities. For instance, some studies have found that LGBTQ POC feel excluded or treated as second-class citizens in predominantly white LGBTQ spaces (Díaz et al., 2006; Han, 2009, 2021; Ibañez et al., 2009; Mosley et al., 2019; Patel, 2019) and that LGBTQ POC may encounter racism in their dating lives and sexual or romantic relationships (Han, 2009, 2021; Han & Choi, 2018; Ibañez et al., 2009; Stacey & Forbes, 2022; Winder & Lea, 2019). On the other hand, LGBTQ POC may also feel excluded or treated as second-class citizens within their racial and ethnic communities, particularly by those heterosexual group members who want to deny or silence their sexuality or who overtly discriminate against them (Cerezo et al., 2020; Nadal & Corpus, 2013; Patel, 2019). While these may not have been labeled as such, many of the examples provided in these studies fall in line with the definitions of microaggressions.

Intersectional Microaggressions and LGBTQ People of Color

There are a few known studies that focused on intersectional microaggressions toward LGBTQ POC. The first is a quantitative study by Balsam et al. (2011), who created the Lesbian, Gay, Bisexual, and Transgender People of Color Microaggressions Scale—an 18-item self-report scale with questions on (a) racism in LGBTQ communities, (b) heterosexism in racial/ethnic minority communities, and (c) racism in dating and close relationships. Preliminary findings included: (a) gay and bisexual men of color reported more instances of microaggressions than gay and bisexual women, (b) lesbians and gay men scored higher than bisexual women and men, and (c) Asian Americans scored higher than Black and Latinx Americans. Although the scale was created and normalized on a mostly gay and lesbian cisgender people of color sample, a subsequent study found that it was statistically relevant for transgender people of color too (Orphanidys, 2018).

Another quantitative measure, the Intersectional Microaggressions Scale (IMS), was created to examine microaggressions that occur because of both sexual orientation and racial identities (Fattoracci et al., 2021). With a sample of 843 queer people of color participants, the researchers reviewed items from the Homonegative Microaggressions Scales (Wright & Wegner, 2012) and the Racial Ethnic Microaggressions Scales (Nadal, 2011) to create new intersectional items. For instance, one item read: "I overheard jokes about [race/ethnicity] people who are [sexual orientation]," while another read: "Someone avoided close proximity to me because I am a/an [race/ethnicity] person who is [sexual orientation]" (Fattoracci et al., 2021). Factor analyses yielded six subscales: (a) alien in own land, (b) denial of experiences, (c) exoticization, (d) gendered stereotypes, (e) negative treatment, and (f) being pathologized. Findings revealed that people who encounter more intersectional microaggressions are significantly more likely to report anxiety and social isolation, and that combining items to reflect intersectional identities was a more reliable way to measure microaggressions for LGBTQ people of color than just using microaggression measures on singular identities.

Regarding qualitative studies, my research team at the City University of New York published two qualitative studies on intersectional microaggressions. The first study (Nadal et al., 2015) utilized focus group data from our previous microaggression studies with women, queer people, transgender people, multiracial individuals, Muslims, and Filipino Americans, with the goal of identifying participants' perspectives with microaggressions that were based on more than one identity. With 80 participants in 19 focus groups, participants were initially asked only about microaggressions based on one identity (e.g., the Muslim participants were asked specifically about microaggressions based on being Muslim). Yet, because many participants described how other identities influenced their experiences with microaggressions, an analysis was conducted to explore intersectional microaggressions. Of the seven themes that emerged, three intersectional microaggressions directly involve LGBTQ people: (a) assumption of gender-based stereotypes for lesbians and gay men; (b) disapproval of LGBTQ identity by racial, ethnic, and religious groups; and (c) invisibility and desexualization of Asian American men. These themes are described below.

Assumption of Gender-Based Stereotypes for Lesbians and Gay Men

In the first theme, participants' narratives demonstrated how gender influenced the types of microaggressions experienced by gay men and women. So, despite having a similar sexual orientation (being attracted to people of their same sex), their gender led to nuanced microaggressions not experienced by others. As an example, lesbians describe being assumed to act "butch" and not feminine. One lesbian disclosed:

> I often have people be like "Oh well you're very feminine, so how are you a lesbian?" But yeah I get that a lot where people say that I'm too feminine to be gay and I'm like that has nothing to do with it . . . like not all lesbians are like really butch . . . or they didn't seem happy because I'm not a butch lesbian. (Nadal Davidoff, et al., 2015, p. 155)

Similarly, gay men identified microaggressions in which they were presumed to be feminine or uninterested in traditionally masculine activities. One male participant shared:

> I'm one of the only guys in the area and I feel like the women always compete for me to give them compliments on what [they're] wearing. [Laughter]. Like . . . if I actually, I said to someone, "Wow, I really love that dress." She was like, "Oh my God, if you love this dress, then it must be really great." (Nadal, Davidoff, et al., 2015, p. 154)

Taken together, these examples demonstrate how the intersection of gender and sexual orientation may change what types of microaggressions people experience, which may affect processes and coping mechanisms too.

Disapproval of LGBTQ Identity by Racial, Ethnic, and Religious Groups

Another theme, "disapproval of LGBTQ identity by racial, ethnic, and religious groups," involved microaggressions that LGBTQ POC and LGBTQ Muslims experienced from their families and ethnic/religious communities. One male participant simply stated, "If you're a minority gay, it's way worse" (Nadal, Davidoff, et al., 2015, p. 155). Many participants described how cultural factors prevented them from coming out or led to both microaggressions and overt discrimination. For example, one woman explained,

> I was going out with uh, a girl—she's Cuban. . . . Her family is Catholic, and she was married and now was getting a divorce. Her whole family actually came up to me and they thought that I was the one trying to convince her to become gay. (Nadal, Davidoff, et al., 2015, p. 155)

Invisibility and Desexualization of Asian American Men

Finally, through the theme "invisibility and desexualization of Asian American men," one gay Asian American man revealed how Asian American men are viewed as undesirable in gay male spaces:

> If you mention that you're an Asian, it's like listening to crickets on the internet. I mean, gay men are just that shallow. Particularly Caucasian. . . . So, it's a little hard. It's like thinking, damn! I can't even get laid on the internet! (Nadal, Davidoff, et al., 2015, p. 156)

Similarly, a gay Filipino American man shared his perceptions of how Asian men are portrayed in the media: "Can't we just see one really butch Asian male? We are not all feminine" (Nadal, Escobar, et al., 2012, p. 164). Both examples demonstrate how Asian American males face racial microaggressions in general American society and LGBTQ community spaces.

While the remaining themes did not include perspectives from queer or trans participants, they do have implications for LGBTQ people. For instance, women of color described being exoticized, aligning with previous studies (Lewis et al., 2016; Nadal, Escobar, et al., 2012; Sue, Bucceri, et al., 2009) that reveal women of color are exoticized or oversexualized in general (and typically by white heterosexual men). However, future studies can examine if this intersectional microaggression is also commonly faced by trans and queer women of color—perpetuated by other white, queer women or white, **transamorous** men. Similarly, women of color describe being distressed when they are treated as intellectually, physically, or socially inferior to others. Such experiences have been reported by queer and trans women of color in academia who navigate microaggressions and isolation because of minoritized identities (Nadal, 2019c). Finally, because men of color describe being criminalized, future studies can explore how queer and trans men of color may undergo intensified distress because of their **dual minority status**. In fact, Nadal (2020) described the many ways that queer BIPOC men are unfairly treated in the criminal justice system, with one example being the case of Michael Johnson, a young Black man who was convicted for not informing consensual sexual partners of his HIV status, all while being subjected to racialized and sexualized tropes during his trial. Across all these themes, future researchers

FIGURE 5.2. A Gay Couple Relaxing in Central Park in New York City

Note. Photo courtesy of Ketut Subiysanto.

can investigate how a **multiple minority stress** may result in more mental health issues for LGBTQ POC.

Given the limitations of the previous study, my research team conducted a qualitative study that involved collecting new data with LGBTQ POC—specifically probing participants about intersectional microaggression incidents based on race, sexual identity, or both (Nadal et al., 2017). With a sample of 16 queer people of color, four focus group interviews were conducted with participants representing a variety of minoritized racial and ethnic groups. Participants were able to identify microaggressions they experienced based on race, sexual orientation, and more than one identity (e.g., race and sexuality; race and gender). For instance, one queer man of color perceived how a white male healthcare professional did not want to help him with a health issue because of both his race and sexuality. Finally, LGBTQ POC participants described their emotional and behavioral processes in reacting to microaggressions in the moment, as well as the impact of such incidents on their mental health.

VOICES OF LGBTQ PEOPLE OF COLOR

In reviewing academic literature, contemporary narratives, and media, I propose a few major themes of intersectional microaggressions that affect LGBTQ POC. Because of the limitations of covering LGBTQ POC of different racial, ethnic, and religious backgrounds, as well as genders and sexual orientations, this cannot be a complete depiction of all LGBTQ POC experiences. However, I hope these examples will provide an overview of the intersectional microaggressions experienced by LGBTQ POC, potentially inspiring future research.

Exclusion Within LGBTQ Communities and the Normalization of Whiteness

Previous research found that LGBTQ POC people have encountered exclusion in mainstream LGBTQ spaces, primarily because they tend to center predominantly white LGBTQ values and perspectives. Previous literature (e.g., Díaz et al., 2006; Han, 2009; Patel, 2019) highlights the racial politics that ensue within a mainstream LGBTQ community when it comes to the LGBTQ social scene, romantic relationships, and online dating. For example, one gay Asian American male participant (Han, 2009) described the types of microaggressions he perceives:

> It's not so blatant, I mean, people don't come up to you and call you "chink" or anything like that. But it's definitely there, you can feel it. . . . Like little

things, like if a lot of Asians go to a bar, then they start calling it a "rice bar" or something. And like the personal ads that say, "No Asians," or whatever, so it makes it hard to approach guys at bars because you never know if they're going to reject you because you're Asian. (p. 276)

Similarly, in a study with gay and bisexual Latino men (Díaz et al., 2006), one participant shared:

Well, my experience in growing up in a gay world . . . it's kind of almost like if you are not Caucasian, you do not even deserve to be gay. . . . These are gay Caucasian kinds of clubs, and unless you go to a specific Hispanic club, I personally feel that you're not treated equally, not only as an individual, but because you are a different race. (p. 213)

In another study, a queer Black Muslim cisgender man shared:

And yet our queer spaces in the city are overwhelmingly white. I know the majority people in my life are queer folks of color. So why aren't they in these spaces? Often, it's because they've been made to feel unwelcome. And so, we go elsewhere and create spaces outside of the [gay neighborhood]. (Golriz, 2021, p. 366)

Similar sentiments were shared by queer women of color. A Filipina lesbian asserted: "I was (and am) always that one Filipina. . . . The lesbian social scene consists of bars that are primarily full of white girls" (Corpus, 2010, p. 190). Finally, a South Asian woman added: "When I was [in white queer spaces] in the past . . . you don't feel understood, lack of sense of belonging, and just like disconnected. It's a different experience as a [South Asian] queer person" (Patel, 2019, p. 9).

In all five of these examples, the narrators perceive subtle or coded racism in LGBTQ spaces; one common thread that they appear to have learned is that what is deemed to be general LGBTQ culture centers on whiteness and "white normativity" (i.e., communication styles and standards of beauty of white people) regardless of the actual racially diverse makeup (Ward, 2008, p. 563).

LGBTQ white people are typically unaware of the subtle racism that occurs (particularly the ways that LGBTQ POC are expected to conform to white norms) or of the privileges they have as part of the dominant group. In fact, one study found that white liberal LGBTQ people were significantly less likely than LGBTQ POC to believe that racism still exists or to be in support of policies that support poor or disenfranchised people (Hinkson, 2021).

Moreover, when LGBTQ POC do engage in white LGBTQ spaces, such experiences may be detrimental to their mental health. One study found that while white LGBTQ people report less depression and victimization after engaging in LGBTQ campus organizing, LGBTQ POC report the opposite (Kulick et al., 2017). In this way, LGBTQ organizations that fail to welcome or affirm LGBTQ people of color may be psychologically damaging.

One last example that demonstrates the exclusion faced by LGBTQ POC involves the ways that LGBTQ social spaces enact policies or promote behaviors that discriminate or exclude trans or queer people of color. For instance, in a foundational research study on experiences of Black lesbians and gay men, a common theme was the difficulty in finding validation or community among other gays and lesbians. For instance, a gay Black man described:

> I would go into a bar . . . behind young whites who looked a hell-of-a-lot younger than me, and they would have no problem getting in. Whereas I would be stopped, and they would ask for at least two forms of [identification]. Also, just the attitudes of the bartenders. They would wait on others before they would wait on me . . . and it really saddened me because I thought we were all gay, we were all fighting for equality. You know, we would pull together. But I found more racism among white gays than I did among just whites period . . . which really upset me. (Loiacano, 1989, p. 23)

While this perspective was from three decades ago, casual racism is still rampant in LGBTQ spaces today. Han (2021) revealed how many gay bars change their music or enforce dress codes to limit clientele of color from patronizing their businesses; further, an unspoken code exists for white men to warn other white men about which bars have clientele of color.

One environmental microaggression that exemplifies the normalization of whiteness in LGBTQ culture is through the media. Apart from one television show (*Noah's Arc*), most of the well-known "mainstream" lesbian or gay American television shows (e.g., *Will and Grace, the L Word, Queer as Folk*) have historically focused on the lives of almost all white lesbian and gay characters. One author wrote about this lack of diversity in lesbian depictions in the media: "Lesbian bar representations in the twentieth century depict bars as primarily white spaces. Save for a few nonwhite women, the women who populate the lesbian bars . . . are white." (Hankin, 2002, p. 112). Similarly, when the television show *Queer Eye for the Straight Guy* premiered in 2003, there was some of controversy not only because of the lack of diversity on the show (Jai Rodriguez, a multiracial Latino, was the only person of color on the show) but also because the lone Black host (James Hannaham) was replaced after the pilot. When the show rebooted in 2016, two people of color (Karamo Brown and Tan France) were cast—an improvement, but still far from an accurate representation.

Exclusion Within Communities of Color

Previous academic literature has found that LGBTQ POC often feel excluded from their racial and ethnic communities, who may not be accepting of their sexual identities (Cerezo et al., 2020; Nadal & Corpus, 2013; Patel, 2019). Often, this lack of acceptance first begins within one's family. In a study on queer Latinx women and nonbinary people (Cerezo et al., 2020), one participant revealed:

> My mom, I remember, when she found out, she would make statements about, "What are your cousins going to think? What is your family going to think?" She was adamant that I wouldn't be able to get a job, or I wouldn't be able to go to college for some reason. As far as she was concerned, my future was just done. Aside from the handful of people that I was closest to, I didn't really feel compelled to come out to anybody. (p. 73)

However, such exclusion can also occur in one's general racial or ethnic community. For example, Gloria Anzaldúa (2012), a Latina lesbian writer, wrote about feeling excommunicated from her racial and ethnic community because of her sexual identity:

> As a mestiza, I have no country, my homeland cast me out; yet all countries are mine because I am every woman's sister or potential lover. As a lesbian I have no race, my own people disclaim me; but I am all races because there is the queer of me in all races. (pp. 102–103)

Being excluded by one's various communities can be isolating; one Black queer woman shared:

> For me, it was always a little bit harder because sometimes it feels like the African American community and the LGBT community can be at odds. It feels that African Americans as a whole are slower to adopt like that same-sex marriage really is equal and things like that. A lot of times I feel like mainstream feminism has kind of forgotten women of color. (Cerezo et al., 2020, p. 76)

In these ways, having multiple minoritized identities can cause significant psychological stress, particularly when one does not feel included in certain spaces and situations.

Experiencing heterosexism by people of one's racial group can feel particularly insulting or shocking, especially when the perpetrator is a loved one. In another example (Mobley & Pearson, 2005), a gay Black man described a time when he felt excluded and hurt by a heterosexual Black American woman colleague. When the two were to give a presentation, he noticed that she had removed all the PowerPoint slides that were related to sexual orientation. When he confronted her, she replied, "I cannot be gay affirming" (p. 89). He continued:

> Hearing this, I was immediately shocked, angered, and I felt a deep sense of disbelief followed by an internal rage. My gay cultural identity was being deleted, denied, and dejected in my very presence. . . . I feared that [she] represented one of those African Americans who gave lip service to being friends with an African American lesbian, gay, or bisexual (LGB) person but in reality, was obviously not fully comfortable and accepting due to "the church." (p. 89)

While the interaction eventually led to an intense discussion as well as a deeper friendship between the two parties, this type of conflict represents one that is very common between LGBTQ POC and heterosexual people of color (particularly those who are religious). When communities of color espouse homophobic biases, LGBTQ POC have difficulty in feeling accepted in these spaces. When heterosexual family and other community members discriminate against them, it may be especially hurtful for LGBTQ POC, who recognize that their loved ones know firsthand what it is like to experience exclusion and discrimination due to racism.

Denial of Existence in Communities of Color

There are many ways that LGBTQ POC are denied their existence altogether. Historically, many leaders of many countries throughout the world have claimed that queer and trans people don't exist, or that they did not exist until their contact with the Western world. These sentiments are shared by many of the citizens of those countries who are still staunchly unsupportive of LGBTQ people or LGBTQ rights. Poushter and Kent (2020) found that while many Western, industrialized countries (e.g., Canada, the United States, Australia) are generally supportive of diverse sexual orientations and gender identities, that many regions (e.g., Eastern Europe, Russia, the Middle East, and sub-Saharan Africa) still maintain blatant homophobic or transphobic views. In many countries, homosexuality and transgenderism is considered a criminal act and may even be punishable by death.

In the United States, this denial of the existence of LGBTQ POC can persist through immigrants who maintain these beliefs from their countries of origin, and such biases can manifest on all levels, such as community organizations, groups, and families. When whole societies do not discuss or acknowledge LGBTQ people in their government policies, educational systems, or media, they communicate the false belief that LGBTQ people do not exist, or they communicate the societal bias that it is taboo to talk about diverse gender identities or sexual orientations. For example, Patel (2019) described how the lack of queer representation in South Asian culture has resulted in the common myth that "Brown girls can't be gay" (p. 10).

Within families, common microaggressions that occur are when parents and other relatives may deny that their loved one is really LGBTQ or reject their children or relatives after they disclose their identities. Through many media (academic writings, personal narratives, films, and other artforms), many LGBTQ POC have described the fear of "coming out" to their family members. For instance, in a study (Singh & McKelroy, 2011) with transgender people of color, one Black transgender man stated, "It's shocking when you know your very own family might not be around to accept who you really are" (p. 38). It is for these very reasons that for LGBTQ POC, coming out may feel superfluous or unnecessary or like a pressure instilled by white LGBTQ people who come from different circumstances. In one study (Nadal & Corpus, 2013), a Filipina woman shared:

> Filipinos are the last people I would tell that I was a lesbian and that's the way that it's come about because of not wanting to be separated from my family. It's sort of like . . . it's all about family ultimately. (p. 171)

In another study (Patel, 2019), one South Asian woman related:

> [white queers] all emphasize coming out so much. . . . Next time a white person tells me to come out to my parents I'm going to tell them to make sure "cause of death: coming out because a white person told her to" is included in my obituary." (p. 11)

When some LGBTQ POC disclose their identities to their families, they are met with dismissal or denial. For example, in a personal narrative, a Filipina woman wrote:

> I thought I came out to my mom when I was 24 years old, but apparently, I didn't. You see, in my household (and in many other Filipino households), coming out doesn't really mean anything. It just encourages my mom to work harder at being in "denial" that I'm gay. . . . Since I came out, I've been receiving Catholic prayer books, rosaries (that she got blessed by her priest at St. Athanasius), and panties on a frequent basis. In her indirect way of communicating to me, her subtext has always been clear. She believes prayer could solve everything, even my sexuality. (Corpus, 2010, p. 188)

Similarly, in one of my studies (Nadal, Wong, et al., 2011), a Latina bisexual woman shared, "My family doesn't really know I'm bisexual. But it's because they're Latin. I tried once to tell my mom and she stopped me right there when I tried to tell her" (p. 34).

Some families of color may demonstrate a general acceptance of their trans or queer relatives' sexual orientations or gender identities; however, they may still demonstrate discomfort or communicate a culture of silence surrounding those identities. For instance, in one study (Nadal et al., 2017), a participant shared:

> My parents are Sudanese, so being around them, you know, they're accepting of me, but when we're around the family, you know, I'm forced to act as, you know, like a straight guy; something that I'm not, you know what I mean? (p. 146)

So even if the narrator perceives that his parents are generally accepting, their encouragement or coercion for their child to hide their identity when others are around might indicate otherwise.

Denial of Racism in LGBTQ Communities

Because of the white normalization within LGBTQ community spaces, it is common for LGBTQ POC to feel as if racism goes unaddressed and sometimes even denied. In an older study with lesbian and gay Black Americans (Loiacano, 1989), one Black lesbian described her perceptions of the mainstream LGBTQ community: "Some of us [women of color] end up dropping out of planning groups or raising hell. We might want to work on the racism that's going on there, but racial issues are tough, and people don't really want to talk about them" (p. 22). Similarly, in a narrative by a gay female Filipina American woman, the author stated: "The sad thing is that it seems like my 'lesbian community' does not even recognize this plight that I may experience. I've felt invalidated by white lesbian women who claim that racism is nonexistent in the lesbian community" (Corpus, 2010, p. 190). When LGBTQ POC are invalidated or gaslit based on their lived racialized experiences, they may feel even more alienated within or excluded from what is supposed to be an inclusive LGBTQ community.

Exoticization and Sexual Racism

As mentioned earlier in this chapter, people of color can feel exoticized in general society and within LGBTQ spaces. Previous research has found that Asian American women are viewed as being sexually submissive (i.e., obedient to their sexual and romantic partners) or as being "Madame Butterfly" characters in that they are sexually conniving or odd (Nadal, Escobar, et al., 2012; Sue, Bucceri, et al., 2009). Meanwhile, Black American women are sometimes perceived as being sexually seductive "Jezebel" characters (Lewis & Neville, 2015, p. 291). LGBTQ POC may experience exoticization in similar yet nuanced ways to these general stereotypes, because of the intersections of their racial, gendered, and sexual identities.

Some scholars have used the term **sexual racism** when describing micro-aggressions involving dating, sex, or romance. For various subgroups of trans and queer people of color, sexual racism/exoticization microaggressions may manifest differently. First, as aforementioned, Asian American men in general are stereotyped as being demasculinized or effeminate. As a result, queer Asian and Asian American men are often said to uphold similar stereotypes as Asian and Asian American women in that they are viewed as sexually submissive or obedient "bottoms" (i.e., those that would be the recipients of anal sex), feminine, and dainty (i.e., small-statured, smooth-skinned, and with small penises). For example, one gay Asian man said:

> A rice queen is a white guy, usually a white guy, who likes Asian men. That's the short definition. But then there's the whole stereotype of what a rice queen is supposed to be. He's the older white guy who's not so attractive and he goes for younger Asian guys because that's all he can get. But then, the counter-stereotype is that Asian guys go for rice queens because that's all they could get. (Han, 2009, p. 276)

These sorts of microaggressions may further lead to a sense of exclusion for LGBTQ people—perpetuating the normalization of white standards of beauty and the "otherness" of Asian Americans and other people of color.

On the other hand, while Black and Latino queer men may be **hyper-sexualized**, in that they are presumed to be sexually promiscuous or sexually satisfying, due to racial sexual biases. Some men of color are also **hyper-masculinized**, in that they are viewed as being ultramasculine, dominant in bed, or having large penises. For example, Black men are reduced to having big Black penises, as evidenced by a Black man who revealed:

> I've seen some profiles, like "I want a big, Black man with a big, Black dick to fuck me" and stuff like that, and it just seems pretty weird. It just seems pretty odd. It seems like you're fetishizing me. There's this thing in their eye. I don't lust after white men like that. If I see a white guy, I'm not going to automatically drool for him, even if I find him attractive. But I've seen a lot of white guys who will drool over any Black guy. (Stacey & Forbes, 2022, p. 8)

Another Black man recalled: "We were flirting, so he made some comments like 'Yeah, you know I like Black guys a lot. And he goes 'Well you know you guys have big cocks'" (Follins, 2014, p. 56). Latino men are exoticized and stereotyped in a similar way. A gay Latino stated:

> With some white gay men, it's like they see you as, again, a piece of meat. Something they could go to bed with, you know, they had their Latino boy

or whatever and I've been in situations where I start talking and they're like, "Oh, you can think too?" (Díaz et al., 2006, p. 213)

A gay Latino man shared another sexual encounter: "We were having sex [and] he kept calling me Salvadorian . . . like exoticizing me and reminding me I'm Latino" (Follins, 2014, p. 55).

Relatedly, in another study, one bisexual Black man shared:

> I also had specifically gotten messaged by one Caucasian who was a little bit older, and he wanted me to be his "slave," his "bedroom slave." So, I did react through anger and I just basically [responded], "I am no one's slave." (Winder & Lea, 2019, p. 231)

These examples all demonstrate the type of casual sexual racism that queer men of color are exposed to in their dating interactions. Interestingly enough, these racial tropes have persisted over the decades and appear to have only increased with the use of online dating and social media apps (Stacey & Forbes, 2022; Winder & Lea, 2019).

Queer men of color also endure general racial stereotypes in queer white spaces—reflecting people's racial biases or tokenizing of racial groups. One Black male shared:

> When I'm in a bar, you know, drinking, white people would come up to me, asking me questions. . . . Uh, just because I'm Black, I'm supposed to be raised in the "hood." . . . I'm like, you know, I wasn't raised in the "hood," so why are you coming up to me asking me these crazy questions? I'm always offended. (Nadal et al., 2017, p. 164)

In another study (Stacey & Forbes, 2022), a Latino participant described: "They tend to fetishize me sometimes because I am Latino and white-passing, and they think it's cute. It's not cute. They'll want to speak Spanish to me even though I don't speak Spanish" (p. 7). While these examples both reflect stereotypes held about certain groups based on their multiple identities, they are all centered on the notion that white standards are the norm and all others are different. Even when such stereotypes are meant to be positive, they reduce people of all groups to a single trope—one that often involves their dehumanization or objectification.

Exoticization also targets queer women of color. Hankin (2002) described how lesbian and bisexual women of color, particularly Black and Latina lesbians, are often sexualized:

> Exoticized black lesbian bar patrons repeatedly appear in pulp fiction, journalistic exposes, and scientific studies. . . . Most notable are the bar scenes in [the movies] *Living Out Loud* and *Boys on the Side*. [The] white heterosexual protagonist in *Living Out Loud* "finds herself" after being caressed by scantily clad women of color in a lesbian bar. In *Boys on the Side*, the multicultural

depiction of the lesbian bar contributes to the film's overall fetish of the Southwest's Hispanic culture. (p. 113)

Relatedly, Black queer women face both racial and gendered stereotypes based on their gender presentation (particularly regarding how they dress). Scholars have described how Black lesbian, bisexual, and queer women may experience gendered racial discrimination based on whether they present more femininely, more masculinely, or in more gender-fluid or nonconforming ways (Brassel et al., 2020; Moore, 2006). In one study (Moore, 2006), a masculine-performing Black lesbian shared:

> People call us out . . . threaten us, all because of who we are and what we look like, what we represent. . . . They've spent their whole lives with one idea of who they are, and then they look at us with our men's shirts, our men's shoes, and realize gender is something that is taught. (pp. 132–133)

Queer women of color may face the same types of casual sexual racism described by queer men of color. In one study (Patel, 2019), a South Asian woman divulged:

> I feel like [white women] either want me to be white or they show their "appreciation" in extremely racist ways. I've gone on dates where white women . . . start doing all the Bollywood moves they know . . . that's just super racist. (p. 9)

In these ways, it appears that queer women of color may encounter an array of **gendered, racial microaggressions** (Lewis et al., 2016) that are like their cis heterosexual counterparts. However, their queerness (which may include gender presentation) may add another level of bias that exacerbates their experiences.

Finally, trans women of color are exoticized in similar ways as cis women of color, particularly regarding romantic or sexual partners. In one study (Sevelius, 2013), a Black trans woman divulged:

> You walk down the street after you done turned the trick and you feel like you're the grand diva 'cause somebody stopped 'cause you're pretty. But see what I realize is that it's not the beauty on the inside that they see. All they see you for is a piece of ass. . . . All they think that transgenders are good for is sex and drugs. (p. 681)

In the same study, another Black trans woman described how some cisgender men are only interested in having a sexual relationship with her, while maintaining a romantic relationship with a cisgender women. She revealed:

> He figures he can go to the picnics with his [non-transgender] girlfriend, take her around to his parents, his family, take her to the movies, and then I would be on the back burner. He's only going to want to have sex with me. (p. 681)

Such perspectives are shared by many trans people, particularly trans women who may face an array of microaggressions in the context of their romantic relationships (Pulice-Farrow et al., 2017). For transgender women of color, these interactions may be exacerbated by race. In the critically acclaimed television series, *Pose*, there are several examples of the exoticization that Black trans women experience. First, the character Elektra is in a long-term romantic relationship with a wealthy white man who breaks up with her and kicks her out of her apartment (which he finances) after she discloses that she completed gender-affirming **bottom surgery**. Second, in the first season, the character Angel dates a white man who enjoys their romantic and sexual relationship in private but is unwilling to commit to her beyond that. The first example demonstrates exoticization in that Elektra's boyfriend can easily dispose of her when she undergoes her bottom surgery— despite knowing that such a procedure helps her to feel complete. Meanwhile, the second scenario exemplifies exoticization, in that Angel's boyfriend may enjoy the benefits that come from being in a private sexual relationship with a trans Latina woman but is unable to reciprocate her emotional needs.

Microaggressions Based on Both Racial/Ethnic and Sexual Identities

Finally, there are microaggressions in which LGBTQ POC may feel marginalized or discriminated against because of the intersection of their racial/ethnic and sexual identities. Sometimes they may be treated as second-class citizens or intellectual inferiors, and sometimes they may be assumed to be criminal or pathological. With these types of occurrences, people may be unclear if the microaggression transpired because of one of their social identities, both their racial/ethnic and sexual identity, or because of some other combination with other factors (e.g., age, social class). As an illustration, a Black American transgender woman described how she feels negatively stereotyped because of her race, ethnicity, and gender identity:

> Society put me in a place where I am a minority and doesn't think I have the talent or potential because of who I am [racially/ethnically]. When I was a child, didn't think my ethnicity was anything to be proud of—I was looked down on because I was Black. And then being transgender made it even worse. Now that I am older, I am proud of everything I am. I am an African American transsexual woman. No one can tell me I am less than anyone else. That helps me no matter what bad things happened to me. Some days, just getting out of bed is a revolutionary act to deal with the world. And I *make sure* I get out of bed. (Singh & McKleroy, 2011, p. 38)

Similarly, a Latina transgender woman described how she reacts to people who may treat her negatively because of both her race and gender identity:

I decided that just because I was transsexual Hispanic woman didn't mean that people could treat me any type of way. I didn't know if anyone would ever love me. I realized that I had to fight just to live my life as who I am—in school, at work, with my family, everywhere! That's also why I knew I couldn't just stay in an abusive relationship. I had to accept myself 100%. (Singh & McKleroy, 2011, p. 38)

As a final example, I return to the television show *Pose*. In the first season, Blanca (an Afro Latina transwoman) decides she wants to have drinks at a gay bar with her friend, Lulu (another trans woman of color). While there, they are harassed by both patrons and servers (all cisgender men and majority white men), who directly and indirectly communicate that they don't want them there (Mulkerin, 2018). Although a fictional scene, such experiences are common for transgender women—especially trans women of color—in white LGBTQ spaces. Even if it is likely that their transgender identities are the primary reason for the gay men's prejudice, their races (and especially because Blanca is Black) may exacerbate the severity and speed of their reactions. Perhaps if she were a white trans woman, they might still communicate that they didn't want her there; however, there is a possibility that they would have been less hostile or violent about it.

The previous examples demonstrate three main themes about LGBTQ POC within white LGBTQ spaces. First, it may be impossible to examine only singular identities when understanding discrimination towards LGBTQ POC. While there are some situations when a singular identity may be a primary factor when microaggressions occur, other identities may influence the situation as well. For instance, if a transgender woman of color is called a derogatory, transphobic slur, her transgender identity may be the primary factor behind the discriminatory statement. However, perhaps the perpetrator was even more hurtful or offensive because of the transgender woman's race (or age, social class, physical appearance, etc.).

Second, an individual's dual minority identity may also influence one's ability to react to and cope with the incident, which in turn may affect their mental health. For example, one study found that Black and Latina lesbian and bisexual women who accepted discrimination in their lives and did not discuss discrimination with others were more likely to be diagnosed with psychiatric disorders, and that Black lesbian and bisexual women particularly were likely to be diagnosed with mood and anxiety disorders when they accepted discrimination and did not talk about their experiences with others (McLaughlin et al., 2010). Thus, LGBTQ POC must find support when they encounter discrimination to protect their own mental health.

Finally, because LGBTQ people of color hold these dual minority statuses, it is evident that they may be more cognizant of the different ways that they navigate certain communities than their counterparts with only one marginalized identity (e.g., LGBTQ white people or heterosexual people of color). LGBTQ POC may be more able to identify racism in the general LGBTQ community than LGBTQ white people, while being more able to identify heterosexism in their families and communities of color than heterosexual people of color. As a result, further research may examine if LGBTQ POC (a) encounter more microaggressions, (b) perceive more microaggressions in their lives, and (c) are more distressed because of the higher prevalence of encountering or perceiving these microaggressions.

CASE STUDIES

To demonstrate the various types of intersectional microaggressions experienced by LGBTQ POC, three fictional case studies are provided. In reviewing these cases, consider how each of the person's identities (gender, sexual orientation, race, ethnicity, and more) may influence the types of discrimination they encounter and how people's identities may impact how they navigate various microaggressions.

The Intersection of Culture, Gender Identity, and More: The Case of Lorenzo

Lorenzo is a 30-year-old Latino, Dominican American, transgender man who grew up in New York City. He is the only child of his parents, who both worked full-time and emigrated from the Dominican Republic. He had a large extended family that lived within a few miles of his home, and his family had remained in good contact with their family members back abroad.

Although assigned a girl at birth (and given a feminine name), Lorenzo knew that he was transgender ever since he was a little child. He rejected the gender role norms that his family, who wanted him to live the life of a "normal girl," attempted to instill in him. When his mother tried to make him wear dresses, Lorenzo always refused, saying that he wanted to dress like "the other boys" and wear pants. While this was a common argument between Lorenzo and his mother during most of his childhood, Lorenzo's mother eventually became more lenient and accepting of whatever Lorenzo chose to wear.

As an adolescent, Lorenzo lived a life that seemed somewhat typical for a teenage girl. He had several female friends; he participated in both sports and the arts; and he even dated boys. He did not feel like a lesbian, particularly because he was indeed attracted to boys. However, as a girl, Lorenzo felt incomplete; he felt more like a boy. While there was an LGBTQ student club that existed at his high school, Lorenzo did not feel comfortable attending its meetings. He recognized that even though there was a "T" in the title of the organization, there were not any out "T" people who were involved. He also noticed that most of the people in the organization were white. So, instead of telling anyone about how he was feeling, he began to do some research online about transgender people and identities. When he entered transgender chat rooms and read online discussion boards regarding transgender experiences, he began to gain a better understanding about himself and how he identified. In college, he made some transgender friends and met several transgender role models who were leaders in the community. It was at this point that he made some major changes. He decided that he wanted everyone to refer to him as "Lo" instead of his birth name; he also started wearing stereotypically masculine clothes, like baggy sweatshirts and jeans. While his family noticed some of the differences, they just assumed that he was going through a "stage," making the assumption that Lo was a lesbian.

When Lo was in college, he eventually made the decision to officially come out to his family as a transgender man. Because Lorenzo was the only child and because his family was Latino and Catholic, he worried that his parents would have a difficult time accepting his transgender identity. During the winter break of his sophomore year, he decided to tell his parents that he was transgender and that he was planning on physically and medically transitioning into a man. At first, his parents were very shocked, stating that it was just a "phase" and that he would change his mind eventually. They also asked if he was sure that he wasn't just a lesbian and told him that being transgender "simply wasn't natural." Lo was hurt, angry, and invalidated; he told his parents that he was going to start his transition with or without their support. He returned to college, got a part-time job, and applied for more financial aid, so that he could save as much money as possible to begin his transition.

After several years of hormone treatment (and no contact with his parents), Lo returned home to try to reconnect with his parents. Upon arriving, he informed them that he now identifies as Lorenzo, and that he would appreciate it if everyone referred to him as such. Surprisingly, Lorenzo's parents reacted differently this time around. They apologized for not being initially accepting and shared that they loved him and supported him in his decisions. Noticing his notable change in physical appearance (i.e., Lorenzo could "pass" as a cis man), they asked him incessant questions about his experiences and his medical procedures. Lorenzo shared he had been taking hormone treatment, but he had not yet completed gender affirming **top surgery**. Lorenzo's mother suggested that he not undergo the surgery, stating: "This way, if you decide that you really don't want to be a man, you can always go back to being normal."

The Intersection of Race, Sexuality, and More: The Case of Tuan

Tuan is an 18-year-old Vietnamese American living in the Pacific Northwest. He recently disclosed his identity as "pansexual" to his closest friends at school—many of whom identified as queer or pansexual. While he decided he could not tell his immigrant family anytime soon (due to cultural and religious reasons), he felt good about starting to explore this new part of himself.

One thing that some of his queer friends recommended was to try some of the dating apps like Grindr or Scruff. His friend Patrick, a queer white man from his class, was especially adamant about how fun the apps were—sharing that he had met lots of cute guys online and that he even hooked up with a few of them. Tuan immediately created a profile on both sites—excited at the potential of meeting someone attractive whom he could date or experiment with.

Tuan quickly learned that his experience differed significantly from Patrick's. He messaged men around his age but would not get many replies. One user replied with "Sorry, not into Asian guys. Just a preference," while another said, "Not trying to get COVID." Some users immediately blocked him after he sent a message. The few users who initiated contact were much older (i.e., men in their 40s or 50s), whose opening lines were usually racially charged (e.g., "Asian guys are hot"); sexually brash (e.g., "Let me see that ass!"); or both (e.g., "You want this white daddy cock inside you?").

These types of messages (or lack of messages) were how Tuan experienced the apps for the first few days. He was incredibly discouraged and saddened—not just because he did not have any luck in meeting anyone his own age but also because he didn't realize that race would be such a prominent part of his dating process. Tuan also began to question whether he was attractive enough; while he had never questioned his looks before (mostly because he had heard compliments about his looks throughout his life from his class-mates and people from his Vietnamese American community), he started to feel horrible about himself.

One day, Patrick texted Tuan to find out how many guys he had met. Tuan informed him that he had not really chatted with anyone worthwhile. He added that only older guys are messaging him; that he thinks the apps are "racist against Asians" and that he might delete his accounts. Patrick replied, "That's crazy! You're probably doing something wrong. I promise it's easy to meet guys. Let me look at your profile later."

CASE STUDY DISCUSSION

Both scenarios demonstrate the complexities of intersectional identities, particularly the impact that these identities can have on one's exposure to microaggressions. The first scenario focuses on Lorenzo, a transgender man who is faced with several microaggressions before and after his transition. Many of these incidents match some of the gender-identity microaggressions described in Chapter 4. For example, when Lorenzo's parents tell him that his gender identity is "just a phase," it could be classified as their "discomfort/disapproval with transgender experience." Similarly, when they ask him intrusive questions about his genitalia, the incident can be categorized as a "denial of bodily privacy." However, the scenario is heavily influenced by other identities—namely his family's Dominican culture and his Catholic religion. Because Latino culture promotes rigid gender roles for men and women—in which Latino men are typically expected to subscribe to *machismo* gender roles (i.e., to be masculine, providers, and emotionally restrictive), while Latina women are typically expected to subscribe to *marianismo* gender roles (i.e., to be feminine, self-sacrificing, and like the Virgin Mary)—his immigrant parents may not comprehend how someone who was raised a girl would want to become a boy. Furthermore, because Catholicism preaches heterosexuality and procreation as the norm, his family may struggle to accept anything that goes against what they have been taught.

The second scenario, involving Tuan, a Vietnamese American man, includes microaggressions that many queer Asian American men have reported encountering online. While some of the dating apps have changed policies to ban users from using phrases like "No Asians" from their profiles (Truong, 2018), racial microaggressions are still rampant on dating app sites (Han, 2021; Han & Choi, 2018; Stacey & Forbes, 2022; Winder & Lea, 2019). For queer Asian American men, sexual racism usually manifests through invisibility, exclusion, or presumptions of sexual stereotypes (e.g., all queer Asian men are passive, bottoms, submissive to white men, hypersexual, etc.). **Blocking** (the act of preventing someone from further seeing their profile or communicating with them) or **ghosting** (the act of ignoring someone's messages) is a common experience for queer Asian Americans and other LGBTQ POC (Han, 2021). While both are permissible actions and can be used as a protective factor (e.g., many people use the features to prevent harassment or unwanted contact), such acts toward entire groups can feel hostile and dehumanizing—especially for queer Asian Americans who already notice a lack of positive representation in media or feel excluded from general LGBTQ community spaces.

Furthermore, these two scenarios demonstrate how some microaggressive incidents may appear to be much more blatant and obvious, while other incidents might seem more well-intentioned and not malicious in any way. For example, Lorenzo's initial rejection from his parents can be construed as overtly transphobic, in that they are unsupportive of his gender identity and transition. However, when he returns to them, and his mother encourages him to not undergo gender-affirming medical surgeries in case he wants to return to "normal," his mother may be unaware of her hurtfulness. Similarly, while some comments Tuan reads online are blatantly biased (e.g., "Not trying to get COVID"), some comments are guided in benevolence (e.g., "It's just a preference"). Further, while his friend Patrick wanted to help or be encouraging, he also invalidated him by not acknowledging his racial concerns. In this way, Patrick committed a microinvalidation; he communicated that racism is not real or that Tuan is imagining it. In the next chapter, we continue our discussion on intersectional identities, but now integrating ability status and age.

DISCUSSION QUESTIONS

For General Readers

1. What types of intersectional microaggressions do you believe occur often with LGBTQ people of color? Do microaggressions occur differently for LGBTQ people of color of diverse racial groups (e.g., Black, Asian, Indigenous, Latinx, etc.)?

2. Do microaggressions towards LGBTQ POC feel worse when they are perpetrated by LGBTQ white people? By family members?

3. What part of Lorenzo's or Tuan's story do you identify with most? Identify with least?

For Psychologists, Educators, and Other Experts

1. What institutional policies would help in addressing intersectional microaggressions in your workplace?

2. If you met Lorenzo or Tuan in a therapeutic setting, how would you approach your work?

GLOSSARY OF KEY TERMS

blocking On dating apps, the act of preventing someone from further seeing one's profile or communicating with them.

bottom surgery A gender-confirming medical procedure in which a transgender person has their genitalia altered. For trans women, this typically includes a vaginoplasty or vulvoplasty; for trans men, this usually includes a phalloplasty or metoidioplasty.

dual minority status The identity in which an individual belongs to two marginalized groups (e.g., gay/Black, bisexual/Asian American).

gendered, racial microaggressions Subtle forms of discrimination experienced by women of color based primarily on sexist and racist biases.

ghosting The act of ignoring someone's messages altogether; never replying to someone who messages you.

hypermasculinze To unnecessarily accentuate or concentrate on another person's masculine features, typically due to stereotypes or biases about one or more identity/identities held by the person.

hypersexualize To unnecessarily accentuate or concentrate on a person's sexuality or sexual traits, typically due to stereotypes or biases about one or more identity/identities held by the person.

intersectional microaggressions Everyday forms of discrimination that are based on individuals' multiple social identities.

intersectionality theory A theory proposed originally for Black women that describes how people with multiple marginalized identities navigate interlocking forms of systemic and interpersonal oppression.

MSM An abbreviation for the term "men who have sex with men"—which includes men who are open about their sexuality (e.g., out gay, bisexual, or queer men) and those who may conceal their sexual identities, relationships, or behaviors.

multiple minority stress The psychological distress that one experiences when they belong to two or more marginalized groups.

sexual racism Biases, prejudices, or discrimination based on race, that occur in the context of dating, sexual encounters, or romantic relationships.

top surgery A gender-confirming medical procedure in which a transgender person has their chest altered. For trans women, this typically includes breast augmentation or breast reduction surgery; for trans men, this usually includes breast reduction surgery (sometimes known as a transgender mastectomy or a masculinizing chest surgery).

transamorous A term used to describe someone who is romantically or sexually attracted to (and/or seeks relationships with) transgender, gender nonconforming, or nonbinary people.

6

INTERSECTIONAL MICROAGGRESSIONS

Experiences of LGBTQ People With Disabilities, LGBTQ People of Diverse Sizes, Older LGBTQ People, and LGBTQ Youth

FIGURE 6.1. A Group of Diverse Friends Enjoying Each Other's Company at a Bar

Note. Photo courtesy of Elevate.

https://doi.org/10.1037/0000335-007
Dismantling Everyday Discrimination: Microaggressions Toward LGBTQ People, Second Edition, by K. L. Y. Nadal

As outlined in Chapter 5, intersectional identities may complicate the ways in which microaggressions are committed and experienced. When people with multiple marginalized identities encounter microaggressions, they may wonder if they are being targeted because of one singular identity (e.g., their race or their gender) or a combination of their identities (e.g., their race, their gender, their sexual orientation, or more). For instance, when a trans woman of color working as an executive in a corporation is excluded by her white male colleagues or peers (e.g., she doesn't get invited to happy hour gatherings, her coworkers don't engage in the same social banter with her as they do with each other, and so on), she may wonder if it is because of her transgender identity, her race, her identity as a woman, or some combination of all of these categories. If she maintained other identities (e.g., having a disability, being much older or younger), her story might result in even more complex dynamics and potentially more microaggressions.

While the Chapter 5 focused primarily on the microaggressions that manifest due to the interaction of one's race, gender identity, and sexual orientation, this chapter focuses on anti-LGBTQ microaggressions that are also influenced by one's ability, size, and age. Specifically, this chapter covers **ableist microaggressions** (i.e., everyday forms of discrimination based on ability status, experienced by people with disabilities [PWDs]), **sizeist microaggressions** (i.e., everyday forms of discrimination based on size), and **age-related microaggressions** (i.e., everyday forms of ageist discrimination, experienced most by older people and youth). These microaggressions may intersect with race (e.g., an LGBTQ person of color who lives with a disability), or they may even intersect with each other (e.g., an able-bodied LGBTQ person develops a disability as they grow older, or an LGBTQ PWD reports increased symptoms as they age).

To best understand **ableism, sizeism, ageism** (and the intersection of all three), it is crucial to first provide some definitions. First, scholars have described how the concept of ableism has been defined very differently, usually dependent on the identities of the writers or the political intentions regarding the content being shared. For instance, according to Patel and Brown (2017), the medical model of disability is based on a disease or health condition that limits someone's ability to carry out expected individual and societal obligations, while the social model of disabilities considers the ways that societal expectation and built environments interfere with an individual's ability to engage in a productive role in society. In comparing these two definitions, one can observe how medical models tend to pathologize PWDs (i.e., comparing them with able-bodied people, who are considered the "norm" or "standard" group); meanwhile, the social model holds environmental and societal factors accountable for limiting PWDs' capacity to function or thrive (i.e., normalizing PWDs and pathologizing systems that fail or hinder their opportunities).

Related to disability is the idea of **impairment**, which is defined as "any psychological, structural, or functional abnormality at an individual level" (Patel & Brown, 2017, p. 248). People who have impairments are not necessarily considered PWDs; instead, people may be considered to have a disability if their impairment negatively impacts or interferes with their ability to function in their everyday lives. For example, some PWDs have impairments that are physical (e.g., visual impairments, hearing impairments, or the use of a wheelchair for mobility), while others have impairments that are mental or psychological (e.g., one who has cognitive deficiencies or attention-related difficulties). Some people with visual impairments may be blind (which prohibits their ability to see altogether), while others may have visual impairments that can be assisted with other devices, treatments, or procedures (e.g., corrective lenses, surgeries). Thus, some people with visual impairments are PWDs and others are not.

Another important note is the usage of the terms "people with disabilities" versus "disabled people." While both are generally considered appropriate and inclusive terms, they may be used differently by people who identify as such. In recent years, community leaders and scholars have described the difference between "identity-first" language versus "person-first" language, particularly when describing people who belong to historically marginalized groups (American Psychological Association [APA], 2021, p. 6). Identity-first language places an emphasis on an identity group (e.g., disabled people, autistic people), whereas person-first language places the emphasis on the person first (e.g., people with disabilities, people with autism). Proponents of identity-first descriptors may use it as a term of cultural pride or a reclamation of the identity that is often denigrated or pathologized. Meanwhile, proponents of the people-first approach may believe that it is important to acknowledge people as human beings first and then use other descriptors to identify unique aspects about them (especially when those descriptors are stigmatizing or dehumanizing). For instance, APA (2021) recommended saying "person without housing" instead of "homeless person," "person who is incarcerated" instead of "prisoner," and "person with a substance use disorder" instead of "addict" (p. 6). Either term is acceptable under APA guidelines, unless one knows which term is preferred by the individual or group under discussion, in which case those terms should be used and respected. For the remainder of the text, the terms PWDs and disabled people are used interchangeably.

Until recently, discussions on disabled people have focused heavily on people's impairments or pathologies—often concentrating only on disparities and less on capabilities or strengths. However, there have been moves for psychologists and other mental health practitioners to support person–environment approaches, which acknowledge that there are several external and environmental factors (that go above and beyond one's bodily capabilities) that influence people's lives (Patel & Brown, 2017; Pledger, 2003). Because of this, it is important to recognize that a disability is merely a part of a person's experience and should not be the only way that they are defined or understood.

In recent years, psychologists have defined the term *ubiquitous ableism* as "social prejudice and discrimination against disabled individuals in favor of nondisabled persons" (Andrews et al., 2021, p. 452). So, just as just as manifestations of racism (e.g., systemic racism, hate crimes, microaggressions) and sexism (e.g., systemic sexism, sexual violence, benevolent sexism, micro-aggressions) can be expressed in many ways, discrimination toward people with disabilities may also take multiple forms. While studying the ways that people with disabilities have been oppressed via systems and blatant dis-crimination every day, we discover further, covert forms of ableism too.

Related to ableism is ageism, which is defined as "prejudice against some-one based on their age" (Nelson, 2016, p. 338). While ageism can target people of any age group, most ageism-related research focuses on discrim-ination targeting older adults. An older person is older than middle age, with middle age typically referring to people whose age is between 40 and 60 years old. Yet, definitions of who is considered older vary depending on who is using such terms. For instance, various studies and public polls have described how adults over 65 years old may still consider themselves young or middle-aged, or that adults over age 65 dislike terms like "elderly," "seniors," or "old" (Pinsker, 2020). Further, APA (2021) suggested avoiding terms like "seniors" or "elderly" because such terms can be viewed as biased language that excludes or negatively differentiates the group from people of other age groups. Hence, throughout this text, the term "older adults" and "older people" are used to describe people over age 65.

Although this is understudied, there is a growing amount of literature supporting that the concept that young people may be discriminated against because of their age. One study found that young people were more likely than middle-aged and older adults to report ageism in work-related contexts and that they encountered ageism most often by coworkers (Chasteen et al., 2021). Other scholars have described how young people are often viewed as "too young and inexperienced" in workplace settings, often limiting oppor-tunities for professional growth (Macdonald & Levy, 2016, p, 173). At the same time, some scholars have described how ageism directed toward younger people can increase performance and efficacy—signifying that age discrimination toward younger people may be felt differently than toward older people (Hehman & Bugental, 2013), especially since it is likely more temporary and will minimize over time (Garstka et al., 2004).

REVIEW OF MICROAGGRESSIONS BASED ON ABILITY, SIZE, AND AGE

This section highlights the literature involving microaggressions experienced by people with disabilities, people of diverse sizes, and people of various age groups. While people of these groups may encounter unique and nuanced types of microaggressions in their lives, some common themes demonstrate how biases and discrimination stem from societal norms about people's bodies, appearances, and functioning.

Ableism

Over the past several decades, there has been a growing amount of literature that has focused on the types of institutional ableism that PWDs experience in various aspects of their lives—from the workplace to healthcare facilities (Nario-Redmond, 2019). In recent years, there has also been an increase in understanding the categories of microaggressions that disabled people encounter. First, utilizing a qualitative method, Keller and Galgay (2010) described several microaggression themes that PWDs encounter. These include (a) denial of identity (e.g., when people overemphasize one's disability, instead of perceiving the individual as a human being), (b) denial of privacy (e.g., when people ask intrusive questions about people's disabilities), (c) **desexualization** (e.g., when a PWD is automatically assumed to be asexual or not have sexual interests), (d) **patronization** (e.g., when able-bodied people tell disabled people how "heroic" they are for accomplishing minor tasks), and (e) second-class citizenship (e.g., when a PWD receives substandard or less favorable treatment, in comparison to an able-bodied person).

Using a quantitative design, Conover et al. (2017) created a measure to examine the kinds of microaggressions encountered by PWDs. Four factors emerged: (a) helplessness, or microaggressions in which disabled people are presumed to be incapable, useless, dependent, or broken; (b) minimization, or microaggressions in which people are presumed to be exaggerating their impairments or disabilities; (c) denial of personhood, or microaggressions in which people are reduced to one's physicality; and (d) otherization, or microaggressions in which people are pathologized or viewed as abnormal.

Previous microaggression literature has focused on two specific subgroups of people with disabilities. First, Gonzales et al. (2015) conducted a qualitative study to explore the sorts of microaggressions encountered by people living with severe mental illness or other psychological disorders. Through focus groups, participants shared personal instances of microaggressions; coded themes included: experiences of invalidation, being presumed to be inferior, people acting fearful due to biases about mental illness, encounters related to the shaming of mental illness, and being treated like a second-class citizen. Second, focusing on people living with HIV/AIDS (a group that is considered a protected class under the Americans With Disabilities Act of 1990), Vitiello and Nadal (2019) theorized the types of microaggressions based on **serostatus**. Reviewing previous literature on biases and discrimination toward people living with HIV/AIDS, the authors hypothesized six themes: (a) stigmatized language, (b) desexualization and dating/sex-related microaggressions, (c) dehumanization and second-class citizenship, (d) pathology of HIV/AIDS, (e) romanticizing of HIV/AIDS, and (f) criminalization of HIV/AIDS. Taken together, this existing scholarship exemplifies the many microaggressions that PWDs may face. However, using an intersectional lens, one might wonder how LGBTQ identities may exacerbate these microaggressive encounters—particularly for LGBTQ PWDs, LGBTQ older adults, and LGBTQ youth.

Sizeism

Related to ableist microaggressions are the discriminatory ways in which fat people and others who have been deemed overweight have been treated in society—also known as **sizeism** and **fatphobia**. While sizeism is a term that describes oppression toward people based on size in general, fatphobia is used to describe the biases about and discrimination enacted toward fat people and others who have been deemed overweight. Sizeism and fatphobia can manifest in institutional ways (e.g., standardized seating on airplanes or in theaters) and interpersonal ways (e.g., blatant discrimination and microaggressions).

Of note, disability-related microaggressions and fat-related microaggressions often manifest in very similar ways—especially in health care systems—due to societal notions of what is considered "normal" in society and the biases that manifest as a result.

Though sizeism has been used primarily to demonstrate prejudices against fat people and others who have been deemed overweight, it is a system of oppression that affects people of all sizes. For instance, research on people living with **dwarfism** (also known as **little people** or **LPs**) experience all sorts of systemic and interpersonal discrimination based on sizeist stereotypes (Heider et al., 2013). Further, because of societal standards of beauty, people of all genders, ages, races, sexual identities, and other groups may encounter size-related or appearance-related microaggressions—with people receiving messages about fatness, slimness, muscularity, facial disfigurement, baldness, and more (Cash & Smolak, 2011). Some groups may experience size-related microaggressions because of their intersectional identities; for instance, scholars have described that Black women of all body types experience intersectional microaggressions based on race, gender, and size (Watson et al., 2020). So, while fat people and others deemed overweight may regularly encounter microaggressions and overt forms of discrimination due to their size, skinny and slim people (and others deemed underweight) may also learn (and internalize) negative messages about their bodies too.

Further, it is important to note the challenge in finding the most appropriate or commonly used terms when describing people of various sizes. First, while the term "fat" was first used as a term of empowerment by fat activists in the late 1960s as a way of combatting the clinical terms "overweight" or "obese" (Rothblum, 2012), it is still common for people of all sizes to feel uncomfortable in using the term "fat" as a neutral descriptor. In fact, many people who fit clinical definitions of being overweight or obese have difficulty in self-identifying as fat—which can be detrimental to their own body affirmation or feelings of ingroup belonging, while also serving as protective factors against general health or self-esteem issues (Wellman et al., 2022). Accordingly, throughout this text, I use the phrase *fat people and others who have been deemed overweight* as a way of being inclusive of (a) those who self-identify as fat and (b) those who experience fatphobia but do not identify, or have difficulty in identifying, as fat. Relatedly, when describing other people who are discriminated against due to their size, I will either name the group (e.g., little people) or identify how the person is targeted by systemic sizeism.

While the field of **fat studies** has increased significantly since the 2010s (Rothblum, 2012), the literature on sizeism and fatphobia in the field of psychology remains sparse. In fact, using the PsycINFO database (an abstracting and indexing database of psychology-related literature from the 1600s to the present), a keyword search in May 2022, using the search terms "sizeism," "fatphobia," and "fat prejudice" yielded 34, 13, and 29 entries respectively. While the term "dwarfism" yielded 276 entries, only five entries included the words "discrimination," "prejudice," or "stereotypes." This lack of inclusion in literature about sizeism is presumed to mirror the lack of exposure to such topics in training programs; accordingly, many psychologists and other practitioners are not trained to examine their own biases about sizeism in general or fatphobia specifically.

As a final note on sizeism, there is a growing area of literature on sizeist or antifat microaggressions. First, Hunt and Rhodes (2018) described how fat professors experience microaggressions that communicate that they are not seen as being as smart or credible as their thin counterparts. Second, Akoury et al. (2019a) uses microaggression theory as a way of conceptualizing people's experiences with antifat discrimination. Specifically, Akoury et al. (2019b) described how fat women encounter numerous weight-based microaggressions in psychotherapy, resulting in a lack of therapeutic rapport or even distrust in psychotherapy processes. Third, Munro (2017) used microaggression theory to examine antifat biases, namely, microassaults (e.g., someone writing "No fat chicks" on their dating profile) or microinsults (e.g., asking a fat person or someone deemed overweight, "Are you sure you want to eat all of that?"). Further studies on antifat microaggressions and sizeist microaggressions in general are needed to understand the various ways in which discrimination manifests toward and detrimentally impacts these groups.

Ageism

Although ageism has been studied extensively over the past several decades, there remains a dearth of scholarship examining it through the lens of microaggressions. Despite this, previous literature on ageism can be applied to the current conceptualization of microaggressions. For instance, early theorists on ageism described concepts like malignant ageism versus benign ageism (see Nelson, 2016); the former might involve more overt dislike, resentment, or anger towards older people, whereas the latter may involve more unintentional or benevolent manifestations of bias towards older people. For instance, elder abuse (sometimes referred to as elder bashing) may be considered a malignant form of ageism, while **parentalism** (i.e., the act of asserting a parental role over someone else) or **infantilization** (i.e., the act of treating older adults or adults with disabilities as children) may be considered a form of a benign ageism (Kagan, 2017). Ubiquitous ageism may manifest both systemically (e.g., policies that do not offer resources for older people) or interpersonally (e.g., young or middle-aged people who show frustration when having to accommodate older adults). Utilizing concepts from microaggression research, malignant ageism may be considered violent or overt forms of bias, while benign ageism and ubiquitous ageism may be more aligned with microaggressions.

Some literature has examined the manifestation of ageism through microaggressions. Gendron et al. (2016) analyzed public tweets to understand how ageist language may be used online; results indicate that Twitter users implement various types of ageist language in referring to older adults, with themes such as making broad generalizations about older people, infantilization, viewing older people as different, or reducing older people to "uncharacteristic characteristics" (p. 1001), or comments in which older adults are complimented or celebrated for behaviors that are presumed to be outside the norm for older people. An example may include seeing an older relative and patronizingly saying, "You're looking alive and well" or "Look at you, still being able to drive and go grocery shopping!").

Gordon (2020) examined how age-related microaggressions may occur in families, particularly when discussing the care of older adults; the author cited that there were differences between sharing a concern about an older family member (a comment that considers a person's well-being and functioning as well as potential actions or assistance), while a microaggression may involve an opinion that has little or no positive benefit to the older family member. Both authors described how biases toward older adults are embedded in greater societal discrimination toward older people, as well as the biases people develop accordingly.

Intersectionalities

Finally, a few scholars have examined the types of intersectional microaggressions experienced by LGBTQ people based on their age, size, ability status, or more. First, Miller and Smith (2020) conducted a qualitative study with 25 queer or trans people disabled people and found that participants were able to identify both anti-LGBTQ microaggressions and ableist microaggressions as described in previous literature (e.g., Gonzales et al., 2015; Keller & Galgay, 2010; Nadal et al., 2010). One main finding was that participants were able to easily identify microaggressions based on their LGBTQ identities or their disabled identities; however, participants had difficulty providing examples of microaggressions based on both identities. Second, using a queer narratives approach, Davies and Neustifter (2021) described how their various identities as queer, nonbinary, neurodiverse, or fat influence how they are treated as faculty members in academia; they cite themes related to invisibility and queer relationality (i.e., the cultivation of relations and connections that are necessary for queer people to survive or thrive against microaggressions and systemic oppression). Finally, Kum (2017) examined how LGBTQ older adults of color encounter myriad forms of discrimination—from systemic oppression in health care settings to microaggressions—because of their interlocking identities related to race, age, and sexual orientation.

SYSTEMIC OPPRESSION AND THE COVID-19 PANDEMIC

In addition to the microaggressions (or interpersonal forms of discrimination) people face based on their ability, size, and age, these groups also continue to encounter institutional and systemic discrimination. As an example, the COVID-19 pandemic, which began in 2020, demonstrates some of the systemic barriers still faced by disabled people, fat people or others deemed overweight, and older adults. First, at the onset of the pandemic, a limited number of ventilators or critical care units meant some hospitals made decisions about triaging patients and rationing the use of equipment for those who were expected to have a better chance of surviving (Andrews et al., 2021; Wong, 2020). In these ways, many groups (e.g., PWDs, older adults) feared that they were deemed expendable and that their lives would be valued less if they were to seek hospital care during the pandemic. Alice Wong (2020) wrote,

> Were I to contract coronavirus, I imagine a doctor might read my chart, look at me, and think I'm a waste of their efforts and precious resources that never should have been in shortage to begin with. He might even take my ventilator for other patients who have a better shot at survival than me. (p. 8)

Further, many able-bodied people became vocal about not wanting to comply with best practices (e.g., social distancing, wearing masks) because they did not fear death or illness upon contracting the virus; they also pushed for "reopening" because only older adults, disabled, or chronically ill people are at risk for COVID-19 (Denk, 2020: Monahan et al., 2020). Similarly, when it became known that obesity was a risk factor for mortality for COVID-19, biases against fat people and others deemed overweight became more rampant (Pearl & Schulte, 2021).

Specific to older adults, the COVID-19 pandemic revealed long-term inadequacies affecting older adults—particularly those from lower socioeconomic backgrounds or communities of color. Such systemic and institutional problems ranged from barriers and discrimination in the health care industry (e.g., ageism in triage protocol) to common discriminatory employment practices (Monahan et al., 2020). In fact, the hashtag #BoomerRemover went viral on social media—indicating that people were less empathetic about older adults contracting the virus, especially if it meant inconveniencing themselves (Monahan et al., 2020). The notion that certain groups of humans (e.g., PWDs, older adults, fat people and others deemed overweight) were deemed disposable or expendable—and the fact that such discourse was public and overt—demonstrates the pervasiveness and ubiquity of oppressions like ableism, fatphobia, and ageism in U.S. society.

Youth or young people were another subgroup that was found to be negatively impacted by the COVID-19 pandemic. In general, studies found that mental health disparities increased significantly for youth during the pandemic, with prevalence rates of depression and suicidal ideation higher than any other time in recent history (Hill et al., 2021; Loades et al., 2020). Certain subgroups of youth that reportedly exhibited more difficulties at the onset of the COVID-19 pandemic included children living with disabilities and families experiencing high levels of conflict (Gabrielli & Lund, 2020). Many scholars described how mental health issues were more prevalent for numerous reasons, including the social isolation from one's friends and support groups, the stressors involved in switching to online or virtual classes, economic issues that arose from not being able to work, and the conflicts that arose from being in isolation with one's family.

Further, recent studies found that LGBTQ youth (particularly transgender and nonbinary youth) had significant increases in mental health issues (especially suicidal ideation) during the pandemic, particularly if they reported having unsupportive families (Gonzales et al., 2020; Hawke et al., 2021; Salerno et al., 2020). So, while youth in general were susceptible to a plethora of psychological stressors because of the COVID-19 pandemic, LGBTQ youth were at even higher risk—especially if they were forced to quarantine or shelter in place with family members who did not know about their gender identities or sexual orientations and were unable to connect with people who were affirming of their identities (Gonzales et al., 2020).

VOICES OF LGBTQ DISABLED PEOPLE AND LGBTQ PEOPLE OF DIVERSE SIZES

In this section, I include a few themes that have emerged in narratives from LGBTQ people with various disabilities, including LGBTQ individuals who use wheelchairs for mobility, are blind or deaf, have cognitive or developmental impairments, or who live with chronic illness. Because the literature on LGBTQ people of various sizes—such as fat people and others deemed overweight, as well as little people—reveals such similar themes as LGBTQ people with disabilities, I include their narratives in this section too. The notion that both groups encounter such similar types of microaggressions demonstrates how uncomfortable people are with those who are considered "abnormal" or "different" from those who are considered "normal" or "standard."

Where there are still very few representations of LGBTQ PWDs in the media and general society altogether (Guter & Killacky, 2014), there has been an increase in academic literature that has examined how microaggressions affect LGBTQ people with disabilities. For instance, Dispenza et al. (2018) highlighted the status of queer and trans people living with disabilities—citing how LGBTQ people are more likely to report a disability than non-LGBTQ people. Other studies have examined how LGBTQ disabled people perceive their own health (Dispenza, Harper, & Harrigan, 2016), as well as how rehabilitation counselors approach their work with LGBTQ PWDs (Dispenza, Viehl et al., 2016). Several studies (e.g., Dinwoodie et al., 2020; Hunter et al., 2020) examined how LGBTQ PWDs were able to navigate discrimination, develop positive disability and sexual identities, and increase resilience throughout their lives. Meanwhile, the representations of or conversations about LGBTQ people of diverse sizes remain minimal in academic writings, mainstream media, educational systems, and even within LGBTQ spaces.

Before delving further, it is important to acknowledge that the few pieces of literature that do focus on this intersectionality among LGBTQ people still tend to concentrate on gay men and lesbian women who are predominantly white and cisgender. In other cases, literature tends to omit discussions about gender identity or race altogether—promoting false notions of a monolithic umbrella LGBTQ community (even when exploring specific subgroups like LGBTQ people with disabilities or LGBTQ people of size). Thus, I must reemphasize that the following examples are limited and much more literature (empirical and theoretical) needs to emerge in the future so that the experiences of queer and trans PWDs are better understood.

Exclusion Within LGBTQ Community Spaces

Like other marginalized subgroups within the LGBTQ umbrella, it is evident that LGBTQ disabled people and LGBTQ people of diverse sizes may feel excluded by their privileged counterparts. One physical way this may manifest is through the lack of accessibility in LGBTQ spaces; for instance, many LGBTQ bars and clubs do not have accessible doors or ramps (Dispenza et al., 2018), physically preventing LGBTQ PWDs from entering the facility. However, there are some more metaphorical ways that people feel excluded from the community. For example, one gay man with an intellectual disability shared about the difficulty in dating within LGBTQ community: "When you've got a disability, they don't want to know you because they think it's wrong" (Dinwoodie et al., 2020, p. 9). Deaf queer people shared similar sentiments, with participants in one study divulging: "I don't state that I am Deaf in my profile because I have noticed that when I do, people do not want to talk to me," and "If I am direct and tell them up front that I am Deaf, they will block me on the apps" (Cheslik & Wright, 2021, p. 1031). In another study, a deaf participant stated: "Hearing people sometimes view Deaf culture with disdain and have no respect and understanding. They don't like our culture or are not able to fully appreciate it" (Sinecka, 2008, p. 481). Through these perspectives, feeling rejected results in feeling less community with other LGBTQ people as well as feelings of hurt or isolation.

Fat LGBTQ people and others deemed overweight have described the ways that they have been excluded in LGBTQ communities. One mixed-method study focusing on **body image** among gay men found that men of all sizes reported **antifat biases**, but that men who were overweight or obese experienced these most frequently (Foster-Gimbel & Engeln, 2016). In the study, the most common form of antifat bias was rejection by a potential sexual or romantic partner due to size. Participants reported microaggressions that were blatant (e.g., "This attractive but overweight man had bought a younger and thin man a drink. The younger man had returned the drink and told him that he didn't accept drinks from fatties"; Foster-Gimbel & Engeln, 2016, p. 66) to subtle (e.g., "At a bar I saw an overweight guy get rejected immediately by a much thinner guy. As the guy walked away, the thinner guy started laughing with his friends at the bar"; p. 66). Some participants shared personal scenarios, with one gay man sharing: "At a gay bar I tried to hit on a guy, and he ignored me. When I tried talking to him, he told me I was not his type and walked away" (p. 66). While the perpetrator did not explicitly reject the speaker due to his size, the speaker deduced that weight was the main reason. With research finding that eating disorders and other body image issues are rampant among LGBTQ people (Chow, 2021; Parker & Harriger, 2020), future research can further investigate how antifat microaggressions contribute to this disparity.

In one interview, a self-identified gay dwarf drag performer revealed the bigotry he experienced from both sides—homophobia from his little people community and sizeism from his LGBTQ community (Chester, 2015). Specific to other LGBTQ people, he divulged being bullied by other gay kids during his high school years and his reactions to standards of beauty imposed by LGBTQ media during his adult years:

> When I was in high school, I would get bullied by the Gay–Straight Alliance members. They would constantly be on me, trying to make sure that I fit impossible standards because they thought I embarrassed all the gay kids at that school. I think it was because I was obviously different and they wanted to be seen as regular people. (para. 4)

Finally, LGBTQ people living with HIV/AIDS are one subgroup that has described discrimination or exclusion within the general LGBTQ community.

Vitiello and Nadal (2019) reviewed the various ways that people living with HIV/AIDS might be discriminated against, ranging from people who still stigmatize HIV/AIDS to people who criminalize those with HIV/AIDS. For instance, a gay man described how his serostatus has affected his dating behaviors:

> I'm HIV positive and it scares me. Like, I won't date a negative guy. I won't even go near negative guys because I'm afraid, like, that if I have a bad breakup, he's gonna say to the police that I assaulted him with a deadly weapon. (Nadal, Quintanilla et al., 2015, p. 472)

Sometimes biases against LGBTQ people living with HIV/AIDS may manifest in more subtle ways (e.g., using "clean" to describe people who are HIV-negative; Vitiello & Nadal, 2019) as well as more systemic ways (e.g., men who have sex with men not being allowed to donate blood unless they are celibate).

Microaggressions in Health Care and Rehabilitation Settings

Among PWDs and LGBTQ fat people and others deemed overweight—especially those who are in frequent contact with health care and rehabilitation settings—some have reported feeling targeted because of their sexual orientation or gender identity. In a study focusing on lesbians with disabilities who go to rehabilitation therapy (Hunt et al., 2009), participants described how discrimination is subtle but still felt. For example, one woman reported: "There wasn't a lot of really blatant, you know, 'We don't like dykes and get out of our hospital' kind of stuff, but there was a clear sort of criticalness of people's expressions and lack of understanding through that" (Hunt et al., 2009, p. 174). Another woman shared how health care workers reacted after discovering her sexual orientation: "Then when they figure it out, you can sort of see the looks, you can see the level of uncomfortability" (p. 174).

In a more recent study (Dinwoodie et al., 2020), a gay man with an intellectual disability described reactions from health care workers upon learning about his sexuality:

> People look at me as if I am some sort of a monster and I know I am not. I know I am not. . . . It feels as if I actually come from another planet, it's as if I don't belong on Earth anymore. (p. 9)

In another recent study (Hunter et al., 2020), a queer white woman with a disability described how her parents learned that she was in a relationship and threatened to cut off providing her care:

> I can't be in a relationship or do any of these things because I do need help, and I must choose. What do you choose? Do you choose being happy in a

fulfilling relationship with someone you really care about, or do you choose being able to physically survive, to live? (p. 37)

While both examples demonstrate heterosexist biases by caretakers, the latter scenario depicts the abusive and manipulative behaviors PWDs and older adults encounter from their caretakers.

Sometimes health care workers may create a heterosexist environment that prohibits LGBTQ people from feeling comfortable in expressing their sexual identities. In a different study that focused on lesbians with disabilities (Hunt et al., 2006), one participant described her perceptions of the heterosexist biases of health care workers:

> There was some level of uncomfortability definitely in the psych hospital because when my partner would come and visit, we were the only couple there that was gay, and people would stare. . . . The staff, they just didn't really want to talk about it. They were more into straight people who've got kids and were married. (p. 169)

Similarly, another lesbian with a disability in the same study described:

> And, uh, it's just that sort of atmosphere where if I had said anything when we were talking about family members and husbands and wives or their lack of understanding or whatever the effect on them, I could never, ever have brought . . . [my partner] up. (p. 174)

Finally, many LGBTQ people with disabilities described how health care workers normalized heterosexuality through their presumptions and behaviors. For instance, one lesbian described a scenario that occurred with a physician: "He asked if she was my sister, and [my partner] didn't feel comfortable, so she interjected that she was a friend . . . We didn't feel free to put it out there." (Hunt et al., 2009, p. 175). In Chapter 3, this volume, this type of microaggression was described as a "endorsement of heteronormative culture and behaviors"; for example, asking a woman. "Do you have a husband and children?" assumes that she would be heterosexual and interested in raising children. Nonetheless, all these examples point to the need for health care workers to become more culturally competent when working with LGBTQ people, particularly with LGBTQ PWDs. While health care workers (particularly those involved in rehabilitation therapy) are taught to be compassionate and competent in working with PWDs, they must also be compassionate and competent in relation to their sexual identities.

One sizeist microaggression experienced in health care facilities revolves around weight and body image. Many studies have described how sexual minority cis women (e.g., lesbians, bisexual women, queer women) and trans men tend to have higher body mass indexes (BMIs) than cis heterosexual women (McPhail & Bombak, 2015). As a result, many queer women and trans men are presumed to be "high risk"; they are also stigmatized in health care settings, particularly when they are fat or deemed overweight (McPhail & Bombak, 2015; Paine, 2021). A queer fat white cis woman said:

> I do realize if I lost weight, I'd have less knee pain. I'm not oblivious to what's going on with my body, but . . . certain things are not directly related to being a fat person. And those health concerns should also be valid. For me as a fat person being in a doctor's office, seeing at what point that gets brought up and to what extent and how far it gets pushed makes you wonder, sort of gauge the quality of care you might anticipate. (Paine, 2021, p. 3)

Similarly, a Black trans man shared his perspective on going for health care visits:

> Everything is about being fat. I never got diagnosed with diabetes, because people always just chalked it up to me being fat. They were like, "Well, have you tried not being fat?" And so, you know, there are probably articles out there about trans broken arm syndrome as they call it—fat people have the same experience, if not amplified, depending on their level of fatness. (Paine, 2021, p. 4)

The fatphobia that manifests in medical facilities—coupled with the heterosexism or transphobia LGBTQ people face—may be reasons why many trans and queer people do not trust the medical or healthcare industry, potentially resulting in further health disparities for these communities (McPhail & Bombak, 2015; Paine, 2021).

Desexualization and Exoticization

LGBTQ PWDs, much like their heterosexual counterparts, may also be viewed or treated as asexual beings, deemed as sexually unattractive, or denied the opportunity to be sexually active beings. Being excluded in this way may feel distressing because LGBTQ PWDs can be (and feel) just as sexual as their able-bodied counterparts. Furthermore, when LGBTQ PWDs are desexualized, they may feel even more isolated and distant from the general LGBTQ community. Ryan O'Connor—creator and star of the television show *Special* (as well as a gay man living with cerebral palsy) described how PWDs have been desexualized in the media. In a 2021 interview, he proclaimed: "Society had castrated disabled people . . . It [is] really important that we don't shy away from that, that we give them sexual agency and desire and humanity" (Roppolo, 2021, para. 2). Because of this societal stigma, the show attempts to counter the narrative by displaying the many sexual situations that Ryan (a gay man with cerebral palsy) finds himself in as well as the numerous microaggressions that the protagonist faces in each episode.

Similarly, LGBTQ fat people and others deemed overweight report experiencing romantic rejections within LGBTQ community spaces. For example, when gay men are rejected by thin men in bar settings (Foster-Gimbel & Engeln, 2016), it may lead to feelings of exclusion in general LGBTQ community spaces, while also making them question their own sexual attractiveness or sexual worth. Similarly, one study on queer fat femme women revealed similar results, with women reporting experiences of both sexual rejection and fetishization, which led to feelings of undesirability and failure (Taylor, 2022). When only slim or muscular bodies are promoted as sexual symbols within both mainstream and LGBTQ communities, LGBTQ fat people and others deemed overweight may internalize negative messages about their own bodies and their views of themselves as sexual beings. As an example, in the Tony-award winning musical *A Strange Loop*, the protagonist (a fat, Black, gay man) engages the audience in consistent self-loathing dialogues, involving the multiple negative messages he internalized about anti-Blackness, homophobia, and fatphobia (Oladipo, 2022).

For people with cognitive or developmental disabilities, sexuality is something that is often avoided altogether, particularly when same-sex sexual acts are involved. For instance, in a study that examined perceptions of health care staff who work with people with developmental disabilities, one participant described how the institution dealt with two men who were found having sex: "The local day center found a couple having sex in the shed and guess what the day center did to deal with the problem? They took down the shed. I think that says it all, doesn't it?" (Abbott & Howarth, 2007, p. 119). While it is possible that the institution is uncomfortable when any of their patients with developmental disabilities have sex, there is a possibility that they are especially uncomfortable when a person with a developmental disability identifies as LGBTQ or engages in same-sex sexual acts. Thus, such an instance could be considered an intersectional microaggression because it is based on both disability and sexual orientation.

One notable court case that demonstrates the biases that may occur due to the intersection of developmental disabilities and sexual orientation is the trial of Matthew Limon. In 2000, Limon, an 18-year-old with a developmental disability was sentenced to 17 years in prison for engaging in a sexual act with a 14-year-old boy who also had a developmental disability (Higdon, 2009). Both residents at a mental health facility, the boys were said to have verbally agreed upon the sexual act and to be sexually experimenting. Because Limon had just turned 18 years old the week prior to the act (and therefore was legally an adult), he was arrested for statutory rape. Typically, if an adult under 19 years old engages in sex with a minor who is 3 or 4 years younger than themselves, they are likely to receive shorter prison terms due to a legal clause that has been deemed the "Romeo and Juliet" exceptions. However, because Limon's case involved two people with developmental disabilities engaged in a same-sex sexual act, the court was not forgiving of him (Higdon, 2009).

Contrary to desexualization is the notion of tokenism or exoticization—or the notion of people being dehumanized or objectified because of one of their identity groups. For PWDs, Keller and Galgay (2010) referred to these types of microaggressions as *patronization*. In American slang, this category of microaggressions has also been referred to as "inspiration porn" (Grue, 2016), which has been defined as "the representation of disability as a desirable but undesired characteristic, usually by showing impairment as a visually or symbolically distinct biophysical deficit in one person, a deficit that can and must be overcome through the display of physical prowess" (p. 838). When a PWD is told they are "brave" or "inspiring" for doing mundane tasks, the intention might be benevolent, but the interaction feels patronizing or condescending.

For LGBTQ PWDs, exoticization/patronization microaggressions may manifest through dating or romantic relationships, with some LGBTQ PWDs divulging interactions in which they felt fetishized. For instance, one queer Deaf man shared:

> I had an experience with one guy who asked me if I knew these other Deaf guys after I disclosed my status to him. He had already slept with them. He loved sleeping with Deaf guys and felt that they were better in bed. . . . It seems that there is a Deaf fetish out there. People want to sleep with Deaf people. (Cheslik & Wright, 2021, p. 1034)

LGBTQ people living with dwarfism have also described these feelings of exoticization or sexual tokenism. In an interview, a gay man living with dwarfism mentioned: "There are people that contact me for fetishes, like, 'Oh my god, I always wanted to try a little guy'" (Juzwiak, 2015).

A final example of this oversexualization or sexual exoticization occurred on the television show *Special*. The protagonist Ryan meets a **neurotypical** actor who is enamored with him; when they finally have sex, he makes objectifying comments about Ryan's body and disability—making Ryan feel tokenized, dehumanized, and used.

ENVIRONMENTAL MICROAGGRESSIONS

While there are many interpersonal microaggressions that PWDs may face regularly, it is evident that there are several environmental microaggressions that may have a negative influence on their everyday lives. Wheelchair access may be a huge obstacle for many individuals with disabilities and may result in them feeling excluded in general society but also within general LGBTQ community spaces. One lesbian living with visual impairment wrote about her feelings about the ableism that she perceived in her workplace, especially when she tried to include her partner, who also lives with a disability:

> My partner uses a wheelchair for mobility, and this added another level of complexity to the social aspects of the organizational environment. For example, departmental celebrations and events that included significant others were often hosted in inaccessible environments. The failure to attend to additional disability-related accessibility issues resulted in an air of exclusion. (Wiebold, 2005, p. 133)

A Black lesbian said, "When I am in queer spaces, they are usually inaccessible. If the space is physically accessible, I get stared at and asked, 'Why are you here?'" (Hunter et al., 2020, p. 36). Another major environmental microaggression that may occur for LGBTQ PWDs involves health care. One lesbian with a disability described a situation she and her partner had had when same-sex marriage was not legal yet:

> To fill out my disability forms, [my partner] could help me, but she couldn't go seek out my info. No one would give it to her, so I had to go. . . . It would have been great to say: "Here, go get me that information." (Hunt et al., 2009, p. 175)

A final environmental microaggression that LGBTQ PWDs may experience is invisibility. One of the reasons why this community goes unnoticed is because both of their identities (i.e., as LGBTQ people and PWDs) tend to be overlooked in our heterosexist and ableist society. In a collection called *Queer Crips: Disabled Gay Men and Their Stories* (Guter & Killacky, 2014), the editors gathered short stories, poetry, and other writings to share the intersectional identities of those who are "queer" (i.e., gay, bisexual, transgender) and "crip" (i.e., with a disability). In their introduction, they described the need for the stories of LGBTQ PWDs to be told:

> As queer crips, we've been isolated from society at large and even from one another, by under-employment, institutionalization, poverty, and internalized cripophobia. All these factors have not merely discouraged us from telling our stories, they have brainwashed us into believing we have no stories to tell. . . . Fearing we are wordless; it becomes easy for us to believe we are worthless. (p. xviii)

When LGBTQ PWDs are invisible in the media (and society in general), many people from this community may feel invalidated and isolated, which may in turn have a negative effect on their mental health and self-esteem.

MICROAGGRESSIONS BASED ON DISABILITY, SIZE, AND/OR SEXUAL IDENTITY

As with the other intersectional identities presented in the previous chapter, some microaggressions may be influenced by both one's disability and one's sexual identity. In these situations, the offender's behavior may be due to the person's disability, sexual orientation or gender identity, or some combination of both. Such a sentiment can be exemplified by a Black bisexual woman with a disability, who shared the following:

> In college, I initially identified as a lesbian. I remember someone remarking, "She's Black, so she already has a strike against her. She's a woman, so she has another strike against her, and she has a disability, so that's yet another strike against her. Why would she want to be a lesbian?" (Hunter et al., 2020, p. 36)

A trans/nonbinary PWD described how disability and gender affects how people treat them:

> Because I'm a wheelchair user, people see me as incapable of having a gender identity, so often they will correctly avoid using gendered language or pronouns to refer to me, but it's not because they're recognizing and respecting my identity as a nonbinary person (i.e., male or female)—it's because they think my wheelchair automatically makes me genderless. (Timmons, 2021, p. 258)

In these sorts of situations, the behavior of the perpetrator is subtle and indirect, in that they may not intentionally say anything hurtful, overtly transphobic, or overtly ableist. However, the speaker picks up on the discomfort (and meaning by the avoidant behavior), which still results in their feelings of dehumanization.

In a performance piece, one author wrote about something a woman said to him as a gay white man with a disability:

> You have to understand that the choice that you have made in your life is a sin. Your body is crippled, because it is crippled with sin. Don't you see? If you go to church God will help you. God can heal you. God gave you a disability, because he knew that you were going to be gay. Now don't take offense at what I'm saying. (Walloch, 2014, p. 3)

While the comment is clearly biased and hurtful, this type of statement may be considered a microaggression, particularly because the woman asks him to not "take offense" at what she was saying. She may genuinely believe that her comment would be helpful for the speaker and that she was helping him to find God and "cure" him. This example also demonstrates an intersectional microaggression, in that her bias is based on both his disability and his sexual orientation.

A gay, deaf young man described how both of his identities negatively affected his relationship with his father:

> My father did not care, I don't remember him trying to educate me or bring me up. He could not cope with the fact that first, I am Deaf, and second, that I am gay. . . . My dad does not accept that I am gay, just does not accept it! (Sinecka, 2008, p. 480)

In this case, it appears that the narrator's father already had such a difficult time with his son's deafness that their relationship became even more strained when he came out of the closet too.

Finally, people with intersectional identities report feeling not fully understood or accepted because others cannot grasp both identities. One butch, fat, nonbinary person described the following:

> While I would still face many obstacles, I have no doubt that my queerness would be more recognized and respected if I were thin and fashionable, instead of fat, muscular, visually disruptive, and butch. (Davies & Neustifter, 2021, p. 12)

Relatedly, in a study with lesbians with disabilities (Hunt et al., 2006), participants described how some counselors "get it" and some do not:

> Gay professionals that I tried to go to cared about the disability and stuff and had never done their own work on that, so I couldn't go to them, and straight

FIGURE 6.2. A Same Gender Loving Black Man in Los Angeles

Note. Photo courtesy of Rodnae Productions.

people couldn't deal with the lesbian thing. I've never found anybody who could get the lesbian and the disability pieces together. (p. 169)

Another woman in the study stated, "Talking about disability was not something they were comfortable with and my treatment modalities . . . I mean I sensed that immediately and then talking about being lesbian was secondly [their] least [favorite topic]" (Hunt et al., 2006, p. 169). In these cases, both participants perceived that their counselors were uncomfortable in addressing sexuality and disability. When clients in therapy have to worry about their counselors' biases about their social identities, they may feel invalidated and find it difficult to build a rapport with their therapists. They may also leave treatment altogether, which means that the reason that they went to therapy (e.g., depression, anxiety) would remain unaddressed.

VOICES OF LGBTQ OLDER ADULTS

To understand LGBTQ older adults, it would be helpful to recognize who this category refers to, as well as some of their common, general experiences. First, despite the lack of official data collected via the U.S. Census, it is estimated that in 2020 there were at least 2.75 million LGBTQ older adults (over age 60) in the United States (Burton et al., 2020). However, other community reports estimate that there are potentially 4 million LGBTQ older adults in the United States and that there will be a growth of up to 5 million LGBTQ older adults by 2030 (Choi & Meyer, 2016). In recent years, there has been an increase in literature on LGBTQ older adults, describing a range of sociocultural issues they may face (Chan & Silverio, 2021). One major issue includes living in isolation; it has been reported that three fourths of this population live alone (Adelman et al., 2006) and are less likely to have adult children or other family members to care for them during times of illness (de Vries, 2009). Other issues include mistreatment in health care settings, with fears of discrimination, stigma, and traumatization by medical staff (Burton et al., 2020). Further, LGBTQ older adults are likely to report more health disparities, mental distress, disabilities or impairments, financial stressors, or housing issues than cisgender, heterosexual older adults (Chan & Silverio, 2021; Czaja et al., 2016). The dual minority status of being an LGBTQ person and an older adult can lead to three types of discrimination: (a) ageism within the general LGBTQ community, (b) heterosexism and transphobia within the older adult community, and (c) discrimination based on dual or multiple identities that they could feel throughout general society.

Ageism Within LGBTQ Communities

While ageism may exist throughout various sectors of society, it may play a unique role within LGBTQ communities—creating divides between (a) queer and trans people who are older and (b) queer and trans people who are younger. Youth is promoted in almost every aspect of that general LGBTQ community, particularly through norms of social behaviors and standards of beauty. Gay bars and clubs are frequent gathering places for many LGBTQ people, including LGBTQ middle-aged adults and older adults (Wight et al., 2015), often contributing to a party culture of binge drinking (Wong et al., 2008) and substance abuse (Theodore et al., 2014). Some researchers have examined the notion of accelerated aging among LGBTQ people and, specifically, gay men, citing that many gay men feel "that they are old even when they are relatively young because youth and physical attractiveness are disproportionately valued in the gay male community" (Wight et al., 2015, p. 201).

Related to aging is the idea of the notion of body image, or the internalized feelings that people may have about their physical appearances. Within communities of gay, bisexual, and queer men, there is also emphasis on a "gay muscled body" as the ideal body image (Chow, 2021, p. 1), and the subsequent "gym culture" it creates—which typically consists of "excessive dieting, meal supplementation and exercising limits" (Chow, 2021, p. 12). Such pressures may contribute to queer men feeling pressured to be or appear younger—which may contribute to the normalization of both ableism and ageism within general gay male communities. In fact, research has consistently revealed that gay men and gay adolescent boys were more likely than their heterosexual counterparts to report clinical eating disorders (Parker & Harriger, 2020).

Age influences standards of beauty for other LGBTQ communities as well. First, according to objectification theory, which purports that "women's life experiences and gender socialization routinely include experiences of sexual objectification" (Moradi & Huang, 2008, p. 377), women of all sexual orientations and gender identities would internalize the notions of body surveillance and body comparison (Moradi & Huang, 2008; Sevelius, 2013). In other words, because society has put such an emphasis on sexualizing or objectifying women's bodies, women may learn that they must always be aware of what their bodies look like and that they may feel compelled to compare their bodies to others. Such pressures may be felt even more with age, as exemplified by a 41-year-old bisexual woman's narrative:

> I'm 41 and newly single, with two kids who I nursed for a long time, so my breasts sag. Recently I was in a hot tub with a male friend and his roommate.

My female roommate was there, too. She's a lot younger than me, and her breasts don't sag. It was the first time that I picked up the feeling that aging breasts are not attractive. I am also aware that I don't think a woman would be as concerned with how my breasts look as men are. . . . I realize that now I'm going to have to deal with what getting older means for my body image. (Orndorff, 1999, p. 65)

While body image issues are prevalent for women of all sexual orientations, some studies have found that lesbian, bisexual, and queer women may engage in more restrictive eating and other disordered eating behaviors, such as bingeing, purging, or using laxatives (Parker & Harriger, 2020). However, further research directions may include examining how these behaviors may change or remain the same over the lifespan.

Transgender women (especially trans women of color) have described the pressures they may feel because of the standards of beauty they have internalized—typically based on cisgender and white norms (Sevelius, 2013). Further, with the tendency to "constantly monitor and compare their body to that of other trans and non-trans women," trans women are particularly at risk for "engaging in risky body modification procedures, such as street hormone use and injection silicone use" (Sevelius, 2013, p. 686). More recent research has found that transgender and nonbinary people were more likely to engage in disordered eating than their cisgender counterparts (Parker & Harriger, 2020); further research would be needed to understand how this may affect aging processes.

Age may also influence whether trans or queer people may continue with certain behaviors that were deemed more enjoyable or common when they were younger. For instance, one trans woman sex worker stated,

It's not like before, it's not like I enjoy doing [sex work] now. And each day that passes by I'm trying to walk away from it because I'm getting older and I don't know, I think I value myself a little more now. (Nadal, Vargas, et al., 2012, p. 140)

While it may be that the participant has grown tired of the sex work, one may wonder how her age or perception of her appearance may affect whether she continues to succeed as a sex worker.

While ageism exists in the heterosexual community, such microaggressions can be particularly hurtful to an LGBTQ person who at one point may have felt so connected and involved in the general LGBTQ community. Many of these LGBTQ elders were at the forefront of the Stonewall Uprisings or the forming of the Castro in the 1960s. They have been arrested, harassed, and beaten for standing up for their beliefs. They watched their friends die in the name of civil rights. Thus, being isolated and excluded by LGBTQ younger people can be especially distressful for LGBTQ older adults who fought for many rights that LGBTQ youth and young adults benefit from today.

Ageism Within Retirement Homes and Other Health Care Settings

LGBTQ older adults may face both overt and covert discrimination in nursing homes and other health care settings. First, some scholarship has examined how some LGBTQ older adults report "going back into the closet" (Kum, 2017, p. 232), out of a fear of being mistreated by caregivers in nursing homes, hospitals, or other settings. In one study that focused on LGBTQ senior citizens and their perceptions of the health care system (Stein et al., 2010), several participants described the discrimination that they fear. One participant shared, "I have to think very carefully about the possible repercussions when I let each doctor know, because I have been discriminated against and worse" (p. 429). Another participant added,

> I'm afraid to have a stranger in my home, someone who may be very anti-gay, and then what if they find out about my life and now, they're in my home regularly, and could somehow take advantage or mistreat me. (p. 429)

Because of this fear of being discriminated against (either blatantly or covertly), many LGBTQ senior citizens may prefer to be isolated or alone. For example, one senior said, "I feel I'd be better off home and alone than feeling humiliated by other residents or even worse, the people I'd depend on for my health care, my medicine" (Stein et al., 2010, p. 429).

Transgender older adults may encounter even more disparities than their cisgender queer counterparts, with one study finding significantly more health disparities, disabilities, depressive symptoms, and psychological stress (Fredriksen-Goldsen et al., 2015). Another study found that trans older adults were more likely to have difficulty accessing health services or to experience victimization by health care services than were queer cisgender adults (Fredriksen-Goldsen et al., 2014). One trans older person describes their fear of getting older and having to live in a nursing home: "My worst fear is being physically mistreated or neglected, ridiculed, discounted, marginalized, ignored" (Witten, 2016, p. 110). Another trans person shared how they had been treated by medical professionals in the past, which affected their fears of how they will be treated in a home as they age or potentially develop dementia:

> I know with pretty fair certainty I don't ever want to be in a position where I am dependent on medical staff for my care. I have been asked to leave doctor's offices because I am trans. They plead ignorance over minor issues related to my care and I've been treated like an animal in the zoo. My old gynecologist

asked whether or not she could show me to the staff. Also, even minor problems like muscle pulls get blamed on my "situation." (Witten, 2016, p. 115)

This example illustrates how the mistreatment of trans people in health care affects their trust of health care systems—even affecting their willingness to seek help when they need it most.

Ageist Microaggressions Based on Multiple Identities

Being discriminated against because of one's age as well as one's sexual identity or gender identity is a reality for many LGBTQ older adults. Such incidents may be influenced by other identities such as race or social class. As an example, LGBTQ people of color may also undergo additional minority stress in older ages. Some studies report that LGBTQ older adults of color may be at higher risk for victimization or maltreatment (Gardner et al., 2014; Kum, 2017), reinforcing that individuals who hold more marginalized identities are more susceptible to victimization or discrimination or may have poorer life outcomes.

Relatedly, older queer or trans people of color may be targeted by even more discrimination within youth-centered and white-centered LGBTQ spaces due to their age and race. In a study on older Black lesbians and gay men (Woody, 2014), one older Black lesbian said:

> What I find is like being placated because you are older. I have to say things two and three times, not because they don't hear me, but because they don't see me. It's like I've become invisible or something. When I was younger, like even 10 years ago, I would say what I needed to say, and people would hear me. And now I have to raise myself and my voice to be heard [she sits straight in her chair to demonstrate]. Because they see my gray hair or see me walking slowly. It's like I don't know anything (p. 156).

A gay Black man in the study shared a similar sentiment:

> What happens sometimes is again a feeling of isolation and loneliness of clearly being the only Black sometimes in a group is not always comfortable. For example, I've been going to [redacted] meetings and sometimes I'm the only Black person there. It just feels weird because whenever they want diversity, it's me, or they expect me to identify some others for them. I am a token Black person. (p. 157)

So, while exclusion based on age can already be a daunting process for LGBTQ older adults, being discriminated against or tokenized due to multiple identities can be even more distressing.

Further, when people do not have resources when they are older (or have disabilities), their risk increases for socioeconomic issues like homelessness or poverty. For instance, one trans participant worried "that I will become a bag lady living on the street, unable to afford or access testosterone" (Witten, 2016, p. 114). Such a fear is a reality for many trans older adults who may have many additional obstacles to worry about than cisgender (heterosexual or queer) older people. Not only might they face discrimination based on heterosexism in health care settings and ageism in LGBTQ communities, but they must also be concerned about how they can keep up their hormone treatment or how they can deal with discrimination when care workers do not know about their gender identity. Either way, as the LGBTQ population grows over time, more research and advocacy efforts are necessary to best serve LGBTQ older adults.

VOICES OF LGBTQ YOUTH

The last subgroup to be covered in this chapter is LGBTQ youth. In recent years, there has been an increase in literature that has examined LGBTQ youth experiences—citing that LGBTQ youth are more likely than their cisgender, heterosexual counterparts to be homeless, to be involved in the criminal justice or child welfare system, to report mental health issues, and to use and abuse substances (see Torre & Avory, 2021, for a review). Previous studies have also supported that LGBTQ young people may face many of the same sorts of microaggressions that have been illustrated throughout the text (Munro et al., 2019; Nadal, Issa, et al., 2011). Particularly, they may encounter bullying in their school systems and microaggressions within their families, but they may also be victimized by microaggressions because of the intersection of their age and their sexual orientation (Kosciw et al., 2020; McCabe et al., 2013). GLSEN, formerly the Gay Lesbian Straight Education Network (Kosciw et al., 2020), found that LGBTQ-identified students still regularly hear homophobic and transphobic remarks at school, by their peers, their teachers, and other adult staff members. Banks et al. (2022) revealed that LGBTQ and female high school students were much more able to identify racial and heterosexist microaggressions than were heterosexual boys. Meanwhile, Sterzing et al. (2017) found that transgender, genderqueer, and cis queer youth were at great risk of being polyvictimized if they reported higher lifetime experiences of familial microaggressions.

While these microaggressions experienced by LGBTQ youth may be primarily a result of identities like sexual orientation, gender identity, or race, the youth may also encounter more microaggressions than adults because of their age. One qualitative study that examined these types of intersectional microaggressions was conducted by Munro et al. (2019). Young LGBTQ participants in this study were able to describe the previous themes identified by other studies, including (a) endorsement of gender normative/binary culture, (b) use of transphobic language/incorrect gender terminology, and (c) endorsement of heteronormative culture and behaviors, among others. However, their worldviews as young people appear to have influenced the ways that these microaggressions manifested or were perceived. For example, one trans youth participant described how attendance sheets were taken in their classroom and how there are gender markers next to their names:

> They also pass around the attendance during the exam time and me sitting there all I can think of is, I'm stealth in high school, and if somebody were to happen to look at my name and see an F beside it, like, my whole life could be just completely turned upside down. (Munro et al., 2019, p. 1452)

Although problematic gender binaries have been documented in government settings, court settings, and the criminal justice system, this young person was able to describe how gender binaries manifest in their K–12 education.

Similarly, youth participants discussed other microaggressions they encountered in school, particularly from teachers, parents, and other adults who believed that they knew what is best for the young people. For instance, one young participant described:

> I feel like some adults think "Oh my children shouldn't learn this because what if they end up gay?!" And it's like, just because they learn it doesn't mean they will be. If they don't learn it and they are gay, they will still end up gay. But they just might not have the proper education to know what to do, where to go, and all that stuff. (Munro et al., 2019, p. 1456)

Similarly, a young person described a microaggression committed by their parents:

> They were like, "Oh it's just a phase. It will pass. You're mistaking friendship for love" . . . and I just recently came out months ago and then they were like "Oh well we knew it wasn't a phase. We knew it wasn't." (Munro et al., 2019, p. 1457)

Finally, there are several microaggressions that LGBTQ youth may be targeted by in various systems. LGBTQ youth are generally mistrustful of educational systems due to their experiences with blatant and covert homophobia and transphobia (Kosciw et al., 2020; McCabe et al., 2013). Many LGBTQ youth, especially LGBTQ youth of color, have described an array of microaggressions from law enforcement and the justice system—from being presumed to be criminals to not being taken seriously when reporting a crime (Nadal, 2020). In a study with over 6,000 trans and queer youth, nearly one third of participants (32%) who were LGBTQ people of color reported negative contact with police (e.g., harassment, unjustified stops), in comparison with 17% of the white youth (Torre & Avory, 2021). Accordingly, only 5% of the entire youth sample said they would ever turn to the police for help.

So, although the population of LGBTQ youth has increased significantly in recent times (Conron, 2020), and although young people in general are more accepting of people of diverse gender identities and sexual orientations (Poushter & Kent, 2020), it is evident that systems (e.g., schools, workplaces, governments) need to continue to improve their abilities to serve LGBTQ people effectively. Because these systems were not built with LGBTQ people in mind (or people of any minoritized group), LGBTQ people may not feel safe or included in any environment they are in. Thus, it is important for leaders, activists, and general community members to do their part in **queering** various systems (Nadal, 2020)—disrupting or dismantling oppressive systems and binaries that continue to inflict harm onto the people they allegedly are supposed to serve.

CASE STUDIES

Now that we have learned how microaggressions may target people based on ability, size, and age, some case studies are presented as a way of demonstrating how some LGBTQ people experience and react to intersectional microaggressions. As per other chapters, pay attention to all of the factors that may influence how biases manifest, as well as potential approaches that could be used by the people who are targeted.

The Intersection of Sexuality, Ability, Size, and More: The Case of Marcia

Marcia is a 22-year-old, South Asian, Indian American, bisexual woman with a disability. She is the younger of two daughters of two immigrant parents from India (both of whom are physicians) and grew up in an upper middle-class family in a suburb of Denver. When Marcia was 15 years old, a drunk driver hit her with his car one evening when she was walking home after volleyball practice. She sustained many injuries, including severe damage to her spinal cord. As a result, Marcia has used a wheelchair for mobility ever since.

Despite her disability, Marcia has been able to live a typical life. While she couldn't play sports in the same way she could when she was able-bodied, she tried to remain physically active however she could. When she started to gain weight a year or so after her accident, she often felt insecure about her body and sometimes would enter depressive states when thinking about her disability or her body image.

Interpersonally, Marcia always had a good social network with many friends, and she maintained her interests in arts and music. In high school, she graduated with honors and was even accepted into a prestigious university. As a result of the legal battles that she and her family faced with the drunk driver, she became very interested in law. After 4 years of undergraduate studies, she graduated with a degree in political science and was accepted into law school.

It was during her junior year of college that Marcia started to question her sexual orientation. While she always had crushes on boys, she found herself fascinated by the many lesbian and bisexual women she began to meet in college. Although she was still attracted to some men, she found other lesbian and bisexual women to be much more compassionate and kinder than the men she was meeting at school. She also started to wonder if a man could ever want to be in a relationship with her because of her disability or size. So, she started to explore her sexuality and meet other queer people by volunteering at the school's LGBTQ Center, disclosing to other students that she was "**bicurious.**"

Throughout her last 2 years of college, Marcia had made many LGBTQ friends, including many lesbian and bisexual women to whom she felt very attracted. One time, she started to develop feelings for a female friend named Cara and decided to tell her after many weeks of spending time together. Cara replied, "Marcia, I think you're really sweet, but I really only see you as a friend." As this was the first time that she had been rejected, Marcia felt hurt, but she was still optimistic. Yet, after similar situations ensued with repeated results, she started to feel much more pessimistic, wondering if these women would react differently if she were able-bodied or thin.

Furthermore, Marcia struggled with telling her family that she was bi-curious. She worried that they would not accept her primarily because of their conservative South Asian background and the potential shame it would bring to the family. After she graduated from college, Marcia finally decided to tell someone in her family. She chose to tell her sister Fran, who was 2 years older. She had known Fran to be liberal and had heard that she has at least one gay male friend; thus, she assumed her sister would be supportive. However, when Marcia finally told Fran the news, Fran replied, "Wait, what? Why would you choose to be bisexual?" Fran continued, "Your life is already hard enough because of your disability; why would you want to add another obstacle in your life?" While Marcia did not argue with her, she felt incredibly invalidated and alone.

The Intersection of Sexuality, Race, Age, and More: The Case of Adrian

Adrian is a 52-year-old gay Black American man who grew up in a middle-class suburban Maryland neighborhood with a large Black population. He was the youngest of four boys, all of whom identify as heterosexual (and who eventually got married and had children). Although Adrian started to feel same-sex sexual attractions since he was younger, he tried to block out these thoughts as much as he could. Throughout his life, he had heard many times from his family members and his church leaders that "homosexuality was an abomination." So, he tried to repress his sexual feelings for as long as he could, even trying to pretend to be heterosexual by dating girls and sometimes even having sex with them.

Adrian had his first encounters with other "out" gay men when he was 21 years old. He had read about a gay male bar that was a few towns away from where he lived, and he decided to drive there. At the bar, he noticed that many of the people there were white and that there were very few people of color present. He noticed how the young white men got a lot of attention from everyone, including the older white men and the other men of color. While Adrian believed he was attractive and had a fit physique, he sat alone, feeling unattractive and unwanted.

Over the next 5 years or so, Adrian continued to live his life on the "downlow"—frequenting gay bars and bathhouses on occasion, while still hiding his secret from his family. When the internet became more popular for dating and meeting other men, Adrian began to meet men through gay dating sites, bulletin boards, and chat rooms. Like his initial perceptions about the first gay bar he attended, he noticed young white men received the most attention, while men of color were ignored. He especially observed a lot of men's profiles and advertisements that contained messages like "No Blacks or Asians." Every time he saw something like this, he felt almost exactly how he did when he was younger—unattractive and excluded.

When Adrian was 30 years old, he stopped dating women altogether and decided to "stop pretending" to his family. While he never officially came out to his family members, they eventually stopped asking him about girlfriends, which Adrian assumed meant that they knew. Meanwhile, throughout his thirties, Adrian began to feel much more comfortable identifying as a "same gender loving man" and even started to date men and establish meaningful friendships. He became involved in a few LGBTQ organizations and began to volunteer his time for a group that served LGBTQ youth of color. When he was 40, he met James, another Black man, whom he felt very attracted to and connected to. The two started dating and were together for over 10 years. However, their relationship eventually dwindled, and the couple broke up.

Now that Adrian is 52 years old, he has started to realize how much age affects the way that he is perceived in LGBTQ spaces. He hardly frequents gay bars anymore because he feels like he is constantly surrounded by images of young, hard-bodied gay men, which in turn reminds him of his aging body. When he does attend bars and tries to initiate conversations with younger men, many of them are rude to him or ignore him altogether. Adrian is sad that he feels excluded and unattractive not just because of his race anymore but because of his age too.

CASE DISCUSSION

Both scenarios demonstrate the complexities of intersectional identities, particularly the impact that these identities can have on one's experiences with microaggressions. The first scenario involves Marcia, a bi-curious South Asian woman with a disability and body image issues, who also faces microaggressions that were discussed in previous chapters. For instance, her sister denies that her bisexuality and her disability seem to influence so many aspects of her life. First, she perceives that all her female friends, many whom she has crushes on, reject her because of her disability and perhaps also her size. This type of microaggression may be like the examples of desexualization described earlier in this chapter, in which PWDs, fat people, or people who are deemed overweight are often perceived as asexual beings because of their disabilities or size. So, when Marcia's romantic interests view her "just as a friend" Marcia begins to question if it is because of her personality or physical attractiveness (which may be more typical or accept-able reasons in other scenarios) or if it is indeed since she is in a wheelchair. Either way, Marcia feels invalidated and hurt.

The second scenario includes Adrian—a Black man who struggles with his gay identity but who also experiences subtle discrimination within LGBTQ spaces. Similarly, Adrian encounters microaggressions that are described in previous chapters (e.g., he learns that being gay is an "abomination"). However, in this case, we can see how both racial microaggressions and age microaggressions can manifest within LGBTQ community spaces. Adrian encountered racial microaggressions when he first began frequenting LGBTQ spaces, noticing that gay white men are the viewed as the most desirable. Yet, thirty years later, he perceives that young, gay white men are still consid-ered the standard of beauty among the gay male community. These percep-tions have taken a toll on his mental health and self-esteem.

In both cases, Marcia and Adrian perceive that other LGBTQ people may discriminate against them because of one of their identities (their disability, size, race, or age); however, it appears the perpetrators of the microaggressions may be completely unconscious of their behaviors while also remaining oblivious to the impact these behaviors have on others. For instance, when people write "No Blacks or Asians" on their internet dating profiles, they may not believe they are being racist or offending others. However, when Adrian (and others) read such statements, they indeed have negative reactions that can potentially harm their mental health and self-esteem.

Finally, in both scenarios, every single identity has an impact on the individual's experiences. Even if one identity was different, the scenario could change drastically altogether. If Marcia were deaf or blind, or if she were white instead of Asian, her interactions with others would be different. If Adrian had a disability or were transgender, the discrimination he faced would be different too. Because of this, it is important to acknowledge that when examining intersectional microaggressions, every identity is taken into consideration. Thus, in the next chapter, other identities like immigration status, social class, and religion are explored.

DISCUSSION QUESTIONS

For General Readers

1. What types of intersectional microaggressions do you think LGBTQ older adults, LGBTQ PWDs, LGBTQ fat people or LGBTQ people deemed overweight, and LGBTQ young people experience most?

2. What would you do if you were in Marcia's situation? Adrian's situation? What were some of the feelings that arose for you?

3. How would each of these scenarios be different if even one identity (e.g., sexual orientation, gender identity, race, religion, age, size) was different?

For Psychologists, Educators, and Other Experts

1. What are some biases you might have to challenge to increase your work with LGBTQ PWDs, LGBTQ older adults, LGBTQ youth, LGBTQ fat people, or LGBTQ people deemed overweight?

2. What psychotherapy techniques do you think would be most useful in working with Marcia or Adrian?

3. What types of countertransference issues might you have in working with Marcia or Adrian?

GLOSSARY OF KEY TERMS

ableism The negative attitudes, biases, and beliefs held about people with disabilities as well as the discrimination that occurs as a result.

ableist microaggressions Everyday forms of discrimination based on ability status (or perceived ability status)—experienced by people with disabilities.

ageism The negative attitudes, biases, and beliefs held about PWDs as well as the discrimination that occurs as a result.

age-related microaggressions Everyday forms of discrimination based on age (or perceived age)—experienced most often by older people and youth.

antifat biases Prejudices based on weight, directed towards people perceived as overweight.

bi-curious A label used to describe someone who does is interested in exploring a non-heterosexual sexual orientation; usually, the individual might often use this label when they do not want to be labeled as bisexual, heterosexual, or gay.

body image Internalized beliefs about one's own body—often subjective and based on embedded societal standards of beauty.

desexualization The act or process of depriving or taking away one's sexuality.

downlow A term used primarily in Black and Latinx communities to describe a person who is closeted and engages in anonymous or secretive same-sex sexual behaviors.

dwarfism Short stature, due to a genetic or medical condition, generally defined as an adult who has a height between 2 feet to 4 feet and 10 inches.

fat A term used to identify people perceived as overweight. While considered a derogatory term for some, many fat people have reclaimed the word as one of empowerment.

fat studies A scholarly field that examines the societal oppression of people based on weight and body type, while advocating for equities for people of all sizes.

fatphobia Negative attitudes, biases, and beliefs held about fat people, as well as the discrimination that occurs as a result.

impairment A problem with any psychological, structural, or functional organ or part of the body.

infantilization The act of treating someone like a helpless child—usually experienced by older adults or adults with disabilities.

little people People living with dwarfism, often referred to as LPs.

neurotypical A term used to described someone who does not exhibit autistic or other neurologically diverse patterns of thought or behavior.

parentalism The act or process of asserting a parental or authoritative role over someone else, usually in a condescending or manipulative way.

patronization The act or process of treating someone in a condescending manner, often with the intention of showing kindness but communicating judgment or insincerity.

queering The act of disrupting, challenging, or dismantling systems and institutions—particularly norms that are standardized on historically privileged groups while harming historically marginalized groups.

serostatus The state of having (or not having) detectable antibodies against a specific antigen in one's blood—most often used as a term to describe whether people are living with HIV/AIDS.

sizeism The negative attitudes, biases, and beliefs held about people based on size, as well as the discrimination that occurs as a result. Typically, these prejudices are directed towards people perceived as overweight or little people.

sizeist microaggressions Everyday forms of discrimination based on size—experienced most often by people perceived as overweight; little people; and people with other appearances that are considered nonnormative.

7

INTERSECTIONAL MICROAGGRESSIONS

Experiences of LGBTQ Religious and Nonreligious People, LGBTQ Immigrants, and LGBTQ Poor and Working-Class People

FIGURE 7.1. A Proud Immigrant Woman in San Francisco

Note. Photo courtesy of Marcus Silva.

https://doi.org/10.1037/0000335-008
Dismantling Everyday Discrimination: Microaggressions Toward LGBTQ People, Second Edition, by K. L. Y. Nadal

To review, intersectional microaggressions are the types of everyday forms of discrimination that may occur because of one's multiple identities. While there has been an increase in literature focusing on LGBTQ people of color, LGBTQ people with disabilities, LGBTQ older adults, and LGBTQ youth, there remains a limited amount of scholarship on other marginalized LGBTQ subgroups. This chapter focuses on several groups: religious people, nonreligious people, immigrants, and people of lower social classes.

Let's begin by providing some definitions, so that we know which groups we are referring to throughout the chapter. First, when discussing religion, we recognize that there are religious groups and nonreligious groups. While the United States is meant to be a country in which all religions are to be welcomed and accepted, Christianity is the dominant religious group and people of other religions are susceptible to an array of discriminatory experiences—ranging from hate crimes to microaggressions (Cheng et al., 2019; Nadal, 2018). Further, nonreligious groups—or people who do not identify with or practice any organized religion (e.g., **atheists** or **agnostics**)—may also be targeted by bias and discrimination (Cheng et al., 2018). For instance, Cook et al. (2015) found that people perceived atheists to be immoral or threatening, whereas Grove et al. (2020) found that atheists were perceived as distrustful.

Immigrants are people who travel to another country for permanent residence. People migrate for a variety of reasons, including perceived financial and economic opportunities or to escape negative or violent conditions in their home country. Immigrants are often referred to as **first-generation**, whereas their children who are born or raised in the host country are often referred to as **second-generation**. People who are forced to leave their countries of origin to escape war, persecution, or displacement from natural disasters are known as **refugees**. Relatedly, **asylees** are migrants who seek refuge (or **asylum**) or citizenship due to violence or persecution in their home country, typically after already having left their country or origin and entered the new country. Some immigrants are **undocumented** or **unauthorized**, which means that they do not have legal standing in their new host country. Scholars have described how immigrants—especially immigrants of color in the United States—encounter an array of discrimination and traumatic stress because of white nationalism and **xenophobia**, war, violence, and fears of deportation (Armenta et al., 2021; Sissoko & Nadal, 2021).

Socioeconomic status is a classification of persons based on financial income, material wealth, assets, and residence/neighborhood; it is typically determined by census and data collection agencies, who can use such information to categorize people into groups. Meanwhile, **social class** is a personal identifier based on values, assumptions, and beliefs, about (but not limited to) the tangible aspects of socioeconomic status (e.g., financial wealth and assets), but also objective indicators like education, employment, privilege, access to resources, and cultural expectations (Smith & Scott-McLaughlin, 2017; Williams, 2017). Examples of different social classes include upper class, upper middle class, middle class, lower middle class, working class, poor, and people living in poverty—each with varying definitions, classifications, and spoken and unspoken rules of membership. While **classism** is a much less researched form of oppression, research has found classist discrimination affects a variety of outcomes, including psychological distress, educational outcomes, and life satisfaction (see Cavalhieri & Chwalisz, 2020, for a review).

A REVIEW ON MICROAGGRESSIONS BASED ON RELIGION, IMMIGRATION, AND SOCIAL CLASS

Although the literature on microaggressions has been growing for the past 2 decades, there continues to be a dearth of academic literature focusing on religious microaggressions, anti-immigrant microaggressions, or classist microaggressions. However, the literature that does exist illustrates some of the experiences that may be faced by various minoritized people. The first taxonomy on religious microaggressions was proposed by Nadal, Issa, et al. (2010). Considering all religious minority groups, the authors theorized six types of religious microaggressions to exist, including: (a) endorsing religious stereotypes, (b) exoticization, (c) pathology of different religious groups, (d) assumption of one's own religious identity as the norm, (e) assumption of religious homogeneity, and (f) denial of religious prejudice.

Several empirical studies have been conducted to support this religious microaggression taxonomy. Cheng et al. (2019) created a quantitative measure to examine these types of religious microaggressions. Through a factor analysis, three main themes emerged: (a) assumption of inferiority, (b) religious stereotyping, and (c) assumption of nonreligiosity. Other studies have supported how these types of religious microaggressions do occur, particularly with Muslims (Husain & Howard, 2017; Manejwala & Abu-Ras, 2019; Nadal, Griffin, et al., 2012). Cheng et al. (2018) created a quantitative measure to examine the types of microaggressions encountered by nonreligious people. Five factors emerged, including (a) assumption of inferiority, (b) denial of nonreligious prejudice, (c) assumption of religiosity, (d) endorsing nonreligious stereotypes, and (e) pathology of a nonreligious identity.

Specific to immigrants' experiences on microaggressions, Sissoko and Nadal (2021) theorized a taxonomy for racial minority immigrants—based on previous literature on racial microaggressions and religious microaggressions. Eight themes included (a) alien in own land, (b) questioning of cultural authenticity, (c) ascriptions of intelligence and language-related microaggressions, (d) assumptions of homogeneity, (e) the myth of meritocracy/denial of individual and systemic racism, (f) pathologizing cultural values and communication styles, (g) criminalization, and (h) second-class citizenship. Examples of language-related microaggressions would be ones in which people comment on immigrants' accents in both benevolent and malicious ways. A demonstration of pathologizing cultural values is commenting (either benevolently or maliciously) about a person's food, dress, or customs.

Further, classist microaggressions involve everyday forms of discrimination based on social class. With the introduction of the concept by Smith and Redington (2010), classist microaggressions were theorized to manifest as microassaults, microinvalidations, or microinsults. Smith et al. (2016) used narrative data to support how classist microaggressions are especially prevalent for working class or poor students who attend institutions of higher education; participants described feelings of stigmatization (e.g., witnessing stereotypes about people of lower social classes), as well as alienation (e.g., learning to navigate cultural practices they may have never learned). Similarly, Gray et al. (2018) interviewed college students of various social classes and revealed the types of class-based microaggressions encountered by first-generation college students.

Cavalhieri and Chwalisz (2020) created a quantitative method to examine perceived classism with examples of downward classism (e.g., perceived discrimination from people of higher classes) and lateral classism (e.g., perceived discrimination from people of similar social classes). Further, Torino and Sisselman-Borgia (2017) investigated homelessness microaggressions—citing multiple manifestations of bias toward homeless people. Common themes include (a) subhuman status, (b) invisibility, (c) aesthetically unappealing, (d) criminal status/dangerous, (e) assumption of mental illness, (f) assumption of substance abuse, (g) laziness, and (h) intellectual inferiority.

There are only a few known studies that have examined intersectional microaggressions for LGBTQ people based on religion, immigration, or social class. One qualitative study investigated the microaggressions encountered by LGBTQ people of various religious groups, with most participants identifying as Christian (Lomash et al., 2019). Three main themes emerged: (a) LGBTQ identities as inauthentic, (b) religious/spiritual tolerance of LGBTQ identities, and (c) LGBTQ and religious/spiritual identities as incompatible. One sample quote involves one Catholic bisexual genderqueer participant who acknowledged:

> Some of the microaggressions I have experienced within religious spaces: "I didn't know people like you believed in God." "You are so much more than a gay man." "I've never met a homosexual before." "God still loves you." "It must be hard to suffer with same-sex attraction, but honestly we all have crosses to bear, this is just yours." (Lomash et al., 2019, p. 1501)

Additionally, in some studies focusing on the lives of queer Muslims (Golriz, 2021; Minwalla et al., 2005), many participants disclosed personal inter-actions that would be considered microaggressions. Despite this growth of literature on intersectional microaggressions for some LGBTQ religious people, there remains a dearth of literature on microaggressions encountered by LGBTQ people of many other religious groups (e.g., Hindus, Sikhs, Jews) and nonreligious groups (e.g., atheists, agnostics). Understanding how inter-sectional microaggressions like these affect LGBTQ atheists is especially important, given research findings that LGBTQ people are more likely than heterosexuals to identify as atheists or nonbelievers (Brewster et al., 2021; Schwadel & Sandstorm, 2019).

Relatedly, some studies on LGBTQ immigrants have revealed unique incidents of microaggressions, even when not the main purpose for the research. For instance, Cisneros and Bracho (2020) examined safe spaces for undocumented queer Latinx people—many of whom self-identify as **undocuqueers**. In a different study, Cerezo et al. (2014) examined the psycho-social stressors of trans Latina migrants; in sharing their narratives, several participants divulged myriad situations that range from overt discrimination to microaggressions. Despite these insightful studies, further literature explic-itly investigating intersectional microaggressions for trans and queer immi-grants would be crucial in identifying specific discrimination they face.

Finally, studies find that LGBTQ people who are homeless or unhoused may encounter an array of discriminatory experiences because of their LGBTQ identities and housing status. For instance, in homeless shelters, LGBTQ people are often harassed or subjected to violence, and binary facilities often lead to trans or nonbinary people being unsheltered or forced to share housing with others of their sex assigned at birth (Romero et al., 2020). Further, LGBTQ people often have difficulty finding work because of transphobia or hetero-sexism (and racism for LGBTQ people of color), resulting in an inability to earn a living wage or even forcing them into survival behaviors like sex work or crime (Nadal, 2018, 2020).

Taken together, these studies demonstrate promising areas of research; however, there is much still unknown about intersectional microaggressions for LGBTQ subgroups. For instance, how might religious microaggressions be felt uniquely for LGBTQ people (in comparison with their cis heterosexual counterparts)? How might LGBTQ immigrants encounter and manage micro-aggressions based on their immigration status, sexual identities, or gender identities? And finally, how might classist microaggressions manifest uniquely for LGBTQ people living in poverty or identified as working class? In the sections that follow, I share examples from previous literature as a way of highlighting these potential themes.

VOICES OF LGBTQ RELIGIOUS GROUP MEMBERS

Because most major religions are either blatantly heterosexist or transphobic, or are not overtly accepting of LGBTQ people, there are many intersectional microaggressions that can be experienced by LGBTQ people of various religious groups, as well as many stressors that can be felt by LGBTQ people who belong to religious groups (Ford, 2021). First, it is necessary to acknowledge that there are many ways that discrimination toward LGBTQ people is still explicit and blatant. As an example, it has been documented that a common historical practice in The Church of Jesus Christ of Latter-day Saints (LDS) was for gay men and lesbian women to undergo **conversion therapy** or other **sexual orientation change efforts (SOCEs)**, to "cure" them from their homosexuality. In fact, one study found that in a sample of 1,612 current or former LDS members that 73% of men and 43% of women engaged in some form of SOCEs, usually through multiple methods across their lifetimes (Dehlin et al., 2015). When SOCEs are encouraged or enforced among any conservative religious group, it is typically very difficult for members of those groups to come to terms with their sexual orientations and gender identities, especially when they have been taught explicitly that it is "an abomination," "perverse," "sinful" (Barton, 2010, pp. 465–466), or "evil" (p. 473). Further, because empirical research has found that SOCEs are ineffective and damaging, such practices were deemed unethical by all leading professional health and mental health organizations in the United States and many parts of the world (Glassgold, 2017).

Sometimes these anti-LGBTQ sentiments that are preached in the Christian religions are based on older interpretations of passages from the Bible (see Chapter 1) that current theologians may interpret differently. However, when such hateful rhetoric is still preached by current religious leaders, it may have detrimental effects on LGBTQ members of church congregations. Fahs and Swank (2021) contacted 255 leaders of Christian churches and inquired about their current teachings about homosexuality; findings included that many churches still follow literal interpretations of the Bible. One response read:

> We believe that the Bible addresses homosexuality as being a lifestyle that is not in line with God's design for our lives. We do not condemn anyone who identifies as gay, but we also teach what we believe the Bible says on this (and every other subject) even when it is difficult to hear. (p. 110)

The researchers also found that many churches preach that nonheterosexual identities and behaviors are sinful or deviant. "We see homosexuality going against God's plan for humankind. It is one of many sins" (Fahs & Swank, 2021, p. 111). In both cases, the speakers may not be intentional in conveying homophobic biases, but someone who hears these messages may certainly interpret the hateful undertones.

Hearing explicitly homophobic teachings can cause psychological distress to anyone questioning their LGBTQ identities. A lesbian who grew up in a fundamentalist church shared:

> The preacher would preach on homosexuality. He would always group us in with the so-called perverts, you know, like child molesters and just awful people. Of course, since I was having feelings about me being different, I felt like I needed to go to the altar and just pray and ask God to forgive me every Sunday. And every Sunday I would get on my knees and just cry and pray. (Barton, 2010, p. 472)

Because of anti-LGBTQ teachings, many individuals may feel immense amounts of guilt and shame if they stay with their religion, often choosing to leave their religious groups altogether (Barton, 2010; Dehlin et al., 2015). Given these blatantly homophobic and exclusionary beliefs, it should not be surprising that queer people who sought advice from conservative leaders were more likely to attempt suicide (I. H. Meyer et al., 2015).

Although there remains a dearth of research that focuses on the perspectives of LGBTQ people from various religious groups, I will highlight a few themes of religious microaggressions encountered by LGBTQ from religious backgrounds—specifically focusing on the subtler and covert messages that may be communicated. I will attempt to include a spectrum of examples from various LGBTQ subgroups, including perspectives from Christian, Jewish, Muslim, and Hindu faiths, as well as atheists and nonreligious people. Again, this is not an inclusive list, because not all groups are represented; yet, it is hoped that more research emerges in this area.

Rejection and Exclusion From Religious Communities

Being excluded from one's religious community can be overtly taught in official writings, via sermons or lessons of ministers or church leaders, or by blatant communications from family or community members. In one study

(Barton, 2010), a Black lesbian who grew up in a Black Orthodox Pentecostal church shared: "To be a full-fledged member you have to be saved, and to be saved you can't be gay. Just being gay, period, points you to hell" (p. 473). Similarly, in a study on same-sex Hindu couples, some participants described being cast out by their families; one queer Hindu woman described how her parents reacted after hearing she was married to a woman:

> They disowned me. They wrote me a letter and literally disowned me. They had given me a piece of property, a flat, and they took it back. They were afraid I would come out to everyone in their club. They tried to get the rest of my family to have nothing to do with me. (Khan, 2011, p. 394)

So, messages of exclusion can come from observing the culture of the religion or because of interpersonal conflicts and verbal confrontations.

However, sometimes these messages of exclusion are communicated implicitly or unintentionally. A Black gay man who grew up Baptist shared how his childhood church refused to hold a funeral for its music director because he died of AIDS, which the church referred to as "the gay disease." While they did not explicitly say why the funeral was not allowed, the speaker interpreted their behavior as meaning: "If you are gay, you are not part of us" (Barton, 2010, p. 473). Relatedly, one Jewish lesbian described a subtle form of bias they felt:

> The most common one has been people advising me that they're not homophobic because they "hate the sin, love the sinner," typically in the context of opposing gay marriage and/or denying services to LGBTQ people. (Lomash et al., 2019, p. 1504)

These examples demonstrate how some perpetrators of anti-LGBTQ microaggressions are not aware of how their religious beliefs convey heterosexist or cissexist bias; in fact, many deny their comments are oppressive or harmful, or use religious convictions as an excuse to discriminate.

Moreover, some anti-LGBTQ biases from religious people may be communicated through coded behaviors. A gay Hindu man described a microaggression that occurred from his family after his same-sex wedding:

> I'll tell you about a little episode that happened a day after the ceremony. It was my eldest brother's twenty-fifth [wedding] anniversary, and to celebrate that they had a banner made on which they had the entire family's names except for [my husband] Kunal's. (Khan, 2011, p. 393)

Similarly, in another study, a gay Muslim male participant shared:

> When I was probably 17 or 18, I was struggling because I was attracted to men. There was a sense of guilt . . . [I would] escape from socializing [with]

my cousins, even with my parents, because each time we met as an extended family, there was talk about girls or marriage—it was just too much for me. (Minwalla et al., 2005, p. 118)

Both examples demonstrate the presumption of heterosexuality as the norm. In the first, the message communicated was that only heterosexual couples were deemed legitimate; in the second, family members made assumptions that all men were heterosexual and interested in dating or marrying women. While both categories of microaggressions caused negative emotions for the person who was targeted, it is worth noting that there isn't anything explicit in Hinduism or Islam that preaches heterosexism or cissexism. However, heteronormativity that is promoted culturally and intergenerationally may isolate those who question their sexual identities.

Finally, although the literature is sparse, LGBTQ atheists or nonbelievers may experience a double rejection from their families or religious communities, due to their sexual identities (Brewster et al., 2021). As nonreligious nonbelievers, their religious or theist families may view them as evil, immoral, or sinful; and as queer or trans people, their religious or theist families may have similar stereotypes too, causing exacerbated stress and discrimination.

Exclusion and Religious Stigmas From LGBTQ Communities

Some LGBTQ people from religious groups report how they are excluded from LGBTQ communities because of their religious identities or how their religions are stereotyped as extremely heterosexist or transphobic. For instance, a gay Indigenous trans man stated:

> I get more issues from LGBTQQ people for being religious than the other way around. I've been told many times that being religious is somehow a betrayal to the community or that I'm complicit in abuse and harassment because I'm religious. While I do understand most of these comments are made because people fail to separate many of the world's major religions from religion in general and that most people making these comments have been a victim of religious abuse or harassment, but it's frustrating to see. LGBTQQ people can (be) and are religious. (Lomash et al., 2019, pp. 1505–1506)

In the same study, a gay Christian shared:

> I have been called "self-hating" by queer people in "safe spaces" because I am religious. I have also been told that I shouldn't be allowed in LGBTQ safe spaces because I am religious. It makes me feel terrible and like I don't have a place where I don't have to hide who I am. I try to ignore those kinds of comments and spaces, I even quit going to the GSA during college. (Lomash et al., 2019, p. 1506)

Finally, a Protestant lesbian trans woman revealed: "I've had other members of the trans community who poke fun at me for still keeping my faith. It's hard to have no home for my faith" (Lomash et al., 2019, p. 1506). Through these examples, we learn that LGBTQ people who practice religion are judged by nonreligious LGBTQ people. While it is possible that these LGBTQ non-religious people may have experienced trauma with religion, their comments frustrate, hurt, or insult LGBTQ people who have found peace and connection to religion.

Similarly, queer and trans Muslims report experiencing microaggressions in which people make broad generalizations about their religion, without recognizing that such biases are harmful and problematic. As an example, a Black queer Muslim cis man stated:

> Sometimes the narrative that we get is that Muslims are inherently homophobic or misogynistic. It's important for us to resist that narrative because we know it's not true: we know that homophobia and misogyny know no boundaries, and we know that it's not essential to our communities. (Golriz, 2021, p. 366)

Later, the same participant divulged:

> I have had white gay men tell me "aren't you afraid that god will send you to hell? Doesn't the Quran say that?" And I'm like, "have you read the Quran?" And they are like "of course not!" and then I say, "then what are you talking about?" [Laughs]. But there are these deep-seeded understandings of what Islam says about our lives that people have taken up and continue to take up and continue to perpetuate unto our bodies. (Golriz, 2021, p. 367)

Some queer Muslims reported how racist, xenophobic, or **Islamophobic** comments make them feel uncomfortable in mainstream LGBTQ spaces. A Muslim nonbinary person divulged:

> People are really racist and will say a thing like "[body hair] is disgusting" without realizing how racialized it is. I went to a queer space recently, and one of the white guys there was talking about how he thinks hair is so dirty. And I was like "I have worked so hard to love myself and this is so disrespectful." So, do I want to expose myself to these microaggressions? (Golriz, 2021, p. 369)

Meanwhile, a queer Muslim cis woman of color added: "Some of our members go to queer spaces wearing hats instead of their hijabs because they feel safer. It's pretty bad. I don't think non-Muslim queer folks recognize how bad queer-Muslims have it in queer spaces" (Golriz 2021, pp. 368–369). These sentiments illustrate how unwelcoming many LGBTQ communities are toward Muslims (and other marginalized groups). While LGBTQ safe spaces are supposed to be open to people with shared or similar sexual orientations and gender identities, these participants view them as exclusionary, discriminatory, and even violent.

Use of Religion as Intervention

When LGBTQ people of conservative religious backgrounds do come out to their families, their families may react in many ways. It appears that one common reaction from those family members who are religious is to have some sort of religious intervention to "eliminate" the homosexuality from their loved one. As mentioned previously, many LGBTQ people from conservative religions have reported undergoing conversion therapies, as forced by their families or church leaders, when their sexual identities were discovered. In the movie *Prayers for Bobby*, Sigourney Weaver plays Mary Griffith, a devout Christian mother in a traditional white middle-class American family who discovers her son Bobby's gay identity. Instead of accepting him, she turns to the Church, and encourages him to do the same. In one scene in the movie, she claims:

> Homosexuality is a sin. Homosexuals are doomed to spend eternity in hell. If they wanted to change, they could be healed of their evil ways. If they would turn away from temptation, they could be normal again if only they would try and try harder if it doesn't work. (Mulcahy, 2009)

Because of this lack of acceptance by his family, Bobby eventually dies by suicide. After this tragedy, Ms. Griffith aims to become more educated on LGBTQ experiences and later becomes an activist for LGBTQ people. However, this story reflects how using religion as a way of pathologizing a loved one's sexuality or gender identity can result in fatal consequences.

Some research has highlighted similar scenarios in which LGBTQ people encounter religious interventions. For instance, one trans woman of color participant shared:

> I don't consider myself a religious person. A punishment from my mom was being forced to read passages condemning homosexuals to hell. She thought I was gay but being forced to read that hurt me. I am a very spiritual person though. Eventually, I established my own personal relationship with my creator that I don't have to justify to anyone who I am. My spirituality helps me with that—practicing meditation and having faith that I am not a mistake [as a transgender person of color]. That gives me hope—the terrible things that have happened to me don't have to *become me.* (Singh & McKleroy, 2011, p. 39)

Meanwhile, in a study with LGBTQ Filipino Americans (Nadal & Corpus, 2013), one gay male participant revealed:

> I started coming out to cousins, female cousins, not male cousins . . . except for one . . . but then about last year, all my cousins wanted to have a family intervention. It became religious in scope. I think that the hardest blocks to coming out was the religious aspect. (p. 170)

While these "interventions" might be well intentioned (in that these family members may claim to be genuinely concerned about their LGBTQ loved ones' souls), they end up causing significant distress and trauma for the loved ones they claim to want to help.

MICROAGGRESSIONS BASED ON BOTH RELIGIOUS AND SEXUAL IDENTITIES

Aligning with the literature on LGBTQ people of color, LGBTQ people of religious minority groups may encounter microaggressions that may be due to both their religious and sexual identities. Simply stated, when they face certain microaggressions from others, it may be due to their religious identity, their sexual identity, or both concurrently.

As an example, one Jewish bisexual woman described the treatment that she received in her academic department as an untenured professor:

> Christian literature showed up at my office door. A student asked to pray with me and prayed that I give up not only my "homosexuality" but also my Judaism, as she hoped I would "accept Jesus as my savior." The chair of my department informed me that calls were received demanding my dismissal. While the faculty all openly supported me, my file for retention, tenure, and promotion was questioned. It was suggested that I remove all evidence of the scholarly and professional work I had been doing on gay and lesbian issues from the file. I refused. (Dworkin, 2005, p. 66)

While it is evident that this professor was experiencing bias due to her bisexual identity, Jewish identity, or both, some of the microaggressions may or may not have had malicious intentions by the offender. For example, when a Christian person encourages another to become a Christian, the individual's intentions are unlikely to be malicious (Nadal et al., 2010); however, while they may attest to being genuinely concerned about a person's well-being, they communicate that their religion is the norm and all other belief systems are pathological or inferior.

A similar type of discrimination may occur for nonreligious people—especially atheists or nonbelievers. Because of all the stigmas associated with LGBTQ people and atheists, the stigma, prejudice, or hate they encounter might be greater both in quantity and quality. In her book entitled *Queer Disbelief: Why LGBTQ Equality is an Atheist Issue,* Camille Beredjick (2017) posited:

> As both an atheist and a queer person, I'm doubly baffled by the intensity of religious hatred against my people—all my people. I write a lot about LGBTQ

FIGURE 7.2. Three Gay Friends From the Philippines Who Identify as Chosen Family

Note. Photo courtesy of Slaytina.

issues, and I've received countless anonymous messages (and some not anonymous) outlining all the reasons I'm a hellbound dyke. (p. 11)

So, when a religious person asks a queer atheist why they don't believe in a higher power, their line of questioning may be due to the queer atheist's sexual identity, nonreligious identity, or both. And even if such incidents are well-intended, the religious person's behaviors may be indicative of biases that queer people, nonbelievers, or both, are immoral or unwise—potentially causing psychological distress and other harmful outcomes for the target.

VOICES OF LGBTQ IMMIGRANTS

Many of the microaggressive experiences of LGBTQ immigrants are likely to match those of LGBTQ people of color; Sissoko and Nadal (2021) described how immigrants in general may encounter microaggressions related to being treated like perpetual foreigners, being exoticized, or having their racial and cultural realities invalidated. However, one's additional identities as queer or trans might result in a few nuanced realities. Skinta and Nakamura (2021) provided a comprehensive overview of the various obstacles encountered by LGBTQ immigrants—citing factors that contribute to their leaving their home countries and obstacles faced when they arrive in the United States. For instance, queer or trans immigrants—especially immigrants of color—escape persecution from their countries of origin (where they may encounter violence or death due to their LGBTQ identities); however, when they arrive, they may have difficulty attaining asylum status in the United States (Nadal, 2020; Nakamura & Morales, 2016). One gay asylum-seeker from Kenya described:

> I naively faced the process of seeking asylum, believing I would present my case and that I would be questioned in a non-adversarial manner. However, when the Immigration Officer interviewed me, I was surprised and offended by the battery of queries, particularly those designed to determine whether or not I was truly a gay man as I had asserted. From the start the interview felt like an inquisition. (Randazzo, 2005, p. 46)

One major critique of the asylum process is that it is up to the migrant to prove both their sexual identity and their history of violence. With policies like these in place, asylum seekers can be subject to **victim blaming**, which is described as "assigning fault to people who experience violence or wrong-doing and is used as a tool to discredit people of marginalized groups who speak out against microaggressions or any injustices" (Johnson et al., 2021, p. 1024). Further, interactions in which they are invalidated or gaslit about their perspectives may result in a retraumatization as well as a total mistrust of the system.

One final critique of the asylum process is that it is a lengthy one—often enduring for years; thus, many trans and queer immigrants are often detained at immigration borders for a significant amount of time. At these detention centers, many asylees have described how they are housed according to their sex assigned at birth—resulting in harassment and assault, especially for trans women. Moreover, residents in these detention centers have cited inhumane living conditions and violence from both staff and other detainees, with some reports of transgender women being brutalized and killed (Nadal, 2020; Skinta & Nakamura, 2021). So, while these LGBTQ migrants come to the United States to seek better conditions than in their home countries, they instead encounter violence, harassment, and threats to their lives.

Another group of LGBTQ immigrants who are exposed to intersectional microaggressions are undocuqueers—a term used to describe trans or queer people who are also undocumented. In recent years, there have been studies that have examined the unique perspectives of undocumented trans or queer people (e.g., Cisneros & Bracho, 2019, 2020). Several participants underscored how not having proper documentation (e.g., driver's licenses or state-issued identification) resulted in microaggressions and other forms of harassment. One common example involved having to show identification to be admitted into queer spaces:

> When they don't take your fucking *matricula* (foreign documentation) at the club . . . they be like: "Oh, I am sorry you cannot get in." I'm like: "Dude, I live in San Francisco. You are supposed to be like a progressive city, and you don't let undocumented people in your club? Because allegedly queers are not undocumented? I don't understand." And it's not even just about the club. It is more about how people perceive you as something of a lesser level than them simply because of that. (Cisneros & Bracho, 2020, p. 1500)

While queer spaces are known by many LGBTQ people to be sanctuaries that keep them safe from heterosexism and cissexism in the outside world (Nadal, 2020), they can be a source of unnecessary distress for many undocumented LGBTQ people who are dehumanized and prevented from participating in community spaces.

Other undocumented queer or trans people revealed how their unauthorized status may result in interpersonal forms of discrimination. One queer Latinx man recalled:

> I had a boyfriend that I was dating for two and a half years, and that boyfriend ended up cheating, and he told me, "You can't leave me because who else is going to marry you for your papers?" He also had said, "If you leave, I'm going to call the police." . . . When you're placed in a vulnerable spot with individuals who try to use your undocumented status against you, that's when it all builds up. (Cisneros & Bracho, 2020, p. 1503)

While such behavior may be viewed as a form of manipulation or even extortion, the conscious behavior of the perpetrator could be considered a form of microassault.

One mainstream example of an undocuqueer is from the television sitcom *Superstore*. The character Mateo is a gay Filipino American who reveals that he is undocumented. Many of his storylines involve systemic issues with his immigration status—including having to give up a promotion because he can't produce a social security card (Kang, 2018). However, he does encounter some microaggressions too. As one illustration, in an episode about the Olympics, his supervisor questioned why he would be supporting the Philippines, instead of just the United States, making comments that "America is #1." Eventually, Mateo is arrested by Immigration and Customs Enforcement—demonstrating a scary reality for many undocumented immigrants.

Trans women, especially trans Latina immigrants, may also encounter all forms of discrimination within the criminal justice system—ranging from sexual assault in prisons to police brutality and harassment to microaggressions. In a study on trans Latina perspectives, one participant revealed: "There is a lot of harassment from the police, a lot. . . . Policemen would tell me 'cutie, cutie, come here'" (Cerezo et al., 2014, p. 175). Some undocumented trans migrants have revealed how police officers abuse their power, with one trans woman from Central America revealing:

> We have a government where the police officers themselves are the delinquents. They are the ones that pursue us, they beat us, they force us to do immoral acts. They force us to do . . . sex at gunpoint. (Nakamura & Morales, 2016, p. 53)

In addition to overt forms of violence, police bias can also manifest in more microaggressive ways. For instance, trans and nonbinary people describe misgendering as a common microaggression experienced from police officers. As an example, one trans woman described: "When I told them my real name, Rachel, [the police officers] refused to recognize that and continued to call me by my male name" (Amnesty International, 2005, p. 73). Trans women immigrants are also stereotyped by police as sex workers, often being harassed or falsely arrested (Nadal, 2020). One trans Latina shared:

> While they were handcuffing me, my boyfriend was also thrown to the wall, and they frisked him. They told me I was being arrested for sex work. I told them that I was not doing anything like that. After they frisked my boyfriend, they frisked me and found 3 condoms, after seeing the condoms they asked if I was sure that I was not working. I told them that I was with my boyfriend, and they said that he was not my boyfriend . . . I was taken to court and was accused of sex work. (Daum, 2015, p. 566)

Because of incidents like this, it is clear why one trans Latina shared the following: "Since I was younger, other transgender women taught me to not trust the police" (Cerezo et al., 2014, p. 176).

Systemic barriers may also result in many disparities for undocumented trans and queer immigrants. Across different studies, trans undocumented immigrants illustrated how institutional discrimination makes it difficult to attain employment. One participant shared:

> It is difficult. It's very difficult because of the situation that I am in right now. I want to find a job, but everyone wants you to show legal documentation, like a work permit. I don't want to work with documents that are not mine because I don't want to have any problems with the police. It is very difficult to find a job. (Cerezo et al., 2014, p. 176)

Meanwhile, another trans Latina reflected:

> Apart from being part of the LGBT community, we are Latinas, we are people that do not speak English. When we find work, they don't pay us well, and they don't give us work for not having papers, and sometimes even for being transgender within the LGBT community. They just don't. So, we are the ones that suffer the most, no? We know these are issues that affect the undocumented

community, but if you identify as LGBT, it is going to affect you twice as much. (Cisneros & Bracho, 2019, p. 726)

Another participant described similar sentiments:

I couldn't get a job. I kept looking for jobs and it was really hard to get jobs. You know people didn't want to give me jobs because I didn't have papers. So, you know, I just felt like, well, I think this is not . . . I don't know, it just felt like I can't, I just can't do this. And I was really afraid. (Cisneros & Bracho, 2019, p. 723)

Finally, because of these institutional barriers, some undocumented immigrants describe having to turn to other means of survival. One participant admitted:

I have all the intentions to work and do everything the right way. I have reached the point that if I don't find a job, I have to work as a prostitute to survive. Because no one is going to support me for free. (Cerezo et al., 2014, p. 176)

While these perspectives speak to some of the intersectional forms of discrimination faced by undocumented trans and queer immigrants, they all support the need for research. Future studies could examine perspectives of other specific LGBTQ undocumented subgroups—including trans and queer immigrants from Asia, Africa, South America, the Caribbean, and the Middle East.

VOICES OF LGBTQ PEOPLE FROM POOR AND WORKING-CLASS BACKGROUNDS

LGBTQ people of lower social classes (e.g., those who are poor, living in poverty, or working class) may face many barriers that affect their qualities of life and abilities to thrive. As mentioned in Chapter 4, transgender people tend to be unemployed at rates much higher than the general population, and they also tend to have higher poverty levels and unemployment rates than the general population (Grant et al., 2011). In general, LGBTQ people have higher poverty rates than their cisgender heterosexual counterparts, with trans people and bisexual cisgender women having the higher rates among LGBTQ subgroups (Badgett et al., 2019; Wilson et al., 2020). LGBTQ youth also tend to be overrepresented in homeless populations—comprising up to 40% of homeless youth, despite LGBTQ people presumed to represent only about 10% of the population (Quintana et al., 2010). Research has found that LGBTQ youth with histories of homelessness are more likely to be survivors of physical, emotional, or sexual abuse in their families of origin, while also being more likely to report greater disparities in mental health, substance use, and physical health (Coolhart & Brown, 2017; Quintana et al., 2010; B. A. Robinson, 2018). While much of the literature on LGBTQ people of lower social classes tends to focus on systemic issues, there are many potential intersectional microaggressions that may occur for people in this group. In this section, I highlight a few themes from the literature.

Unemployment and Survival Behaviors

One of the reasons why poverty rates are particularly high for LGBTQ people—especially trans people, LGBTQ youth, and LGBTQ people of color—is because of their inability to obtain steady and gainful employment. Across many studies, trans participants (especially trans women of color) have described how transphobia in hiring practices may contribute significantly to these employment disparities. As noted in Chapter 4, in one study (Nadal, Davidoff, & Fujii-Doe, 2014), a Black trans woman declared:

> I remember a lot of them looking at me . . . and taking the paper. I gave them my resume, and "If we have an opening we'll call you." Even though in the window it says, "Now Hiring," they go, "If we have an opening, we'll call you." So, they would say that, but they didn't just come out and go "how dare you, hell no we ain't gonna hire you." But they did not say it, it was just they watch what they say cause there were witnesses. (p. 173)

Similarly, a Black nonbinary person shared:

> So walking in the places, they're like, "They?" I'm like, "Yes, they." So, a lot of places aren't—they don't know how to handle that either, so instead of hiring you and figuring out what "they" is, they'd just rather not hire you. (Wilson et al., 2020, p. 5)

In both instances, the targets confidently recognized that transphobia affected their ability to get hired for jobs, demonstrating how commonplace and even expected such experiences are for trans people (and especially trans Black people).

Trans and nonbinary people also recognize the limitations in employment opportunities—due to other people's perceptions of them. One queer nonbinary Asian American divulged:

> My gender identity and expression that keeps me from ever working at . . . a job that a cis straight person can work at. Like, I can't work at the bank . . . I can only be front-facing staff in very, very specific situations. And I probably will not get hired by a white man because I'm not sexy . . . I'm not like passable enough to play that card, and I don't hide enough to like pass as cis if I wanted to do that whole thing. So, yeah, I think my identity—like, my refusal to tone it down, to play either side keeps me from a lot of like mainstream jobs. (Wilson et al., 2020, p. 59)

In a further example, one participant shared:

> I've gotten discriminated [against], not only because I'm Black, but I'm Black—
> I'm a Black trans woman. So, I've gotten a lot of jobs turned down. Like,
> I—I'm not supposed to be doing hair and makeup. I'm supposed to be working
> at the bank. (Wilson et al., 2020, p. 28)

Further, some LGBTQ people reveal how employment discrimination negatively impacts their psychological health. A Latinx bisexual trans woman shared:

> I've been denied jobs before because I'm trans, and I think it's affected me
> emotionally to the point where even if I didn't have a physical disability,
> I don't think that mentally I'm prepared to work because of all of the things
> that I've been through related to me being trans. (Wilson et al., 2020, p. 28)

When people are living in poverty or have less ideal financial situations, they are often accused of being lazy or are victim-blamed for their circumstances (Torino & Sisselman-Borgia, 2017). However, it is evident that many systems are oppressive and make it difficult for certain people to succeed—especially when they have multiple marginalized identities.

Finally, scholars have described how employment discrimination may result in LGBTQ people engaging in **survival behaviors**, or activities that are performed as a means of obtaining money, shelter, food, or other resources, usually when one is in extreme need (Kattari & Begun, 2017; Nadal, 2020). Also known as survival crimes or survival economies, the most common examples include sex work, selling drugs, or stealing. Grant et al. (2011) found that 16% of trans people have participated in some form of survival sex or other survival behaviors. While many trans sex workers have described some positive elements of sex work, many also cite that they entered the industry because they felt they had no other choice (Nadal, Davidoff, & Fujii-Doe, 2014; Nadal, Vargas, et al., 2012).

Homelessness

For the past 2 decades, researchers have found that there is a disproportionate number of LGBTQ youth who become homeless or unhoused (Nadal, 2020). Studies suggest that the main reason for this disparity is that LGBTQ youth are being kicked out of their homes due to their LGBTQ identities or are running away from home to escape violent, heterosexist or cissexist situations (Quintana et al., 2010; B. A. Robinson, 2018). A gay Black male youth stated:

> I was in the 4th grade [when my dad started calling me "twinkle toes"]. I dealt
> with this stuff all my life. He had such a negative connotation for me that I have

extremely low self-esteem because of it now. . . . When I came out, things got even worse; that's when he started kicking me out. (B. A. Robinson, 2018, p. 8)

When LGBTQ people seek help at homeless shelters, they often meet an array of obstacles—many stemming from both overt and covert heterosexism and transphobia. In fact, some LGBTQ people (especially trans people and LGBTQ youth) have reported that shelters do not protect their physical safety or do not have LGBTQ-affirming staff who are aware of LGBTQ issues or respect gender pronouns (Coolhart & Brown, 2017; Kattari & Begun, 2017). For instance, one gay male adolescent reported an interaction at a shelter:

> After they realized I was gay, they kind of put me with the girls, where they had like a separation thing. Guys go with girls. Girls go with guys. And I know there was this one kid there that, she was gay, and they put her with the guys so that way she wouldn't be with the girls. I don't know; I just felt like it was really awkward. Because once you find out someone's sexual orientation, you have to shift everything because you think that they're gonna do something sickening or whatever. (Coolhart & Brown, 2017, p. 233)

While not explicitly stated, the participant viewed this policy to be homophobic, based on the stereotype that LGBTQ people would be sexual predators or harass their heterosexual peers.

Conversely, some LGBTQ homeless youth have reported more overt instances of homophobia or transphobia. A LGBTQ youth case manager revealed, "I've had youth tell me that staff at various shelters have told them that they'll have to get on their knees and . . . repent for their LGBT lifestyle" (Coolhart & Brown, 2017, p. 234) So, despite young people being in vulnerable situations (e.g., being homeless after being kicked out of their homophobic homes), some service providers can inflict even more homophobia or transphobia—causing additional psychological stressors or potentially even retraumatizing them.

Future studies are needed to better comprehend how intersectional identities influence lived experiences of LGBTQ homeless people. One possibility is to utilize Torino and Sisselman-Borgia's (2017) taxonomy on homeless microaggressions and to examine how themes may apply to LGBTQ people. For instance, while homeless people in general are often treated as "subhuman" or "criminal" or presumed to have "mental illness" (Torino & Sisselman-Borgia, 2017, p. 153), future researchers can examine if LGBTQ homeless people are viewed as doubly subhuman, even more dangerous, or stereotyped to have more mental health issues, due to the intersection of their perceived LGBTQ identities and homeless statuses. Finally, given that people with severe mental illness are found to be stereotyped as dangerous and violent, especially when they are people of color and homeless (Gonzales et al., 2015), further studies can investigate how race and mental illness influence LGBTQ homeless people's lives too.

Economic Barriers to Gender-Affirming Care

One primary issue for transgender people living in poverty is the inability to afford gender-affirming health care, particularly regarding medical or hormonal treatments. Not having the financial resources to transition (if they choose) can cause significant psychological stress. In one study focusing on resilience among transgender people of color, a trans male participant shared that he "had no place to turn to get help in transition—and worked five jobs trying to save money for surgery that [he] never knew if [he] would be able to afford. (Singh & McKleroy, 2011, p. 38). In the same study, one trans woman shared:

> For a long, long time I didn't have money and that meant no hormones. I was looking for acceptance in my relationships—but a lot of them [partners] just thought they could abuse me because no one else would want to be with me. (p. 38)

Not having access to these gender-affirming treatments meant that these trans people would not be able to live in their truths. The latter participant even appeared to put up with abuse from partners, believing that no one would desire her, since she was not on hormones. For both participants, it is evident that not having money or resources can be a big obstacle, particularly for trans people who want their gender presentations to match their gender identities.

CASE STUDIES

Now that we have been presented with ways that intersectional microaggressions may affect LGBTQ people of diverse religions, social classes, and immigration statuses, the following case studies are presented to elucidate the complexities when encountering such discrimination. Readers are encouraged to reflect upon their own identities and experiences, particularly paying attention to the ways that they may relate to the cases, as well as the ways they may have limited knowledge or biased reactions to the scenarios.

The Intersection of Gender Identity, Religion, and More: The Case of Kainoa

Kainoa (they/them pronouns) is a 24-year-old queer Native Hawaiian *māhū* (a word used to describe a third gender in Native Hawaiian and Tahitian cultures). Kainoa was born and raised on the Big Island in Hawai'i; they were raised in a big family, which consisted of their parents, their five siblings, and grandparents, as well as multiple uncles, aunts, and cousins who all lived in the neighborhood and whom they saw weekly at family dinners.

Kainoa was raised nonreligious; their parents identify as Protestant, but they hardly ever attended any church services or asked their children to. Kainoa's parents and grandparents also instilled a strong sense of ethnic identity in Kainoa and their siblings—teaching them about Indigenous values, histories, and cultural traditions. So, when Kainoa disclosed their identities to their parents and grandparents, they were quite accepting, due to their understanding that Native Hawaiian culture had historically held fewer rigid views of gender and sexuality, especially prior to Western colonization.

When Kainoa opened up about their queer identities to the extended family, people were generally accepting. At first, some family members struggled with switching to "they" pronouns, while others had to learn to alter some subtle gendered language (e.g., saying "Brah" when talking to Kainoa). Nonetheless, when Kainoa corrected their family members, they seemed to be receptive and caring; they told Kainoa they loved them and wanted Kainoa to feel that.

Despite this overall support, Kainoa knew there would be one family member who might not be as LGBTQ-affirming. Their maternal aunt, Aunty Leilani, had moved to Oahu 5 years earlier with her husband (Uncle Scott), shortly after they were married. When Aunty Leilani and Uncle Scott got married, she also converted to his religion—a fundamentalist Christian church that was known to preach about the sins of homosexuality, abortion, and other conservative issues. However, when Aunty Leilani had come to visit the family for holidays and other major events over the years, Kainoa never heard her say anything overtly homophobic or transphobic.

Kainoa decided to come out to Aunty Leilani when she was going to be in town for Easter. They were hopeful that she would be supportive, or that she would at least be kind in her response. When Aunty Leilani arrived at the house, Kainoa asked if they could speak in private. As they mustered up the energy to tell her, Aunty Leilani stopped Kainoa abruptly and said, "I already heard. You don't need to tell me anymore." Confused, Kainoa said, "So, does that mean you accept my identities?" Aunty Leilani replied, "I think God made you exactly the way you are and don't think you need to pretend to be something you are not." Kainoa rebutted, "But this *is* who I am." Aunty Leilani responded, "Well, then, I'm sorry to know that your soul won't be saved." She then left the room, leaving Kainoa devastated and despondent.

The Intersection of Immigration, Class, and More: The Case of Amina

Amina is a 33-year-old queer woman from Iran who first came to the United States as a 25-year-old graduate student on an F-1 student visa. Part of her initial motivation to study in the United States was because she knew that same-sex sexual activity was illegal in her home country, and she wanted to have freedom in exploring her sexual orientation identity. While she pursued a doctoral degree in economics at a university in Texas, she encountered an array of microaggressions. As an example, when revealing her last name ("Hosseini"), acquaintances would make comments about the former Iraqi dictator with a similar (but obviously different) last name. Similarly, when people learned she was Muslim, classmates asked her ignorant questions (e.g., "Did they teach terrorism when you were a kid?"). On dating apps, white women tokenized her (e.g., "I didn't know there were queer women in the Middle East") or exoticized her (e.g., "I've always wanted to kiss a Muslim girl"). Despite these incidents, she felt happier being in the United States than being in Iran, where she feared having to conceal her identity.

While Amina excelled as a student and finished all her classes, she took her time in completing her dissertation—partially because she knew that to stay in the country after she graduated, she'd be tasked with finding a job that was willing to sponsor her. Further, while her program covered her tuition and a small stipend for the first 5 years (the average time for most students to complete the degree), she knew she'd have to find alternative forms of income beyond that fifth year. Complicating her situation was the fact that as an international student, she could not apply for federal funding, nor could she legally obtain a work permit. So, she needed to find a job that was willing to pay her "under the table"; this way, she could earn money to pay for her tuition and basic costs of living, while still legally following the guidelines of her visa.

After asking around her social circles, Amina was able to obtain a job at a local lesbian bar as a barback and host. Her job involved mostly physical duties like keeping stock of liquor, clean glasses, and ice; bringing dirty dishes to the kitchen; and emptying trash. She worked almost every single night— often getting home at 4 a.m. On some nights, she stuck around and drank with some of the staff, getting home even later. While she did not have any scheduled classes or meetings in the daytime, these late shifts prevented her from doing all the tasks necessary for her dissertation. Yet, she did not mind this schedule; not only did she enjoy the sense of community she felt with all the queer women staff and patrons, but she also appreciated the financial rewards. At the end of the night (after splitting tips with the bartender), she often took home a couple of hundred dollars—enough to pay for rent, expenses, and tuition.

A whole year passed, and Amina had not made any significant progress toward graduation. Her doctoral advisor (Dr. Cunningham, an older white heterosexual woman professor) emailed her and asked to meet. At this meeting, she asked Amina about why she had not finished her dissertation. To be fully transparent, Amina was truthful about her work schedule and the limitations in the types of jobs she could obtain. She also described that she liked working in an all-queer female environment where she could be herself. Professor Cunningham replied with, "Well, is there anyone in your family who could send you money so that you don't have to work?" She added: "And can't you find a more respectable job with normal hours? There has to be something better than working in a dirty bar where everyone is drunkenly lusting after each other."

CASE STUDY DISCUSSION

These two cases demonstrate how well-intentioned people can communicate an array of biases. In the first scenario, Kainoa's aunt exhibits hostility after learning about their queer sexual orientation and nonbinary gender identity. While some might view her behavior as being overtly biased, many religious people might not feel that they are being discriminatory. When they assert that people with LGBTQ identities are bad or immoral, they claim it is out of care or concern for the person's soul. In this way, their behaviors may be best labeled as a microassault—they are overt or intentional in their commentary but are unaware or unwilling to understand the impact or hurt inflicted. In fact, if Aunty Leilani was confronted even further by Kainoa or another family member, she might have become defensive—possibly even doubling down on why her comments were neither problematic, nor biased.

In the second scenario, Dr. Cunningham may perceive her commentary to Amina as helpful advice—not realizing that in just a few sentences she participated in microaggressions that were classist, heterosexist, and insensitive to immigration issues. Yet, it is important to note that her statements reflect many biases held by members of the privileged groups she belongs to. First, many people of higher social classes do not recognize that normalized opportunities for them are not accessible or common for others; in fact, some privileged people may believe that everyone might have someone they can turn to—such as a family member for money—simply because that was a privilege they had themselves. Gray et al. (2018) described this process as "contexts and status symbols invoking awareness of class differences" (p. 1233). In their sample, people of lower social classes were very cognizant of how their more privileged peers discussed class- or income-related behaviors and traditions (e.g., frequently going on family vacations and spring break trips) or accessing materials or resources (e.g., purchasing the newest smartphones or laptops). Meanwhile, people of upper classes did not seem to be aware of how such traditions or resources were uncommon for people of lower social class backgrounds, nor regarding the impact of their assumptions and privileges onto others.

Second, in suggesting that Amina should simply obtain a new job with better hours, the professor demonstrated some potential class bias against service industries or people who perform manual labor. Previous studies have found that many people hold biases about occupations in which people serve others, such as waitstaff and bartenders (Fisk & Neville, 2011). Sometimes this sentiment is referred to as "servitude perception"—or the idea that people in service industries are inferior or deserving of dehumanizing treatment (Wildes, 2005). Because people often believe that service industry jobs should be merely a "stopover to something better" (Wildes, 2005, p. 214), they mistreat service workers or exhibit entitled behaviors—resulting in workers feeling "objectified," "diminished," "small," and "demeaned, degraded, disrespected, and inferior" (Fisk & Neville, 2011, p. 400). So, even if her advisor wasn't intentional in diminishing Amina's job, her words may have resulted in any of these emotional reactions.

Furthermore, when Dr. Cunningham did not even acknowledge the limitations of securing employment as an international student, she exhibited her lack of knowledge or compassion about the systemic barriers affecting foreign-born students. And finally, her coded use of the words "dirty bar" and "lusting after each other" might be reflective of her heterosexist biases about lesbians, queer women, or LGBTQ people in general.

Both scenarios also demonstrate the importance of social support when people encounter microaggressions. Amina appears to be alone in the ways she must navigate both systemic barriers and microaggressions. While she might have coworkers or classmates whom she likes, it might be hard for her to process her reactions or even share her perspectives with others, if she doesn't believe they can relate. On the other hand, Kainoa appears to have lots of familial support, yet having even one unsupportive relative can feel daunting and painful. Some people may ruminate on the negative and minimize the positive. However, it is hoped that Kainoa's family members can serve as allies or accomplices—pushing Aunty Leilani on her homophobic or transphobic biases, while supporting Kainoa with validation and emotional support.

Finally, one last consideration with Kainoa's situation is how their aunt's homophobia is embedded in a religion that was imposed onto their cultural group. Prior to Western colonization, Indigenous peoples across North America, the Pacific Islands, and Asia were known to be more accepting of diverse gender identities and sexualities. In Hawai'i, fundamentalist Christianity was introduced via U.S. colonization. Thus, when people hold any anti-LGBTQ beliefs—especially when those beliefs are religiously-embedded—it is crucial to reflect on the colonialism involved. In fact, perhaps if more people were aware of how heterosexism and cissexism are systemic forms of colonialism (and individual forms of colonial mentality), they might be more willing to combat these forms of oppression on both societal and internalized levels. Nonetheless, in the next chapter, we will examine the processes LGBTQ people undergo when they encounter and navigate microaggressions in their everyday lives.

DISCUSSION QUESTIONS

For General Readers

1. What types of intersectional microaggressions do you think LGBTQ religious people experience most often? Nonreligious LGBTQ people? LGBTQ immigrants? LGBTQ people of lower social classes?

2. What would you do if you were in Kainoa's situation? Amina's situation?

3. How would each of these scenarios be different if even one identity (e.g., sexual orientation, gender identity, race, religion, age, size) was different?

For Psychologists, Educators, and Other Experts

1. What are some biases you might have to challenge to increase your work with LGBTQ religious people, LGBTQ nonreligious people, and LGBTQ immigrants?

2. What psychotherapy techniques do you think would be most useful in working with Kainoa or Amina?

3. What types of countertransference issues might you have in working with Kainoa or Amina?

GLOSSARY OF KEY TERMS

agnostic A term used to describe an individual with nonreligious belief—typically someone who claims neither faith nor disbelief in a higher being.

asylee A person seeking asylum in a new country, due to past persecution or violence in their home country or substantiated fears of future persecution if they return.

asylum The process of being granted refuge or citizenship in a new country—typically after experiencing past violence or persecution (or the threat of violence/persecution in the future) in one's country of origin.

atheist A term used to describe an individual who does not believe in any higher being.

classism The negative attitudes, biases, and beliefs held about people of lower social classes or socioeconomic status, as well as the discrimination that occurs as a result.

conversion therapy An outdated, unethical, and ineffective sexual orientation change effort that attempts to change a person's sexual orientation or gender identity. Sometimes referred to as reparative therapy or reorientation therapy.

first generation A term used to describe people who seek permanent residence in another country—often starting families who are born and raised in that country.

immigrants People who seek permanent residence in another country—often for increased financial or economic opportunities.

Islamophobia Negative attitudes, biases, and beliefs held about Muslim people, or anything related to the Islamic religion, as well as the discrimination that occurs as a result.

refugees Migrants who are forced to permanently leave their countries of origin to escape war, persecution, or displacement from natural disasters.

sexual orientation change efforts A variety of outdated, unethical, and ineffective methods used by mental health professionals and nonprofessionals with the goal of changing sexual orientation or gender expression. All major professional mental health organizations have denounced the use of these methods, citing the lifelong psychological harm and trauma that is caused.

second generation A term used to describe children of immigrants who are born in the country that their parents migrated.

social class A term used to categorize people based on common values, assumptions, and beliefs, derived from economic privilege, education, access to resources, and cultural expectations.

socioeconomic status A term used to categorize people and groups based on financial income, material wealth, assets, and residence/neighborhood.

survival behaviors Activities that are performed as a means of obtaining money, shelter, food, or other resources, usually when one is in extreme need; also called "survival crimes" or "survival economies" and can include sex work, selling drugs, or stealing.

unauthorized A term used to describe immigrants who do not have legal standing to permanently reside in a country.

undocumented A term used to describe immigrants who do not have legal standing to permanently reside in a foreign country—regardless of the actual amount of time they have spent in that country or participated in civic duties.

undocuqueers LGBTQ immigrants without legal authority to reside in a country.

victim blaming Assigning fault to people who experience violence, wrong-doing, or systemic oppression; used to discredit people of historically marginalized groups who speak out against injustice or microaggressions.

xenophobia Fearful or hateful biases about people perceived as foreigners or strangers, especially those from different cultural or national groups; in the United States, this includes targeting people of color and those from non-Christian religious groups.

8

THE PROCESSES OF DEALING WITH MICROAGGRESSIONS

Considerations for Targets and Allies

FIGURE 8.1. A Queer Latino Couple Contemplating About Life

Note. Photo courtesy of Los Muertos Crew.

https://doi.org/10.1037/0000335-009
Dismantling Everyday Discrimination: Microaggressions Toward LGBTQ People, Second Edition, by K. L. Y. Nadal

For the past 15 years or so, I have been fortunate in having opportunities to speak to hundreds of audiences at college and universities, hospitals, community centers, conferences, and other venues where people are interested in hearing my work on microaggressions and other areas of multicultural psychology. During the question-and-answer portion of any of these lectures, I am usually met with an audience member who discusses a microaggression they faced (or are currently dealing with), followed by: "What should I have done?" or "What should I do?" When asked questions like these, I first tend to wonder if providing a direct answer of what I personally would do would be particularly helpful to the person. Given that situations are all so unique, that personalities and contexts impact interpersonal dynamics, and that I could not possibly understand everything from a very short description, I generally steer clear of ever giving direct advice to people. Nevertheless, I try to gather as much information as I can, while being cautious of how much the person wants to disclose, the setting in which we are currently discussing the problem, and the time constraints in our conversation. It is necessary for me to collect as much data as possible, so that I am fully aware of the many players involved as well as the potential consequences when addressing certain microaggressions.

Even after I feel comfortable that I have as much knowledge as possible and appropriate, I tend to say something like, "Well, here are a few options you could consider." I have never told someone explicitly what to do, and I can't recall a scenario where I offered only one suggestion. When I finish sharing some of my thoughts, I usually say something like, "I hope this is helpful," and I wish them luck—encouraging them to continue to seek alternative support systems and resources if possible or available and knowing that they may still have a lot of things to consider before or if they decide to do something.

As I think back on these types of interactions, I realize that the dialogue that I am having in the moment (i.e., between me and the audience member) is likely an internal monologue that they have already engaged in. The person has probably already thought about the details of the microaggression, the players involved, and the possible consequences. Yet, I usually wonder if these thoughts remain internalized or if they ever have had an opportunity to discuss their feelings with anyone else. Over time, I've viewed the value in engaging in this type of overt and drawn-out thought process, because I think it's important for individuals to verbalize their internal thoughts and to gain perspective from others, as they make decisions on how to handle these conflicts. I also believe that participating in this dialogue in front of others can be useful in providing a model for what a loved one or ally can do when someone in their life comes to them after experiencing a microaggression.

In the previous seven chapters of this book, I have provided numerous examples and case scenarios of the types of microaggressions that LGBTQ people encounter. However, this chapter takes a different approach in that it focuses on the processes of dealing with microaggressions. What do people do when they are targets of a microaggression? How do they usually feel? What would make them feel better? I begin by reviewing some foundational studies that involve the ways that various groups cope with and react to microaggressions in their lives. I then share a model that hypothesizes the various ways that people can navigate microaggressions when they occur. Finally, I share three last case vignettes from my own personal life, as a way of describing my own process of dealing with microaggressions. In doing so, I hope to convey my own internal monologues, the factors in decision making, and the speed needed to act or react to various conflicting situations.

Understanding the process of navigating microaggressions can be helpful for several audiences. First, LGBTQ people and people from other marginalized groups may find some value in learning about the ways that most people struggle when encountering microaggressions. Hearing someone else's internal monologue about what they are experiencing, their decision-making processes, and how they may be emotionally affected by microaggressions may be validating for some who are struggling with their own processes or who may be experiencing feelings of blame, shame, regret, or guilt. Second, people who care about LGBTQ people (e.g., practitioners, educators, family members) might find it useful to read about the complexities and struggles that people go through when they are subjected to these anti-LGBTQ microaggressions. Perhaps learning about these experiences can help to increase awareness of their relationship dynamics with LGBTQ people and assist in the decreasing or even erasure of microaggressions in their lives. Perhaps understanding these processes can also be helpful for allies and accomplices who want to be **upstanders** and assist their LGBTQ clients, students, or loved ones when they experience these microaggressions. Such allies and accomplices may include psychotherapists, teachers, professors, social workers, youth leaders, community organizers, parents, or other family members. In learning of some examples of how people react to microaggressions, they might be able to offer similar strategies or practical support when someone they care about goes through something similar.

PREVIOUS RESEARCH ON COPING WITH MICROAGGRESSIONS

Four foundational studies examined the psychological processes and coping mechanisms that people undergo when they experience a microaggression. These qualitative studies involved microaggressions toward lesbian, gay, bisexual, and queer people (Nadal, Wong, et al., 2011); transgender people (Nadal, Davidoff, Davis, & Wong, 2014); women (Nadal et al., 2013); and Black Americans (Sue, Capodilupo, & Holder, 2008). While all these studies focus on individuals' coping with different categories of microaggressions (e.g., sexual orientation, gender identity, gender, and racial microaggressions), there are a few themes that are clear among all of them. Thus, it is likely that some of these can also be applied to other groups including transgender people and LGBTQ people of other intersectional identities.

In Nadal, Wong, et al. (2011), queer participants reported their behavioral, emotional, and cognitive reactions when they were targeted by microaggressions. In terms of behavioral reactions, some participants reported how they were passive, choosing not to react to microaggressions; meanwhile, others shared how they protected themselves after microaggressions occurred (e.g., by avoiding certain areas where they knew they could be harassed). To illustrate this, one gay male participant stated:

> I think it is more open now, but at the same time you still gotta be careful and I could just forget about it one day and then all of a sudden a situation— I'm walking down the street, and someone looks at me with a group of boys and they look at me really dirty and it brings me back to reality . . . that "Ok . . . I have to protect myself." (Nadal Wong et al., 2011, p. 29)

This example and others demonstrate how participants were particularly conscious of the potential violence they could experience, likely because of their familiarity with the number of hate crimes that occur toward LGBTQ people. Protecting oneself may be like the "felt stigma" (Herek, 2007) that was described in Chapter 1, in which LGBTQ individuals may change their behavior to protect themselves from danger or discomfort.

On the other hand, some participants stated how they were confrontational in reaction to microaggressions (e.g., some would overtly vocalize their anger, while others might assertively question the intentions of the offender). One gay male participant recalled:

> I heard one of the kids say "flamer," and my reaction was different—I actually walked up to the kid . . . and I said: "'What did you say?" [because] I knew he'd probably back down . . . I don't think things like that should go unaddressed. (Nadal, Wong, et al., 2011, p. 29)

Examples like these demonstrate how some queer people find success when directly addressing microaggressions.

Furthermore, participants described four major categories of emotions: discomfort/lack of safety, anger and frustration, sadness, and embarrassment/ shame. They also shared two opposite thought processes: (a) acceptance and conformity and (b) resilience and empowerment. One bisexual female participant describes how she has just accepted heterosexism to be a norm in her family: "I figure that that's just the way they are. But you know. It happens. You have to accept the way they are you can't do nothing about it" (Nadal, Wong, et al., 2011, p. 30). On the other hand, a lesbian female participant reported being resilient:

> I've already been there and done the whole closeted thing I am so over that. That was miserable for me, I'm never going back to that and if people can't accept me that's their problem as far as I'm concerned and not mine. (Nadal, Wong, et al., 2011, p. 30)

So, although there were times where participants accepted that heterosexism was a reality and they conformed to or surrendered to the continuation of such norms, some participants shared that they felt resilient and empowered as queer people.

Nadal, Davidoff, Davis, and Wong (2014) explored transgender participants' emotional reactions, behavioral reactions, and cognitive reactions to transphobic microaggressions. Emotions included anger, betrayal, distress, hopelessness, and exhaustion. One example of betrayal was a participant who described how a friend ignored her in public:

> I happened to walk down the same block he was, and he moved to the left and I kept moving forward . . . but the way he moved, you know? He waved hi, but it was like he was ashamed . . . as if I was diseased. I felt very uncomfortable. I was definitely hurt. (p. 76)

An example of distress is demonstrated by a trans man: "It's hard to figure out—how do you balance being between who you are and wanting to be respected?" (p. 76).

Further, many cognitive reactions were identified, such as rationalization (e.g., justifying or understanding people's actions), vigilance and self-preservation (e.g., always being aware of their safety or people's perceptions of them), and resilience and empowerment (e.g., recognizing the need to be confident or using positive self-talk). Finally, trans participants identified their behavioral reactions to microaggressions—which ranged from direct behaviors, indirect behaviors, and passive coping. An instance of direct confrontation included a trans person actively educating someone on their transphobia: "He was extremely, extremely transphobic when we first met and I kind of felt an obligation to break him out of that and through time and dedication I did, where he then fell in love with me" (Nadal, Davidoff, Davis, & Wong, 2014, p. 78). An instance of indirect confrontation was a trans person who deflected questions with answers like, "We have to be friends for me to answer that question" (p. 78), whereas a demonstration of passive coping was a participant who revealed: "It's always that moment like, how do I minimize the attention?" (p. 78).

In Nadal et al. (2013), 10 women participants in various focus groups described their behavioral reactions, emotional reactions, and cognitive reactions when they encountered microaggressions. Behavioral reactions ranged from passivity (i.e., not responding to the microaggressions at all) to confrontation (i.e., vocalizing their frustration directly when a micro-aggression occurred). An example of passivity includes one participant who said, "My friends [and I] would . . . either laugh it off or put our heads down. . . . Or like somebody would throw up the middle finger. I don't know. What could we do? What were we supposed to say?" (p. 208). Meanwhile, an example of a confrontation included a woman who describes how she reacted to a man who catcalled her: "Basically, I just go tell him to screw off. (Laughter) The guy, the guy always is like, 'Oh yeah, whatever then I didn't need to know your number anyway.' [Then], he just walks away, just like that" (p. 210).

Parallel to the study on queer people, the women participants were also concerned with their safety. They tended to be avoidant at times (e.g., evading potential environments where microaggressions may occur) and protective (e.g., calling someone on their cell phone or walking in groups with male friends to avoid being catcalled). One participant asserted how she often feels when she is a potentially unsafe environment with a man:

> After a while it's like, okay, am I comfortable with the guy or not? What's the escape plan? What do you do now? How are you going to protect yourself? So, I think when you go through those experiences you never you never feel safe 100% even if you know the person or not. (p. 209)

Women participants reported many emotional reactions, such as feelings of humiliation, discomfort, anger, fear, and guilt. Sometimes these women would be more vocal about their feelings and externalize them to others, while other times these feelings were internalized or repressed. Finally, the women spoke of similar types of cognitive reactions as those in the prior study on queer people and microaggressions (Nadal, Issa, et al., 2011); some accepted gender microaggressions as a regular part of life, while others asserted how overcoming such incidents made them feel more resilient.

Finally, in a qualitative study with 13 self-identified Black participants, there were four major themes that participants reported when describing their reactions to microaggressions, with the first being a "healthy paranoia" that they felt (Sue, Capodilupo, & Holder, 2008, p. 329). Simply stated, they shared how they often questioned the role of race in many situations that made them feel uncomfortable. Participants viewed this as being "healthy" because they knew that many interactions were influenced by race—a schema deduced from their own personal histories and shared perspectives from Black family members and friends. Second, participants shared a "sanity check" (p. 332), in which they turned to loved ones and allies when they perceived subtle discrimination. Getting such social support was necessary to validate the person's experience and to counter any self-doubts. As one example, a participant shared:

> As opposed to being paranoid—I have people in my sphere of influence that I can call up and share my authentic feelings with, so that there's sort of this healing, there's just this healing circle that I have around myself, and these are people who I don't have to be rational with if I'm battling racism. (Sue, Capodilupo, & Holder, 2008, p. 332)

A third theme involved empowering and validating oneself; participants reported a process in which they would soothe themselves after they were targeted by microaggressions, often reminding themselves that they were not at fault. To illustrate this, one Black woman stated, "I find that is keeping your voice. . . . If I decide I want to do an intervention, I'm not necessarily doing it for them. I'm doing it for me" (Sue, Capodilupo, & Holder, 2008, p. 332). The final theme was "rescuing offenders," which is a thought process that occurs when participants consider the aggressor's feelings over their own. Many participants reported that because they were aware of stereotypes others had about Black people, that they made sure that their body language communicated nonthreatening behavior. This cognition could be considered a protective factor, in that these individuals take measures to prevent certain negative outcomes from occurring (e.g., arguments, perpetuating of stereotypes).

With all four studies, it is evident people of various marginalized groups may cope with microaggressions uniquely. Across the four groups, participants were able to illustrate the behavioral reactions, emotional reactions, and cognitive reactions that they experienced when a microaggression occurred. Behaviorally, it seemed that some individuals were passive and did nothing at all, while others were more confrontational toward the perpetrator. The emotional reactions ranged from sadness to anger to humiliation and guilt. Finally, cognitively, some participants learned to just accept things the way they were, while others learned to be resilient and to empower themselves whenever a microaggression occurred.

In all four groups, it was evident that when people were targeted by microaggressions, they were psychologically affected. While some say that they have become resilient and others claim they learned to be accepting or tolerant of others' prejudice or microaggressive behavior, they may, rather, have learned to rationalize as a way of alleviating any other negative feeling that they have. Some might consider such a coping mechanism to be a positive one, in that the person is not dwelling on their negative emotion. On the other hand, others may consider rationalizing to be a negative process, in that they are repressing or avoiding their emotions altogether. Regardless, it is up to the individual to decide which coping mechanism would be most psychologically healthy and beneficial for them. But perhaps it may be helpful for them to be cognizant of which type of coping mechanism they tend to utilize most often, as well as which ones seem to be the most effective in different types of situations.

Years after these qualitative findings on coping with microaggressions were first published, there has been a significant amount of literature exploring how people cope with or manage reactions to microaggressions. In a quantitative study with 144 college students, Sanchez et al. (2018) found that while racial microaggressions predicted psychological distress, engagement coping mechanisms (e.g., problem-solving behaviors, positive cognitive reframing, emotional support seeking) helped to decrease psychological distress. In a mixed method study with 228 college students, Ingram and Wallace (2019) revealed eight themes of "coping, bouncing back, and healing" (p. 90), including (a) strategies involving cognitive coping, cognitive reframing, and distraction; (b) involvement in advocacy, education, organizing, and activism; and (c) participating in stress reduction and self-care activities, to name a few. Specific to heterosexist microaggressions, Scharer and Taylor (2018) used a sample of 229 queer participants and found that two coping styles mediated the relationship between microaggressions and psychological distress—internalization (e.g., believing one did something wrong or should be held responsible for something bad) and detachment (e.g., disconnecting and not sharing emotions with others). In other words, while people who experienced microaggressions were more likely to report mental health symptoms, two less healthy coping mechanisms (e.g., self-blame and ignoring feelings) made those symptoms worse.

Related to coping with and managing microaggressions, Sue et al. (2019) identified microintervention strategies, which are defined as "a new strategic framework developed for addressing microaggressions that moves beyond coping and survival to concrete action steps and dialogues that targets, allies, and bystanders can perform" (p. 128). Some of these responses may include (a) remaining passive or retreating, (b) retaliating or hurting the perpetrator, (c) stopping or deflecting a harmful act, (d) educating the enactor, (e) seeking outside help from an authority figure, (f) seeking social support, and (g) acting as an ally. With each of these options, the authors note the objectives, the rationales, and the tactics involved, as well as some of the risks, benefits, and potential outcomes involved.

Relatedly, it is important to note that each microintervention strategy has its pros and cons. For instance, while passivity or retaliation are valid emotional responses that people employ after experiencing a microaggression, neither option might be an effective teaching method compared with a more assertive or diplomatic approach (e.g., educating the perpetrator). Yet it is important to acknowledge why people choose to react in such ways. Some people choose passivity as a protective act; they choose to not engage in addressing the microaggression because they want to avoid stressful or challenging interactions or the behavioral or psychological consequences they perceive will occur (e.g., arguing, getting emotionally upset, ruminating about the event later). Meanwhile, some people may choose retaliation or confrontation because they are emotionally exhausted and do not have time for **respectability**. In fact, some people of historically marginalized groups may choose not to be diplomatic as an overt act of teaching their microaggression perpetrator that their behavior was harmful.

Finally, in recent years, researchers have described the process of reacting and coping with subtle discrimination as a "microaggression tax"—which they defined as "the social, physiological, and psychological toll that microaggressions levy upon persons regarded as 'other' (e.g., people of color and LGBT populations)" (Robinson-Wood et al., 2020, p. 49). Meanwhile, the vigilance that goes into preparing for microaggressions—particularly when one knows or presumes they will be the only minoritized person (or only one of a few)—has been labeled an "armored resistance" or "a state of high alert and mimics anxiety. One anticipates an offense and holds a stance that is analogous to being in battle" (Robinson-Wood et al., 2020, p. 52). To demonstrate these concepts, one Black man revealed:

> For me, the physical symptoms are probably heightened blood pressure and anxiety because I typically enter a room and I do not see people like myself. So, I know going into that situation what my experience is going to be like. But I think even though I know that the anxiety is still there in terms of wondering if people will respect what you will be saying. (Robinson-Wood et al., 2020, pp. 49–50)

For trans people, scholars have labeled this vigilance as a "transgender identity defense stress" or "the ongoing need for trans people to defend the validity of their gender identity" (Parr & Howe, 2019, p. 464). Thus, managing microaggressions involves constantly assessing situations to avoid distress. Such hypervigilant behaviors appear to be lifelong processes—or a microaggressive tax historically marginalized people pay (emotionally or psychologically) for existing.

A MODEL IN DEALING WITH MICROAGGRESSIONS

In the *American Psychologist* article in which racial microaggressions were reintroduced to the literature, Sue et al. (2007) illustrated the "Catch 22" that people of color experience when they witness or are recipients of racial microaggressions. In other words, recipients of microaggressions may question if they should respond or react to the microaggression because of the many negative consequences that could potentially transpire. Because microaggressions are so often ambiguous, innocuous, and covert, they may wonder if they are just being paranoid or if the instance really did occur. They may even question if the perpetrator was aware of their actions, if they intended to be offensive or hurtful, or both.

This may cause the individual significant distress, particularly depending on the context, the players involved, the environment they are in, and the amount of time in which they must react. In this moment in time, they may have to instantaneously weigh their options, knowing that there can potentially be unfavorable consequences with whatever they decide to do. If they do choose to say something, an argument may ensue, which may then lead to psychological discomfort (and potentially even physical safety issues). If they choose not to say something, there is a potential of feeling regretful and ruminating on the fact that they did not say anything.

In 2010, I presented a model that involved several internal questions an individual may ask themselves in the few seconds after they observe a microaggression. This three-step model includes: (a) Did this microaggression really occur? (b) Should I respond to this microaggression? (c) How should I respond to this microaggression? (Nadal, 2010b). Let's review each of these questions.

Did This Microaggression Really Occur?

Sometimes microaggressions may be so glaringly apparent that a person can identify them easily. For example, in Chapter 3, when I described the case of

Daniel, the 14-year-old Latino boy who was constantly bullied by his class-mates, the majority of the microaggression incidents were obvious (e.g., his classmates calling him a "sissy" or a "fairy" and saying that he "played sports like a girl"). His classmates were intentionally trying to insult Daniel, and it was clear that the word choices that they used were all homophobic or transphobic. However, many incidents may occur in which individuals may question whether a microaggression really was indeed a microaggression. For instance, in the case of Marcia, the bi-curious South Asian woman with a disability, it is unclear whether her romantic crushes did not feel similarly about her because she was in a wheelchair. Similarly, Adrian, the gay Black man in Chapter 5 who feels subtle racial discrimination at gay bars, may have difficulty "proving" that his perceptions are correct. Finally, Sid, the transgender man in Chapter 4 who heard his coworker Liz use the word "trannies," may have initially wondered if he had heard her correctly or if she said something completely different. These are the types of incidents in which the LGBTQ individual may need more information or support to definitively realize that something was truly microaggressive.

When microaggressions occur in the presence of other friends and allies, it could be much easier for an individual to ask someone else if they heard, saw, or experienced the same incident. For instance, if Sid's coworker, Liz, did make the transphobic comment in front of other people at the office, Sid might ask a coworker if they heard the word that Liz used. However, when an individual is alone and experiences a microaggression, they may be confused or even feel paranoid about whether something really happened. In this case, it may be helpful to (a) trust one's instincts, (b) ask someone (e.g., bystanders or passersby) if the potential microaggression really occurred, or (c) seek support from others for validation (Nadal, 2010b). For example, perhaps Marcia just needs to trust her instincts that she does face a lot of ableist microaggressions because of her disability; because it happens so often (to her and to other people with disabilities), perhaps she can learn to feel confident that she is not just being paranoid. If she does want or need more external validation, maybe she can seek support from another friend with a disability or an ally, who can hopefully validate her experiences or serve as a "reality check" if there is indeed another factor that may be involved.

Similarly, Adrian may need to trust his instincts as well, particularly because his experience is one that is shared by so many other LGBTQ people of color and because he has similar encounters regularly. However, if he needs extra external validation, he can ask other passersby or loved ones. Let's say that Adrian noticed a specific incident in which a Black man was treated as a second-class citizen at a gay bar; perhaps he may scan the room to see if anyone (e.g., another person of color or a white ally) saw the same thing that he did. At that point, he might directly ask the other person if they had the same perception. Sometimes even a confirming facial expression from a stranger or passerby can be enough validation that someone needs to identify something as a microaggression.

Should I Respond to This Microaggression?

If the individual is at least minimally confident that the incident was indeed a microaggression, there may be two more questions to consider: (a) If they respond to this person, what are the potential risks, consequences, or both? (b) If they do not respond to this person, what are the risks, consequences, or both? (Nadal, 2010b).

There are a few factors that one might think about at this stage in the process. First, there is the very real issue of safety. If there is a potential for physical harm, the individual may wonder if confronting the person would be worth it. Given the constant high rate of hate violence toward LGBTQ people (Herek, 2017; Nadal, 2020), this is a crucial consideration, particularly for people with more marginalized identities (e.g., trans people, LGBTQ people of color). Thus, the individual must consider two more factors: (a) the environment that they are in (e.g., whether they are in a public setting with others around or not) and (b) their perceptions of the perpetrators' physical threat (e.g., the physical size and stature of the perpetrators, the number of perpetrators present, and the aggression levels or personality styles of the perpetrators; Nadal, 2010b).

Let's revisit the case of Daniel—the high school student who is being bullied and who may not want to confront his bullies at all because he may indeed worry about his safety. However, there are probably places and situations in which he especially would not want to confront his bullies; he likely would never want to confront them in a place where there were no authority figures, nor would he likely want to confront them when there were several boys there at the same time (particularly if they appeared violent or aggressive). This same type of thought process may occur for an adult LGBTQ person who overhears someone make a disparaging remark like "faggot" or "tranny" or "she-male." If the LGBTQ person was walking alone at night and overheard the slur(s), it might not be worth it to confront that individual; however, if the word was used jokingly at a workplace or university environment, perhaps they may feel safer in confronting the perpetrator directly and instantaneously.

In addition to physical safety, one may consider the psychological consequences that may occur when responding to microaggressions. Because it is likely that the perpetrator of the microaggression could become defensive, angry, and argumentative, the individual may wonder if getting into an argument would be worth it at all. Do they even have the time or energy to engage in an argument with this person? Could this microaggression lead to another microaggression? If a microaggression takes place in public (e.g., an individual overhears someone on the subway or at a grocery store say something transphobic), confronting the person (who is a stranger) may consume a significant amount of time and energy, and may not have many benefits (e.g., the target may never see the perpetrator ever again).

In other spaces, microaggressions could have practical consequences or retaliations. If a microaggression occurs in a school setting (e.g., a professor makes a heterosexist comment), a student may hesitate to confront their instructor because they may worry about their grade. If a microaggression occurs in a workplace setting (e.g., a coworker says something like, "No homo"), responding may cause potential tension in the individual's working relationship with the perpetrator, but also may damage one's potential for promotion opportunities or even threaten one's job security. Finally, sometimes confronting microaggressions might be more stressful than the actual microaggression itself; thus, perhaps a target might just walk away from a microaggression because they view it as the least stressful consequence.

Despite all of this, there are negative consequences that may occur if a person does not confront the perpetrator of the microaggression. As mentioned previously, the individual may regret not saying anything, potentially even ruminating about the scenario and about what they should have or could have said. Let's consider the earlier scenario in which an LGBTQ individual overhears a transphobic comment on the subway. If the individual walks away without saying anything to confront the perpetrator, they may feel disappointed or guilty, perhaps even worrying that the perpetrator may continue using such discriminatory language in the future. In fact, many LGBTQ people and others may feel compelled to confront perpetrators because they feel it is their responsibility to educate others about what is unacceptable and discriminatory, to prevent such behavior from continuing. Because of this, some LGBTQ people might intentionally challenge or confront microaggressions— even in the slightest ways—to avoid feeling responsible for not doing anything at all.

How Should I Respond to This Microaggression?

Once individuals do indeed decide to respond to a perpetrator, they must consider *how* they would want to react. If they are aggressive or confrontational in their approach, there may be consequences that are not constructive.

In fact, angrily yelling at someone who makes a homophobic remark may lead to a potentially destructive or exhaustive argument (that may even compromise one's safety or one's mental health). When a victim of a microaggression turns around and insults a perpetrator in reaction to feeling hurt or offended, the action may be counterproductive because now the perpetrator has a reason to be upset with the victim. For instance, if a lesbian who is being teased by her sister for being a "dyke" counteracts by teasing her sister about her weight or her intelligence, her sister may now be unable to hear how she was originally at fault for using homophobic language.

At the same time, it might be understandable when LGBTQ people (and other people of marginalized groups) do become confrontational toward perpetrators. When individuals experience many microaggressions throughout their lifetime, it is only human for them to react intensely. In fact, scholarship on **microaggressive trauma** posits that the accumulation of microaggressions may be a form of **complex trauma** (Nadal, 2018). In other words, when microaggressions are so consistent, they can feel violent and life-threatening and result in trauma symptoms like avoidance, difficulty concentrating, and nightmares.

Further, some microaggressions might be **triggers** to the greater trauma of systemic oppression or interpersonal discrimination. In the same way that a loud sound could trigger a war survivor with posttraumatic stress disorder to become **emotionally dysregulated**, a microaggression could trigger one's cumulative experiences with discrimination too (Nadal, 2018). For example, an LGBTQ young person who is bullied daily might finally "fight back" after years of being harassed. Furthermore, sometimes survivors of microaggressions may be intentional in aggressively responding to their perpetrators, to prove they are strong and resilient (e.g., because Asian American women are often stereotyped as being meek and submissive, an Asian American lesbian might vocalize her anger to prove the stereotype wrong).

When a person is targeted by a microaggression, another tactic might be to use an assertive approach by engaging in a composed and deliberate dialogue with the perpetrator. This may involve the victim calmly approaching the perpetrator, asking about their intention, and directly divulging how the microaggression made the individual feel. Perhaps this type of technique may be easier in some settings than in others. For instance, if a microaggression is committed by someone with whom the victim already has an existing relationship, it might not be difficult to directly point out the hurtful statement or behavior to this person. If the perpetrator has a history of being open-minded, reflective, and nondefensive, then perhaps the task of assertively confronting them might cause very little distress. However, if the perpetrator is a stranger, and/or if the perpetrator is one who has been known to be defensive, less reflective, or closed-minded in the past, it may be challenging to have a rational conversation about the topic.

One technique that might be helpful if one does decide to confront a perpetrator is to attack the behavior, not the person. A common tool in conflict management in general, this method involves the following:

- pointing out the behaviors of the perpetrator/offender
- using "I" statements
- emphasizing that you are not judging the individual's personality or morality

First, pointing out behaviors (or statements) involves identifying exactly what transpired. Using all facts to describe the series of events is helpful in engaging in a rational and sound dialogue and can assist in even just clarifying what happened, for example, saying, "I just want to point out that you said a term that is outdated and is considered homophobic" or "I just want to acknowledge that you used Rohan's incorrect pronouns." Next, using "I" statements means that the target or observer will accentuate how they felt in reaction to the behaviors or statements. For example, a person can say, "When you said that phrase, I felt really hurt" or "I'm having a reaction to what just happened." Sharing your own personal perspectives helps the enactor to realize the impact their behavior had on you individually and directly; so, even if the perpetrator still tries to excuse or explain their behavior, they will still know that it had a personal effect on you. Finally, emphasizing that you are only focusing on the individual's behavior and not questioning their personality or morality is useful because people in general believe they are "good" or "moral" people. Thus, when someone challenges them, they may become defensive. When people are guarded in this way, they may not actually listen to any feedback or criticism; rather, they may just start to think about the ways that they can retort or justify their actions and behaviors.

Another element that is helpful in engaging in dialogues about other sensitive issues, such as discrimination, is to ensure that both parties are actively listening. One tip that I have found to be very helpful when I have participated in such dialogues is to paraphrase what someone had said immediately after they are done speaking, as a way of clarifying that I understand their perspective. I then ask the individual to do the same after I speak my opinion or share my feelings, because I want to make sure that they know exactly where I am coming from. Using this method can be helpful because both parties must actively listen to the other's opinion instead of already formulating arguments in their head.

I must emphasize that while these are two ways of attempting to confront a microaggression, these techniques may not always be successful (and sometimes may not be successful at all). The ways that conflicts are dealt with in general are contingent on a few factors, namely, the parties involved, the history and relationship between the parties, the communication styles that are used, the environment in which the conflict takes place, and the emotions. Thus, other factors may also complicate microaggression confrontations, including the relationship between the two individuals prior to the microaggression and the emotions and communication styles of both parties. Accordingly, it may be necessary for targets of microaggressions to take all these factors into consideration when confronting an individual, to prepare for any potential stress that may emerge from the dispute.

Finally, regardless of how people handle microaggressions, it may be necessary for them to find support and resources that may help them practically but also psychologically. In terms of practical support, it may be important for people to familiarize themselves with different places, groups, and institutions that can be helpful in addressing microaggressions. For example, if a person is targeted by microaggressions in a workplace, they may want to turn to their human resources department and become acquainted with the company's policies regarding issues of discrimination and harassment. Furthermore, LGBTQ people who experience microaggressions in workplaces, school systems, and other institutions may want to be connected to local LGBTQ community or legal organizations that can assist in advocating for them if necessary (e.g., if they decide to pursue legal action when microaggressions or overt discrimination has negatively affected their work environment and ability to thrive).

At the same time, targets of microaggressions may also need social support that can be beneficial in meeting their mental health needs. Hopefully, most LGBTQ individuals have family, friends, and allies in their social support network that they can turn to when they are targets of microaggressions. However, when they are shunned by their families and friends, it would be especially beneficial for them to seek social support from LGBTQ people. In many major cities across the United States, there are LGBTQ community centers with an array of programs for many sectors within the community (e.g., counseling services, substance abuse treatment, senior support groups). There are many national LGBTQ hotlines that people can call when they need support, and there are also many websites and community organizations that can provide resources and validation to LGBTQ people in need. Finally, perhaps it would be especially helpful for LGBTQ people and allies to be more vocal and visible in their neighborhoods, workplaces, churches, and school systems so that isolated LGBTQ people know that there are indeed others who care about their well-being.

FIGURE 8.2. A Lesbian Elder Celebrating at a Pride Parade

Note. Photo courtesy of Ronê Ferreira.

CASE VIGNETTES

Throughout the chapter, I have provided several cases that have demonstrated the kinds of microaggressions that may be common for various LGBTQ people to experience. Because this section involves the processes of dealing with and coping with microaggressions, I thought it would be most beneficial for me to describe personal microaggressions that have occurred in my life as a way of illustrating how someone initially reacts to a microaggression, feels when a microaggression occurs, and decides whether to respond or confront the perpetrator. As I mentioned in the previous model, people must take several things into consideration. They must first identify that the micro-aggression did indeed occur and was indeed a microaggression. They must weigh out whether they should respond, given the environment, the parties involved, and the potential consequences. If they do choose to confront the perpetrator, they might try to be strategic in their approach. Sometimes confronting microaggressions can be successful; other times the individual may walk away from the situation feeling much more distressed than they did by the actual microaggression itself. Thus, I share these examples to demonstrate that there is not a "right" answer of how to respond to micro-aggressions. In any circumstance, there are potential negative consequences. However, it is up to the individual to make the decision that would be best for them in any given situation.

Before I begin, I must share a bit about who I am as a way of providing a context for these situations. I am a self-identified gay or queer, Filipino American, able-bodied, cisgender man who uses he, they, or *siya* pronouns. I am in my mid-40s, I have an average build, and a clean-shaven, bald head. In addition to being recognized as Filipino American, I am typically mis-taken for several other racial and ethnic groups, including Latino, Asian, Pacific Islander, Middle Eastern, and Multiracial/Black. I have grown more flexible in gender over the years (I wear makeup regularly and more femi-nine clothing sometimes), and I have been told that I have both masculine and feminine behaviors, traits, and style of speech. I have been out to all my family and friends since my mid-20s, but I know that I sometimes "pass" (mostly to people who assume that everyone is heterosexual). I have a doctoral degree in counseling psychology, and I currently identify as upper-middle class, even though my family has working- to middle-class roots. I have lived in New York City, in various parts of Manhattan, for over 20 years, but spent my whole childhood and adolescence in California. I tend to get along well with people, and I've been told that I am outspoken and out-going; however, I also admit that I tend to lie low and try not to stand out in many situations. Finally, I am married to a man of color, and we are currently parents to small children—which means we are often walking around New York City with a stroller, a baby carrier, or both.

The following three scenarios are actual situations that have occurred in my life. Some of the identifying characteristics of people and locations have been changed to protect people's privacy and identities. Pseudonyms are used when necessary.

Case Vignette 1: Returning to an Old Workplace

About 10 years ago, I was asked to speak at an LGBTQ conference that was coincidentally taking place on a college campus where I had once worked. It was the first time that I had come back to the campus in over a year, although I hadn't worked there for a few years. The conference took place on a typical workday and was attended mostly by undergraduate students. The lecture itself went very well, and I was very happy to be able to connect with the various LGBTQ student leaders that I met and engaged with. I was also excited because a former coworker of mine, Yvonne, who worked with LGBTQ students at a different institution, was in attendance too. Yvonne (a heterosexual, cisgender white woman) and I had actually worked together in the same office on this campus. She informed me that she also had not been back on campus for a while, so we both decided to go to our former department and visit any of our former coworkers who still worked there.

When we arrived at our old department, we saw several familiar faces, including the office secretary and several staff members who still worked there. Each of these staff members, who are all cisgender white women of various sexual orientations, greeted us each with a big hug. We then walked to other individuals' offices to see if there were any open doors. When we noticed that the office door of George (one of the senior staff members) was open, we knocked, and he excitedly asked us to come inside. George is a heterosexual, cisgender white man in his 40s. I always had a nice relationship with him, apart from a few minor instances of office politics that I considered typical. Thus, I was excited to see him.

Yvonne entered first and he greeted her with a big hug. Thinking it was my turn next, I approached him too, and he stuck his hand out—gesturing that he was only going to give me a handshake. Confused and taken aback, I said, still smiling, "What's with the handshake, George?" He replies, "Come on, Kevin. I'm a dude."

Many things run through my mind at this point. Why was he so willing to give a hug to Yvonne and not to me? Was it just based on gender? Did he just not hug men in general? Was it based on my sexual orientation? And is there any chance it could also be based on race?

For seconds, thoughts still flew throughout my mind. He does know that I am gay, right? I know I talked about it when I worked here years before. But I also don't know if he ever really talked about it with me or told me that he was "okay" with gay people. There were definitely a lot of times when I worked in the office that I felt like the "other" (because I was not only the only gay man in the office, but I was one of only two people of color). Why wouldn't he want to hug me? Did he think that I was going to molest him or something?

My thought process continued. Should I say something? He knows that I study microaggressions, right? Does he know he's committing a micro-aggression right now? He's an educated person in a helping profession, and he works with students. He needs to know that this is not okay. I don't work here anymore. I have nothing to lose.

I finally replied laughing: "Forget the handshake. Give me a hug!"

George then proceeds to give me a hug but does one of those "masculine" hugs where there is brief touching only in the upper body (with waists intentionally pulled away) and ends with two pats to the back. Meanwhile, my thoughts continue. Should I say anything else? I do.

"George, so is there a reason why you didn't want to give me a hug? Is it because I'm gay?" I asked, in a consciously nonthreatening way.

He said, "No, no, no. It's because I don't hug men."

"Are you sure?" I replied. "Well, how come you don't hug men?"

"I just don't," he affirmed.

"Okay. I'll let this go but know that when you do that to a gay man, it can be construed that you are scared that we are going to molest you or something."

We continued to chat about nonsense for an obligatory 3 minutes or so, before Yvonne and I both left the office. As we left the building, I turned to Yvonne and said, "What was that all about?" She validated me and we discussed what had happened for a few more minutes, before moving onto another topic. We both agreed that it was good that I said something, but we both were unclear about whether he was telling the truth.

Case Vignette 2: A Car Ride Home

After attending a birthday party with my husband and my kids, I used a rideshare app to call for a car to take us home. Our driver—a South Asian man who appeared to be in his 50s—pulled up to the curb in his large SUV. When I opened the door and confirmed my identity, he smiled and noticed that we had a stroller, several bags, and children. He offered to help, but we politely declined. As New Yorkers who don't own cars, my husband and I have become experts at quickly getting our kids into cabs or rideshares—installing car seats and fastening seat belts in record speeds. My husband sat in the back row with our toddler, and I sat in the middle row with our 10-month-old daughter, who was strapped into a car seat.

With this positioning, I was also now the sole passenger whom the driver is communicating with, as my husband and toddler were in the back. As we are finally settled and the car takes off, our 10-month-old daughter begins crying. Not knowing why she was upset, we attempted everything (e.g., a rattle, a bottle, making silly faces); however, nothing seemed to be working. At a stoplight, the driver turns around and lightheartedly says: "Maybe he is just looking for his mom."

"Um, okay." I hesitantly replied, as I started thinking about how awkward and annoying the comment was. This is a common experience for me. While walking around with my kids solo, some people will make general comments like, "Mom must have the day off, huh?" or "Your wife is so lucky that you take the kids out. My husband never does that." But when I'm walking with my husband and my kids, these types of comments are even more shocking because they can see that there are two parents equally and actively caring for the children, likely suggesting that both are invested parents (at least to people who are aware that two people of the same perceived sex could possibly be raising children).

My mind then focused on the fact that he also incorrectly gendered my daughter—referring to her with "he" pronouns. While this does not even come close to the experiences of transgender or nonbinary people when they are misgendered (especially if such microaggressions occur after they assert the pronouns they use), I presumed that the driver used "he" pronouns for a few reasons. First, our baby girl is wearing a neutral-colored parka and hat, with no signs of pink or purple. So not only is she not wearing anything that would be considered "girly" or feminine, but she is also very covered. In this way, boys are still considered the norm or default, unless there is reason to demonstrate otherwise. Second, I wonder if there was a language issue. In Tagalog, there are no "she" or "he" pronouns, but instead a gender neutral "*siya*"; so, although I presumed that he probably was not Filipino, perhaps there was some linguistic error in speaking what I presumed was not his primary language. All these thoughts rushed through my head, but I simply ignored the comment and chose not to respond, especially since I was actively trying to calm our baby. Also, I just wanted to go home—I had had a long day with the kids and wanted to make sure that this ride is as smooth and quick as possible.

Just as she eventually stopped crying (after we gave her a bottle), he persisted: "Where is the baby's mother?" asking in a tone that seemed somewhat sincere and curious. I replied, "I have no idea." I was not telling a lie; I really did not know where my children's biological mother was, and I probably never will. But I did not want to tell him the full truth because I did not think I had to. "It isn't fair," I thought. "Why do LGBTQ people always have to announce personal parts of their lives? Heterosexual couples never have to announce that they are straight, and most of them have to ever explain their family makeup or history." I was annoyed that I was even having this internal dialogue—trying not to make any eye contact with my husband or show any obvious frustration, so that my toddler would not ask me any questions.

"Is she at home?" he asked.

"Probably" I replied. I hope she is at home—her home. I hope she is safe and taking care of herself.

Then I started to think that maybe I should not be embarrassed or reluctant to tell him the full truth—to disclose that we are a queer couple raising small children. Why should I be embarrassed or annoyed? We are a proud family. I love my family. I would talk about my kids to anyone who is willing to listen to me.

Yet, I retracted that thought immediately. Maybe it's because I perceived him to be an older immigrant, and maybe I thought he would judge me. Maybe it was because I didn't think it was fair that I must "out" myself or my identities when it was not even a relevant part of the conversation. Maybe I was just annoyed because I was tired, and any open-minded or logical person could deduce that we were an LGBTQ family.

With only 5 minutes left in our ride, my heart and mind started to calm. Because the driver didn't ask any questions in hostile or threatening ways, I started to realize that he is probably just trying to engage in small talk. I still believe that his bias was embedded in subtle heterosexism, but there was no reason to do anything further. Not only would I not gain anything personally by educating him, but I also wanted to avoid any hostile or awkward confrontations, as a way of ensuring that our family got home as quickly and safely as possible.

Case Vignette 3: A Conversation With Younger Family Members

When I was in my early 30s, I was sitting in the living room of my apartment with three of my younger cousins, Andrew, Mark, and Veronica. At the time, Andrew and Mark were teenage boys (cisgender and presumably heterosexual), while their sister Veronica (also cisgender and presumably heterosexual) was a college student. I had never come out officially to any of them, but by this point in our lives, they all knew I was gay or queer, and they each often turned to me for advice or even just an escape from home. As we were watching TV and I was catching up with Veronica, the boys were horsing around with each other, in a way that a lot of teenage boys seem to do. Then suddenly, I hear Andrew teasing: "Stop being so gay!"

I immediately reacted: "What did you say?" I couldn't believe my ears. I thought that my own family members would know what is acceptable and unacceptable to say. Didn't he know that would be offensive to his gay older cousin sitting 5 feet away?

Andrew replied, embarrassingly, "Nothing."

"Did you call him 'gay'?" I calmly asked.

"Yeah, but I didn't mean it like that."

"Well, what did you mean then?" I started to notice that he was visibly uncomfortable, which made me realize that he did feel remorseful for his words. But then I started to think that if he said it at that moment, he probably said it in his everyday life with his friends. Perhaps he just knew to not to say it in front his gay older cousin, but he didn't realize how offensive the term is.

Andrew then told me that he and his friends do say things like "That's so gay," but that it has "nothing to do with gay people." He shared, "We mean it to mean things that are bad or dumb. . . . If someone was gay, I would never call him that." Mark, my other male cousin, agreed with him, sharing similar sentiments and behaviors of his own friends.

"Okay, I understand," I emphasized. "And I know you probably aren't intending to hurt a gay person's feelings when you use the word like that. But when you say things like that, you allow people to continue to think that gay people *are* bad or dumb or weird. And worse yet, if you say that in front of someone who may be gay (but in the closet), you're basically telling them that you think it's okay to make fun of gay people. And maybe that person won't come out of the closet to you because they think you'll be homophobic, when I know that you are not."

Veronica, my female cousin, chimed in and shared how she stopped saying "gay" in a negative context when she first started college. She said that she made some LGBTQ friends in her dorm and that she learned how hurtful saying "That's so gay" is. I asked her to tell me about everything that she has learned about LGBTQ people. I smiled as she told me that she knew words like "transgender" and "pansexual" and "queer," and I smiled even more as her brothers listened to her. The boys and I continued to talk about the term, and they promised me that they wouldn't use the term anymore. They also promised me that they would try to correct their friends too. We changed the subject and continued watching TV.

CASE VIGNETTE DISCUSSION

In all three of the scenarios, I attempted to illustrate the sorts of microaggressions that may occur, as well as the internal thought processes that can accompany them. In each scenario, you can notice each step that occurred. First, I had to decide if the microaggression did occur. Did my former coworker intentionally avoid giving me a hug? Did the car driver reporter really ask about where our baby's mother was? Did my cousin really use "gay" in a negative context? Next, I had to question if heterosexism or other bias was involved. Was my former coworker being heterosexist in not wanting to hug me? Was the driver demonstrating heteronormative bias in assuming that one of us was married to the mother of our children? Was my cousin's comment reflective of a heterosexist bias that gay people were bad or weird?

When I did recognize that the incident was a microaggression, I had to decide if I wanted to reply. For the first scenario, I thought to myself, "I had nothing to lose" because I no longer worked in the department. So even if my former supervisor did become very defensive, I would not have to deal with him on a regular basis after that. If I had still worked there, perhaps I would not have said anything, to avoid any potential tension or retaliation. Perhaps I also realized that he might be willing to engage in a conversation with me because I knew that he is an educated person in a helping profession, which would hopefully mean that he would have good communication skills, good self-awareness, or both. Perhaps I also felt safe because my friend Yvonne was present, and I trusted that she would come to my aid if the conversation needed another perspective. Given all these factors, I decided to say something. However, it is important to acknowledge that if the circumstances were even slightly different, perhaps I would not have said anything at all.

In the second scenario, I chose to barely do or say anything at all. Sure, I answered his questions in a way that I felt comfortable with. Yet, I did not address why his comments were offensive and presumptuous (and embedded in heteronormative biases). So, while my silence might mean that he may continue to act upon those biases with others in his life (especially future LGBTQ passengers), I chose not to say anything because I determined that it "wasn't worth it." I wanted my family to get home safely, and I didn't have the emotional capacity to provide a lesson on queer families for a stranger whom I would never see again. Perhaps I also thought that a brief conversation about heteronormativity would not have made a difference in his life and that maybe he would have to learn about it another time. Perhaps the cultural dynamics negatively influenced my ability to openly talk about being gay. Because Asian American cultures may tend not to talk about LGBTQ issues (and sexuality in general), and because elders are to be revered, I likely wanted to avoid any conflicts or awkwardness.

In this second scenario, my interaction with the car driver matches a common microaggression for LGBTQ parents. Previous research indicates that many LGBTQ people who are raising children are deemed to not be a "real family" because they don't match the heteronormative standard that dictates that a family includes a cisgender mother and a cisgender father (Haines et al., 2018, p. 1138). These kinds of heterosexist microaggressions can be especially frustrating for LGBTQ parents, as many must undergo numerous systemic obstacles to adopt children and form their families legally (Estrellado et al., 2021).

In the final scenario, I decided to confront the microaggression directly and instantaneously for a few reasons. First, it involved my family members, whom I genuinely care about and whom I want to be aware about LGBTQ issues and power and privilege issues in general. Second, because I was the oldest person in the room (with the most education and the most material wealth) and because it was my home, I had the most power in the room, which likely meant that I felt comfortable leading a conversation about the topic. If the perpetrator of the microaggression was an older person in my family, or if the conversation took place in the home of the perpetrator of the microaggressions, perhaps I would not have been as forthright with initiating the conversation.

In all three scenarios, I also illustrated different ways of handling certain situations. While I did directly confront my former coworker in the first scenario, I consciously tried to be as nonthreatening as possible; I did not raise my voice, and I attempted to keep a light-hearted attitude, by maintaining the demeanor I held just before the interaction occurred. I imagine that if I became aggressive in any way, George could have used that as an excuse to dismiss my point. I also realize that he may have viewed any aggression from a person of color as potentially threatening—a common occurrence for many people of color (Johnson et al., 2021; Sue, Capodilupo, Nadal, & Torino, 2008; Sue, Lin, et al., 2009). So, I simply asked him directly about his intention and his behavior. And whether George was being honest with me about his intention, I walked away feeling satisfied that I assertively confronted him.

While I did not take much action at all in the second scenario, I did try to answer the driver's questions as truthfully as possible. In some ways, I was entertaining myself by stretching the truth with my answers. When I processed the whole situation with my husband after the kids were asleep, we laughed at the creativity in my answers. Sometimes being able to laugh at certain difficult situations can be a healthy way of dealing with them. While there are certain microaggressions with consequences that might not be funny at all, there might be some instances in which people use humor to overcome some of the nonsense that they have to deal with. As an example, my friends and I have laughed about the horrible race-based pickup lines that men use to try to pick us up at the bar and have shared our common responses (e.g., when someone curious about my ethnicity has asked, "So, what are you?" I have often replied, "I'm a Taurus!"). Sometimes, using humor can be a way of bonding with others who encounter similar microaggressions, while validating others who may take comfort in knowing they are not the only ones who are targeted by certain microaggressive incidents.

As a final note, the way that I chose to handle the third scenario was again to remain calm and collected. I did not want to shame my cousin, nor did I want it to seem that I was punishing him. So, I tried to validate him by telling him that I didn't think that he was homophobic but that his behavior might be perceived that way. I also wanted him to hear my perspective and to teach him about how to be a better person toward LGBTQ people. I also made sure to listen to his perspective (even repeating his words for clarification), so that he knew that I understood him too. Either way, I was very happy to say that the conversation felt good and effective. I was even happier when both reported how they taught their friends to stop saying "That's so gay!" too.

Now that we have examined the various processes that LGBTQ people may undergo when encountering microaggressions, the last chapter will help the reader understand some of the ways that all people (including LGBTQ people and cisgender or heterosexual allies) can help to decrease microaggressions on individual and systemic levels.

DISCUSSION QUESTIONS

For General Readers

1. What goes through your mind when you are targeted by a microaggression?
2. Do you tend to confront microaggressions when they occur?
3. Are there certain people that you avoid confronting? How come?

For Psychologists, Educators, and Other Experts

1. What were your reactions to each vignette? What would you have done differently?

2. Have you experienced similar types of microaggressions in your life? How did you handle these instances? Were you happy about how you handled these microaggressions?

3. If one of your LGBTQ clients, students, or other constituents shared with you that they experienced a microaggression in their families, workplaces, or communities, how would you respond?

4. If one of your LGBTQ clients, students, or someone else challenged you on a microaggression that you committed, how would you respond?

GLOSSARY OF KEY TERMS

complex trauma The exposure to multiple (often repeated) traumatic events and the range of long-term effects of this exposure; the term was used initially to refer to the repeated traumas (and enduring trauma symptoms) experienced by survivors of childhood sexual abuse.

emotional dysregulation The inability to manage one's emotional or behavioral responses to psychological distress.

microaggressive trauma Excessive and continuous exposure to subtle discrimination (both interpersonal and systemic) and the subsequent symptoms that develop or persist as a result.

respectability The state or quality of being proper, correct, and socially acceptable—often used by historically marginalized groups to describe the ways in which they are encouraged to assimilate or appease the dominant group.

trigger A person, place, or event—often a reminder of a previous trauma—that affects an individual's emotional or psychological state and results in extreme feelings of psychological distress.

upstander People who intervene when violent or discriminatory behavior occurs—typically sacrificing their own comfort and self-preservation in the name of justice and equity.

9

CONCLUSION

Recommendations for LGBTQ People, Allies, and Upstanders

FIGURE 9.1. A Multigenerational LGBTQ Chosen Family

Note. Photo courtesy of Pavel Danilyuk.

https://doi.org/10.1037/0000335-010
Dismantling Everyday Discrimination: Microaggressions Toward LGBTQ People, Second Edition, by K. L. Y. Nadal

It has often been said that academics and researchers, particularly those in the social sciences, "preach to the choir" because we conduct our studies and publish our findings for the rest of the academic community to see and read, without general society members ever really discovering what we have found. I have found myself being guilty of this. While I know that I have published an extensive amount of academic literature regarding multicultural issues in psychology, my guess is that most of the people who read it are other professors, other researchers, graduate students, and maybe a few other practitioners (e.g., teachers, nonprofit directors, student services personnel). I sometimes wonder if the people who might be most influenced by our work know that we are even doing it—or if the work we are doing affects them. For example, do the young LGBTQ kids who are bullied everyday know that there are so many people who care about their physical and psychological safety and are trying our best to advocate for their needs? Does the transgender person of color who is being discriminated against every day because of their race and gender identity know that there are people out there who are writing about "intersectional identities" and the psychological distress that stems from having dual minority statuses? Does the LGBTQ person who constantly hears homophobic phrases like "That's so gay," "No homo," or "tranny" at their workplaces or schools know that this is called a "microaggression," that it is a real and common experience for LGBTQ people and other marginalized groups, and that it can negatively impact their mental health? While the internet and social media have increased people's access to knowledge over past 2 decades, I presume many people still have never heard about terms like "intersectional identities" or "microaggressions." And with conservative politicians' fight to keep queer studies, ethnic studies, and critical race theory out of classrooms, I fear that perhaps many never will.

Because it can be so easy for psychological literature to remain stuck in PsycInfo and other academic databases, it is important for scholars and researchers to make our work much more accessible to the people who might directly benefit from it. We cannot just write in academic jargon any longer and reserve our words of wisdom for professional conferences and college-level classes. We cannot remain complacent when we get another manuscript accepted in a peer-reviewed journal, even if we know that it will help us with our tenures or promotions. We cannot simply encourage students to critically think about multicultural or social justice issues and hope for the best. If we are truly passionate about our work (as I know most of us claim to be), we must make sure that our work somehow gets translated and applied.

Specific to psychologists, I once wrote of the importance of us all becoming "psychologist–activists" and ensuring that we integrate social justice principles into every aspect of our work and our everyday lives (Nadal, 2017). We can do this by using our roles as researchers to influence policy—via sharing our expertise in court cases or pushing elected officials to advocate for equitable laws. We can use our roles as educators to teach young people about our country's history of colonialism, genocide, slavery, and oppression—and how that history persists in our laws, educational systems, and normalized cultural practices today. We can use our roles as therapists to validate clients' perceptions of discrimination and providing emotional and psychoeducational support that can lead to their healing and empowerment. We can also use our personal roles as parents, family members, friends, and neighbors to teach people about the various atrocities still happening in the world—encouraging them to be accomplices and upstanders for justice.

I recognize that these words might seem too idealistic, and that whenever a social issue or problem starts to be recognized by general society, it can be very easy for people to simply think, "Well, what can I really do about that?" It can be easy to feel apathetic and to believe that there are few things that one individual can do to make real change in the world. Issues like war, hate violence, HIV/AIDS, poverty, and homelessness may be difficult to tackle alone as one individual. However, I am a firm believer that if every single person did their part, big or small, we could collectively make a difference and instill change. And even if that change comes slowly, or not at all, we still need to be active however we can, because at least we would be trying to do something, instead of nothing.

My mentor, Derald Wing Sue, and his colleagues (2019) introduced the concept of microinterventions, or the everyday actions that people can take to disarm microaggressions and advocate for social justice. Sue et al. (2020) highlighted an array of tactics that people can employ in their everyday lives, including naming incidents (e.g., "That was a microaggression."); restating phrases or actions (e.g., "So you're saying that because I'm a lesbian, I must be more masculine presenting?"); and reversing, redirecting, or mimicking statements to perpetrators (e.g., after a white person asks an Asian American "Where are you really from?," responding with the same line of questioning).

This final chapter focuses on what *you* can do to help combat microaggressions. Whether you're a parent or educator who is always aiming to teach your children or students about justice, or you're a mental health practitioner or community leader who wants to assist your clients or constituents when they face discrimination, there are many actions that you can take to advocate against microaggressions and the systems that perpetuate them. Some of these recommendations might feel too big to tackle—especially when a person does not have the power or resources to make it happen; these strategies may require finding other accomplices to assist in the cause and engaging in some community organizing. However, some of these recommendations are not difficult at all. They might just require some courage and the conviction to overcome a bit of discomfort. But if you know that you can take some action to make even a little bit of change in the world, wouldn't you want to take it? If you knew that you could make even a little difference to help an LGBTQ person avoid feeling a lifetime of psychological distress, wouldn't you want to make that difference?

RECOMMENDATIONS FOR FAMILIES

To first tackle microaggressions, it is necessary to start with the home. Families are where children first learn about their values and where they initially start to develop their personalities. It is also where they learn their first messages about anything that is different (e.g., race, religion, gender, or sexual orientation), which may in turn have an impact on their values and personalities. Thus, it is necessary for parents to openly discuss issues of diversity and difference with their children from a very early age—directly addressing the reality of power, oppression, and fairness in the world. Perhaps the easiest thing to do is prevent microaggressions before they happen. When parents have dialogues about discrimination, prejudice, and diversity from an early age, they can start with elementary lessons (e.g., how hateful words and behaviors can hurt others). They may also initially discuss diversity of all sorts, ranging from gender to sexual orientation, to race and ethnicity, to religion, ability, social class, and size, so that their children already have familiarity with other groups.

Studies on racial socialization (or the ways that children and young people are taught about race) are critical in understanding how race negatively influences the biased thoughts and behaviors of children and adolescents (see Wang et al., 2020, for a review). Studies have found that Black American children are likely to learn about race and racism from their parents from a very early age; furthermore, when Black American children have more awareness of race, they have been found to attain better grades in school, have fewer behavioral problems, and develop healthier racial identities (Brown & Tylka, 2011). On the other hand, white students who learn about historical racism in the United States during elementary and middle school are more likely to have less biased attitudes towards Black people than those who do not. Thus, learning about discrimination from an early age has its advantages for both those of the dominant group and the target group.

Applying this knowledge in order to teach our children about acceptance of LGBTQ people and experiences can be helpful for children in two ways. First, like the white adults who learned about racism from an early age, perhaps a heterosexual adult who was taught as a child to be accepting of all people, including those of diverse sexualities and genders, maintains fewer biases and becomes a more empathetic, compassionate, and socially conscious human being. In fact, research has found that people who identify as heterosexual allies attribute these values to childhood upbringings of normalized LGBTQ-affirming messages and parents who conveyed open-mindedness and egalitarianism—in addition to witnessing or experiencing discrimination themselves (Goldstein & Davis, 2010). Thus, teaching children to be LGBTQ-affirming can result in them becoming the types of adults who might be less likely to commit sexual-orientation and gender identity micro-aggressions, who might be less defensive and more open to admitting fault if or when they do commit microaggressions, or who might be more able to stand up against microaggressions when they witness them.

On the other hand, if a child does later identify as LGBTQ, growing up in a family with normalized LGBTQ experiences can be validating, can lead to healthier self-esteem and positive psychological outcomes, and can prevent or reduce one's propensity to internalize oppressive messages about themselves or their identity groups. Like the Black Americans who were taught about race from an early age and were better equipped to navigate racism accordingly (Brown & Tylka, 2011), it is possible that LGBTQ children who are taught to love themselves may develop good self-esteem, have healthier senses of themselves, and perhaps even perform better in school. Further, LGBTQ children who learn about how transphobia and heterosexism are societal problems (instead of learning that queerness is bad or pathological) might be better at externalizing negative emotions (like shame or guilt), instead of internalizing them (e.g., blaming themselves; Nadal & Mendoza, 2014). Thus, when they encounter microaggressions, they might better identify the event as being heterosexist or transphobic and use myriad coping mechanisms and inner strength to respond effectively. Given the number of mental health issues faced by LGBTQ children and youth (Torre & Avory, 2021)—the feeling of isolation in particular (Garcia et al., 2020)—it is crucial for families to provide LGBTQ-affirming environments where they can feel accepted, celebrated, and empowered.

Parents and other family members must also recognize the biases they hold and how those biases may unintentionally affect those that are around them. For example, because many people tend to have assumptions about gender role norms and what is considered "acceptable" for boys or girls, they may act (or react), consciously or unconsciously, when another family member, particularly a child, engages in gender nonconforming behaviors. Previous research finds that LGBTQ people were more likely to encounter microaggressions in their families when they identified as transgender or nonbinary or when they had higher levels of gender nonconformity; people also experienced more familial microaggressions when their families had higher level of child maltreatment or religiosity (Gartner & Sterzing, 2018).

Given this, messages about gender roles can affect both trans and cisgender children. Imagine a situation in which a young child, who was assigned male at birth, wears a dress. A family member might violently tell them, "Dresses are only for girls!" or "Be a man!"—communicating that gender roles are rigid and that boys have limited ways of dressing. Such messages can negatively affect the child regardless of their gender identity. If the child is transgender or nonbinary, the accumulation of messages like these can take a negative toll on their self-esteem, perhaps even impacting the child's development and mental health. If the child is not transgender (i.e., identifies as a boy), hearing statements like these can reinforce the stereotypes that boys are supposed to be masculine and emotionally restrictive. As a result, perhaps this child might not be able to express healthy emotions during adolescence or adulthood because he believes it would make him less of a man. So, instead of dealing with problems in healthy ways, he may turn to anger, violence, or even substance abuse—common behaviors for cisgender men when they are emotionally dysregulated.

It is also important for parents and other family members to set a tone for what is acceptable language and behavior in the home. If a child calls another a "fag" or a "dyke" as a synonym for "bad" or "weird," and a parent does not say anything to correct that, the child is unconsciously learning that such language and behavior is accepted, not just in the home but also in any environment. Because of this, addressing microaggressions like these in direct and straightforward ways can help to extinguish negative behaviors. Engaging in nonpunitive conversations when directly confronting microaggressions would be ideal, so that children can learn *why* they should not be using homophobic or transphobic language, instead of just stopping to be politically correct. As an example, in Chapter 8, I shared the story of a conversation that I had with a younger teenage family member about his use of the term "gay." While I easily could have punished him and told him to stop, I instead engaged him in a conversation so that he could understand my perspective and why use of the term was hurtful.

Dealing with microaggressions in families does not just consist of promoting safe and accepting environments with children, it also means confronting microaggressions with other adults in the family. Sometimes I hear people say things like, "Well, she's my grandma and she's 80 years old, so there is no use even trying to talk to her about it," or "Well, my uncle is really religious, so I just don't listen to him when he says homophobic things." While each family is different, with a huge spectrum of dynamics involved, allowing anyone in the family (regardless of age, generation, religion, or life experience) to make offensive microaggressive comments can create a hostile environment. If "grandma" or "uncle" or someone else makes these upsetting comments, perhaps you personally have the emotional strength to dismiss them, but what about the young LGBTQ teenager in the room who is struggling with their identity? If you do not say anything, that teenager may assume that you agree with that person or are at least tolerant of their views. While you may not be able to change that person's mind, you can at least vocalize something like, "I know that this is your opinion, but I don't agree with what you are saying, and I'd appreciate it if you didn't say things like this around the family." In doing so, you become an accomplice or upstander in the room for anyone who might identify as LGBTQ, and research suggests that you also create a safer environment, one in which your confrontation can minimize the potential of further microaggressions from occurring (LeMaire & Oswald, 2016).

One last recommendation for families is to normalize the experiences of LGBTQ people. Instead of treating them as an outside group, perhaps getting to know more about LGBTQ history, LGBTQ communities, and LGBTQ people's lives can help someone to feel more comfortable with LGBTQ people instead of viewing them as the "other." Research has found that heterosexual people who are more exposed to lesbian and gay people are more likely to hold less biased attitudes; similarly, people who are more educated, less religious, and have fewer rigid views about gender roles are also less likely to be heterosexist (Burgess & Baunach, 2014). Thus, it would be beneficial for people to become more educated about LGBTQ people by attending LGBTQ community events, watching LGBTQ films, and reading LGBTQ literature. If your town or community offers it, take your child or teenager to a queer-affirming theater space or a spoken word night at an LGBTQ poetry space. If they don't, seek age-appropriate LGBTQ-affirming animated short films (e.g., *Out* or *In a Heartbeat*) movies (e.g., *Moonlight*; *Camp*; *Pariah*; or *Love, Simon*), or television shows (*Pose*; *Glee*; *The Fosters*; or *Love, Victor*). Teaching loved ones about oppression and normalizing LGBTQ people's lives can decrease people's biases. Such efforts may also minimize others' micro-aggressive behaviors; promote safer and more inclusive spaces; and even decrease LGBTQ people's cumulative encounters with microaggressions, hate violence, and other forms of discrimination.

Getting to know LGBTQ people can be another way of increasing familiarity with the group, which in turn can minimize your own biases and the biases held by other family members. Introducing LGBTQ people to your family can be another way of fostering the acceptance of LGBTQ people in general, while also decreasing microaggressions that may occur within your home and your loved ones' lives outside of the family. While I am not saying to "go out and make a token LGBTQ friend," I am instead suggesting for everyone to consider organically fostering friendships with LGBTQ people, while genuinely getting to learn about their life experiences and realities. Exposure to people or things that are different from you can be the best way to eliminate the fear or trepidation that you may have had about them.

RECOMMENDATIONS FOR SCHOOLS

Besides families, school systems are the other primary places where children learn about issues of diversity and difference. Because of this, it is necessary that such issues be taught in competent and appropriate ways to foster the most optimal levels of acceptance while minimizing the potential of microaggressions toward students. It is first necessary to acknowledge that there are many systemic and institutional obstacles that need to be addressed. In doing so, individuals will have more informed data in how to approach the problem—recognizing that there may be many policies and bureaucratic barriers that may hinder their ability for advocating for justice. For example, does the school have an antidiscrimination policy, an antibullying policy, or both? Are these policies effective and conducive to creating a safe environment for their students? If the answer is yes, then perhaps more of the focus needs to be on enforcing these policies. If the answer is no, then perhaps the school community needs to create these policies to ensure that they have the best interests of the children in mind. In fact, if a school does not have an antibullying policy, then perhaps the parent-teacher association needs to advocate for it.

As I mentioned in Chapter 1, nearly nine out of 10 LGBTQ students reported harassment at school and about two thirds felt unsafe because of their sexual orientation. As a result, many LGBTQ students skip school regularly, and those who were harassed regularly had lower grade point averages than those who were less harassed (Kosciw et al., 2020). If children do not feel safe in their own schools, how can we expect them to learn and perform well? And if these policies do not exist (or are not enforced), who will advocate for them if parents and teachers do not?

Further, when students are bullied for being (or being perceived to be) LGBTQ, it can be extremely devastating for them to report such incidents to their teachers or principals for two main reasons: First, they may fear that their bullies may retaliate, and second, they may have to admit to being LGBTQ or that the bullying involved their sexual orientation or gender identities (something they may not be comfortable to talk about). So, it cannot simply be that school systems rely on LGBTQ students to advocate for themselves; there must be preventative measures to make changes on institutional levels.

Relatedly, it is necessary to acknowledge that most educational systems operate on heteronormative structures and pedagogies—isolating LGBTQ students who are struggling with their identities. For instance, "abstinence-only-until-marriage" programs are one type of programming that can be very isolating for LGBTQ students while also enabling the heterosexist bullying and harassment that occurs in school hallways and classrooms (O'Quinn & Fields, 2020). Because children and adolescents are taught that sexuality is acceptable only in the context of heterosexual marriage, students may view heterosexuality and gender conformity as the norm (resulting in heterosexual and cisgender students feeling normalized, while LGBTQ students may learn that they are different or inferior). Thus, it is important for educators on all levels to recognize that if they want their LGBTQ students to feel included, they need to revisit the programs and pedagogies they are teaching and promoting.

There are many things that teachers can do to create a safe environment to promote diversity and minimize microaggressions. Understanding Prejudice (2021) provides a helpful list called "Tips for Elementary School Teachers" that can be very useful for educators hoping to inspire justice-oriented students. Some recommendations include the following:

- creating an inclusive environment (e.g., ensuring that classroom posters, pictures, books, music, toys, dolls, and other materials are diverse in terms of race, ethnicity, gender, age, family situations, disabilities, and so on)

- integrating children's own experiences (e.g., avoiding a "tourist approach" to multiculturalism that limits diversity to holidays, special events, and history months)

- addressing children's questions and concerns (e.g., directly answering diversity-related questions rather than side-stepping the question or changing the topic)

- dealing with discriminatory behavior (e.g., explicitly stating and explaining why racial, ethnic, religious, sexual, or other offensive jokes, slurs, or behaviors are not tolerated)

I appreciate this list because there are practical techniques for teachers to use; they can also be applied to all levels: middle school, high school, and even college and graduate school.

Of the many recommendations, these four tips seem most salient for me. First, creating an inclusive classroom is important for children as a way of combating the power and privilege that can be taught in classroom settings. Peggy McIntosh (2003) wrote about "white privilege" and how one of the privileges of being white is that they see images of themselves everywhere (e.g., in magazines, television, picture books), which in turn allows them to feel normalized and perhaps unconsciously superior. Thus, children must be exposed to literature that depicts LGBTQ people in positive lights so that (a) heterosexual children learn to be inclusive of LGBTQ experiences and (b) LGBTQ children do not feel excluded, which then may negatively influence their learning. When reading books to children about families, perhaps it might be useful to integrate books with same-sex parents or divorced parents or grandparents as the primary guardians; in doing so, children who belong to these types of families can feel accepted and those who do not can become more educated that all types of family are common and just as good as their own.

Second, I appreciated that the list included "avoiding a tourist approach." When diversity becomes an afterthought that is discussed only on special occasions, teachers may inadvertently communicate that it is not as important as topics that get integrated regularly. As an example, teaching children about discipline is not something that is only reserved for special occasions; it is something that is integrated into everyday curriculum. Sometimes it may not be planned, and it may be something that the teacher must suddenly integrate into the lesson plan for the day. Teaching discipline is usually inconvenient and stress-provoking; however, teachers also know that it is a crucial part of students' learning and development. Diversity should be taught the same way. LGBTQ examples can be introduced into all school subjects, including everything from social studies to math problems to reading assignments. Again, when LGBTQ people's (and other groups') experiences are normalized, minoritized students may feel validated, privileged students' biases might be reduced, and microaggressions might be minimized.

Furthermore, my thoughts about addressing children's questions and concerns directly and dealing with discriminatory behaviors are akin to how I feel they should be treated in the family. First, students should not be punished when they commit a microaggression; rather, it is important that they understand why it is hurtful for others when they make certain comments. Second, being direct and vocal when a microaggression occurs is necessary because silence can convey acceptance, agreement, or tolerance. If a teacher hears a homophobic or transphobic slur being used, it is necessary that they address it right away. Even if a teacher hears a homophobic or transphobic slur being used by another teacher—which Kosciw et al. (2020) reported was a common occurrence for LGBTQ students—it is necessary for the teacher for be vigilant that such language is not viewed as acceptable. In this way, **restorative justice**, or "an approach to discipline that engages all parties in a balanced practice that brings together all people impacted by an issue or behavior" (Gonzalez, 2012, p. 281), would be most effective. Perpetrators of microaggressions might not learn why their behaviors are harmful, if they are merely punished; helping them to understand the effects of their hurtful actions instead (potentially from the target themselves or from upstanders who are personally impacted by the behaviors) might lead to more empathy and understanding.

In applying restorative justice principles, it is critical to be flexible and to center the needs or perspectives of an individual who was clearly violently targeted or oppressed. For instance, that targeted person may not want to meet face-to-face with their abuser—out of fear of retraumatization, retaliation, or some other negative emotion. In this way, the engagement from the perspective of the survivor or targeted person might include asking what types of actions or accountability would be needed for them to feel the most healing from the situation.

One last consideration regarding educational settings is to understand that microaggressions can endure on all educational levels. Prior research has indicated that LGBTQ college students and graduate students encounter a great deal of microaggression on campus—often influencing psychological and behavioral issues like physical health issues, drinking, substance use, depression, and suicide (Kalb et al., 2018; Winberg et al., 2019; Woodford et al., 2012, 2018). Further, another study found that LGBTQ college students who reported more microaggressions often reported greater discomfort in their classrooms and reported fewer intentions to continue studying at their university (Crane et al., 2022). Thus, institutions may even lose their students if they fail to address microaggressions on campus.

RECOMMENDATIONS FOR WORKPLACES

Workplaces and other organizations are also places where microaggressions can occur frequently. One of the difficulties with microaggressions that occur in the workplace is that there are so many factors involved that may influence the ways that they manifest and the ways that people react to them. First, because of power dynamics among employers, employees, and coworkers, it may be difficult to confront microaggressions because one might be concerned about the security of their employment, as well as other potential tension that may transpire. Second, because microaggressions are so subtle and innocuous, it can be difficult for an individual to "prove" their intent, particularly if they want to report such instances to human resources. Because of these factors, workplace discrimination cases—especially those involving LGBTQ identities—are often very challenging and often result in unjust outcomes (Nadal, 2020).

Thus, there are few things that employers can do to promote comfortable and culturally competent work environments and also prevent microaggressions from occurring. Perhaps the most important thing is to integrate education about microaggressions into multicultural competence training models and other workplace conduct trainings in all employment settings. While some trainings on sexual harassment or discrimination may be mandated for certain workplaces across various jurisdictions, some work environments may also require their employees to attend some sort of "diversity training" when they are newly hired. However, because many individuals attend grudgingly because many of them may believe that racism and other forms of discrimination no longer exist, it may be important for these trainings to focus on microaggressions (i.e., subtle discrimination) and how their unconscious and unintentional biases and behaviors may negatively influence their professional relationships. Moreover, because diversity seminars may tend to focus on race and often may not include issues related to sexual or gender identity, employers must ensure that LGBTQ people (and other marginalized groups) are included and that intersectional identities are always considered.

It is necessary for employers and supervisors to remain aware of microaggressions and the ways that such instances can affect workplace dynamics. First, with microaggressions specific to LGBTQ people, employers and supervisors must model what is appropriate language and behavior to use in the office. For instance, using phrases like "partners" instead of "husbands and wives" can be so beneficial in promoting an LGBTQ-friendly environment. Second, when microaggressions do occur, supervisors and other workplace leaders should learn to enact and model effective interpersonal skills in coping with microaggressions (e.g., acting nondefensive when confronted by an employee or coworker on microaggressive behaviors). Some of the techniques that I discussed in Chapter 8 (e.g., using "I" statements, active listening) can be useful in supporting employees to feel heard and validated.

Creating an open environment in which it would be comfortable and safe to discuss microaggressions is necessary for promoting an accepting work environment. For instance, when multicultural topics (e.g., issues related to race, gender, sexual orientation) are integrated openly into staff meetings and other work interactions, employees may feel safe and open to address microaggressions when they do occur. Perhaps open dialogues can be facilitated in which coworkers can voice their opinions about issues related to diversity. Either way, discussing microaggressions can be helpful because they promote safe environments while preventing future microaggressions from occurring.

Finally, policies regarding anti-LGBTQ microaggressions can be instilled in any and every work environment. Such measures are especially important, since the U.S. Supreme Court ruled in 2020 that gender identity and sexual orientation should be considered protected classes in Title VII of the Civil Rights Act of 1964 and that any workplace discrimination based on sexual orientation or gender identity was unconstitutional (Liu et al., 2021).

FIGURE 9.2. Two Gay Men Joyfully Strolling Through the Park

Note. Photo courtesy of Ketut Subiyanto.

Thus, workplaces and other institutions should be encouraged to develop their own policies to prevent any type of discrimination against LGBTQ people—not just to create inclusive spaces, but also to adhere to federal law. Specific to microaggressions, companies may consider creating procedures and protocol for dealing with incidents involving the subtle forms of discrimination while promoting LGBTQ-affirming environments (e.g., policies for promoting pronoun inclusivity, policies regarding homophobic or transphobic language). If employers themselves do not take initiative in implementing such policies, unions or other employee organizations can advocate for these policies to protect their fellow LGBTQ employees in the workplace.

RECOMMENDATIONS FOR NEIGHBORHOODS AND COMMUNITIES

When I refer to neighborhoods and communities, I am speaking about any environment outside of the home, school, or workplace. This can include public spaces (e.g., shopping malls, restaurants, public parks), religious institutions (e.g., mosques, temples, churches), and other organizations (e.g., sports leagues, community centers). Many of the microaggressions that occur in public spaces may be those types of incidents that are instantaneous and/or are enacted by strangers, as well as acts that people do not know how to react to immediately. Such an experience may contrast the types of microaggressions that happen among the families, schools, and workplace settings where individuals may have time to react or at least have opportunities to deal with the microaggression when they have had time to process and return to the setting. Meanwhile, in other community settings, there may be factors that differ from those in families, schools, and workplaces, such as whether or not the target knows the perpetrator (e.g., a churchgoer experiences a microaggression from a longtime family friend vs. an acquaintance) or the frequency in which they might come into contact with the setting (e.g., a person who goes to a community center sporadically vs. someone who is well connected to the center's leaders or members).

In addition to all the other techniques that I have shared regarding families, schools, and workplaces (e.g., addressing the microaggression directly, creating a safe environment), I offer a few further thoughts about how to deal with microaggressions in one's community. First, microaggressions often go unaddressed because bystanders engage in what has been referred to as **abandonment** and **microaggressive neglect.** *Abandonment* refers to a bystander's "failure to act on behalf of a target of microaggressions despite having noticed the transgression," whereas *neglect* is defined as "the failure to act on behalf of a target because of a failure to recognize that a microaggression took place"; Johnston et al., 2021, p. 1032). It is important for accomplices to not just act in the moment (e.g., confronting microaggressions even when they are not targeted directly) but to provide emotional support to targets afterward. Validate their experiences by affirming that a microaggression occurred. Allow them to share their thoughts and feelings about the incident and be a sounding board, especially if they may not have someone in their own network to serve this purpose. Further, having conversations with the perpetrator in the moment (or later) may be very beneficial in assisting the person to understand their behavior.

Such upstander behaviors would likely be easier in community spaces in which someone knows all the parties involved (e.g., being on the same sports team or member of the same youth group). However, these behaviors can even be applied to spaces and situations in which an individual does not personally know the others involved. For example, if someone witnesses a microaggression in public (e.g., at a movie theater, on public transportation), an accomplice can use any number of microinterventions to address or challenge the situation. After doing so, that person can certainly check on the target and offer support or validation. If they are feeling bold or fervent, they may also make efforts to educate the perpetrators about their actions. Such convictions might possibly be most effective when the upstander has privileged identities or does not fear any repercussions. For instance, a heterosexual cisgender man might not feel threatened in challenging another heterosexual cisgender man; in fact, his message might be better received than if it were to come from an LGBTQ person or cisgender woman.

My second thought about microaggressions in the community is to prevent them from occurring. One way that you can prevent future microaggressions is by educating others about microaggressions in general. Because members of general society, particularly those who are not familiar with social justice issues, may not recognize the subtle forms of discrimination that may occur, they will also be unable to recognize the harm that microaggressions may have on peoples' mental health. Perhaps providing a definition of "microaggressions" and emphasizing how they are often unconscious and unintentional may be met with less resistance or defensiveness. Perhaps labeling something as a "potential microaggression" instead of as "racist," "sexist," or "homophobic" may be an easier way to have dialogues about discrimination and prejudice. And if that person reacts negatively to the concept of microaggressions in general, it might be helpful to inform them of the thousands of articles that scientifically support the presence of microaggressions and their impact on people and communities. If everyone educated their families and social circles about the concept of microaggressions, such conversations might become more normalized—resulting in more empathy, more inclusion, and less psychological distress.

One thought regarding religious or spiritual communities is the notion that religious leaders or their constituents do not have to be homophobic or transphobic, regardless of what these institutions had taught throughout history. For example, Reverend Jacqui Lewis of Middle Church in New York City wrote a compelling piece in *Harper's Bazaar* in response to Lil Nas X's music video *Montero (Call Me by Your Name)*. While naysayers proclaimed the short film as blasphemous because of sexual themes involving the devil, Lewis (2021) instead asserted how Lil Nas X is "reclaiming his queerness to proclaim his own blessedness" (para. 1). She cites how religion has been used as a tool to oppress trans and queer people, proclaiming that "generations of kids entered churches asking to be loved, and we offered them chains. What a joy it is to see Lil Nas X break those shackles and demand a love that calls him by his name" (para. 9). It is hoped that other Christian ministers (and leaders of other religions) could follow in Reverend Lewis's lead. In doing so, they practice what they preach by loving everyone for who they are and accepting them as they are.

Finally, one last consideration regarding communities in general involves the notion of how to manage the notion of "cancel culture"—which initially was used as a way for people of historically marginalized groups to hold people in power accountable for their problematic comments or behaviors, primarily using social media or other online platforms (see Romano, 2021, for a review). To "cancel" someone meant that people who were initially advocating for justice were using their collective voices to attempt to prevent high-profile people (e.g., politicians, celebrities) from maintaining their careers or their platforms. In response to these efforts, those who believe they have been "cancelled" have often fought back (instead of, or in addition to, apologizing)—with claims that their free speech was infringed upon, that they were the real victims of the situation, or both.

Eventually, the act of cancelling someone became a tool for people in various communities to "call out" people who were not in the public sphere (e.g., teachers, principals, peers, coworkers)—sometimes even sharing personal details about their home addresses or families' addresses. While I firmly believe that it is important to hold people (especially people in power) accountable for their actions—especially when those actions harm or detrimentally affect people from historically marginalized groups—it is important for social justice advocates to reflect upon the utility of applying the concepts of cancel culture to all people. For instance, while it could be effective to publicly condemn people who engage in violent acts (e.g., people who engage in sexual assault or hate violence), it may be worth examining whether the same type of response is necessary for someone who commits a microaggression. Further, while being vocal against a public figure who continues to harm LGBTQ communities via their work (e.g., J. K. Rowling or Dave Chappelle, who succeed despite their blatant transphobia) may feel necessary and important, initiating or engaging in a smear campaign against a community organizer who committed a microinsult (and who has since apologized) may seem extraneous and even counterproductive. In fact, some may argue that doing so demonstrates the use of a person's power (or people's collective power) to destroy someone—which may then be viewed as a form of bullying or harassment.

Thus, when dealing with microaggressions among any sort of community— whether it be a local neighborhood community, a school community, or social media community—it is important to consider that everyone has the capacity to commit a microaggression. Because we have all been socialized to have biases about different groups, we have the capacity to commit microassaults, microinsults, or microinvalidations. Some people may not have had opportunities for others to educate them or "call them in" to talk about problematic language or beliefs. Further, as humans, we are all prone to mistakes— mistakes that hopefully we will learn from and grow from. And perhaps in those cases, showing people some empathy and grace could assist them in recognizing the errors of their ways, instead of making them more defensive and unable to understand their impact on people.

RECOMMENDATIONS FOR GOVERNMENT

The last set of recommendations that I have is for governmental officials and policy makers. First, I hope that leaders recognize how biased legislation (both overt and covert) has a negative impact on the lives of LGBTQ people. When trans or nonbinary people are denied access to health care or the ability to use the restroom that matches their identities, a message is communicated that they are second-class citizens or that their lives are inferior. When same-sex couples who want to adopt children are told by religious organizations that they will not serve them, a message is sent that they are immoral, deviant, or evil. When public officials do not stand up against this type of discrimination, their silence equals complicity. When government leaders actively or passively support laws that target or oppress marginalized peoples, they must recognize or be held accountable for the direct consequences of their actions. For example, if the passing of laws that prevent trans youth from seeking gender-affirming health care correlates with a higher prevalence of trans suicides or mental health problems, then government leaders must recognize their part in contributing to that problem.

One historically biased form of government involves the use of majority public opinion to inform civil rights laws. While voting is an essential part of the democratic process, voting on the rights of a numerical minority group can be problematic, if most of the population has biases about that minority group. For instance, when Proposition 8 was passed in California in November 2008, banning same-sex marriage throughout the state, many government officials stated that it was the "will of the people" because the majority voted. However, when the majority holds an opinion that is not in the best interests of the minority, do they really have the right to decide for them? If the majority made every decision throughout the history of the United States, it is possible that our country would still legally allow for inhumane conditions like slavery, lack of voting rights or property owner-ship rights for women and people of color, and antimiscegenation laws that prevented interracial couples from getting married. Throughout the various historical eras in which these laws were changed, most of the general popu-lation (namely, white, upper class, men) did not want any of those things to happen. However, because of judicial leaders who believed in civil rights for all, all those laws were overturned. Thus, my primary recommendation for government officials (both elected and appointed) is to ensure that the laws of the land are just and promote equity for all people. If all people, including LGBTQ people, are indeed equal citizens in the United States, then all laws need to reflect that.

Finally, although it would be ideal for governmental officials and policy-makers to promote social justice and instill changes themselves, it is important for constituents to advocate for these changes. Thus, this section provides recommendations for three talking points citizens can use when meeting with or writing letters to their elected officials: (a) describing concrete harms, (b) emphasizing why LGBTQ voices matter, and (c) telling your personal stories.

Describe Concrete Harms

Throughout the book, many examples (both empirically based and anec-dotal) describe how discrimination may have a negative impact on the lives of LGBTQ people. For instance, some of the research has described how LGBTQ people are at higher risk for attempting or dying by suicide, developing mental and physical health problems, being targeted by hate violence, or becoming homeless. When choosing to contact an elected official, be sure to have a specific issue in mind, so that they can take concrete and actionable steps in addressing that issue. For instance, in Chapter 4, I shared how transgender people experience higher rates of unemployment, poverty, and homelessness, in comparison to cisgender people. Use statistics like these as a way of supporting your argument that discrimination on inter-personal, institutional, and systemic levels negatively affects LGBTQ people. Cite research articles, particularly those that utilize large sample sizes or are consistent across time, to provide the empirical evidence that LGBTQ people have needs that are remaining unmet.

Emphasize Why LGBTQ Voters Matter

While politicians may have competing political ideas and stances, it is hoped that many elected officials would care at least minimally about the people they are supposed to represent. Yet, perhaps even more important, many elected officials (especially those who seek reelection) may be interested in appeasing their constituents, especially if those communities make up powerful voting blocs. Describe how more people are identifying as LGBTQ nowadays (up to 10 percent of the population in some jurisdictions; Conron & Goldberg, 2020) and how LGBTQ voters have been deciding factors in many federal, state, and local elections (Flores et al., 2020). Perhaps hearing such numbers may clarify why they should consider making LGBTQ issues a priority platform, especially since LGBTQ people can help or hurt future elections.

Tell Your Personal Stories

Personal anecdotes can be used to illustrate the many ways in which people are affected by oppression. Emphasize how LGBTQ people just want to have the same types of rights and opportunities as cisgender and heterosexual people, and describe how discrimination negatively impacts your life or the lives of your loved ones. When telling your stories, make sure to connect them to a political issue. For instance, discuss how not having learned about LGBTQ people in your school systems affected your ability to develop healthy self-esteem and how mandating LGBTQ-affirming curricula in public school systems (i.e., queer studies) would be beneficial in addressing the disparities affecting LGBTQ youth. Further, share how you feel when public officials and policymakers do not stand up against biased laws and how their silence communicates acceptance, agreement, or tolerance of these laws.

Storytelling can also dispel any misconceptions that elected officials may have about LGBTQ people. If political leaders believe that bullying is not any different than it was 30 years ago or that bullying does not affect LGBTQ kids more than it does heterosexual kids, then they may not see a need for antibullying legislation. However, if they hear a personal story about a child who has been bullied and the torment and trauma that they endured, perhaps they would have different perceptions of the problem. Similarly, if government leaders believe that housing discrimination does not exist or that LGBTQ people do not face any disparities in the criminal justice system, then they likely will not feel passionately about endorsing laws or policies to prevent these injustices. However, perhaps a letter to your congressperson with a personal recollection of a time that you were discriminated against when trying to buy a home or rent an apartment would be helpful in pushing for federal laws on anti-LGBTQ discrimination.

Further, perhaps telling an elected official about the time you (or someone you love) were treated unfairly or violently by a police officer or while in the prison industrial complex could help them to see how real these experiences are for LGBTQ people.

Finally, being a face or voice to the problems faced by LGBTQ people can sometimes help to humanize a problem—not just in lobbying to elected officials, but in educating loved ones and peers. While no one should ever feel forced to share or relive their trauma for the sake of educating others, one might also feel empowered by sharing stories as a way of helping others. Thus, in continuing to tell stories—including your own or the many voices you have read throughout this text—I hope that more people will listen, and I hope that more LGBTQ people will feel validated and understood.

DISCUSSION QUESTIONS

For General Readers

1. What are some practical ways that you can advocate for LGBTQ people in your families, schools, workplaces, and communities?

2. What are some LGBTQ issues you might advocate for to your government officials?

For Psychologists, Educators, and Other Experts

1. What are some of the systemic barriers that prevent you from becoming more of an activist in your profession?

2. How would you handle the topic of political activism in your therapy sessions with clients? In your classrooms?

GLOSSARY OF KEY TERMS

abandonment The inability to confront or challenge a violent, unjust, discriminatory, or problematic behavior, despite having recognized that it had occurred.

microaggressive neglect The inability to recognize that an injustice, microaggression, or violent act occurred and the failure to notice that the incident caused harm towards someone.

restorative justice An approach to discipline or rehabilitation that engages all parties involved in a violent or harmful act (e.g., perpetrators, targets, and loved ones) with the intention of discussing the impact of the behaviors.

AFTERWORD

A Personal Message to LGBTQ People

FIGURE 10.1. A Diverse Group of LGBTQ People Marching in NYC Pride

Note. Photo courtesy of Following NYC.

https://doi.org/10.1037/0000335-011

Dismantling Everyday Discrimination: Microaggressions Toward LGBTQ People, Second Edition, by K. L. Y. Nadal

To conclude this text, I send my personal message to my lesbian, gay, bisexual, transgender, nonbinary, and queer sisters, brothers, siblings, and friends. I wrote this book in hopes that heterosexual and cisgender people would be more cognizant of the ways in which hate hurts and negatively impacts our lives. I also wrote this book to honor all of you and your experiences. I hope that you can relate to some of the incidents that I have described throughout the text, and I hope that reading about some of these microaggressions has validated that you were not paranoid or irrational for feeling or reacting the way that you did.

As a general community, we have gone through so much. In some parts of the world, it is still illegal to be us. And sadly, in other parts of the world, we could even be killed for just existing. Regardless of all the hardships that all of us have had to endure, I hope that you have learned that there is nothing wrong with you. You are not evil or immoral. You are not an abomination. You are not psychologically disordered or deficient. In fact, you are perfect. You're amazing just the way you are. You are a firework. You are beautiful. You were born this way. I hope that you can accept that, and I hope that you can help me to teach this to all of those who are still struggling with knowing that.

I also think it is important for us to acknowledge two major things. First, there are some major divides in our community, which we sometimes do not want to talk about. There is so much discrimination and tension between LGBTQ subgroups—between the men and the women; the cisgender and the transgender and the nonbinary; the monosexuals and the bisexuals; the white people and the people of color; the able-bodied and people with disabilities; the older and the younger; and the list goes on. If you are part of the group with power or privilege in any of these combinations, I hope that you can recognize that you too, despite your own oppression and marginalization, can sometimes be an oppressor and commit microaggressions. I hope that you can be open to hearing when others point out your mistakes, in the same way that you would want people to hear you when you are victimized. We can no longer deny that there are power structures (and struggles) within the general LGBTQ community and between LGBTQ subgroups. We must do our parts to address these issues, if we really do want to mobilize and advocate for our needs. This may require recognizing our own biases and stereotypes and engaging in difficult and tense dialogues. But I believe these are necessary, if we want to move in the right direction. And I believe that since we all know what it is like to be marginalized in the greater society, that we do genuinely want what is best for the entire community.

The second issue that needs to be addressed is the need for more activism and change in our communities. Because we now live in a world where we have much more privilege and equality, and in which many of us may feel safe in living as our most authentic selves, it can be so easy to be complacent. However, there are still thousands of LGBTQ children who are being kicked out of their homes on a regular basis. They sometimes run away to cities where they think they will be accepted; but because they don't have jobs or educations, they end up homeless on the streets or turn to drugs or sex work as a means of coping or survival. There are still LGBTQ people living in poverty, LGBTQ children who are being bullied, and LGBTQ older adults who are being abused. There are LGBTQ immigrants who cannot attain their documentation, which impacts their ability to attain employment and thrive. There are still thousands of LGBTQ people who are addicted to drugs and other substances and thousands of LGBTQ people who are contracting HIV/AIDS daily. The COVID-19 pandemic demonstrated how vulnerable our communities are—especially in our limited access to health care and other resources. So, although LGBTQ people have obtained a lot of wins in the past decade (including victories like marriage equality, federal employment non-discrimination, hate crime legislation, the right to serve in the military), some of us are still struggling to even be alive.

There is so much more work to be done, and we all must do our parts. I know that I must channel the spirits and convictions of the LGBTQ pioneers and other civil rights leaders who came before us. I must fight for justice everywhere—even where it does not affect me personally. I need to use my voice and privilege when it can help and amplify and support others when their voices would be most effective. I must do everything I can—not just to assist in my own healing, but to ensure that young LGBTQ people never have to suffer. If I indeed want to "make it better" for future generations of LGBTQ people, then I must do more. And I hope you realize that you do too.

In solidarity,
Kevin Leo Yabut Nadal, PhD

References

Abbott, D., & Howarth, J. (2007). Still off-limits? Staff Views on supporting gay, lesbian and bisexual people with intellectual disabilities to develop sexual and intimate relationships? *Journal of Applied Research in Intellectual Disabilities, 20*(2), 116–126. https://doi.org/10.1111/j.1468-3148.2006.00312.x

Adelman, M., Gurevitch, J., de Vries, B., & Blando, J. (2006). Openhouse: Community building and research in the LGBTQ aging population. In D. Kimmel, T. Rose, & S. David (Eds.), *Lesbian, gay, bisexual, and transgender aging: Research and clinical perspectives* (pp. 247–264). Columbia University Press. https://doi.org/10.7312/kimm13618-014

Akoury, L. M., Schafer, K. J., & Warren, C. S. (2019a). Everyday indignities: Using the microaggressions framework to understand weight stigma. *Journal of Law, Medicine & Ethics, 45*(4), 502–509. https://doi.org/10.1177/1073110517750584

Akoury, L. M., Schafer, K. J., & Warren, C. S. (2019b). Fat women's experiences in therapy: "You can't see beyond . . . unless I share it with you." *Women & Therapy, 42*(1–2), 93–115. https://doi.org/10.1080/02703149.2018.1524063

Almeida, J., Johnson, R. M., Corliss, H. L., Molnar, B. E., & Azrael, D. (2009). Emotional distress among LGBT youth: The influence of perceived discrimination based on sexual orientation. *Journal of Youth and Adolescence, 38*(7), 1001–1014. https://doi.org/10.1007/s10964-009-9397-9

American Psychological Association. (2021). *Inclusive language guidelines.* https://www.apa.org/about/apa/equity-diversity-inclusion/language-guidelines.pdf

Americans With Disabilities Act of 1990, 42 U.S.C. § 12101 et seq. (1990). https://www.ada.gov/pubs/adastatute08.htm

Amnesty International. (2005). *USA: Stonewalled: Police abuse and misconduct against lesbian, gay, bisexual and transgender people in the U.S.* https://www.amnesty.org/en/documents/AMR51/122/2005/en/

Andrews, E. E., Ayers, K. B., Brown, K. S., Dunn, D. S., & Pilarski, C. R. (2021). No body is expendable: Medical rationing and disability justice during the

COVID-19 pandemic. *American Psychologist, 76*(3), 451–461. https://doi.org/10.1037/amp0000709

Anzaldúa, G. (2012). *Borderlands/La Frontera: The new mestiza* (2nd ed.). Aunt Lute.

Arayasirikul, S., & Wilson, E. C. (2019). Spilling the T on trans-misogyny and microaggressions: An intersectional oppression and social process among trans women. *Journal of Homosexuality, 66*(10), 1415–1438. https://doi.org/10.1080/00918369.2018.1542203

Armenta, A. D., Alvarez, M. J., & Zárate, M. A. (2021). Wounds that never heal: The proliferation of prejudice toward immigrants in the United States. In P. Tummala-Narra (Ed.), *Trauma and racial minority immigrants: Turmoil, uncertainty, and resistance* (pp. 15–30). American Psychological Association. https://doi.org/10.1037/0000214-002

Badgett, M. V. L., Choi, S. K., & Wilson, B. D. M. (2019). *LGBT poverty in the United States: A study of differences between sexual orientation and gender identity groups.* Williams Institute, University of California, Los Angeles. https://williamsinstitute.law.ucla.edu/wp-content/uploads/National-LGBT-Poverty-Oct-2019.pdf

Balsam, K. F., Molina, Y., Beadnell, B., Simoni, J., & Walters, K. (2011). Measuring multiple minority stress: The LGBT People of Color Microaggressions Scale. *Cultural Diversity & Ethnic Minority Psychology, 17*(2), 163–174. https://doi.org/10.1037/a0023244

Banks, B. M., Cicciarelli, K. S., & Pavon, J. (2022). It offends us too! An exploratory analysis of high school-based microaggressions. *Contemporary School Psychology, 26*(2), 182–194.

Barton, B. (2010). "Abomination"—Life as a Bible Belt gay. *Journal of Homosexuality, 57*(4), 465–484. https://doi.org/10.1080/00918361003608558

Baur, B. (2016, March 14). 16 blockbusters you forgot were homophobic. *The Advocate.* https://www.advocate.com/film/2016/3/14/16-blockbusters-you-forgot-were-homophobic

Beck, A. J. (2014). *Sexual victimization in prisons and jails reported by inmates, 2011–12, Supplemental tables: Prevalence of sexual victimization among transgender adult inmates.* U.S. Department of Justice, Bureau of Justice Statistics. https://bjs.ojp.gov/content/pub/pdf/svpjri1112_st.pdf

Bell, J. G., & Perry, B. (2015). Outside looking in: The community impacts of anti-lesbian, gay, and bisexual hate crime. *Journal of Homosexuality, 62*(1), 98–120. https://doi.org/10.1080/00918369.2014.957133

Ben-Ezra, M., Hamama-Raz, Y., Mahat-Shamir, M., Pitcho-Prelorentzos, S., & Kaniasty, K. (2017). Shattering core beliefs: Psychological reactions to mass shooting in Orlando. *Journal of Psychiatric Research, 85*, 56–58. https://doi.org/10.1016/j.jpsychires.2016.09.033

Beredjick, C. (2017). *Queer disbelief: Why LGBTQ equality is an atheist issue.* Friendly Atheist Press.

Bith-Melander, P., Sheoran, B., Sheth, L., Bermudez, C., Drone, J., Wood, W., & Schroeder, K. (2010). Understanding sociocultural and psychological factors affecting transgender people of color in San Francisco. *The Journal of the Association of Nurses in AIDS Care, 21*(3), 207–220. https://doi.org/10.1016/j.jana.2010.01.008

Bjork, D. (2004). Disclosure and the development of trust in the therapeutic setting. In J. M. Glassgold & S. Iasenza (Eds.), *Lesbians, feminism, and psychoanalysis: The second wave* (pp. 95–106). Harrington Park Press.

Black, C. (2021, April 23). What offends me most about transphobic jokes is how lazy they are. *Junkee*. https://junkee.com/transphobic-jokes-are-lazy/293132

Bolwell, A. (2021). *Discrimination, mental health, and stress-related growth of sexual minorities* (Publication No. 28547673) [Doctoral dissertation, University of La Verne]. Proquest Dissertations and Theses Global. https://www.proquest.com/dissertations-theses/discrimination-mental-health-stress-related/docview/2565164733/se-2

Boroughs, M. S., Bedoya, C. A., O'Cleirigh, C., & Safren, S. A. (2015). Toward defining, measuring, and evaluating LGBT cultural competence for psychologists. *Clinical Psychology: Science and Practice, 22*(2), 151–171. https://doi.org/10.1111/cpsp.12098

Bostwick, W., & Hequembourg, A. (2014). 'Just a little hint': Bisexual-specific microaggressions and their connection to epistemic injustices. *Culture, Health & Sexuality, 16*(5), 488–503. https://doi.org/10.1080/13691058.2014.889754

Brassel, S. T., Davis, T. M., Jones, M. K., Miller-Tejada, S., Thorne, K. M., & Areguin, M. A. (2020). The importance of intersectionality for research on the sexual harassment of Black queer women at work. *Translational Issues in Psychological Science, 6*(4), 383–391. https://doi.org/10.1037/tps0000261

Brathwaite, L. F. (2016, November 15). *Insecure* asks, "Why can't black men explore their sexuality without being labeled?" *Out.* https://www.out.com/popnography/2016/11/15/insecure-asks-why-cant-black-men-explore-their-sexuality-without-being-labeled

Brewster, M., Velez, B., Sawyer, J., Motulsky, W., Chan, A., & Kim, V. (2021). Family religiosity, support, and psychological well-being for sexual minority atheist individuals. *Psychology of Religion and Spirituality, 13*(3), 266–275. https://doi.org/10.1037/rel0000356

Briones-Robinson, R., Powers, R. A., & Socia, K. M. (2016). Sexual orientation bias crimes: Examination of reporting, perception of police bias, and differential police response. *Criminal Justice and Behavior, 43*(12), 1688–1709. https://doi.org/10.1177/0093854816660583

Bronski, M. (2011). *A queer history of the United States*. Beacon Press.

Brown, D. L., & Tylka, T. L. (2011). Racial discrimination and resilience in African American young adults: Examining racial socialization as a moderator. *The Journal of Black Psychology, 37*(3), 259–285. https://doi.org/10.1177/0095798410390689

Budge, S., & Orovecz, J. (2017). Gender fluidity. In K. L. Nadal (Ed.), *SAGE encyclopedia of psychology and gender* (pp. 660–662). SAGE Publications. https://doi.org/10.4135/9781483384269.n223

Buenavista, T. L., Cariaga, S., Curammeng, E. R., McGovern, E. R., Pour-Khorshid, F., Stovall, D. O., & Valdez, C. (2021). A praxis of critical race love: Toward the abolition of cisheteropatriarchy and toxic masculinity in educational justice formations. *Educational Studies, 57*(3), 238–249. https://doi.org/10.1080/00131946.2021.1892683

Burgess, E. O., & Baunach, D. M. (2014). Heterosexual allies? Understanding heterosexuals' alliance with the gay community. *Sexuality & Culture, 18*(4), 936–958. https://doi.org/10.1007/s12119-014-9230-9

Burn, S. M., Kadlec, K., & Rexer, R. (2005). Effects of subtle heterosexism on gays, lesbians, bisexuals. *Journal of Homosexuality, 49*(2), 23–38. https://doi.org/10.1300/J082v49n02_02

Burton, C. W., Lee, J. A., Waalen, A., & Gibbs, L. M. (2020). "Things are different now but": Older LGBT adults' experiences and unmet needs in health care. *Journal of Transcultural Nursing, 31*(5), 492–501. https://doi.org/10.1177/1043659619895099

Cachero, P. (2020, February 20). Rappers Boosie and Young Thug's response to Dwayne Wade's trans daughter expose transphobia in hip hop. *Insider.* https://www.insider.com/dwayne-wades-acceptance-trans-daughter-zaya-reveals-hip-hop-transphobia-2020-2

Capodilupo, C. M., Nadal, K. L., Corman, L., Hamit, S., Lyons, O. B., & Weinberg, A. (2010). The manifestation of gender microaggressions. In D. W. Sue (Ed.), *Microaggressions and marginality: Manifestation, dynamics, and impact* (pp. 193–216). Wiley.

Capous-Desyllas, M., & Loy, V. (2020). Navigating intersecting identities, self-representation, and relationships: A qualitative study with trans sex workers living and working in Los Angeles, CA. *Sociological Inquiry, 90*(2), 339–370. https://doi.org/10.1111/soin.12350

Carrubba, M. D. (2005). Invisibility, alienation, and misperceptions: The experience of being bisexual. In J. M. Croteau, J. S. Lark, M. A. Liddendale, & Y. B. Chung (Eds.), *Deconstructing heterosexism in the counseling professions: A narrative approach* (pp. 41–46). SAGE Publications. https://doi.org/10.4135/9781452204529.n5

Casey, L. S., Reisner, S. L., Findling, M. G., Blendon, R. J., Benson, J. M., Sayde, J. M., & Miller, C. (2019). Discrimination in the United States: Experiences of lesbian, gay, bisexual, transgender, and queer Americans. *Health Services Research, 54*(Suppl. 2), 1454–1466. https://doi.org/10.1111/1475-6773.13229

Cash, T. F., & Smolak, L. (Eds.). (2011). *Body image: A handbook of science, practice, and prevention.* Guilford Press.

Cavalhieri, K. E., & Chwalisz, K. (2020). Development and initial validation of the perceived classism experiences scale. *The Counseling Psychologist, 48*(3), 310–341. https://doi.org/10.1177/0011000019899395

Cerezo, A., Cummings, M., Holmes, M., & Williams, C. (2020). Identity as resistance: Identity formation at the intersection of race, gender identity, and sexual orientation. *Psychology of Women Quarterly, 44*(1), 67–83. https://doi.org/10.1177/0361684319875977

Cerezo, A., Morales, A., Quintero, D., & Rothman, S. (2014). Trans migrations: Exploring life at the intersection of transgender identity and immigration. *Psychology of Sexual Orientation and Gender Diversity, 1*(2), 170–180. https://doi.org/10.1037/sgd0000031

Chan, C. D., & Silverio, N. (2021). Issues for LGBTQ elderly. In K. L. Nadal & M. R. Scharrón-del Río (Eds.), *Queer psychology* (pp. 237–256). Springer. https://doi.org/10.1007/978-3-030-74146-4_13

Chang, S., & Skolnik, A. (2017). Transgender day of remembrance. In K. L. Nadal (Ed.), *The SAGE encyclopedia of psychology and gender* (pp. 1698–1699). SAGE Publications. https://sk.sagepub.com/reference/the-sage-encyclopedia-of-psychology-and-gender/i8582.xml

Chang, T. K., & Chung, Y. B. (2015). Transgender microaggressions: Complexity of the heterogeneity of transgender identities. *Journal of LGBT Issues in Counseling, 9*(3), 217–234. https://doi.org/10.1080/15538605.2015.1068146

Chappell, T. (2018, July 15). "Pose" takes place in the 1980s, but conversations about LGBTQ homelessness and AIDS are still so important. *Teen Vogue.* https://www.teenvogue.com/story/pose-damon-lgbtq-homelessness

Chasteen, A. L., Horhota, M., & Crumley-Branyon, J. J. (2021). Overlooked and underestimated: Experiences of ageism in young, middle-aged, and older adults. *Journal of Gerontology: Series B, 76*(7), 1323–1328. https://doi.org/10.1093/geronb/gbaa043

Chauncey, G. (2008). *Gay New York: Gender, urban culture, and the making of the gay male world, 1890–1940.* Basic Books.

Cheng, Z. H., Pagano, L. A., Jr., & Shariff, A. F. (2018). The development and validation of the Microaggressions Against Non-Religious Individuals Scale (MANRIS). *Psychology of Religion and Spirituality, 10*(3), 254–262. https://doi.org/10.1037/rel0000203

Cheng, Z. H., Pagano, L. A., Jr., & Shariff, A. F. (2019). The development, validation, and clinical implications of the Microaggressions Against Religious Individuals Scale (MARIS). *Psychology of Religion and Spirituality, 11*(4), 327–338. https://doi.org/10.1037/rel0000126

Cheslik, B., & Wright, S. J. (2021). The impact of gay social networking applications on dating in the deaf gay community. *Sexuality & Culture, 25*(3), 1025–1040. https://doi.org/10.1007/s12119-020-09807-4

Chester, N. (2015, March 30). Life can be tough for LGBT little people: An interview with a gay dwarf. *Vice.* https://www.vice.com/en/article/7bdp3z/lgbt-little-people-729

Choi, S. K., & Meyer, I. H. (2016). *LGBT aging: A review of research findings, needs, and policy implications.* Williams Institute, University of California, Los Angeles. https://williamsinstitute.law.ucla.edu/publications/lgbt-aging/

Chonody, J. M., Rutledge, S. E., & Smith, S. (2012). "That's so gay": Language use and antigay bias among heterosexual college students. *Journal of Gay & Lesbian Social Services*, *24*(3), 241–259. https://doi.org/10.1080/10538720.2012.697036

Chow, J. (2021). No fats, no fems, no problems? Working out and the gay muscled body. *Sexualities*. Advance online publication. https://doi.org/10.1177/13634607211018331

Chung, G. (2021, July 1). Demi Lovato thanks 'Queen' Lizzo for correcting paparazzo after misgendering: 'I Love You'. *People*. https://people.com/music/demi-lovato-thanks-lizzo-for-correcting-paparazzo-after-misgendering/

Cisneros, J., & Bracho, C. (2019). Coming out of the shadows and the closet: Visibility schemas among undocuqueer immigrants. *Journal of Homosexuality*, *66*(6), 715–734. https://doi.org/10.1080/00918369.2017.1423221

Cisneros, J., & Bracho, C. (2020). Undocuqueer stress: How safe are "safe" spaces, and for whom? *Journal of Homosexuality*, *67*(11), 1491–1511. https://doi.org/10.1080/00918369.2019.1607684

Coco, N. A. (2021). *Gender identity, discrimination, and adjustment among college students* [Honors undergraduate thesis, University of Central Florida]. https://stars.library.ucf.edu/honorstheses/969

Conover, K. J., & Israel, T. (2019). Microaggressions and social support among sexual minorities with physical disabilities. *Rehabilitation Psychology*, *64*(2), 167–178. https://doi.org/10.1037/rep0000250

Conover, K. J., Israel, T., & Nylund-Gibson, K. (2017). Development and validation of the Ableist Microaggressions Scale. *The Counseling Psychologist*, *45*(4), 570–599. https://doi.org/10.1177/0011000017715317

Conron, K. J. (2020). *LGBT youth population in the United States*. Williams Institute, University of California, Los Angeles. https://williamsinstitute.law.ucla.edu/publications/lgbt-youth-pop-us/

Conron, K. J., & Goldberg, S. K. (2020). *Adult LGBT population in the United States*. Williams Institute University of California, Los Angeles. https://williamsinstitute.law.ucla.edu/wp-content/uploads/LGBT-Adult-US-Pop-Jul-2020.pdf

Conron, K. J., O'Neill, K. K., Vasquez, L. A., & Mallory, C. (2022). *Prohibiting gender-affirming medical care for youth*. Williams Institute, University of California, Los Angeles. https://williamsinstitute.law.ucla.edu/publications/bans-trans-youth-health-care/

Cook, C. L., Cottrell, C. A., & Webster, G. D. (2015). No good without God: Anti-atheist prejudice as a function of threats to morals and values. *Psychology of Religion and Spirituality*, *7*(3), 217–226. https://doi.org/10.1037/rel0000013

Coolhart, D., & Brown, M. T. (2017). The need for safe spaces: Exploring the experiences of homeless LGBTQ youth in shelters. *Children and Youth Services Review*, *82*, 230–238. https://doi.org/10.1016/j.childyouth.2017.09.021

Corpus, M. J. H. (2010). I am a tomboy. In K. L. Nadal (Ed.), *Filipino American psychology: A collection of personal narratives* (pp. 187–192). Author House.

Cowan, G., Heiple, B., Marquez, C., Khatchadourian, D., & McNevin, M. (2005). Heterosexuals' attitudes toward hate crimes and hate speech against gays and lesbians: Old-fashioned and modern heterosexism. *Journal of Homosexuality*, *49*(2), 67–82. https://doi.org/10.1300/J082v49n02_04

Cox, L. (2009, April 16). 'Smear the queer': Gay students tell their stories. *ABC News Online*. https://abcnews.go.com/Health/MindMoodNews/story?id=7352070&page=1

Crane, P. R., Swaringen, K. S., Rivas-Koehl, M. M., Foster, A. M., Le, T. H., Weiser, D. A., & Talley, A. E. (2022). Come out, get out: Relations among sexual minority identification, microaggressions, and retention in higher education. *Journal of Interpersonal Violence*, *37*(9–10), NP8237–NP8248.

Crawford-Lackey, K., & Springate, M. E. (2019). *Identities and place: Changing labels and intersectional communities of LGBTQ and two-spirit people in the United States*. Berghahn Books. https://doi.org/10.2307/j.ctv1dwq1hj

Crenshaw, K. (1989). Demarginalizing the intersection of race and sex: A Black feminist critique of antidiscrimination doctrine, feminist theory, and antiracist politics. *University of Chicago Legal Forum*, *1989*(1), 8. https://chicagounbound.uchicago.edu/cgi/viewcontent.cgi?article=1052&context=uclf

Cyrus, K. (2017). Multiple minorities as multiply marginalized: Applying the minority stress theory to LGBTQ people of color. *Journal of Gay & Lesbian Mental Health*, *21*(3), 194–202. https://doi.org/10.1080/19359705.2017.1320739

Czaja, S. J., Sabbag, S., Lee, C. C., Schulz, R., Lang, S., Vlahovic, T., Jaret, A., & Thurston, C. (2016). Concerns about aging and caregiving among middle-aged and older lesbian and gay adults. *Aging & Mental Health*, *20*(11), 1107–1118. https://doi.org/10.1080/13607863.2015.1072795

D'Emilio, J. (2012). *Sexual politics, sexual communities* (2nd ed.). University of Chicago Press.

Daum, C. W. (2015). The war on solicitation and intersectional subjection: Quality-of-life policing as a tool to control transgender populations. *New Political Science*, *37*(4), 562–581. https://doi.org/10.1080/07393148.2015.1089030

Davies, A. W. J., & Neustifter, N. (2021). Heteroprofessionalism in the academy: The surveillance and regulation of queer faculty in higher education, *Journal of Homosexuality*. Advance online publication. https://doi.org/10.1080/00918369.2021.2013036

Davis, L. S. (2017). Passing. In K. L. Nadal (Ed.), *SAGE encyclopedia of psychology and gender* (pp. 1279–1280). SAGE Publications. https://doi.org/10.4135/9781483384269.n426

Davis, L. S. (2018). *Bias-motivated homicides: Toward a new typology* [Doctoral dissertation, City University of New York]. CUNY Academic Works. https://academicworks.cuny.edu/gc_etds/2813

Denk, A. (2020, May 28). 9 ways ableism is showing up during the COVID-19 outbreak. *Healthline*. https://www.healthline.com/health/9-ways-ableism-is-showing-up-during-covid-19

de Vries, B. (2009). Aspects of life and death, grief, and loss in lesbian, gay, bisexual, and transgender communities. In K. Doka & A. S. Tucci (Eds.), *Living with grief: Diversity and end-of-life care* (pp. 243–257). Hospice Foundation of America.

Dehlin, J. P., Galliher, R. V., Bradshaw, W. S., Hyde, D. C., & Crowell, K. A. (2015). Sexual orientation change efforts among current or former LDS church members. *Journal of Counseling Psychology, 62*(2), 95–105. https://doi.org/10.1037/cou0000011

Deutsch, T. (2018). *Asexual people's experience with microaggressions* [Master's thesis, City University of New York]. CUNY Academic Works. https://academicworks.cuny.edu/jj_etds/52

Díaz, R. M., Bein, E., & Ayala, G. (2006). Homophobia, poverty, and racism: Triple oppression and mental health outcomes in Latino gay men. In A. M. Omoto & H. S. Kurtzman (Eds.), *Sexual orientation and mental health: Examining identity and development in lesbian, gay, and bisexual people* (pp. 207–224). American Psychological Association. https://doi.org/10.1037/11261-010

Dinwoodie, R., Greenhill, B., & Cookson, A. (2020). 'Them two things are what collide together': Understanding the sexual identity experiences of lesbian, gay, bisexual and trans people labelled with intellectual disability. *Journal of Applied Research in Intellectual Disabilities, 33*(1), 3–16. https://doi.org/10.1111/jar.12252

Dispenza, F., Harper, L. S., & Harrigan, M. A. (2016). Subjective health among LGBT persons living with disabilities: A qualitative content analysis. *Rehabilitation Psychology, 61*(3), 251–259. https://doi.org/10.1037/rep0000086

Dispenza, F., Hunter, T. L., & Kumar, A. (2018). The needs of gender and sexual minority persons living with disabilities. In K. B. Smalley, J. C. Warren, & K. N. Barefoot (Eds.), *LGBT health: Meeting the needs of gender and sexual minorities* (pp. 143–159). Springer.

Dispenza, F., Viehl, C., Sewell, M. H., Burke, M. A., & Gaudet, M. M. (2016). A model of affirmative intersectional rehabilitation counseling with sexual minorities: A grounded theory study. *Rehabilitation Counseling Bulletin, 59*(3), 143–157. https://doi.org/10.1177/0034355215579916

Dixon, E., Frazer, S., Mitchell-Brody, M., Mirzayi, C., & Slopen, M. (2011). *Hate violence against lesbian, gay, bisexual, transgender, queer, and HIV-affected communities in the United States in 2010: A Report from the National Coalition of Anti-Violence Programs*. National Coalition of Anti-Violence Programs. https://avp.org/wp-content/uploads/2017/04/2011_NCAVP_HV_Reports.pdf

Dover, K. J. (2016). *Greek homosexuality*. Bloomsbury.

Dovidio, J. F., Gaertner, S. L., & Pearson, A. R. (2016). Racism among the well intentioned. In A. G. Miller (Ed.), *The social psychology of good and evil* (2nd ed., pp. 95–118). Guilford Press.

Drescher, J. (2015). Out of *DSM*: Depathologizing homosexuality. *Behavioral Sciences, 5*(4), 565–575. https://doi.org/10.3390/bs5040565

Dunn, T. R. (2010). Remembering Matthew Shepard: Violence, identity, and queer counterpublic memories. *Rhetoric & Public Affairs, 13*(4), 611–652. https://doi.org/10.1353/rap.2010.0212

Dworkin, S. H. (2005). Jewish, bisexual, feminist in a Christian heterosexist world: Oy vey! In J. M. Croteau, J. S. Lark, M. A. Liddendale, & Y. B. Chung (Eds.), *Deconstructing heterosexism in the counseling professions: A narrative approach* (pp. 65–70). SAGE Publications. https://doi.org/10.4135/9781452204529.n9

Ellis, S. J., Bailey, L., & McNeil, J. (2016). Transphobic victimization and perceptions of future risk: A large-scale study of the experiences of trans people in the UK. *Psychology and Sexuality, 7*(3), 211–224. https://doi.org/10.1080/19419899.2016.1181669

Eng, D. L., & Puar, J. K. (2020). Introduction: Left of queer. *Social Text, 38*(4), 1–24. https://doi.org/10.1215/01642472-8680414

Estrellado, J. E., Felipe, L. C. S., Nakamura, N., & Breen, A. B. (2021). LGBTQ parenting: Building families on the margins. In K. L. Nadal & M. Scharrón-del Río (Eds.), *Queer psychology: Intersectional perspectives* (pp. 199–215). Springer.

Eyerman, R. (2012). Harvey Milk and the trauma of assassination. *Cultural Sociology, 6*(4), 399–421. https://doi.org/10.1177/1749975512445429

Fahs, B., & Swank, E. (2021). Pray the gay will stay? Church shopping and religious gatekeeping around homosexuality in an audit study of Christian church officials. *Psychology of Sexual Orientation and Gender Diversity, 8*(1), 106–118. https://doi.org/10.1037/sgd0000416

Fallon, K. (2020, September 23). "That's so gay": How 'pen15' nailed the heartbreaking experience of the closeted Y2K middle-schooler. *Daily Beast.* https://www.thedailybeast.com/thats-so-gay-how-pen15-nailed-the-heartbreaking-experience-of-the-closeted-y2k-middle-schooler

Fattoracci, E. S. M., Revels-Macalinao, M., & Huynh, Q.-L. (2021). Greater than the sum of racism and heterosexism: Intersectional microaggressions toward racial/ethnic and sexual minority group members. *Cultural Diversity & Ethnic Minority Psychology, 27*(2), 176–188. https://doi.org/10.1037/cdp0000329

Feder, S. (Producer/Director), & Scholder, A. (Producer). (2020). *Disclosure: Trans lives on screen* [Documentary]. Field of Vision.

Federal Bureau of Investigation. (2021). *Uniform crime reports: Hate crime reporting statistics, 2020.* Government Printing Office. https://www.fbi.gov

Ferguson, A. (2021). Intersectional approaches to queer psychology. In K. L. Nadal & M. Scharron-del Río (Eds.), *Queer psychology* (pp. 15–32). Springer. https://doi.org/10.1007/978-3-030-74146-4_2

Fiani, C. N., & Han, H. J. (2019). Navigating identity: Experiences of binary and non-binary transgender and gender non-conforming (TGNC) adults. *International Journal of Transgenderism, 20*(2–3), 181–194. https://doi.org/10.1080/15532739.2018.1426074

Fisher, C. M., Woodford, M. R., Gartner, R. E., Sterzing, P. R., & Victor, B. G. (2019). Advancing research on LGBTQ microaggressions: A psychometric scoping review of measures. *Journal of Homosexuality, 66*(10), 1345–1379. https://doi.org/10.1080/00918369.2018.1539581

Fisk, G. M., & Neville, L. B. (2011). Effects of customer entitlement on service workers' physical and psychological well-being: A study of waitstaff employees. *Journal of Occupational Health Psychology, 16*(4), 391–405. https://doi.org/10.1037/a0023802

Flentje, A., Heck, N. C., Brennan, J. M., & Meyer, I. H. (2020). The relationship between minority stress and biological outcomes: A systematic review. *Journal of Behavioral Medicine, 43*(5), 673–694. https://doi.org/10.1007/s10865-019-00120-6

Flores, A., Magni, G., & Reynolds, A. (2020, December 1). Had LGBT voters stayed home, Trump might have won the 2020 presidential election. *The Washington Post.* https://www.washingtonpost.com/politics/2020/12/01/had-lgbt-voters-stayed-home-trump-might-have-won-2020-presidential-election/

Flores, A. R., Meyer, I. H., Langton, L., & Herman, J. L. (2021). Gender identity disparities in criminal victimization: National Crime Victimization Survey, 2017–2018. *American Journal of Public Health, 111*(4), 726–729. https://doi.org/10.2105/AJPH.2020.306099

Follins, L. D. (2014). Young Black and Latino gay men's experiences with racial microaggressions. In S. C. Howard (Ed.), *Critical articulations of race, gender, and sexual orientation* (pp. 47–63). Lexington Books/Rowman & Littlefield.

Ford, D. (2021). The salve and the sting of religion/spirituality in queer and transgender BIPOC. In K. L. Nadal & M. Scharron-del Rio (Eds.), *Queer psychology: Intersectional perspectives* (pp. 275–290). Springer. https://doi.org/10.1007/978-3-030-74146-4_15

Foster-Gimbel, O., & Engeln, R. (2016). Fat chance! Experiences and expectations of antifat bias in the gay male community. *Psychology of Sexual Orientation and Gender Diversity, 3*(1), 63–70. https://doi.org/10.1037/sgd0000159

Fredriksen-Goldsen, K. I., Cook-Daniels, L., Kim, H. J., Erosheva, E. A., Emlet, C. A., Hoy-Ellis, C. P., Goldsen, J., & Muraco, A. (2014). Physical and mental health of transgender older adults: An at-risk and underserved population. *The Gerontologist, 54*(3), 488–500. https://doi.org/10.1093/geront/gnt021

Fredriksen-Goldsen, K. I., Kim, H.-J., Shiu, C., Goldsen, J., & Emlet, C. A. (2015). Successful aging among LGBT older adults: Physical and mental health-related quality of life by age group. *The Gerontologist, 55*(1), 154–168. https://doi.org/10.1093/geront/gnu081

Freeman, J. (2018, July 3). LGBTQ scientists are still left out. *Nature.* https://www.nature.com/articles/d41586-018-05587-y%E2%80%AC https://doi.org/10.1038/d41586-018-05587-y

Gabrielli, J., & Lund, E. (2020). Acute-on-chronic stress in the time of COVID-19: Assessment considerations for vulnerable youth populations. *Pediatric Research, 88*(6), 829–831. https://doi.org/10.1038/s41390-020-1039-7

Galupo, M. P., Henise, S. B., & Davis, K. S. (2014). Transgender microaggressions in the context of friendship: Patterns of experience across friends' sexual orientation and gender identity. *Psychology of Sexual Orientation and Gender Diversity, 1*(4), 461–470. https://doi.org/10.1037/sgd0000075

Garcia, J., Vargas, N., Clark, J. L., Magaña Álvarez, M., Nelons, D. A., & Parker, R. G. (2020). Social isolation and connectedness as determinants of well-being: Global evidence mapping focused on LGBTQ youth. *Global Public Health, 15*(4), 497–519. https://doi.org/10.1080/17441692.2019.1682028

Gardner, A. T., de Vries, B., & Mockus, D. S. (2014). Aging out in the desert: Disclosure, acceptance, and service use among midlife and older lesbians and gay men. *Journal of Homosexuality, 61*(1), 129–144. https://doi.org/10.1080/00918369.2013.835240

Garis, M. G. (2016, January 22). These 'SATC' quotes are so anti-feminist. *Bustle.* https://www.bustle.com/articles/137250-14-outdated-sex-and-the-city-quotes-about-feminism-womanhood-and-sexuality

Garstka, T. A., Schmitt, M. T., Branscombe, N. R., & Hummert, M. L. (2004). How young and older adults differ in their responses to perceived age discrimination. *Psychology and Aging, 19*(2), 326–335. https://doi.org/10.1037/0882-7974.19.2.326

Gartner, R. E., & Sterzing, P. R. (2018). Social ecological correlates of family-level interpersonal and environmental microaggressions toward sexual and gender minority adolescents. *Journal of Family Violence, 33*(1), 1–16. https://doi.org/10.1007/s10896-017-9937-0

Gendron, T. L., Welleford, E. A., Inker, J., & White, J. T. (2016). The language of ageism: Why we need to use words carefully. *The Gerontologist, 56*(6), 997–1006. https://doi.org/10.1093/geront/gnv066

Ghaziani, A., & Brim, M. (Eds.). (2019). *Imagining queer methods.* NYU Press.

Glasgow, K., & Murphy, S. (1999). Success stories of a fat, biracial/Black, Jewish, lesbian assistant principal. In W. J. Letts & J. T. Sears (Eds.), *Queering elementary education: Advancing the dialogue about sexualities and schooling* (pp. 217–224). Rowman & Littlefield.

Glassgold, J. (2017). Sexual orientation change efforts. In K. L. Nadal (Ed.), *SAGE encyclopedia of psychology and gender* (pp. 1535–1538). SAGE Publications. https://doi.org/10.4135/9781483384269.n514

Goldstein, S. B., & Davis, D. S. (2010). Heterosexual allies: A descriptive profile. *Equity & Excellence in Education, 43*(4), 478–494. https://doi.org/10.1080/10665684.2010.505464

Golriz, G. (2021). 'I am enough': Why LGBTQ Muslim groups resist mainstreaming. *Sexuality & Culture, 25*(2), 355–376. https://doi.org/10.1007/s12119-020-09773-x

Gonzales, G., Loret de Mola, E., Gavulic, K. A., McKay, T., & Purcell, C. (2020). Mental health needs among lesbian, gay, bisexual, and transgender college students during the COVID-19 pandemic. *The Journal of Adolescent Health, 67*(5), 645–648. https://doi.org/10.1016/j.jadohealth.2020.08.006

Gonzales, L., Davidoff, K. C., Nadal, K. L., & Yanos, P. T. (2015). Microaggressions experienced by persons with mental illnesses: An exploratory study. *Psychiatric Rehabilitation Journal, 38*(3), 234–241. https://doi.org/10.1037/prj0000096

González, T. (2012). Keeping kids in schools: Restorative justice, punitive discipline, and the school to prison pipeline. *Journal of Law and Education, 41*(2), 281–336. Proquest 000035316

Gordon, S. (2020). Ageism and age discrimination in the family: Applying an intergenerational critical consciousness approach. *Clinical Social Work Journal, 48*(2), 169–178. https://doi.org/10.1007/s10615-020-00753-0

Grant, J. M., Mottet, L. A., Tanis, J., Harrison, J., Herman, J. L., & Keisling, M. (2011). *Injustice at every turn: A report of the National Transgender Discrimination Survey*. National Center for Transgender Equality and National Gay and Lesbian Task Force. https://www.thetaskforce.org/wp-content/uploads/2019/07/ntds_full.pdf

Gray, B., Johnson, T., Kish-Gephart, J., & Tilton, J. (2018). Identity work by first-generation college students to counteract class-based microaggressions. *Organization Studies, 39*(9), 1227–1250. https://doi.org/10.1177/0170840617736935

Griffin, K. E. (2010). *Empathy levels for victims of hate crimes versus non-hate crimes: The effects of victim, participant, and hate crime characteristics* [Unpublished master's thesis]. John Jay College of Criminal Justice, City University of New York.

Grove, R. C., Rubenstein, A., & Terrell, H. K. (2020). Distrust persists after subverting atheist stereotypes. *Group Processes & Intergroup Relations, 23*(7), 1103–1124. https://doi.org/10.1177/1368430219874103

Grue, J. (2016). The problem with inspiration porn: A tentative definition and a provisional critique. *Disability & Society, 31*(6), 838–849. https://doi.org/10.1080/09687599.2016.1205473

Guter, B., & Killacky, J. R. (Eds.). (2014). *Queer crips: Disabled gay men and their stories*. Routledge. https://doi.org/10.4324/9781315783833

Gyamerah, A. O., Baguso, G., Santiago-Rodriguez, E., Sa'id, A., Arayasirikul, S., Lin, J., Turner, C. M., Taylor, K. D., McFarland, W., Wilson, E. C., & Wesson, P. (2021). Experiences and factors associated with transphobic hate crimes among transgender women in the San Francisco Bay Area: Comparisons across race. *BMC Public Health, 21*(1), 1053. https://doi.org/10.1186/s12889-021-11107-x

Haines, K. M., Boyer, C. R., Giovanazzi, C., & Galupo, M. P. (2018). "Not a real family": Microaggressions directed toward LGBTQ families. *Journal of Homosexuality, 65*(9), 1138–1151. https://doi.org/10.1080/00918369.2017.1406217

Han, C. S. (2009). Chopsticks don't make it culturally competent: Addressing larger issues for HIV prevention among gay, bisexual, and queer Asian Pacific Islander men. *Health & Social Work, 34*(4), 273–281. https://doi.org/10.1093/hsw/34.4.273

Han, C. S., & Choi, K. H. (2018). Very few people say "No Whites": Gay men of color and the racial politics of desire. *Sociological Spectrum, 38*(3), 145–161. https://doi.org/10.1080/02732173.2018.1469444

Han, C. W. (2021). *Racial erotics: Gay men of color, sexual racism, and the politics of desire*. University of Washington Press.

Hankin, K. (2002). *The girls in the back room: Looking at the lesbian bar*. University of Minnesota Press.

Hanna, K. B. (2017). A call for healing: Transphobia, homophobia, and historical trauma in Filipina/o/x American activist organizations. *Hypatia, 32*(3), 696–714. https://doi.org/10.1111/hypa.12342

Harding, J. E. (2016). *The love of David and Jonathan: Ideology, text, reception*. Routledge.

Hatzenbuehler, M. L. (2016). Structural stigma: Research evidence and implications for psychological science. *American Psychologist, 71*(8), 742–751. https://doi.org/10.1037/amp0000068

Hawke, L. D., Hayes, E., Darnay, K., & Henderson, J. (2021). Mental health among transgender and gender diverse youth: An exploration of effects during the COVID-19 pandemic. *Psychology of Sexual Orientation and Gender Diversity, 8*(2), 180–187. https://doi.org/10.1037/sgd0000467

Hehman, J. A., & Bugental, D. B. (2013). "Life stage-specific" variations in performance in response to age stereotypes. *Developmental Psychology, 49*(7), 1396–1406. https://doi.org/10.1037/a0029559

Heider, J. D., Scherer, C. R., & Edlund, J. E. (2013). Cultural stereotypes and personal beliefs about individuals with dwarfism. *The Journal of Social Psychology, 153*(1), 80–97. https://doi.org/10.1080/00224545.2012.711379

Hendricks, M. L., & Testa, R. J. (2012). A conceptual framework for clinical work with transgender and gender nonconforming clients: An adaptation of the minority stress model. *Professional Psychology, Research and Practice, 43*(5), 460–467. https://doi.org/10.1037/a0029597

Herek, G. M. (2000). The psychology of sexual prejudice. *Current Directions in Psychological Science, 9*(1), 19–22. https://doi.org/10.1111/1467-8721.00051

Herek, G. M. (2007). Confronting sexual stigma and prejudice: Theory and practice. *Journal of Social Issues, 63*(4), 905–925. https://doi.org/10.1111/j.1540-4560.2007.00544.x

Herek, G. M. (2009). Hate crimes and stigma-related experiences among sexual minority adults in the United States: Prevalence estimates from a national probability sample. *Journal of Interpersonal Violence, 24*(1), 54–74. https://doi.org/10.1177/0886260508316477

Herek, G. M. (2017). Documenting hate crimes in the United States: Some considerations on data sources. *Psychology of Sexual Orientation and Gender Diversity, 4*(2), 143–151. https://doi.org/10.1037/sgd0000227

Herek, G. M., Cogan, S. C., & Gillis, J. R. (2002). Victim experiences of hate crimes based on sexual orientation. *Journal of Social Issues, 58*(2), 319–339. https://doi.org/10.1111/1540-4560.00263

Herek, G. M., & Garnets, L. D. (2007). Sexual orientation and mental health. *Annual Review of Clinical Psychology, 3*(1), 353–375. https://doi.org/10.1146/annurev.clinpsy.3.022806.091510

Herek, G. M., Gillis, J. R., & Cogan, J. C. (1999). Psychological sequelae of hate-crime victimization among lesbian, gay, and bisexual adults. *Journal of Consulting and Clinical Psychology, 67*(6), 945–951. https://doi.org/10.1037/0022-006X.67.6.945

Higdon, M. J. (2009). Queer teens and legislative bullies: The cruel and insidious discrimination behind heterosexist statutory rape laws. *Davis Law Review, 42*(1), 195–253. https://lawreview.law.ucdavis.edu/issues/42/1/articles/42-1_Higdon.pdf

Hill, D. B., & Willoughby, B. L. B. (2005). The development and validation of the genderism and transphobia scale. *Sex Roles, 53*(7–8), 531–544. https://doi.org/10.1007/s11199-005-7140-x

Hill, R. M., Rufino, K., Kurian, S., Saxena, J., Saxena, K., & Williams, L. (2021). Suicide ideation and attempts in a pediatric emergency department before and during COVID-19. *Pediatrics, 147*(3), e2020029280. https://doi.org/10.1542/peds.2020-029280

Hinkson, K. (2021). The colorblind rainbow: Whiteness in the gay rights movement. *Journal of Homosexuality, 68*(9), 1393–1416. https://doi.org/10.1080/00918369.2019.1698916

Human Rights Campaign. (2021). *State Equality Index 2021*. https://www.hrc.org/resources/state-equality-index

Hunt, A. N., & Rhodes, T. (2018). Fat pedagogy and microaggressions: Experiences of professionals working in higher education settings. *Fat Studies, 7*(1), 21–32. https://doi.org/10.1080/21604851.2017.1360671

Hunt, B., Matthews, C., Milsom, A., & Lammel, J. A. (2006). Lesbians with physical disabilities: A qualitative study of their experiences with counseling. *Journal of Counseling and Development, 84*(2), 163–173. https://doi.org/10.1002/j.1556-6678.2006.tb00392.x

Hunt, B., Milsom, A., & Matthews, C. R. (2009). Partner-related rehabilitation experiences of lesbians with physical disabilities. *Rehabilitation Counseling Bulletin, 52*(3), 167–178. https://doi.org/10.1177/0034355208320933

Hunter, T., Dispenza, F., Huffstead, M., Suttles, M., & Bradley, Z. (2020). Queering disability: Exploring the resilience of sexual and gender minority persons living with disabilities. *Rehabilitation Counseling Bulletin, 64*(1), 31–41. https://doi.org/10.1177/0034355219895813

Husain, A., & Howard, S. (2017). Religious microaggressions: A case study of Muslim Americans. *Journal of Ethnic & Cultural Diversity in Social Work, 26*(1–2), 139–152. https://doi.org/10.1080/15313204.2016.1269710

Ibañez, G. E., Van Oss Marin, B., Flores, S. A., Millett, G., & Diaz, R. M. (2009). General and gay-related racism experienced by Latino gay men. *Cultural Diversity & Ethnic Minority Psychology, 15*(3), 215–222. https://doi.org/10.1037/a0014613

Ingram, L., & Wallace, B. (2019). "It creates fear and divides us:" Minority college students' experiences of stress from racism, coping responses, and recommendations for colleges. *Journal of Health Disparities Research and Practice, 12*(1), 80–112. https://digitalscholarship.unlv.edu/jhdrp/vol12/iss1/6

Irvine, A., & Canfield, A. (2016). The overrepresentation of lesbian, gay, bisexual, questioning, gender nonconforming and transgender youth within the child welfare to juvenile justice crossover population. *The American University Journal of Gender, Social Policy & the Law, 24*(2), 243–262. https://digitalcommons.wcl.american.edu/cgi/viewcontent.cgi?article=1679&context=jgspl

Jackson, S. D. (2017). "Connection is the antidote": Psychological distress, emotional processing, and virtual community building among LGBTQ students after the Orlando shooting. *Psychology of Sexual Orientation and Gender Diversity, 4*(2), 160–168. https://doi.org/10.1037/sgd0000229

James, S. E., Herman, J. L., Rankin, S., Keisling, M., Mottet, L., & Anafi, M. (2016). *The Report of the 2015 U.S. Transgender Survey.* National Center for Transgender Equality. https://transequality.org/sites/default/files/docs/usts/USTS-Full-Report-Dec17.pdf

Jenkins, B. (Director). (2016). *Moonlight* [Film]. A24/Plan B Entertainment/Pastel Productions.

Johnson, V. E., Nadal, K. L., Sissoko, D. R. G., & King, R. (2021). "It's not in your head": Gaslighting, 'splaining, victim blaming, and other harmful reactions to microaggressions. *Perspectives on Psychological Science, 16*(5), 1024–1036. https://doi.org/10.1177/17456916211011963

Johnston, M. P., & Nadal, K. L. (2010). Multiracial microaggressions: Exposing monoracism in everyday life and clinical practice. In D. W. Sue (Ed.), *Microaggressions and marginality: Manifestation, dynamics, and impact* (pp. 123–144). Wiley.

Juzwiak, R. (2015, November 30). What it's like to be a gay little person. *Gawker.* https://www.gawker.com/what-its-like-to-be-a-gay-little-person-1744667611

Kagan, S. H. (2017). Ageism and the helping professions. In T. D. Nelson (Ed.), *Ageism: Stereotyping and prejudice against older persons* (pp. 165–196). MIT Press. https://doi.org/10.7551/mitpress/10679.003.0011

Kalb, N., Roy Gillis, J., & Goldstein, A. L. (2018). Drinking to cope with sexual minority stressors: Understanding alcohol use and consequences among LGBQ emerging adults. *Journal of Gay & Lesbian Mental Health, 22*(4), 310–326. https://doi.org/10.1080/19359705.2018.1476277

Käng, D. B. C. (2014). Conceptualizing Thai genderscapes: Transformation and continuity in the Thai sex/gender system. In P. Liamputtong (Ed.), *Contemporary socio-cultural and political perspectives in Thailand* (pp. 409–429). Springer. https://doi.org/10.1007/978-94-007-7244-1_26

Kang, I. (2018, February 22). "Superstore" expands TV's understanding of all that Asian American characters can be. *The Village Voice.* https://www.villagevoice.com/2018/02/22/superstore-expands-tvs-understanding-of-all-that-asian-american-characters-can-be/

Kassing, F., Casanova, T., Griffin, J. A., Wood, E., & Stepleman, L. M. (2021). The effects of polyvictimization on mental and physical health outcomes in an LGBTQ sample. *Journal of Traumatic Stress, 34*(1), 161–171. https://doi.org/ 10.1002/jts.22579

Kattari, S. K., & Begun, S. (2017). On the margins of marginalized: Transgender homelessness and survival sex. *Affilia, 32*(1), 92–103. https://doi.org/ 10.1177/0886109916651904

Keller, R. M., & Galgay, C. E. (2010). Microaggressive experiences of people with disabilities. In D. W. Sue (Ed.), *Microaggressions and marginality: Manifestation, dynamics, and impact* (pp. 241–267). Wiley.

Khan, F. A. (2011). Powerful cultural productions: Identity politics in diasporic same-sex South Asian weddings. *Sexualities, 14*(4), 377–398. https://doi.org/ 10.1177/1363460711406789

Kidron, B. (Director). (1995). *To Wong Foo, thanks for everything, Julie Newmar* [Film]. Universal Pictures/Amblin Entertainment.

King, R. D., & Sutton, G. M. (2013). High times for hate crimes: Explaining the temporal clustering of hate-motivated offending. *Criminology, 51*(4), 871–894. https://doi.org/10.1111/1745-9125.12022

Koenig, R. (2020, December 12). Sam Smith responds to Shawn Mendes after he apologizes for using wrong pronoun. *Today.* https://www.today.com/ popculture/sam-smith-responds-shawn-mendes-apology-wrong-pronoun- t203745

Koken, J. A., Bimbi, D. S., & Parsons, J. T. (2009). Experiences of familial acceptance–rejection among transwomen of color. *Journal of Family Psychology, 23*(6), 853–860. https://doi.org/10.1037/a0017198

Kort, M. (2005, September 29). Portia heart & soul. *The Advocate,* 40–46. https:// www.advocate.com/politics/commentary/2005/08/29/portia-heart-amp-soul

Kosciw, J. G., Clark, C. M., Truong, N. L., & Zongrone, A. D. (2020). *The 2019 National School Climate Survey: The experiences of lesbian, gay, bisexual, transgender, and queer youth in Our Nation's Schools* [Report]. GLSEN. https:// www.glsen.org/research/2019-national-school-climate-survey

Kotsopoulos, A., & Mills, J. (1994). *The Crying Game:* Gender, genre and "postfeminism." *Jump Cut: A Review of Contemporary Media, 39,* 15–24.

Kulick, A., Wernick, L. J., Woodford, M. R., & Renn, K. (2017). Heterosexism, depression, and campus engagement among LGBTQ college students: Intersectional differences and opportunities for healing. *Journal of Homosexuality, 64*(8), 1125–1141. https://doi.org/10.1080/00918369.2016.1242333

Kum, S. (2017). Gay, gray, black, and blue: An examination of some of the challenges faced by older LGBTQ people of color. *Journal of Gay & Lesbian Mental Health, 21*(3), 228–239. https://doi.org/10.1080/19359705.2017.1320742

Kupers, T. A. (2005). Toxic masculinity as a barrier to mental health treatment in prison. *Journal of Clinical Psychology, 61*(6), 713–724. https://doi.org/ 10.1002/jclp.20105

Lambda Legal. (2022, March 8). *Lambda legal condemns passage of Florida's "Don't Say Gay" bill* [Press release]. Lambda Legal. https://www.lambdalegal.org/blog/fl_20220308_ll-condemns-passage-of-fl-dont-say-gay-bill

LeMaire, K. L., & Oswald, D. L. (2016). How gender affects heterosexual allies' intentions of confronting sexual prejudice. *Psychology of Sexual Orientation and Gender Diversity, 3*(4), 453–464. https://doi.org/10.1037/sgd0000190

Lewis, J. (2021, April 8). How Lil Nas X is reclaiming queerness to proclaim his own blessedness. *Harpers Bazaar.* https://www.harpersbazaar.com/culture/art-books-music/a36052411/how-lil-nas-x-is-reclaiming-queerness-to-proclaim-his-own-blessedness/

Lewis, J. A., Mendenhall, R., Harwood, S. A., & Browne Huntt, M. (2016). "Ain't I a woman?" Perceived gendered racial microaggressions experienced by Black women. *The Counseling Psychologist, 44*(5), 758–780. https://doi.org/10.1177/0011000016641193

Lewis, J. A., & Neville, H. A. (2015). Construction and initial validation of the Gendered Racial Microaggressions Scale for Black women. *Journal of Counseling Psychology, 62*(2), 289–302. https://doi.org/10.1037/cou0000062

Lewis, J. A., Williams, M. G., Peppers, E. J., & Gadson, C. A. (2017). Applying intersectionality to explore the relations between gendered racism and health among Black women. *Journal of Counseling Psychology, 64*(5), 475–486. https://doi.org/10.1037/cou0000231

Liu, M., Turban, J. L., & Mayer, K. H. (2021). The U.S. Supreme Court and the future of sexual and gender minority health. *American Journal of Public Health, 111*(7), 1220–1222. https://doi.org/10.2105/AJPH.2021.306302

Loades, M. E., Chatburn, E., Higson-Sweeney, N., Reynolds, S., Shafran, R., Brigden, A., Linney, C., McManus, M. N., Borwick, C., & Crawley, E. (2020). Rapid systematic review: the impact of social isolation and loneliness on the mental health of children and adolescents in the context of COVID-19. *Journal of the American Academy of Child & Adolescent Psychiatry, 59*(11), 1218–1239. https://doi.org/10.1016/j.jaac.2020.05.009

Loiacano, D. K. (1989). Gay identity issues among Black Americans: Racism, homophobia, and the need for validation. *Journal of Counseling and Development, 68*(1), 21–25. https://doi.org/10.1002/j.1556-6676.1989.tb02486.x

Lomash, E. F., Brown, T. D., & Paz Galupo, M. (2019). "A whole bunch of love the sinner hate the sin": LGBTQ microaggressions experienced in religious and spiritual context. *Journal of Homosexuality, 66*(10), 1495–1511. https://doi.org/10.1080/00918369.2018.1542204

Lombardi, E. L., Wilchins, R. A., Priesing, D., & Malouf, D. (2002). Gender violence: Transgender experiences with violence and discrimination. *Journal of Homosexuality, 42*(1), 89–101. https://doi.org/10.1300/J082v42n01_05

Lyons, C. J. (2006). Stigma or sympathy? Attributions of fault to hate crime victims and offenders. *Social Psychology Quarterly, 69*(1), 39–59. https://doi.org/10.1177/019027250606900104

Macdonald, J. L., & Levy, S. R. (2016). Ageism in the workplace: The role of psychosocial factors in predicting job satisfaction, commitment, and engagement. *Journal of Social Issues, 72*(1), 169–190. https://doi.org/10.1111/josi.12161

Manalansan, M. F. (2003). *Global divas: Filipino gay men in the diaspora.* Duke University Press. https://doi.org/10.2307/j.ctv12101tn

Manejwala, R., & Abu-Ras, W. (2019). Microaggressions on the university campus and the undergraduate experiences of Muslim south Asian women. *The Journal of Muslim Mental Health, 13*(1), 21–39. https://doi.org/10.3998/jmmh.10381607.0013.102

Mathies, N., Coleman, T., McKie, R. M., Woodford, M. R., Courtice, E. L., Travers, R., & Renn, K. A. (2019). Hearing "that's so gay" and "no homo" on academic outcomes for LGBQ+ college students. *Journal of LGBT Youth, 16*(3), 255–277. https://doi.org/10.1080/19361653.2019.1571981

The Matthew Shepard and James Byrd, Jr. Hate Crime Prevention Act, 18 U.S.C. § 249 et seq. (2009). https://www.govinfo.gov/content/pkg/USCODE-2011-title18/pdf/USCODE-2011-title18-partI-chap13-sec249.pdf

McCabe, P. C., Dragowski, E. A., & Rubinson, F. (2013). What is homophobic bias anyway? Defining and recognizing microaggressions and harassment of LGBTQ youth. *Journal of School Violence, 12*(1), 7–26. https://doi.org/10.1080/15388220.2012.731664

McCormick, A., Schmidt, K., & Terrazas, S. (2017). LGBTQ youth in the child welfare system: An overview of research, practice, and policy. *Journal of Public Child Welfare, 11*(1), 27–39. https://doi.org/10.1080/15548732.2016.1221368

McIntosh, P. (2003). White privilege: Unpacking the invisible knapsack. In S. Plous (Ed.), *Understanding prejudice and discrimination* (pp. 191–196). McGraw Hill.

McLaughlin, K. A., Hatzenbuehler, M. L., & Keyes, K. M. (2010). Responses to discrimination and psychiatric disorders among Black, Hispanic, female, and lesbian, gay, and bisexual individuals. *American Journal of Public Health, 100*(8), 1477–1484. https://doi.org/10.2105/AJPH.2009.181586

McLemore, K. A. (2018). A minority stress perspective on transgender individuals' experiences with misgendering. *Stigma and Health, 3*(1), 53–64. https://doi.org/10.1037/sah0000070

McPhail, D., & Bombak, A. E. (2015). Fat, queer and sick? A critical analysis of 'lesbian obesity' in public health discourse. *Critical Public Health, 25*(5), 539–553. https://doi.org/10.1080/09581596.2014.992391

Meiner, J. C. (2000). Memoirs of a gay fraternity brother. In M. Adams, W. J. Blumenfeld, R. Catañeda, H. W. Hackman, M. L. Peters, & X. Zúñiga (Eds.), *Readings for diversity and social justice: An anthology on racism, anti-Semitism, sexism, heterosexism, ableism, and classism* (pp. 299–301). Routledge.

Mereish, E. H., & Taylor, M. S. (2021). Sexual and gender minority people's physical health and health risk behaviors. In K. L. Nadal & M. Scharrón-del Río

(Eds.), *Queer psychology* (pp. 81–102). Springer. https://doi.org/10.1007/978-3-030-74146-4_5

Meyer, D. (2010). Evaluating the severity of hate-motivated violence: Intersectional differences among LGBTQ hate crime victims. *Sociology, 44*(5), 980–995. https://doi.org/10.1177/0038038510375737

Meyer, I. H. (2003). Prejudice, social stress, and mental health in lesbian, gay, and bisexual populations: Conceptual issues and research evidence. *Psychological Bulletin, 129*(5), 674–697. https://doi.org/10.1037/0033-2909.129.5.674

Meyer, I. H. (2015). Resilience in the study of minority stress and health of sexual and gender minorities. *Psychology of Sexual Orientation and Gender Diversity, 2*(3), 209–213. https://doi.org/10.1037/sgd0000132

Meyer, I. H., Teylan, M., & Schwartz, S. (2015). The role of help-seeking in preventing suicide attempts among lesbians, gay men, and bisexuals. *Suicide & Life-Threatening Behavior, 45*(1), 25–36. https://doi.org/10.1111/sltb.12104

Miller, R. A., & Smith, A. C. (2020). Microaggressions experienced by LGBTQ students with disabilities. *Journal of Student Affairs Research and Practice, 58*(5), 491–506

Minwalla, O., Rosser, B. R. S., Feldman, J., & Varga, C. (2005). Identity experience among progressive gay Muslims in North America: A qualitative study within Al-Fatiha. *Culture, Health & Sexuality, 7*(2), 113–128. https://doi.org/10.1080/13691050412331321294

Mobley, M., & Pearson, S. M. (2005). Blessed be the ties that bind. In J. M. Croteau, J. S. Lark, M. A. Liddendale, & Y. B. Chung (Eds.), *Deconstructing heterosexism in the counseling professions: A narrative approach* (pp. 89–96). SAGE Publications. https://doi.org/10.4135/9781452204529.n13

Monahan, C., Macdonald, J., Lytle, A., Apriceno, M., & Levy, S. R. (2020). COVID-19 and ageism: How positive and negative responses impact older adults and society. *American Psychologist, 75*(7), 887–896. https://doi.org/10.1037/amp0000699

Moore, M. R. (2006). Lipstick or Timberlands? Meanings of gender presentation in Black lesbian communities. *Signs, 32*(1), 113–139. https://doi.org/10.1086/505269

Moradi, B., & Huang, Y. P. (2008). Objectification theory and psychology of women: A decade of advances and future directions. *Psychology of Women Quarterly, 32*(4), 377–398. https://doi.org/10.1111/j.1471-6402.2008.00452.x

Mosley, D. V., Gonzalez, K. A., Abreu, R. L., & Kaivan, N. C. (2019). Unseen and underserved: A content analysis of wellness support services for bi+ people of color and indigenous people on U.S. campuses. *Journal of Bisexuality, 19*(2), 276–304. https://doi.org/10.1080/15299716.2019.1617552

Mulcahy, R. (Director). (2009). *Prayers for Bobby* [Film]. Once Upon A Times Films, Ltd/Permut Presentations/Sladek Taaffe Productions.

Mulick, P. S., & Wright, L. W., Jr. (2002). Examining the existence of biphobia in the heterosexual and homosexual populations. *Journal of Bisexuality, 2*(4), 45–64. https://doi.org/10.1300/J159v02n04_03

Mulkerin, T. (2018, June 11). The second episode of 'Pose' sheds light on trans-phobia in the gay community. *Mic.* https://www.mic.com/articles/189747/the-second-episode-of-pose-sheds-light-on-transphobia-in-the-gay-community

Munro, L. (2017). Everyday indignities: Using the microaggressions framework to understand weight stigma. *Journal of Law, Medicine & Ethics, 45*(4), 502–509.

Munro, L., Travers, R., & Woodford, M. R. (2019). Overlooked and invisible: Everyday experiences of microaggressions for LGBTQ adolescents. *Journal of Homosexuality, 66*(10), 1439–1471. https://doi.org/10.1080/00918369.2018.1542205

Nadal, K. L. (2010a). Gender microaggressions and women: Implications for mental health. In M. A. Paludi (Ed.), *Feminism and women's rights worldwide, Vol. 2: Mental and physical health* (pp. 155–175). Praeger.

Nadal, K. L. (2010b). Responding to racial, gender, and sexual orientation microaggressions in the workplace. In M. Paludi, C. Paludi, Jr., & E. DeSouza (Eds.), *The Praeger Handbook on understanding and preventing workplace discrimination: Vol. 1. Legal, management, and social science perspectives* (pp. 23–32). Praeger.

Nadal, K. L. (2011). The Racial and Ethnic Microaggressions Scale (REMS): Construction, reliability, and validity. *Journal of Counseling Psychology, 58*(4), 470–480. https://doi.org/10.1037/a0025193

Nadal, K. L. (2013). *That's so gay! Microaggressions and the lesbian, gay, bisexual, and transgender community.* American Psychological Association. https://doi.org/10.1037/14093-000

Nadal, K. L. (2017). "Let's get in formation": On becoming a psychologist–activist in the 21st century. *American Psychologist, 72*(9), 935–946. https://doi.org/10.1037/amp0000212

Nadal, K. L. (2018). *Microaggressions and traumatic stress: Theory, research, and clinical treatment.* American Psychological Association. https://doi.org/10.1037/0000073-000

Nadal, K. L. (2019a). A decade of microaggression research and LGBTQ com-munities: An introduction to the special issue. *Journal of Homosexuality, 66*(10), 1309–1316. https://doi.org/10.1080/00918369.2018.1539582

Nadal, K. L. (2019b). Measuring LGBTQ microaggressions: The Sexual Orientation Microaggressions Scale (SOMS) and the Gender Identity Microaggressions Scale (GIMS). *Journal of Homosexuality, 66*(10), 1404–1414. https://doi.org/10.1080/00918369.2018.1542206

Nadal, K. L. (2019c). Queering and browning the pipeline for LGBTQ faculty of color in the academy: The formation of the LGBTQ Scholars of Color National Network. *Journal of Critical Thought and Praxis, 8*(2), 27–46. https://doi.org/10.31274/jctp.8210

Nadal, K. L. (2020). *Queering law and order: LGBTQ communities and the criminal justice system.* Lexington Books/Rowman & Littlefield.

Nadal, K. L., & Corpus, M. J. H. (2013). "Tomboys" and "baklas": Experiences of lesbian and gay Filipino Americans. *Asian American Journal of Psychology*, 4(3), 166–175. https://doi.org/10.1037/a0030168

Nadal, K. L., Davidoff, K. C., Davis, L. S., & Wong, Y. (2014). Emotional, behavioral, and cognitive reactions to microaggressions: Transgender perspectives. *Psychology of Sexual Orientation and Gender Diversity*, 1(1), 72–81. https://doi.org/10.1037/sgd0000011

Nadal, K. L., Davidoff, K. C., Davis, L. S., Wong, Y., Marshall, D., & McKenzie, V. (2015). A qualitative approach to intersectional identities and microaggressions: Understanding influences of race, ethnicity, gender, sexuality, and religion. *Qualitative Psychology*, 2(2), 147–163. https://doi.org/10.1037/qup0000026

Nadal, K. L., Davidoff, K. C., & Fujii-Doe, W. (2014). Transgender women and the sex work industry: Roots in systemic, institutional, and interpersonal discrimination. *Journal of Trauma & Dissociation*, 15(2), 169–183. https://doi.org/10.1080/15299732.2014.867572

Nadal, K. L., Erazo, T., Schulman, J., Han, H., & Deutsch, T. (2017). Caught at the intersections: Microaggressions toward lesbian, gay, bisexual, transgender, and queer people of color. In R. Ruth & E. Santacruz (Eds.), *LGBT psychology and mental health: Emerging research and advances* (pp. 133–152). ABC-CLIO.

Nadal, K. L., Escobar, K. M., Prado, G., David, E. J. R., & Haynes, K. (2012). Racial microaggressions and the Filipino American experience: Recommendations for counseling and development. *Journal of Multicultural Counseling and Development*, 40, 156–173. https://doi.org/10.1002/j.2161-1912.2012.00015.x

Nadal, K. L., Griffin, K. E., Hamit, S., Leon, J., Tobio, M., & Rivera, D. P. (2012). Subtle and overt forms of Islamophobia: Microaggressions toward Muslim Americans. *The Journal of Muslim Mental Health*, 6(2), 15–37. https://doi.org/10.3998/jmmh.10381607.0006.203

Nadal, K. L., Hamit, S., Lyons, O., Weinberg, A., & Corman, L. (2013). Gender microaggressions: Perceptions, processes, and coping mechanisms of women. In M. A. Paludi (Ed.), *Psychology for business success* (pp. 193–220). Praeger.

Nadal, K. L., Issa, M.-A., Griffin, K. E., Hamit, S., & Lyons, O. B. (2010). Religious microaggressions in the United States: Mental health implications for religious minority groups. In D. W. Sue (Ed.), *Microaggressions and marginality: Manifestation, dynamics, and impact* (pp. 287–310). Wiley.

Nadal, K. L., Issa, M.-A., Leon, J., Meterko, V., Wideman, M., & Wong, Y. (2011). Sexual orientation microaggressions: "Death by a thousand cuts" for lesbian, gay, and bisexual youth. *Journal of LGBT Youth*, 8(3), 234–259. https://doi.org/10.1080/19361653.2011.584204

Nadal, K. L., & Mendoza, R. J. (2014). Internalized oppression and the lesbian, gay, bisexual, and transgender community. In E. J. R. David (Ed.), *Internalized oppression: The psychology of marginalized groups* (pp. 227–252). Springer.

Nadal, K. L., Quintanilla, A., Goswick, A., & Sriken, J. (2015). Lesbian, gay, bisexual, and queer people's perceptions of the criminal justice system: Implications for social services. *Journal of Gay & Lesbian Social Services, 27*(4), 457–481. https://doi.org/10.1080/10538720.2015.1085116

Nadal, K. L., Rivera, D. P., & Corpus, M. J. H. (2010). Sexual orientation and transgender microaggressions in everyday life: Implications for mental health and counseling. In D. W. Sue (Ed.), *Microaggressions and marginality: Manifestation, dynamics, and impact* (pp. 217–240). Wiley.

Nadal, K. L., & Scharrón-del Río, M. R. (2021). Introduction to queer psychology. In K. L. Nadal & M. Scharrón-del Río (Eds.), *Queer psychology* (pp. 1–13). Springer. https://doi.org/10.1007/978-3-030-74146-4_1

Nadal, K. L., Skolnik, A., & Wong, Y. (2012). Interpersonal and systemic microaggressions toward transgender people: Implications for counseling. *Journal of LGBTQ Issues in Counseling, 6*(1), 55–82. https://doi.org/10.1080/15538605.2012.648583

Nadal, K. L., Vargas, V., Meterko, V., Hamit, S., & Mclean, K. (2012). Transgender female sex workers: Personal perspectives, gender identity development, and psychological processes. In M. A. Paludi (Ed.), *Managing diversity in today's workplace* (pp. 123–154). Praeger.

Nadal, K. L., Whitman, C. N., Davis, L. S., Erazo, T., & Davidoff, K. C. (2016). Microaggressions toward lesbian, gay, bisexual, transgender, queer, and genderqueer people: A review of the literature. *Journal of Sex Research, 53*(4–5), 488–508. https://doi.org/10.1080/00224499.2016.1142495

Nadal, K. L., Wong, Y., Issa, M., Meterko, V., Leon, J., & Wideman, M. (2011). Sexual orientation microaggressions: Processes and coping mechanisms for lesbian, gay, and bisexual individuals. *Journal of LGBT Issues in Counseling, 5*(1), 21–46. https://doi.org/10.1080/15538605.2011.554606

Nakamura, N., & Morales, A. (2016). 4. Criminalization of transgender immigrants: The case of Scarlett. In R. Fuman, G. Lamphear, & D. Epps (Eds.), *The immigrant other* (pp. 48–61). Columbia University Press. https://doi.org/10.7312/furm17180-004

Nario-Redmond, M. R. (2019). *Ableism: The causes and consequences of disability prejudice*. Wiley. https://doi.org/10.1002/9781119142140

Nelson, T. D. (2016). Ageism. In T. D. Nelson (Ed.), *Handbook of prejudice, stereotyping, and discrimination* (pp. 337–353). Psychology Press.

Noelle, M. (2002). The ripple effect on the Matthew Shepard murder: Impact on the assumptive worlds of members of the targeted group. *American Behavioral Scientist, 46*(1), 27–50. https://doi.org/10.1177/0002764202046001004

O'Brien, J. M. (2005). Sexual orientation, shame, and silence: Reflections on graduate training. In J. M. Croteau, J. S. Lark, M. A. Liddendale, & Y. B. Chung (Eds.), *Deconstructing heterosexism in the counseling professions: A narrative approach* (pp. 97–102). SAGE Publishing. https://doi.org/10.4135/9781452204529.n14

Oladipo, G. (2022, May 17). A Strange Loop review—Michael R Jackson's thrilling Broadway triumph. *The Guardian*. https://www.theguardian.com/stage/2022/may/17/a-strange-loop-review-michael-r-jacksons-thrilling-broadway-triumph

O'Quinn, J., & Fields, J. (2020). The future of evidence: Queerness in progressive visions of sexuality education. *Sexuality Research & Social Policy, 17*(2), 175–187. https://doi.org/10.1007/s13178-019-00395-z

Orndorff, K. (1999). *Bi lives: Bisexual women tell their stories*. See Sharp Press.

Orphanidys, J. C. (2018). To the T: Reliability of the LGBT-POC microaggressions scale (Publication number 10930221) [Doctoral dissertation, Widener University]. ProQuest Dissertations and Theses Global. https://www.proquest.com/docview/2103249424?

Paine, E. A. (2021). "Fat broken arm syndrome": Negotiating risk, stigma, and weight bias in LGBTQ healthcare. *Social Science & Medicine, 270*, 113609. https://doi.org/10.1016/j.socscimed.2020.113609

Palmer, N. A., & Kutateladze, B. L. (2021). What prosecutors and the police should do about underreporting of anti-LGBTQ hate crime. *Sexuality Research and Social Policy, 2021*. Advance online publication. https://doi.org/10.1007/s13178-021-00596-5

Pardo, S., & Devor, A. (2017). Transgender and gender nonconforming identity development. In K. L. Nadal (Ed.), *The SAGE encyclopedia of psychology and gender* (pp. 1689–1692). SAGE Publications. https://doi.org/10.4135/9781483384269.n575

Parker, C. M., Hirsch, J. S., Philbin, M. M., & Parker, R. G. (2018). The urgent need for research and interventions to address family-based stigma and discrimination against lesbian, gay, bisexual, transgender, and queer youth. *The Journal of Adolescent Health, 63*(4), 383–393. https://doi.org/10.1016/j.jadohealth.2018.05.018

Parker, L. L., & Harriger, J. A. (2020). Eating disorders and disordered eating behaviors in the LGBT population: A review of the literature. *Journal of Eating Disorders, 8*(1), 51. https://doi.org/10.1186/s40337-020-00327-y

Parkinson, R. B. (2013). *A little gay history: Desire and diversity across the world*. Columbia University Press.

Parr, N. J., & Howe, B. G. (2019). Heterogeneity of transgender identity non-affirmation microaggressions and their association with depression symptoms and suicidality among transgender persons. *Psychology of Sexual Orientation and Gender Diversity, 6*(4), 461–474. https://doi.org/10.1037/sgd0000347

Pascoe, C. J. (2011). *Dude, you're a fag: Masculinity and sexuality in high school*. University of California Press. https://doi.org/10.1525/9780520950696

Patel, D. R., & Brown, K. A. (2017). An overview of the conceptual framework and definitions of disability. *International Journal of Child Health and Human Development, 10*(3), 247–252.

Patel, S. (2019). "Brown girls can't be gay": Racism experienced by queer South Asian women in the Toronto LGBTQ community. *Journal of Lesbian Studies*, *23*(3), 410–423. https://doi.org/10.1080/10894160.2019.1585174

Paterson, J. L., Brown, R., & Walters, M. A. (2019). The short and longer term impacts of hate crimes experienced directly, indirectly, and through the media. *Personality and Social Psychology Bulletin*, *45*(7), 994–1010. https://doi.org/10.1177/0146167218802835

Pearl, R. L., & Schulte, E. M. (2021). Weight bias during the COVID-19 pandemic. *Current Obesity Reports*, *10*(2), 181–190. https://doi.org/10.1007/s13679-021-00432-2

Phillips, J. C. (2005). Being bisexual in the counseling professions. In J. M. Croteau, J. S. Lark, M. A. Liddendale, & Y. B. Chung (Eds.), *Deconstructing heterosexism in the counseling professions: A narrative approach* (pp. 115–120). SAGE Publications. https://doi.org/10.4135/9781452204529.n17

Pew Research Center. (2019). *Majority of public favors same-sex marriage, but divisions persist* [Report]. https://www.pewresearch.org/politics/2019/05/14/majority-of-public-favors-same-sex-marriage-but-divisions-persist/

Peirce, K. (Director). (1999). *Boys don't cry* [Film]. Hart-Sharp Entertainment/Independent Film Channel/Killer Films.

Pierce, C. M., Carew, J. V., Pierce-Gonzalez, D., & Wills, D. (1977). An experiment in racism: TV commercials. *Education and Urban Society*, *10*(1), 61–87. https://doi.org/10.1177/001312457701000105

Pinsker, J. (2020, January 27). When does someone become 'old'? It's surprisingly hard to find a good term for people in late life. *The Atlantic*. https://www.theatlantic.com/family/archive/2020/01/old-people-older-elderly-middle-age/605590/

Platt, L. F., & Lenzen, A. L. (2013). Sexual orientation microaggressions and the experience of sexual minorities. *Journal of Homosexuality*, *60*(7), 1011–1034. https://doi.org/10.1080/00918369.2013.774878

Pledger, C. (2003). Discourse on disability and rehabilitation issues: Opportunities for psychology. *American Psychologist*, *58*(4), 279–284. https://doi.org/10.1037/0003-066X.58.4.279

Poushter, J., & Kent, N. O. (2020). *The global divide on homosexuality persists: But increasing acceptance in many countries over past two decades*. Pew Research Center. https://www.pewresearch.org/global/2020/06/25/global-divide-on-homosexuality-persists

Pulice-Farrow, L., Brown, T. D., & Galupo, M. P. (2017). Transgender microaggressions in the context of romantic relationships. *Psychology of Sexual Orientation and Gender Diversity*, *4*(3), 362–373. https://doi.org/10.1037/sgd0000238

Pulice-Farrow, L., McNary, S. B., & Galupo, M. P. (2020). "Bigender is just a Tumblr thing": Microaggressions in the romantic relationships of gender nonconforming and agender transgender individuals. *Sexual and Relationship Therapy*, *35*(3), 362–381. https://doi.org/10.1080/14681994.2018.1533245

Quintana, N. S., Rosenthal, J., & Krehely, J. (2010). *On the streets: The federal response to gay and transgender homeless youth.* Center for American Progress. https://www.americanprogress.org/article/on-the-streets/

Ramirez, J. L., Gonzalez, K. A., & Galupo, M. P. (2018). "Invisible during my own crisis": Responses of LGBT people of color to the Orlando shooting. *Journal of Homosexuality, 65*(5), 579–599. https://doi.org/10.1080/00918369.2017. 1328217

Rand, E. J. (2014). *Reclaiming queer: Activist and academic rhetorics of resistance.* University of Alabama Press.

Randazzo, T. J. (2005). Social and legal barriers: Sexual orientation and asylum in the United States. In E. Luibhéid & L. Cantú, Jr. (Eds.), *Queer migrations: Sexuality, U.S. citizenship, and border crossings* (pp. 30–60). University of Minnesota.

Resnick, C. A., & Galupo, M. P. (2019). Assessing experiences with LGBT micro-aggressions in the workplace: Development and validation of the micro-aggression experiences at work scale. *Journal of Homosexuality, 66*(10), 1380–1403. https://doi.org/10.1080/00918369.2018.1542207

Rimes, K. A., Goodship, N., Ussher, G., Baker, D., & West, E. (2019). Non-binary and binary transgender youth: Comparison of mental health, self-harm, suicidality, substance use and victimization experiences. *International Journal of Transgenderism, 20*(2–3), 230–240. https://doi.org/10.1080/15532739. 2017.1370627

Ring, T. (2015, December 14). First out lesbian elected to public office in U.S. finally tells her story. *Pride.* https://www.pride.com/need-know/2015/12/14/ first-out-lesbian-elected-public-office-us-tells-her-story

Roberts, T. S., Horne, S. G., & Hoyt, W. T. (2015). Between a gay and a straight place: Bisexual individuals' experiences with monosexism. *Journal of Bisexuality, 15*(4), 554–569. https://doi.org/10.1080/15299716.2015.1111183

Robinson, B. A. (2018). Conditional families and lesbian, gay, bisexual, transgender, and queer youth homelessness: Gender, sexuality, family instability, and rejection. *Journal of Marriage and the Family, 80*(2), 383–396. https:// doi.org/10.1111/jomf.12466

Robinson, J. L., & Rubin, L. J. (2016). Homonegative microaggressions and post-traumatic stress symptoms. *Journal of Gay & Lesbian Mental Health, 20*(1), 57–69. https://doi.org/10.1080/19359705.2015.1066729

Robinson-Wood, T., Balogun-Mwangi, O., Weber, A., Zeko-Underwood, E., Rawle, S. A. C., Popat-Jain, A., Matsumoto, A., & Cook, E. (2020). "What is it going to be like?": A phenomenological investigation of racial, gendered, and sexual microaggressions among highly educated individuals. *Qualitative Psychology, 7*(1), 43–58. https://doi.org/10.1037/qup0000113

Rogers, B. A. (2019). "Contrary to all the other shit I've said": Trans men passing in the South. *Qualitative Sociology, 42*(4), 639–662. https://doi.org/10.1007/ s11133-019-09436-w

Romano, A. (2021, May 5). The second wave of cancel culture. *Vox*. https://www.vox.com/22384308/cancel-culture-free-speech-accountability-debate

Romero, A. P., Goldberg, S. K., & Vasquez, L. A. (2020). *LGBT people and housing affordability, discrimination, and homelessness*. Williams Institute, University of California, Los Angeles. https://williamsinstitute.law.ucla.edu/publications/lgbt-housing-instability/

Roppolo, M. (2021, May 18). *Netflix star Ryan O'Connell on portraying the "desire and humanity" of disabled relationships*. CBS News. https://www.cbsnews.com/news/ryan-oconnell-netflix-special-disabled-relationships

Rose, S. M., & Mechanic, M. B. (2002). Psychological distress, crime features, and help-seeking behaviors related to homophobic bias incidents. *American Behavioral Scientist, 46*(1), 14–26. https://doi.org/10.1177/0002764202046001003

Rosenblatt, K. (2020, June 11). *J. K. Rowling doubles down in what some critics call a 'transphobic manifesto.'* NBC News. https://www.nbcnews.com/feature/nbc-out/j-k-rowling-doubles-down-what-some-critics-call-transphobic-n1229351

Rothblum, E. D. (2012). Why a journal on fat studies? *Fat Studies, 1*(1), 3–5. https://doi.org/10.1080/21604851.2012.633469

Rothman, E. F., Exner, D., & Baughman, A. L. (2011). The prevalence of sexual assault against people who identify as gay, lesbian, or bisexual in the United States: A systematic review. *Trauma, Violence & Abuse, 12*(2), 55–66. https://doi.org/10.1177/1524838010390707

Ruback, R. B., Gladfelter, A. S., & Lantz, B. (2018). Hate crime victimization data in Pennsylvania: A useful complement to the Uniform Crime Reports. *Violence and Victims, 33*(2), 330–350. https://doi.org/10.1891/0886-6708.v33.i2.173

Salerno, J. P., Devadas, J., Pease, M., Nketia, B., & Fish, J. N. (2020). Sexual and gender minority stress amid the COVID-19 pandemic: Implications for LGBTQ young persons' mental health and well-being. *Public Health Reports, 135*(6), 721–727. https://doi.org/10.1177/0033354920954511

Sanchez, D., Adams, W. N., Arango, S. C., & Flannigan, A. E. (2018). Racial–ethnic microaggressions, coping strategies, and mental health in Asian American and Latinx American college students: A mediation model. *Journal of Counseling Psychology, 65*(2), 214–225. https://doi.org/10.1037/cou0000249

Sandoval, I. (Producer/Director). (2019). *Lingua Franca* [Film]. 7101 Entertainment.

Scharer, J. L., & Taylor, M. J. (2018). Coping with sexual orientation microaggressions: Implications for psychological distress and alcohol use. *Journal of Gay & Lesbian Mental Health, 22*(3), 261–279. https://doi.org/10.1080/19359705.2017.1402842

Scheer, J. R., Breslow, A. S., Esposito, J., Price, M. A., & Katz, J. (2021). Violence against gay men. In E. M. Lund, C. Burgess, & A. J. Johnson (Eds.), *Violence against LGBTQ+ persons* (pp. 135–148). Springer. https://doi.org/10.1007/978-3-030-52612-2_10

Schwadel, P., & Sandstorm, A. (2019). *Lesbian, gay, and bisexual Americans are less religious than straight adults by traditional measures*. Pew Research Center. https://www.pewresearch.org/fact-tank/2019/05/24/lesbian-gay-and-bisexual-americans-are-less-religious-than-straight-adults-by-traditional-measures/

Serano, J. (2007). *Whipping girl: A transsexual woman on sexism and the scapegoating of femininity*. Seal Press.

Sevelius, J. M. (2013). Gender affirmation: A framework for conceptualizing risk behavior among transgender women of color. *Sex Roles, 68*(11–12), 675–689. https://doi.org/10.1007/s11199-012-0216-5

Shatto, R. (2021, September 28). Bethenny Frankel is getting called out over transphobic comments. *The Advocate*. https://www.advocate.com/news/2021/9/28/bethenny-frankel-getting-called-out-over-transphobic-comments

Shelton, K., & Delgado-Romero, E. A. (2011). Sexual orientation microaggressions: The experiences of lesbian, gay, bisexual, and queer clients in psychotherapy. *Journal of Counseling Psychology, 58*(2), 210–221. https://doi.org/10.1037/a0022251

Silverschanz, P., Cortina, L. M., Konik, J., & Magley, V. J. (2008). Slurs, snubs, and queer jokes: Incidence and impact of heterosexist harassment in academia. *Sex Roles, 58*(3–4), 179–191. https://doi.org/10.1007/s11199-007-9329-7

Sinecka, J. (2008). "I am bodied." "I am sexual." "I am human." Experiencing deafness and gayness: A story of a young man. *Disability & Society, 23*(5), 475–484. https://doi.org/10.1080/09687590802177049

Singh, A. A., & McKleroy, V. S. (2011). "Just getting out of bed is a revolutionary act": The resilience of transgender people of color who have survived traumatic life events. *Traumatology, 17*(2), 34–44. https://doi.org/10.1177/1534765610369261

Sissoko, D. R. G., & Nadal, K. L. (2021). Microaggressions toward racial minority immigrants in the United States. In P. Tummala-Narra (Ed.), *Trauma and racial minority immigrants: Turmoil, uncertainty, and resistance* (pp. 85–102). American Psychological Association. https://doi.org/10.1037/0000214-006

Skinta, M. D., & Nakamura, N. (2021). Resilience and identity: Intersectional migration experiences of LGBTQ people of color. In P. Tummala-Narra (Ed.), *Trauma and racial minority immigrants: Turmoil, uncertainty, and resistance* (pp. 245–263). American Psychological Association. https://doi.org/10.1037/0000214-014

Smith, L., Mao, S., & Deshpande, A. (2016). "Talking across worlds": Classist microaggressions and higher education. *Journal of Poverty, 20*(2), 127–151. https://doi.org/10.1080/10875549.2015.1094764

Smith, L., & Redington, R. M. (2010). Class dismissed: Making the case for the study of classist microaggressions. In D. W. Sue (Ed.), *Microaggressions and marginality: Manifestation, dynamics, and impact* (pp. 269–285). Wiley.

Smith, L., & Scott-McLaughlin, R. (2017). Social class and gender. In K. Nadal (Ed.), *The SAGE encyclopedia of psychology and gender* (pp. 1585–1588). SAGE Publications. https://doi.org/10.4135/9781483384269.n532

Solórzano, D., Ceja, M., & Yosso, T. (2000). Critical race theory, racial microaggressions, and campus racial climate: The experiences of African American college students. *The Journal of Negro Education, 69*(1/2), 60–73.

Sonoma, S. (2021, January 7). 44 trans people killed in 2020, marking worst year on record for transphobic violence. *Them.* https://www.them.us/story/44-trans-people-killed-2020-worst-year-for-transphobic-violence

Stacey, L., & Forbes, T. D. (2022). Feeling like a fetish: Racialized feelings, fetishization, and the contours of sexual racism on gay dating apps. *Journal of Sex Research, 59*(3), 372–384. https://doi.org/10.1080/00224499.2021.1979455

Stafford, Z. (2021, August 4). *DaBaby's comments weren't just homophobic— they were dangerous.* MSNBC. https://www.msnbc.com/opinion/dababy-s-comments-weren-t-just-homophobic-they-were-dangerous-n1275964

Stein, G. L., Beckerman, N. L., & Sherman, P. A. (2010). Lesbian and gay elders and long-term care: Identifying the unique psychosocial perspectives and challenges. *Journal of Gerontological Social Work, 53*(5), 421–435. https://doi.org/10.1080/01634372.2010.496478

Stern, K. (2009). *Queers in history: The comprehensive encyclopedia of historical gays, lesbians and bisexuals.* BenBella Books.

Sterzing, P. R., Ratliff, G. A., Gartner, R. E., McGeough, B. L., & Johnson, K. C. (2017). Social ecological correlates of polyvictimization among a national sample of transgender, genderqueer, and cisgender sexual minority adolescents. *Child Abuse & Neglect, 67*, 1–12. https://doi.org/10.1016/j.chiabu.2017.02.017

Stotzer, R. L. (2008). Gender identity and hate crimes: Violence against transgender people in Los Angeles county. *Sexuality Research & Social Policy, 5*(1), 43–52. https://doi.org/10.1525/srsp.2008.5.1.43

Stults, C. B., Kupprat, S. A., Krause, K. D., Kapadia, F., & Halkitis, P. N. (2017). Perceptions of safety among LGBTQ people following the 2016 Pulse nightclub shooting. *Psychology of Sexual Orientation and Gender Diversity, 4*(3), 251–256. https://doi.org/10.1037/sgd0000240

Sue, D. W. (Ed.). (2010). *Microaggressions and marginality: Manifestation, dynamics, and impact.* Wiley.

Sue, D. W., Alsaidi, S., Awad, M. N., Glaeser, E., Calle, C. Z., & Mendez, N. (2019). Disarming racial microaggressions: Microintervention strategies for targets, White allies, and bystanders. *American Psychologist, 74*(1), 128–142. https://doi.org/10.1037/amp0000296

Sue, D. W., Bucceri, J. M., Lin, A. I., Nadal, K. L., & Torino, G. C. (2009). Racial microaggressions and the Asian American experience. *Asian American Journal of Psychology, S*(1), 88–101.

Sue, D. W., Calle, C. Z., Mendez, N., Alsaidi, S., & Glaeser, E. (2020). *Microintervention strategies: What you can do to disarm and dismantle individual and systemic racism and bias.* Wiley.

Sue, D. W., Capodilupo, C. M., & Holder, A. M. B. (2008). Racial microaggressions in the life experience of Black Americans. *Professional Psychology, Research and Practice, 39*(3), 329–336. https://doi.org/10.1037/0735-7028.39.3.329

Sue, D. W., Capodilupo, C. M., Nadal, K. L., & Torino, G. C. (2008). Racial microaggressions and the power to define reality. *American Psychologist, 63*(4), 277–279. https://doi.org/10.1037/0003-066X.63.4.277

Sue, D. W., Capodilupo, C. M., Torino, G. C., Bucceri, J. M., Holder, A. M., Nadal, K. L., & Esquilin, M. (2007). Racial microaggressions in everyday life: Implications for clinical practice. *American Psychologist, 62*(4), 271–286. https://doi.org/10.1037/0003-066X.62.4.271

Sue, D. W., Nadal, K. L., Capodilupo, C. M., Lin, A. I., Rivera, D. P., & Torino, G. C. (2008). Racial microaggressions against Black Americans: Implications for counseling. *Journal of Counseling and Development, 86*(3), 330–338. https://doi.org/10.1002/j.1556-6678.2008.tb00517.x

Sue, D. W., Lin, A. I., Torino, G. C., Capodilupo, C. M., & Rivera, D. P. (2009). Racial microaggressions and difficult dialogues on race in the classroom. *Cultural Diversity and Ethnic Minority Psychology, 15*(2), 183–190. https://doi.org/10.1037/a0014191

Sutter, M., & Perrin, P. B. (2016). Discrimination, mental health, and suicidal ideation among LGBTQ people of color. *Journal of Counseling Psychology, 63*(1), 98–105. https://doi.org/10.1037/cou0000126

Taylor, A. (2022). "But where are the dates?" Dating as a central site of fat femme marginalisation in queer communities. *Psychology & Sexuality, 13*(1), 57–68. https://doi.org/10.1080/19419899.2020.1822429

Theodore, P. S., Durán, R. E., & Antoni, M. H. (2014). Drug use and sexual risk among gay and bisexual men who frequent party venues. *AIDS and Behavior, 18*(11), 2178–2186. https://doi.org/10.1007/s10461-014-0779-y

Timmons, N. (2021). My gender is crip: Engaging the experience of being trans and disabled. In K. Carter & J. Brunton (Eds.), *TransNarratives: Scholarly and creative works on transgender experience* (pp. 249–262). Women's Press/Canadian Scholars Press.

Tomei, J., & Cramer, R. J. (2016). Legal policies in conflict: The gay panic defense and hate crime legislation. *Journal of Forensic Psychology Practice, 16*(4), 217–235. https://doi.org/10.1080/15228932.2016.1192331

Toomey, R. B., Huynh, V. W., Jones, S. K., Lee, S., & Revels-Macalinao, M. (2017). Sexual minority youth of color: A content analysis and critical review of the literature. *Journal of Gay & Lesbian Mental Health, 21*(1), 3–31. https://doi.org/10.1080/19359705.2016.1217499

Torino, G. C., Rivera, D. P., Capodilupo, C. M., Nadal, K. L., & Sue, D. W. (Eds.). (2019). *Microaggression theory: Influence and implications*. Wiley.

Torino, G. C., & Sisselman-Borgia, A. G. (2017). Homeless microaggressions: Implications for education, research, and practice. *Journal of Ethnic & Cultural Diversity in Social Work, 26*(1–2), 153–165. https://doi.org/10.1080/15313204.2016.1263814

Torre, M. E., & Avory, S. (2021). "My wings may be broken, but I'm still flying": Queer youth negotiating expansive identities, structural dispossession, and acts of resistance. In K. L. Nadal & M. Scharrón-del Río (Eds.), *Queer psychology* (pp. 217–236). Springer. https://doi.org/10.1007/978-3-030-74146-4_12

Townsend, C. (2012). Interrogating gender politics and Black power in Newark NJ: An interview with Charles Bennett Brack, producer of *Dreams Deferred: The Sakia Gunn Film Project*. *Transforming Anthropology, 20*(2), 169–171. https://doi.org/10.1111/j.1548-7466.2012.01152.x

Townsend, M., Deerwater, R., Adams, N., Hurwitz, A., Trasandes, M., González, G., & Usher, D. (2022). *Where we are on TV: 2020–2021*. GLAAD Media Institute. https://www.glaad.org/whereweareontv21

Truong, K. (2018, September 22). *After 'sexual racism' accusations, gay dating app Grindr gets 'Kindr'*. NBC News. https://www.nbcnews.com/feature/nbc-out/after-sexual-racism-accusations-gay-day-app-grindr-gets-kindr-n912196

Tucker, D. (Director). (2005). *Transamerica*. [Film]. Belladonna Productions.

Understanding Prejudice. (2021). *Tips for elementary school teachers*. Social Psychology Network. http://www.understandingprejudice.org/teach/elemtips.htm

Upadhyaya, K. K. (2021, May 16). *Pose revisits Pray Tell's past and confronts the contradictions of community*. *AV Club*. https://www.avclub.com/pose-revisits-pray-tell-s-past-and-confronts-the-contra-1846906780

van den Berg, J. (2017). Heterosexist bias in the *DSM*. In K. L. Nadal (Ed.), *The Sage encyclopedia of psychology and gender* (pp. 849–852). SAGE Publications.

Varriage, M. (2019). Continuing stigma: Why the FDA's policy deferring men who have sex with men from donating blood is unconstitutional and a poor policy choice. *Syracuse Law Review, 69*, 611–633.

Velez, B. L., Zelaya, D., & Scheer, J. (2021). Context matters: Minority stress and mental health experiences of diverse LGBTQ people. In K. L. Nadal & M. Scharrón-del Río (Eds.), *Queer psychology* (pp. 103–117). Springer. https://doi.org/10.1007/978-3-030-74146-4_6

Vitiello, M., & Nadal, K. L. (2019). Microaggressions towards people living with HIV/AIDS. In J. Pierce (Ed.), *Living with HIV/AIDS: Challenges, Perspectives and Quality of Life* (pp. 57–82). Nova Publishers.

Walloch, G. (2014). Two performance pieces. In B. Guter & J. R. Killacky (Eds.), *Queer crips: Disabled gay men and their stories* (pp. 1–5). Harrington Park Press.

Walls, N. E. (2008). Toward a multidimensional understanding of heterosexism: The changing nature of prejudice. *Journal of Homosexuality, 55*(1), 20–70. https://doi.org/10.1080/00918360802129287

Walters, M. A., Paterson, J., Brown, R., & McDonnell, L. (2020). Hate crimes against trans people: Assessing emotions, behaviors, and attitudes toward criminal justice agencies. *Journal of Interpersonal Violence, 35*(21–22), 4583–4613. https://doi.org/10.1177/0886260517715026

Wang, M.-T., Henry, D. A., Smith, L. V., Huguley, J. P., & Guo, J. (2020). Parental ethnic–racial socialization practices and children of color's psychosocial and behavioral adjustment: A systematic review and meta-analysis. *American Psychologist, 75*(1), 1–22. https://doi.org/10.1037/amp0000464

Ward, J. (2008). White normativity: The cultural dimensions of Whiteness in a racially diverse LGBTQ organization. *Sociological Perspectives, 51*(3), 563–586. https://doi.org/10.1525/sop.2008.51.3.563

Watson, R. J., Wheldon, C. W., & Puhl, R. M. (2020). Evidence of diverse identities in a large national sample of sexual and gender minority adolescents. *Journal of Research on Adolescence, 30*(S2), 431–442. https://doi.org/10.1111/jora.12488

Weber, A., Collins, S. A., Robinson-Wood, T., Zeko-Underwood, E., & Poindexter, B. (2018). Subtle and severe: Microaggressions among racially diverse sexual minorities. *Journal of Homosexuality, 65*(4), 540–559. https://doi.org/10.1080/00918369.2017.1324679

Wegner, R., & Wright, A. J. (2016). A psychometric evaluation of the homonegative microaggressions scale. *Journal of Gay & Lesbian Mental Health, 20*(4), 299–318. https://doi.org/10.1080/19359705.2016.1177627

Wellman, J. D., Araiza, A. M., Nguyen, T. V. C., Beam, A. J., & Pal, S. (2022). Identifying as fat: Examining weight discrimination and the rejection-identification model. *Body Image, 41*, 46–51. https://doi.org/10.1016/j.bodyim.2022.02.008

White, B. (2021, June 11) Every parent of a queer kid needs to watch 'Love, Victor' season 2. *Decider.* https://decider.com/2021/06/11/love-victor-season-2-ana-ortiz-coming-out-storyarc/

Wiebold, J. (2005). Fluidity in the disclosure and salience of my identities. In J. M. Croteau, J. S. Lark, M. A. Liddendale, & Y. B. Chung (Eds.), *Deconstructing heterosexism in the counseling professions: A narrative approach* (pp. 129–134). SAGE Publications. https://doi.org/10.4135/9781452204529.n19

Wight, R. G., LeBlanc, A. J., Meyer, I. H., & Harig, F. A. (2015). Internalized gay ageism, mattering, and depressive symptoms among midlife and older gay-identified men. *Social Science & Medicine, 147*, 200–208. https://doi.org/10.1016/j.socscimed.2015.10.066

Wildes, V. J. (2005). Stigma in food service work: How it affects restaurant servers' intention to stay in the business or recommend a job to another. *Tourism and Hospitality Research, 5*(3), 213–233. https://doi.org/10.1057/palgrave.thr.6040022

Williams, S. (2017). Social class and sexual orientation. In K. L. Nadal (Ed.), *The SAGE encyclopedia of psychology and gender* (pp. 1589–1592). SAGE Publications. https://doi.org/10.4135/9781483384269.n533

Willis, D. G. (2008). Meanings in adult male victims' experiences of hate crime and its aftermath. *Issues in Mental Health Nursing, 29*(6), 567–584. https://doi.org/10.1080/01612840802048733

Wilson, B. D. M., Gomez, A. G. H., Sadat, M., Choi, S. K., & Badgett, M. V. L. (2020). *Pathways into poverty: Lived experiences among LGBTQ people.* Williams Institute, University of California, Los Angeles. https://williamsinstitute.law.ucla.edu/wp-content/uploads/Pathways-Overview-Sep-2020.pdf

Winberg, C., Coleman, T., Woodford, M. R., McKie, R. M., Travers, R., & Renn, K. A. (2019). Hearing "that's so gay" and "no homo" on campus and substance use among sexual minority college students. *Journal of Homosexuality, 66*(10), 1472–1494. https://doi.org/10.1080/00918369.2018.1542208

Winder, T. J. A., & Lea, C. H., III. (2019). "Blocking" and "filtering": A commentary on mobile technology, racism, and the sexual networks of young black MSM (YBMSM). *Journal of Racial and Ethnic Health Disparities, 6*(2), 231–236. https://doi.org/10.1007/s40615-018-0493-y

Witten, T. M. (2016). Trans* people anticipating dementia care: Findings from the Transgender MetLife Survey. In S. Westwood & E. Price (Eds.), *Lesbian, gay, bisexual and trans* individuals living with dementia* (pp. 110–123). Routledge.

Wong, A. (2020, April). I'm disabled and need a ventilator to live. Am I expendable during this pandemic? *Vox.* https://www.vox.com/first-person/2020/4/4/21204261/coronavirus-covid-19-disabled-people-disabilities-triage

Wong, C. F., Kipke, M. D., & Weiss, G. (2008). Risk factors for alcohol use, frequent use, and binge drinking among young men who have sex with men. *Addictive Behaviors, 33*(8), 1012–1020. https://doi.org/10.1016/j.addbeh.2008.03.008

Woodford, M. R., Chonody, J. M., Kulick, A., Brennan, D. J., & Renn, K. (2015). The LGBQ microaggressions on campus scale: A scale development and validation study. *Journal of Homosexuality, 62*(12), 1660–1687. https://doi.org/10.1080/00918369.2015.1078205

Woodford, M. R., Howell, M. L., Silverschanz, P., & Yu, L. (2012). "That's so gay!": Examining the covariates of hearing this expression among gay, lesbian, and bisexual college students. *Journal of American College Health, 60*(6), 429–434. https://doi.org/10.1080/07448481.2012.673519

Woodford, M. R., Joslin, J. Y., Pitcher, E. N., & Renn, K. A. (2017). A mixed-methods inquiry into trans* environmental microaggressions on college campuses: Experiences and outcomes. *Journal of Ethnic & Cultural Diversity in Social Work, 26*(1–2), 95–111. https://doi.org/10.1080/15313204.2016.1263817

Woodford, M. R., Weber, G., Nicolazzo, Z., Hunt, R., Kulick, A., Coleman, T., Coulombe, S., & Renn, K. A. (2018). Depression and attempted suicide among LGBTQ college students: Fostering resilience to the effects of heterosexism and cisgenderism on campus. *Journal of College Student Development, 59*(4), 421–438. https://doi.org/10.1353/csd.2018.0040

Woody, I. (2014). Aging out: A qualitative exploration of ageism and heterosexism among aging African American lesbians and gay men. *Journal of Homosexuality, 61*(1), 145–165. https://doi.org/10.1080/00918369.2013.835603

Worthen, M. G. (2016). Hetero-cis–normativity and the gendering of transphobia. *International Journal of Transgenderism, 17*(1), 31–57. https://doi.org/10.1080/15532739.2016.1149538

Wright, A. J., & Wegner, R. T. (2012). Homonegative microaggressions and their impact on LGB individuals: A measure validity study. *Journal of LGBT Issues in Counseling, 6*(1), 34–54. https://doi.org/10.1080/15538605.2012.648578

Index

About the Author

Kevin Leo Yabut Nadal, PhD, is a distinguished professor at the City University of New York. The author of 14 books, he is one of the leading researchers on the psychological impacts of microaggressions, or subtle forms of discrimination, toward people of color and lesbian, gay, bisexual, transgender, and queer (LGBTQ) people. He lives in New York City with his husband and their three children.